Motivation and the Struggle to Learn

Motivation and the Struggle to Learn

Responding to Fractured Experience

Theresa A. Thorkildsen
University of Illinois at Chicago

John G. Nicholls
Late of University of Illinois at Chicago

with

Ann Bates
Nancy Brankis
Thyra DeBolt
All of Laura B. Sprague Elementary School

Allyn and Bacon

Boston ▪ London ▪ Toronto ▪ Sydney ▪ Tokyo ▪ Singapore

Vice President: *Paul A. Smith*
Senior Editor: *Arnis E. Burvikovs*
Editorial Assistant: *Matthew Forster*
Marketing Manager: *Kathleen Morgan*
Editorial–Production Service: *Whitney Acres Editorial*
Manufacturing Buyer: *Julie McNeill*
Cover Administrator: *Kristina Mose-Libon*
Electronic Composition: *Cabot Computer Services*

A Pearson Education Company
75 Arlington Street
Boston, Massachusetts 02116

Internet: www.ablongman.com

Between the time Website information is gathered and then published, it is not unusual for some sites to have closed. Also, the transcription of URLs can result in unintended typographical errors. The publisher would appreciate notification where these occur so that they may be corrected in subsequent editions.

Library of Congress Cataloging-in-Publication Data

Thorkildsen, Theresa A.
Motivation and the struggle to learn : responding to fractured experience / Theresa A. Thorkildsen and John G. Nicholls with Ann Bates, Nancy Brankis, and Thyra DeBolt.
p. cm.
Includes bibliographical references and index.
ISBN 0-205-33599-3 (pbk.)
1. Motivation in education—Case studies. 2. Learning disabled children—Education—Case studies. I. Nicholls, John G. II. Title.

LB1065 .T48 2002
370.15'4—dc21 2001022644

Printed in the United States of America

10 9 8 7 6 5 4 3 2 1 06 05 04 03 02 01

To my friends who know that gestures speak louder than words,
the little things you say and do, make me want to be with you.

—Theresa A. Thorkildsen

CONTENTS

PREFACE

Motivation is generally defined as an internal force that activates, guides, and maintains behavior over time. Nevertheless, there is considerable debate about whether motivation is a unidimensional force or whether it is multidimensional. In writing this book, we explored how children fracture their intellectual lives, and found that a multidimensional definition of motivation as a dynamic system was essential to understanding lives in progress.

Focusing on motivation as a unidimensional construct, researchers sometimes use behaviorists' language of "approach and avoidance motivation" to integrate ideas that have traditionally focused on either cognition or action. Historically, this language has been consistent with the idea that affective, conative, and cognitive processes can be studied in isolation, but that the three processes comprise a single force that drives behavior. Some researchers have focused heavily on behavior, whereas others have focused on cognition about behavior. These researchers are currently blending ideas to come up with detailed theories of how cognitive and behavioral processes affect academic performance.

In this book, we define motivation in multidimensional terms and respectfully disagree with the idea that motivation is unidimensional. Like another group of researchers, we focus on individuals' needs, integrating ideas that have traditionally been overlooked with those evident in more mechanistic approaches to motivation. Integrating work from hermeneutic, personality, cross-cultural, and value-driven forms of psychology, we focus on the fact that individuals' needs are complex, varying over time and across contexts. Coordinating empirical findings obtained from various psychological traditions, we define motivation as a dynamic system comprised of numerous dimensions. In describing the dynamic system, we do not distinguish affective, conative, and cognitive modes of thought. Instead, we look for ways to understand how individuals coordinate their personal agendas with the values and expectations of others. A collection of ever-changing forces that are never inert, motivation guides individuals' willingness to approach and avoid particular tasks. The forces are comprised of individuals' beliefs about the world in which they live, understanding of different forms of knowledge, and personal agendas. Like other psychologists, we use the term "needs" to capture the essence of these forces.

Research on children's needs in educational contexts is guided by the assumption that mathematical models of motivation are more useful for policy decisions than for classroom applications. Individuals coordinate their needs by considering the societal norms they confront daily. Local norms rather than theoretical assertions are likely to play a major role in how individuals define and coordinate various aspects of their experience.

Over many years of teaching psychology to students who hope to work in educational settings, we encouraged students who were initially comforted by mechanistic theories of motivation to challenge our concern with children's needs. Once involved in the lives of actual children, these educators quickly learned about the ineffectiveness of mathematical formulas used to predict and control children's motivation. Sadly, we saw many educators interpret this experience as a sign that knowledge of child development was not helpful for organizing fair and effective classrooms. We wrote this book to offer an alternative interpretation.

When those of us involved in exploring children's fractured experience began construing motivation in multidimensional terms, we challenged the assumption that children's needs are easily manipulated by feedback from caregivers. We assumed that information on child development is essential for imagining the perspectives of particular students and that educators need to identify ways to meet the needs of real rather than theoretical children. In our most effective courses, we nurtured conversations on how educators might learn about the lives of actual children. Participants were asked to observe children in educational settings, to read about teachers and parents who are improving the lives of children, and to critique available research findings. Participants conversed with a range of children, families, and school personnel—as well as one another—about topics relevant to their experience in educational settings. In these conversations, participants considered issues of development by imagining how personal reference groups, family structure, schooling, and peer groups influence children's understanding of how they might find a comfortable place in society.

This book is one in a series of collected stories written to facilitate the kinds of conversations about children's needs in school that we promoted in our courses on child development. Guided by the assumption that development is the aim of education, these books involve a synthesis of research findings and direct experience, highlighting exemplary teaching as well as commitments to learning. The first book in the series, *Education as Adventure: Lessons from the Second Grade,*[1] offers a thick description of a year in a second grade classroom. The second book in the series, *Reasons for Learning: Expanding the Conversation on Student-Teacher Collaboration,*[2] offers a more detailed look at why it is important for educators to take seriously students' perspectives. Whereas children's experience with common classroom events and practices are addressed in the first two books, in *Motivation and the Struggle to Learn: Responding to Fractured Experience,* we focus on areas where children have difficulty.

In all three books, children, school personnel, and educational specialists collaborated with us in the quest for new knowledge. Families joined our conversations when we explored children's fractured experience. The information included in *Motivation and the Struggle to Learn* has been carefully selected to offer insight into common struggles involving motivation, moral agency, and intellectual growth faced by most students and their families. The conversations have been edited to focus on what particular children can teach us about the process of learning in school, illuminating the importance of considering children's needs.

Organization of the Book

This book was not conceived as the kind of textbook traditionally written for courses in Educational and Developmental Psychology. It contains relatively few facts that might be memorized. Theoretical arguments and technical jargon are kept to a minimum. And, details about the nature of schooling or the problems educators face in the classroom are introduced only when they are necessary for illuminating children's struggle to learn.

The book is likely to be most useful for future educators, researchers, parents, and teachers who are looking for ideas about how to organize conversations on child development and learning. Written with parents, advanced undergraduate students, and graduate students in mind, it highlights how research findings might be linked with actual experience to facilitate more comfortable lives for children. Rather than encourage readers to imagine problems of motivation as distinct from other aspects of life, the book takes a holistic look at the process of meeting children's needs in relationships with family members, school personnel, and peers.

Chapter 1 introduces the relatively novel way in which this research was conducted, the participants in the conversations about students' fractured experience, and an initial framework established for exploring children's lives in progress. The chapter is followed by two case studies that exemplify the theoretical framework using details from the direct experience of two children, their caregivers, and their peers. These chapters are followed by a more detailed account of how findings from research on child development were incorporated into the theoretical framework. Chapter 4 highlights just how typical some of the concerns raised by children, parents, and educators have come to seem and offers an elaboration of how contextual issues affect development. Two very challenging case studies are then presented, raising concerns that scare many new teachers. One of the cases involves a child with a wide range of disabilities that hampered most aspects of his development. The other case involves a biracial child who was expected to deal with issues of prejudice and identity development that are rarely acknowledged in research reports. Chapter 7 details how decisions were made about the children's future educational experiences and offers a framework for organizing conversations about fractured experience.

All the chapters contain a set of guiding questions after each "parable" or description of experience. The questions are by no means comprehensive, but offer readers some guidance on what to look for when reading about these lives in progress. The questions should help readers who become engrossed in the details of particular lives imagine what they might learn from those lives. Similarly, the end of the book contains a comprehensive reference list and glossary of key terms that researchers take for granted. These features should facilitate readers' ability to look for more details about particular issues and concerns that might be relevant to their intellectual lives.

Acknowledgments

This project was supported in part by a cooperative agreement—Improving Learning Through Home/School Collaboration— from the Office of Special Education and Rehabilitative Services (HO23L10010). John Nicholls held this agreement jointly with Tanis Bryan and Mavis Donahue, and wrote the following acknowledgments:

I am grateful to them for leading me into this, and for providing wise counsel throughout.

The support of Alice Kordek, Dick Best, and Cindy McNitt at the school was indispensable. They were well aware that I was there to look at an aspect of school where strain or difficulty occurs. I was not there to look at and reflect on the many other aspects of the school that would reveal it in a more favorable, let alone a more balanced light. Yet, they were always welcoming, and ready with indispensable local knowledge. It was a pleasure to enter the school each day. I cannot imagine how I would have finished without this support.

The parents of the four boys allowed me to examine a part of their lives where they were encountering more than their usual supply of setbacks. They faced bewildering challenges. Yet, they were always frank, open, and decent. This helped maintain my sense that the work was proving worthwhile.

The teachers did not merely accept my presence, looking for trouble in their classrooms. They made suggestions, raised questions, and tried new things, finding the courage to make themselves vulnerable and strong collaborators. The work of putting together the [first draft of] words in print is largely mine, but the making of this book involved much more than that. Not to acknowledge fully my collaborators would be to exalt the writing of experience over the initial shaping of experience and over the particular themes that, as a result of all this negotiation, emerge in the writing. It would also be to separate and exalt the researcher over the teacher, obscuring the possibilities of teaching itself as a form of inquiry—equal to any in its potential to improve education.

I am also much indebted to Eileen Ball, Joe Kahne, Margy McClain, J. Ron Nelson, and Theresa Thorkildsen for productive conversations and suggestions.

* * *

Since John's death, many individuals helped me gain the courage to reconstruct a manuscript consisting of thoughtfully crafted field notes into a meaningful contribution to the literature. Individuals who organize life at Jamoch's Caffe offered sustenance for the body as well as the spirit. The thoughtful reviews from the educators and families involved in the project, sensitive readers, and editors reinforced my sense that John's manuscript offered more than sentimental value to the research community. In addition to conversations with the families and educators named in the book, productive conversations with Karl Hennig, Karyn LaLonde, Nel Noddings, Susan Bobbitt Nolen, Penny Oldfather, Richard Ryan, Seymour Sarason, Jonas Soltis, Dennis Thiessen, and Lawrence Walker helped me accept the challenge of revising this book and of strengthening John's initial attempt at offering a thoughtful, respectful critique of my preoccupation with understanding children's experience. Arnis E. Burvikovs, my editor at Allyn & Bacon, and Steven J. Condley, University of Florida, offered helpful advice on how the manuscript could be transformed into a textbook. To be able to converse with such thoughtful children, parents, educators, and scholars—all experts on the meaning of their experience—has truly been a pleasure that has enriched my intellectual development.

This edition of the book represents a significantly shorter version of the project than was originally constructed. An unabridged version is available, from the first author, to those individuals interested in more theoretical and empirical details of studying lives in progress.

ENDNOTES

1. See Nicholls and Hazzard (1993).
2. See Nicholls and Thorkildsen (1995).

Motivation and the Struggle to Learn

CHAPTER

1 Learning from Lives in Progress

In Chicago, where this was written, many residents have heard the phrase "God is in the details"[1] so often that it lacks meaning. Nevertheless, the phrase serves as an excellent metaphor for the purpose of this book. Like many intellectuals who have called for a psychology that respects the details of actual lives, we risked doing the kind of scholarship that many merely recommend. We engaged in an interpretive process to document children's fractured experience—outlining ways in which children undermine their motivation and intellectual development.

In understanding the lives of second graders, psychologists have taught many of us to conjure up images of behavior that is typical or normal, and compare that behavior with the unusual or abnormal. To highlight the typical, we construct such images as one hundred and forty second graders standing in a large arc, rehearsing a musical show for their parents. At the music teacher's cue, the room fills with a sweet, strong harmony of childish voices. The children sing music that was written before they were born, yet make the music their own by imposing new meaning on the historical stories represented in the lyrics. Small renaissance angels, wearing the latest popular brand of sneakers, soar with the music. Children's lives gain harmony when they conform to the norms established in such collective enterprises.

In imagining the unusual, we think about the children who would not be uplifted by this collaborative experience. One child might barely whisper the words to the song: A soul in limbo rather than in pain, he would not know what to do with the emotion that flickered on his face. A second child might barely open his mouth, grinning awkwardly, shuffling, and looking around: He would sing occasionally, but only his mouth would contribute. A third child might face stiffly ahead without expression: Trailing behind, lips barely moving, he would have no joyful noise for the Lord or anyone else. A fourth child might fake feeling, and fade in and out as if he knew he should be invigorated, but was not.

In a psychological tradition preoccupied with prediction and control, an academic either looks for ways to help the unusual become "normal" or invents richer descriptions of the typical. This book deviates from that vision, emphasizing a psychology of the individual. As developmental psychologists, we assumed that knowledge of children's uniqueness could unmask important psychological dilemmas that have universal appeal. We sought insight into how individuals become disengaged in environments where group norms are valued over personal agendas. We identified four healthy boys (ages 7–8) who struggled with their uniqueness and could not find meaning in the music and other cultural artifacts their school was charged to impart. Rather than see that educational artifacts can promote lively growth and personal expression, the boys inexplicably seemed wounded by the very tools of school culture that should have helped them find value in learning. Listening to their perspectives, we looked for ways to assist Bruce Johnson, David Richardson, Jack Davis, and Earl Norton in the meaning-making enterprise. The boys and their adult guardians were invited to talk about their experiences, and their audience responded thoughtfully to the concerns raised.

As educational psychologists, we imagined how teaching practices could be more responsive to the perspectives of students who find academic rituals alienating. Like the outstanding teachers we worked with, we asked the question, "What can each of these boys teach us about schooling?" The answers illuminated practical issues associated with revising curriculum to accommodate questions of motivation and the struggle of intellectual growth. We assumed that all children need to read, write, calculate, and communicate orally, even if they do not develop these skills with equal measure. We also assumed that when learners become disengaged from the educational enterprise, it is incumbent upon the people who care about them to ensure that they do not stay that way.

The resulting conversations revealed a double bind that faces parents and teachers who genuinely care about the welfare of particular students. In offering the children extra help, caregivers sometimes undermined initiative. This was evident when we heard the boys speak about their experience, and saw them mistrust their intuitions and fracture their intellectual lives. Fortunately, some conversations also led to healthy transformations when caregivers suspended their commitment to a causal science of prediction and control. Documenting the process of meaning making, it became possible to identify slowly evolving transformations that facilitated children's intellectual engagement.

It would not be surprising, from the perspective of the psychological tradition preoccupied with prediction and control, to learn that the children in this project were labeled *students with learning disabilities.* We challenge that system of thought and critique the usefulness of such labels for constructing a professional language of "ought." Although the psychology associated with the typical and unusual offered a place to begin our inquiries, knowing the results from batteries of diagnostic tests did little to help Bruce, David, Jack, or Earl integrate the various aspects of their intellectual experience into forms that gave meaning and direction to one another.

Comparing the boys' experience with those of the educators involved in this project, we also discovered that preoccupation with labels invariably leads many education specialists, ironically and despite the best of intentions, to become separated from the acts of teaching and parenting. Teachers and parents do not face the general, average, or homogenized students that those of us who invent labels such as "students with learning disabilities" try to imagine. They face the perspectives of particular learners, and "keeping up" may not be an appropriate goal for children whose abilities place them outside the typical range. Effective means for nurturing the growth of particular children may be best left idiosyncratic.

Conscious of the struggle to teach and parent, we experimented with a hermeneutic psychological tradition and described the unique ways in which students may come, at least for a while, to a state of optimum motivation. We sought to make the maintenance of conversations about particular students an essential part of our work—one of the main things we should do well—because individuals are more than mere objects for the application of general theories. We also sought to understand diverse interpretations of the boys' experience—their competencies and the intentions that seemed to prohibit them from finding school learning meaningful.

In attempting to make a similar point, Robert White began the third edition of his book, *Lives in Progress,* with a quote from A. N. Whitehead defining the meaning of truth as a partially distorted representation of the universe.[2] One purpose in writing about children who had difficulty with school is to remind readers that to study the evolution of lives, as White and other eminent psychologists once did, is a valuable tradition that should be preserved. A second purpose is to place limits on the notion of truth that Whitehead promoted because that notion diminishes what might be learned from the study of lives in progress.

Consider the world of Hannah Arendt, who was committed to distinguishing between *truth* as something we can *know* and *meaning making* as the process of *thinking*.[3] In Arendt's world, psychologists would work on meaning making until they came up with a truth. To succeed, the truths sought by Arendt and Whitehead would inevitably have to be limited in scope. Were such truths to be verifiable, they would have to be so global as to be meaningless for use in the struggle to understand particular children. Despite their value for policy decisions, global generalizations are descriptions of statistical averages rather than actual people.

We relied on an alternative vision of truth as the accurate recording of events in the lives of children and those who interact with them. We did not attempt to separate the cognitive, affective, and conative, but sought to identify ways in which these three intrapersonal domains coexisted in the lives of Bruce, David, Jack, and Earl, four living boys who were struggling to master the challenges of second grade.[4] Our work is truthful if, at the time the events were recorded, everyone involved agreed that they had occurred. Audiotape recordings of conversations, drawings, journal entries, and other artifacts serve as evidence for this kind of truth. The four boys and their adult guardians did exist, the boys did complete a range of educational products, and everyone concerned did discuss the lives of these boys in the manner recorded here.

To facilitate our ability to explore the lives of these children in depth, we restricted the number of children involved in this project and chose participants whose behavior reflected diverse and complex personalities.[5] Boys with learning disabilities were chosen as the focus of this project, not to establish a norm to which girls will later be compared, but because, in the United States, boys are more often labeled as having learning disabilities than girls in such ratios as 3:1 and 7:3.[6] We also found no support for gender differences in second graders' motivation.[7]

In this hermeneutic psychology, the goal is meaning making rather than truth seeking. Meaning making requires an endless process of thinking, imagining, and inventing possible interpretations of particular events and personalities. We did not struggle to invent general truths about exactly what happens to boys with learning disabilities. By asking, "What can each of these boys teach us about the struggle to learn in school?" we moved beyond complaints about the ineffectiveness of schooling. By engaging in the process of meaning making, we learned that there are as many detailed answers to our question as there are participants in the conversation. While some perspectives are more useful than others, comparing and contrasting ideas facilitates greater understanding and rich conversations.

We know only some of the participants in this conversation. We know ourselves, the four boys whose lives we documented, and the parents, teachers, and peers who worked to understand the nature of the experiences we explored. Other participants are largely imaginary—anonymous reviewers, a target audience for whom this book was written, and the people who might be influenced by the ideas gleaned from this process.

In representing some of our attempts at meaning making, this book is unusual in that it contains many voices and can be analyzed from many levels. The level that is closest to truth involves biographical and autobiographical accounts from three general positions. First, John Nicholls, a university professor, was the original agent who initiated this project. Second, the perspectives of family members—of the four boys themselves and their parents (pseudonyms are used to protect their privacy)—are revealed in vivid detail. Third, representing the school, Ann Bates, Nancy Brankis, and Thyra DeBolt, the boys' teachers—assisted by others who do not have as direct a voice—participated in this conversation. Each participant said and did the things that are described in this book. Yet, even this level of truth involves appearances and interpretation. Particular questions were posed while others remained unasked. Furthermore, a collection of artifacts from this endeavor remain left out of the story—primarily for editorial reasons, but those reasons were invented.

John Nicholls, the ethnographer for this project, did a second level of meaning making. In writing about the lives of Bruce, David, Jack, and Earl, John included his judgments of the events that occurred, posed questions that were in his own mind, and thus altered the course of events from time to time.

A third level of meaning making involved rule-governed logic. After having recorded events connected with the lives of Bruce, David, Jack, and Earl, including judgments of each incident, John turned copies of his manuscript over to the participants, asking for their critique and conjecture about what "really happened." Everyone openly critiqued this writing—adding detail, and deleting events that did not seem clear enough to those involved. The point of this process was to identify patterns of reasoning and behavior that should be highlighted and speculated about in relation to the experiences of others. Much of that speculation is also included in the book.

A fourth level of meaning making most closely approximated our more general guiding research question of what readers might learn from fully exploring the lives of these four boys. I, Theresa (Terri) Thorkildsen, serve as narrator, charged with identifying and justifying valuable lessons from our conversations. Not having been present for any of the events recorded in the following pages, I tried to imagine more general themes and patterns evident when looking across particular experiences. With the help of the educators at Laura B. Sprague Elementary School, I reconstructed a sense of what was most worthwhile to know about these particular "truths" and to help readers imagine at least one set of conclusions about them. The original narrative has once again been transformed from a story based on a linear progression of time to one of parables in which conclusions are drawn and events are used to support those conclusions. This revision was read again by the families and educators involved in the project to determine whether such conclusions accurately reflected their experience.

The fifth level of meaning making will be left to our readers. Individuals will find a range of uses for these stories; some interpretations we will hear about, and others will remain in the minds of the book's readers. Our goal is not to replace a psychology of prediction and control, but to extend knowledge about students' experience into realms that are difficult to assess with such tools. We hope that, by entering into this conversation, readers can discover some new thoughts and use those discoveries in ways that might be beneficial to themselves and to new students whose interesting lives are worthy of our understanding.

Types of Fractured Experience

The lives of Bruce, David, Jack, and Earl, when coordinated with generalizations from research on child development, highlight at least two types of fractured experience that influence moral and intellectual functioning. The first type involves conflicts among personal needs and orientations toward the world. When adults assume responsibility for children's experience, they can overlook the fact that, like learning, motivation and moral agency are fundamentally intrapersonal processes that are driven by needs. Everyone, whether aware of it or not, responds to internal forces that direct personal experience. Individuals share the same needs for self-determination, competence, and affiliation, yet different orientations to the world affect how such needs are met. Just as it is wise to avoid such language as "teachers learn students," it is probably wise to avoid assuming that "teachers motivate students" and regulate their behavior. Language that overlooks the inner life of a person fosters the first kind of fractured experience by nurturing individuals' tendency to overlook some of their needs or adopt orientations that undermine their potential to meet such needs.

The second type of fractured experience involves conflicts among expectations in various spheres of an individual's life. It is the type of experience that has encouraged adults to invent statements such as "parents control their children," "teachers motivate students," and "peers make children conform." These habits of speech suggest that expectations differ in school, at home, and in peer groups, and everyone must take responsibility for living up to the expectations of others. Such habits also highlight the ways in which individuals can become pawns who are done to and cared for when well-meaning caregivers and friends seek to "learn and motivate" them.[8] Individuals overwhelmed by the second type of fractured experience succumb to pawn-ship, either by failing to identify and respond to others' expectations, or by changing their identities to meet the divergent expectations in various social spheres.

Habits of speech can seem inconsequential but hold serious repercussions for how theories of motivation, moral development, peer relations, and learning are used to facilitate growth. It is our hope that, after finishing this book, you will see why the languages we use to justify our efforts are not trivial. Just as instruction can influence someone's learning, reward contingencies can influence someone's motivation. Expectations are value laden and can influence which aspects of experience someone attends to and which aspects remain ignored. Despite these external influences, intrapersonal aspects of experience remain multidimensional, evolving processes, even when our speech and action do not reflect such awareness. Those of us on the "outside" can only work toward developing a richer understanding of the struggles faced by those on the "inside." We can learn quite a bit from observing individuals' behavior, and even more by also asking them to talk about their lives, but ultimately we are left to construct our own sense of why they think, feel, and act as they do.

When we remain open-minded enough to admit that, at best, we can make educated guesses about another's needs and expectations, we can sustain helpful conversations about nurturing high levels of moral and intellectual engagement. Before introducing a sample of such conversations, it might be helpful to see how existing knowledge of child development offers a framework for organizing the most essential details of particular lives in progress.

Needs and Orientations

Needs form the core of our theoretical framework and are defined as forces that organize how individuals perceive, define, and respond to their experience. There is cultural variation in the orientations that individuals use to prioritize their needs, yet it is human nature to strive for balance or integration when organizing various life events. As individuals strive to maintain states of equilibrium, needs are the forces that guide their reactions. Early motivation theorists distinguished the needs for power, achievement, and affiliation in ways that proved useful for exploring the nature of children's fractured experience.[9] Driven by needs for self-determination, competence, and affiliation, children construct orientations toward their environment and methods of conquering perceived challenges that affect their ability to balance such needs (see Figure 1.1). When children fracture their experience by ignoring some of their needs, they make it difficult to ever attain a comfortable state of equilibrium and make identity-enhancing choices.

When observing the behavior of Bruce, David, Jack, and Earl, John Nicholls had a head full of these notions and a rich sense of the history of motivation research. Accepting a call for research on the struggles of children with learning disabilities,[10] John used his knowledge to explore how these children reconciled their quests for independence, expertise, and relatedness while developing a comfortable sense of identity.

As developmental psychologists, we knew that the ways in which needs have been defined in research on adults were not always adequate for representing the forces that drive children's experience. The forces that drive adults' academic engagement are in many ways significantly more complex than are the forces that drive children's engagement. Although children and adults have the same needs, adults have more knowledge to draw from when interpreting something new. Adults also have greater skill than do children at coordinating the concrete and abstract features of their experience, and more opportunities to assert their autonomy. To emphasize these differences, terms from research on children's needs and orientations that reflect the abilities of second graders will be used throughout the book. In some respects, the initial definitions proposed by theorists are simplified. In other respects, new definitions, consistent with the abilities and opportunities of children, are proposed.

Self-Determination

Children's need for power takes the form of a need for self-determination or independence. They are struggling to sustain high levels of self-efficacy and acquire greater

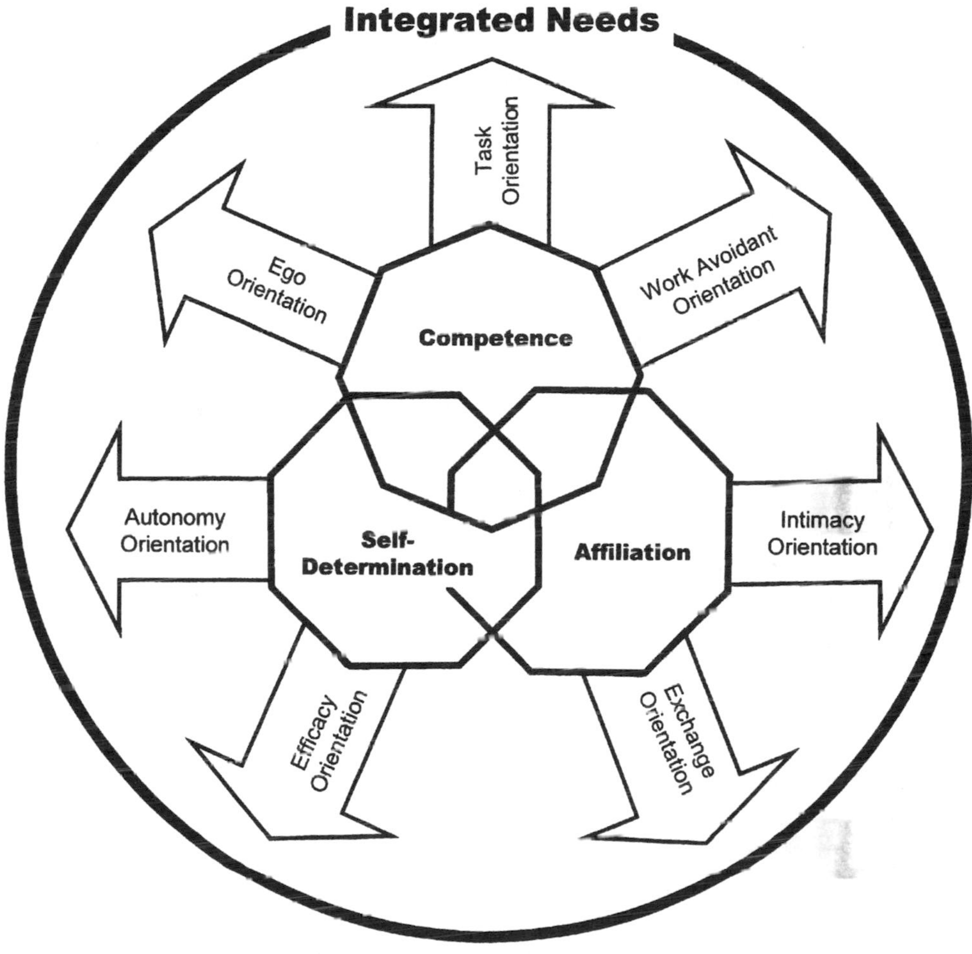

FIGURE 1.1 A Theoretical Model of Integrated Needs Consolidating Three Types of Motivation

autonomy. Specifically, they are learning how to regulate their own behavior, make responsible choices, and avoid relying exclusively on the edicts of powerful others. When self-determination is coordinated with the needs of others, moral agency becomes possible because children are able to step outside their own subjective experience.

Toward those ends, children construct answers to the question of whether they can succeed when devoting energy toward fulfilling a goal. This form of self-efficacy usually involves predefined tasks and addresses children's impulses to engage in such tasks. Because young children generally receive a great deal of adult guidance in how to define and respond to their needs, self-efficacy has the potential to be thwarted if children remain dependent on caregivers. When children learn to control how they approach and avoid assigned tasks, they sustain limited, but age-appropriate forms of self-determination.[11]

Children who are not willing to regulate their own behavior will have difficulty sustaining high levels of the self-efficacy necessary for self-determination.

A second age-appropriate aspect of children's quest for self-determination involves the autonomous ability to select and sustain identity-enhancing interests.[12] Most children are offered a wide range of ideas and activities intended to broaden their intellectual commitments. Finding meaning in some features of the world while feeling comfortable ignoring other features makes it possible to remain committed to particular ideas and values. Noticing themes in how children organize aspects of their experience, spontaneously select activities, and describe their preferences offers clues as to which interests foster high levels of academic engagement. Similarly, high levels of moral engagement are possible when children are encouraged to practice virtuous behavior. Children who cannot sustain interests or commitments to particular moral values will have difficulty exhibiting the autonomy necessary for self-determination.

In the chapters that follow, children differed in their ability to respond to self-determination needs, but those difficulties resisted simple explanations. The children had difficulty coordinating their needs for self-efficacy and autonomy, but the nature of those difficulties could not accurately be represented with simple algorithms. Bruce and Earl, for example, had a tendency to overestimate their ability to self-regulate and make identity-enhancing choices: They sought self-determination by unconsciously resisting many forms of help that most students in their place would have found valuable. David and Jack often underestimated their ability to make identity-enhancing choices: These more reticent boys openly resisted the freedom they were encouraged to embrace.

Competence

In contrast to a need for power, children's need for achievement generally involves the satisfaction of demonstrating moral and intellectual expertise.[13] They are learning how to define and master the task at hand while integrating feelings of competence into their evolving identities. Children still need quite a bit of coaching on what is expected of them, and have difficulty carrying out all the mental processes necessary to reconcile inconsistencies in their performance.[14] Encouraging children to talk about when and why they feel competent may help them determine which steps they skip when deciding how to complete academic tasks or how to treat others.[15] Their general orientations toward tasks reflect their definition of competence.[16]

Like adults, children can embrace a task orientation wherein the task is meaningful in its own right and task mastery generates feelings of success. When task-oriented, children are likely to focus on their interests, effort, and ideas. They are less preoccupied with how their performance compares to the performance of others, and more committed to the new knowledge they might acquire. When collaboration is not defined as a form of cheating, children work eagerly with peers to acquire new ideas rather than to outperform them. When children are task-oriented, they can have difficulty meeting their competence needs if assignments are too difficult and/or they lack information about how to proceed.

Second graders are also learning how to become ego-oriented wherein they seek to outperform their peers or avoid looking incompetent. Children with a strong ego orientation generally see learning as a means to the end of pleasing others. Most second graders do not differentiate the concepts of ability and effort, task difficulty and ability, luck and skill, or fluid and crystallized intelligence sufficiently enough to hold adultlike forms of ego orientation.[17] Nevertheless, they are able to compare their performance to the performance of others well enough to take delight in feeling superior and shame in feeling inferior about their achievement.[18] When children are ego-oriented, they will have difficulty meeting their competence needs if they cannot find others who are willing to observe their performance and/or if they do not succeed in winning.

Children can also become work-avoidant and experience academic alienation, revealing general signs of fractured experience. Task and ego orientations offer distinct means for approaching intellectual projects, yet children are not always willing to attempt the schoolwork before them. This "unmotivated" orientation leads children to feel successful when they are able to avoid learning. When children are alienated, they are also likely to exhibit socially withdrawn behavior, and avoid opportunities for moral agency.[19] Hopefully, when children demonstrate work avoidance in relation to some projects, they will exhibit task and/or ego involvement in alternative activities. In this respect what may appear to be "amotivation" or "helplessness" in one situation can simply reflect a preoccupation with self-determination needs rather than competence needs. Children could well be avoiding projects that they cannot connect to identity-enhancing interests while engaging in projects that facilitate feelings of autonomy.

Bruce, David, Jack, and Earl exhibited all three of these orientations toward achievement. Whereas the boys were all task-involved, ego-involved, and work-avoidant at some point, there were marked differences in their respective orientation profiles over time. Bruce and Earl, for example, generally exhibited a preference for ego orientation, whereas David and Jack generally exhibited a preference for task orientation. The boys fractured their experiences when they were either unable to sustain their preferred competence orientation or could not identify manageable projects well enough to define clear goals.

The attributions children use to explain their performance may influence the development of their competence orientations. By combining causes theoretically linked to power (controllability), competence (stability), and relatedness (locus of causality), researchers have found ways to predict the explanations that individuals offer for their success and failure.[20] This information is helpful when, metaphorically speaking, all individuals choose to play the same game of Monopoly because decisions about which move to make offers insight into an individuals' motives. Nevertheless, children's conceptions of particular attributions affect their ability to use their knowledge when defining experience. When children cannot step outside their own subjective experience, for example, they have difficulty imagining how their performance compares to the performance of others. They assume projects that are difficult for them are also difficult for others. When they work hard, these children assume that others work hard. Such children also struggle to differentiate activities that involve luck from activities that involve skill. As children begin to differentiate their own experience from the activities and expectations outside themselves, their understanding of the challenges before them changes, and the meaning of such attributions as ability, effort, and task difficulty are altered as well.

Attributions also differ in meaning depending upon whether children are task-involved, ego-involved, or work-avoidant. When children are ego-involved, for example, they are preoccupied with hierarchical forms of social comparison, and define ability by focusing on how well they perform relative to others. When children are task-involved, they are preoccupied with identity-enhancing forms of social comparison that reflect personal interests, and define ability in terms of task mastery. Notions of stability take different forms when children are task- and ego-oriented. Children may recognize that their standing in the relative hierarchy of learners is beyond their control, but that their ability to master the task before them is highly controllable. Ego-involved comparisons will always be norm-referenced, and reference groups will be selected to enhance feelings of superiority. Task-involved comparisons, on the other hand, will be self-referenced when task mastery is not associated with a reference group, and norm-referenced when task mastery hinges on knowledge of a reference group. Simple algorithms cannot easily explain children's use of particular attributions.

Like most children, Bruce, David, Jack, and Earl were clearly excited when they felt successful, regardless of their use of attributions. They also talked about failure from time to time. Because we knew that, like many children with learning disabilities, these children had difficulty understanding their own meta-cognitive strategies for learning, we did not explore their failure attributions with the same rigor that we explored their success attributions.[21] Taking the boys' attributions with a grain of salt while combining that information with behavioral observations offered insight into their competence orientations and the ways in which their needs for expertise remained unmet.

Affiliation

The needs for self-determination and competence among children have been studied carefully, yet their need for affiliation has often been taken for granted. Some children are more skilled than others at maintaining relationships, but their relatedness needs typically have been inferred from their behavior toward others.[22] Analyzing children's experience, we found that distinctions among intimacy and exchange orientations, evident in research involving adults, offered helpful language for representing differences in children's need for affiliation.[23] Adults vary in their understanding of and preference for intimacy and for the kinds of interpersonal exchange offered by companionship. Intimacy and exchange can be valued in their own right or valued merely as a means to some extrinsic end.[24] Similarly, children seem to hold the same general approaches to relationships found among adults, even though these orientations take a less complex form.

Less complex than the orientations of adults, for example, children's intimacy orientations reflect the nature of their attachments to caregivers and their ability to construct close friendships with their peers. Children differ in the extent to which they require warm, close, and communicative relationships with their peers.[25] Even so, they generally rely on their caregivers for some form of intimacy.[26] Children who have unstable relationships with caregivers and/or peers undermine their ability to meet affiliation needs.

Like adults, children's exchange orientations involve the willingness to establish, maintain, and restore positive relationships while sharing ideas and interests with others.[27] Interactions with siblings and peers offer ample opportunities for developing comfortable exchange relationships. Even so, children differ in their willingness to participate in positive forms of companionship and teamwork. Children who avoid opportunities for exchange also undermine opportunities for reciprocity and limit their access to new ideas.

Most children differ in how they prioritize issues of intimacy and exchange, but only some children find it difficult to meet their affiliation needs.[28] Children who fracture their experience can ignore their affiliation needs altogether, avoid all forms of intimacy, or avoid all opportunities for exchange. They can also seek inappropriate forms of intimacy and/or fail to notice opportunities for identity-enhancing exchange. These possibilities were evident when we looked at the range of relationships that Bruce, David, Jack, and Earl maintained. The boys exhibited vastly different needs for approval and affection from peers and adults. Some of their needs were met while others languished.

Needs among Students with Learning Disabilities

Generally speaking, a modicum of research has been conducted to determine how children with learning disabilities prioritize their needs for self-determination, competence, and affiliation, but rarely have all three needs been measured in a single study.[29] We know that children with learning disabilities tend to see academic outcomes as controlled by powerful others and have a limited sense of their own efficacy.[30] The resulting anger and frustration from unmet needs can interact with perceptions of control to affect children's classroom behavior.[31] Children with learning disabilities are also more likely to feel incompetent when compared to their nondisabled peers, but hold competency beliefs that are parallel to those of other slower learners.[32] And, a small, emerging literature on relatedness supports the assertion that children with learning disabilities find it difficult to meet their affiliation needs because of their inability to properly attend to the needs of others.[33]

The holistic way in which the lives of Bruce, David, Jack, and Earl were recorded offers a detailed means for imagining multiple ways of coordinating needs and orientations. Each of these boys prioritized his needs for self-determination, competence, and affiliation in unique ways. They also fractured some parts of their experience so that particular needs were more salient than others, and revealed orientations toward meeting their needs that varied over time and place. In writing about the needs of these four boys, we highlighted sample behaviors indicative of each need, details of conversations where the boys labeled their needs, and contradictions in how the boys' needs were manifested in experience. It should be possible to see how Bruce, Jack, and Earl fractured their needs when they became overly concerned with the expectations of others, and how they sometimes expressed needs that could not be addressed simultaneously. It should also be possible to see how David coordinated his needs, but became a different boy at home and at

Challenges and Controversies

- How are children's needs different from those of adults?
- Do children with learning disabilities face unusual dilemmas when striving to meet their needs?
- If all humans need to sustain a sense of self-determination, competence, and affiliation, is it possible for children's needs to be more balanced than those of their caregivers?

school. Each boy fractured his experience in distinct ways that also varied over the course of the year he spent in this project. Linking general research findings with the details of actual lives should facilitate an understanding of common ways in which children express their needs. Becoming conversant with how needs can be expressed in gesture as well as in words, in positive as well as negative ways, and publicly as well as privately makes it possible to encourage children who are struggling to integrate their experience and establish realistic agendas.

Expectations and Responsibilities

It is not enough to simply identify children's needs if caregivers hope to assist them in forming coherent identities by consolidating aspects of their experience. For aspects of experience to give direction and meaning to one another, children must also coordinate their needs with the expectations of others. Ideally, children should seem like the same person to their family members, teachers, and peers and feel comfortable in all of those roles. To do so, they need to be able to coordinate others' hopes and expectations, distinguish others' concerns from their own, and still respond to their own needs. The collection of values that drive this coordination impels an individual's sense of moral and intellectual agency.

Generally speaking, expectations have been defined as the demand characteristics in particular contexts that offer structure to the needs that individuals come to value. There is cultural variation in the degree to which individuals consider the expectations of others when making decisions, yet all strive to anticipate how well their personal agendas correspond to more common agendas. As individuals strive to maintain a sense of equilibrium, they coordinate personal needs and others' expectations. Individuals imagine the probability of events and reactions that are likely to occur when they choose a particular course of action, or their efforts become misapplied. When children fracture their experience, they may be simultaneously responding to contradictory expectations, unaware of some expectations, or unable to accurately identify which features of their experience others are likely to value.

There has been a proliferation of generalizations on how context affects children's actions, facilitating inferences about how others' expectations affect children's ability to consolidate aspects of their experience. The three most common social spheres in which children respond to the expectations of others—the spheres of family, school, and peer groups—have been added to the framework of needs to construct a comprehensive framework for exploring lives in progress (see Figure 1.2).

To highlight idealized roles that involve the integration of needs and expectations, we used an Aristotelian notion of balancing forms of happiness when organizing existing generalizations.[34] In this view, children's lives are ethical when they find happiness as a free and responsible citizen, as a thinker and philosopher, and as an entertainer and artist. Representing the lives of Bruce, David, Jack, and Earl, we looked for generalizations about how children might attain such happiness when responding to others' expectations.

It is difficult for most people to fully grasp the complexities involved in coordinating needs and expectations. The piecemeal way in which research on child development is

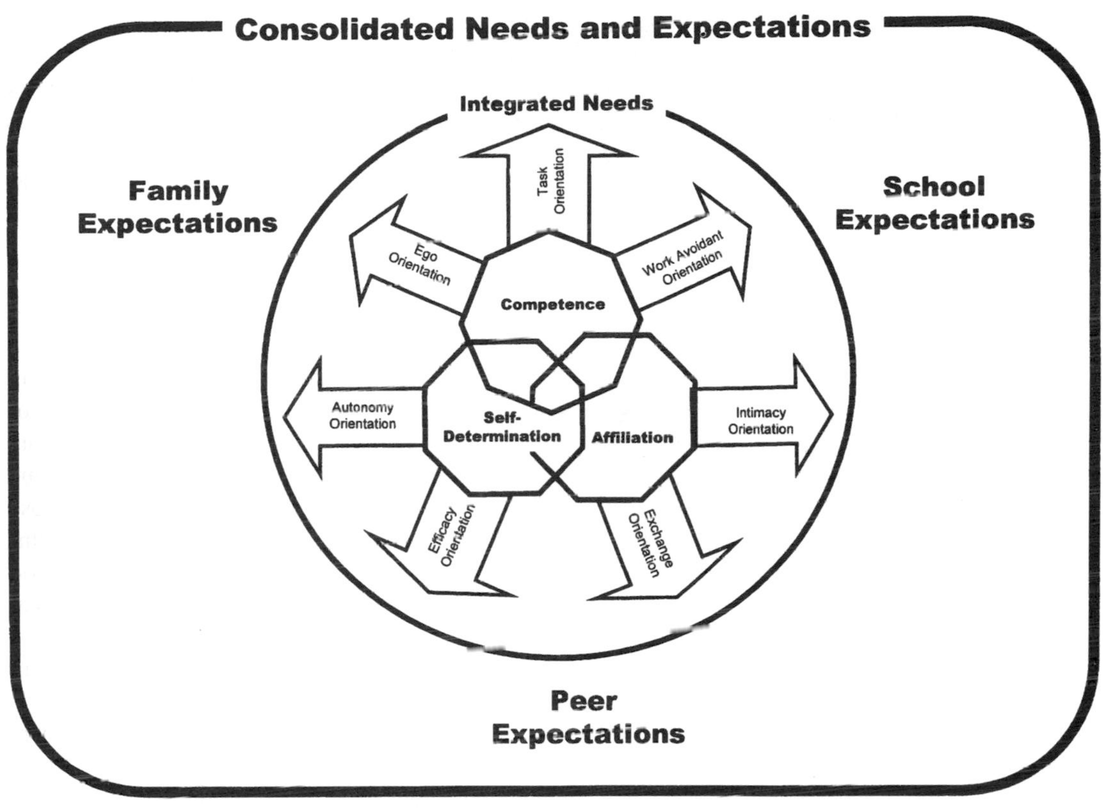

FIGURE 1.2 A Theoretical Model of Integrated Experience Consolidating Needs and Others' Expectations

made available to caregivers exacerbates that challenge. Aware of such tension, we tried to construct a language of synthesis for representing lives in progress. Before elaborating on how our theoretical frame emerged from research, a working language of synthesis will be introduced and exemplified in the next two chapters.

Practicing a Language of Synthesis

In the chapters that follow, children, parents, teachers, and researchers try to coordinate knowledge about needs and responsibilities to better understand children's fractured experience. Details of lives in progress will exemplify how, like many adults, children can find some forms of happiness difficult to attain. No single context offers opportunities for promoting all forms of happiness, nor do individuals respond to each context in identical ways. Bruce, for example, spent more of his class time enjoying the small pleasures of life and working to be a responsible citizen than in the academic pursuit of a thinker. He

Challenges and Controversies

- How do children learn about the expectations of others?
- Is it irresponsible to encourage children to seek Aristotelian notions of happiness?
- Are children responsible for living up to all the expectations others hold for them?
- Although it would be problematic to neglect children's needs, how can caregivers help children consider their responsibilities to others as well as their own needs?

fractured his experience by ignoring some of his needs. David was an active thinker and philosopher at home, but not in school. He fractured his experience by behaving like one person at home and another at school.

After outlining the details of how Bruce and David struggled to find happiness in their roles as son, student, and friend, we will survey some of the expectations that families, schools, and peers typically hold for children. Any caregiver would find it nearly impossible to coordinate all the details of current research on child development with the needs of particular children. Nevertheless, time for reflection made it possible to imagine how the details of particular lives in progress were situated in broader social contexts. Such knowledge of broader contexts should make it possible to understand the pressures faced by Jack and Earl, two boys who fractured their experience in multiple ways.

Whereas Bruce and David fractured only one dimension of their experience, Jack and Earl fractured both their needs and their responses to others' expectations. Jack refused to accept freedom in school, but would release pent-up frustrations by instigating trouble outside of school. Earl was often so busy seeking freedom that he seemed to miss other forms of happiness altogether. Details of these two lives and the means by which caregivers sought to assist the boys in their struggles to learn will be conveyed.

Like Bruce and David, Jack and Earl were fortunate enough to have caregivers who labeled educational experiences and challenged the boys' misguided assumptions. The children were encouraged to behave like educational theorists, speculating about how and why they learn. Caregivers supported the boys' development by calling attention to forms of intellectual and moral engagement and encouraging them to behave like responsible citizens when coordinating their needs.

The book ends with a series of "stock-taking" conversations in which caregivers hold themselves and the children accountable for moral and intellectual growth. The children's experiences are evaluated and plans for the next year are introduced. Caregivers strategize about how to encourage children to coordinate their needs at home, school, and in peer groups while responding to the expectations of others in these contexts. Then, a series of recommendations for constructing a language of synthesis are offered, highlighting our responsibilities to children who fracture their experience. You will notice that constructing a common language is not easy work. The most important lessons we gleaned from our attempts concerned the necessity of breaking a few eggs when creating this proverbial omelet.

ENDNOTES

1. This is a quote regularly attributed to Ludwig Mies van der Rohe and/or the Chicago School of Architecture.

2. See White (1975).

3. See Arendt (1978).

4. Allport (1961) helped readers see the value and the frustrations of using this language to describe people.

5. To protect the boys' privacy, we obfuscate details of their lives that do not affect the integrity of these stories. Three of the boys were Caucasian and the fourth had dual ethnicity.

6. See Kavale & Reese (1992), McLeskey (1992), and Moats & Lyon (1993). Consistent with these trends, at Sprague School, boys and not girls had been labeled LD by second grade.

7. See Cobb, Wood, Yackel, Nicholls, Wheatley, Trigatti, & Perlwitz (1991) and Nicholls, Cobb, Wood, Yackel, & Patashnick (1990).

8. See deCharms (1984), Noddings (1996), and Ryan & Connell (1989).

9. See Atkinson, Heyns, & Veroff (1954), Deci & Ryan (1985), Koestner & McClelland (1992), McAdams (1980), McAdams & Constantian, (1983), McClelland (1985), White (1959), Winter (1996), and Winter & Stewart (1978).

10. See Adelman (1978), Adelman & Chaney (1982), Adelman & Taylor (1983), Kelly (1985), and Kistner & Törgesen (1987).

11. See Bandura (1997), Graham & Hoehn (1995), Schunk (1996), and Weiner (1992).

12. See Cordova & Lepper (1996), Deci & Chandler (1986), Deci, Hodges, Pierson, & Tomassone (1992), Deci & Ryan (1985), Grolnick & Ryan (1990), and Schunk (1989b).

13. See Colby, Kohlberg, Gibbs, & Lieberman (1983), Erikson (1963), Leahy & Hunt (1983), Nicholls (1989), Weiner (1992), and White (1959).

14. See Markman (1979) and Nicholls & Hazzard (1993).

15. See Bandura (1997), Damon (1977), Deci & Ryan (1985), Power, Higgins, & Kohlberg (1989), and Weiner (1992).

16. See Nicholls (1989).

17. See Nicholls (1989).

18. Examples of such evidence are available in Butler (1989), Collins (1996), and Stipek & MacIver (1989).

19. See, for example, Ladd (1990) and Ladd & Profilet (1996).

20. See, for example, Weiner (1992).

21. See Burhans & Dweck (1995), Chiu, Hong, & Dweck (1997), Licht (1983), Miller (1985), Miller & Hom (1990), and Pintrich, Anderman, & Klobucar (1994).

22. See, for example, Asher & Coie (1990), Buhrmester & Furman (1987), Clark & Mills (1993), Crick & Dodge (1994), Dodge, Coie, Pettit, & Price (1990), Eisenberg (1992), Eisenberg & Miller (1987), Graham & Hoehn (1995), Juvonen & Wentzel (1996), Ladd (1990), and Ladd & Price (1986).

23. See, for example, Graziano & Eisenberg (1997) and Hill (1987).

24. Atkinson, Heyns, & Veroff (1954) and McAdams (1980) offer introductory vocabulary for these distinctions.

25. See Laursen, Hartup, & Koplas (1996).

26. Details of such relationships are offered in Grusec & Kuczynski (1997).

27. See, for example, DeVries (1970), Eisenberg (1992), and Selman (1980).

28. Buhrmester & Furman (1987) assumed the existence of this distinction and explored second graders' impressions of who provided them with intimacy and companionship. See also Selman & Demorest (1984).

29. Freeman (1994) offered an exception to this in that she compared all three motives in troubled adolescents and student leaders, some of whom were likely to have learning disabilities.

30. See Chapman (1988), Friedman & Medway (1987), Grolnick & Ryan (1990), Licht (1993), Pintrich, Anderman, & Klobucar (1994), Sabatino (1982), Schunk (1989b), and Wilson & David (1994).

31. See Heavey, Adelman, Nelson, & Smith (1989).

32. See Deci et al. (1992), Grolnick & Ryan (1990), Licht (1993), Lincoln & Chazan (1979), Short (1992), and Skaalvik (1993).

33. See Gresham & MacMillan (1997), Lincoln & Chazan (1979), Pearl (1992), Pearl & Bay (1999), Pearl & Bryan (1992), Pearl & Cosden (1982), Saunders & Chambers (1996), and Siperstein, Leffert, & Wenz-Gross (1997).

34. See VonLeyden (1985). Although Csikszentmihalyi (1990) defined this Aristotelian approach to happiness as the supreme goal in life, characterizing happiness as "optimal experience," we tend to see happiness as one of many important goals.

CHAPTER

2 Little Boy on the Defensive

Like all four of the boys involved in this project, Bruce Johnson did not put various parts of his school and personal experience into satisfactory relation with one another. In many ways Bruce's situation made it easy for John Nicholls and Thyra DeBolt, Bruce's teacher, to facilitate growth in Bruce's understanding of himself. His parents readily understood the reasons why John hoped to coach Bruce toward a more solid commitment to topics of interest. Likewise, Thyra was open to suggestions and looked for ways to help Bruce gain more out of school. Nevertheless, Bruce wounded himself by becoming dependent on adult guidance and undermining his ability to sustain friendships. His minimal sense of self-efficacy, high levels of ego orientation, and preoccupation with exchange rather than intimacy made it difficult to achieve the comfortable levels of self-determination, competence, and affiliation that his classmates took for granted.

Bruce was overly preoccupied with his intellectual standing, relative to his peers, in a way that undermined his ability to build satisfactory relationships and attend to the task at hand. Instead, Bruce appealed to Thyra for support while struggling to defend himself from peers who mocked his poor academic performance. In doing so, Bruce fluctuated from exhibiting the work-avoidant and ego-involved behaviors that exacerbated his academic difficulties to revealing occasional flashes of the task involvement that normally absorbed his peers.

Most of the second graders in Bruce's class exhibited some limitations in their social and intellectual skills and were relatively forgiving of one another's transgressions. Yet, Bruce's behavior, combined with the special attention he received from Thyra, made his peers, at times, seem justified in their hostility. Bruce's machismo attracted attention and led us to speculate about how this limited his personal growth and ability to fully participate in Thyra's classroom.

A Divided Intellectual Life

The most obvious evidence that Bruce fractured his intellectual life came from watching his behavior in class, and comparing that to his reflections and those of his parents. When students' personal and academic lives are in sync, we expect a high degree of concordance among these perspectives. When students fracture their intellectual lives, we expect to find disjointed evidence coming from multiple sources. The equilibrium that is apparent with concordance can enhance students' concentration and commitment to intellectual tasks. However, disequilibrium, apparent when evidence from multiple sources remains disjointed, signals a potential for growth if individuals strive to regain a sense of equilibrium and trouble if they do not. Students with learning disabilities face an additional challenge to this otherwise normal cycle of development because it is natural for students with learning disabilities to be more distractible and exhibit more off-task behavior than their peers.[1] Such distractibility makes it difficult to create meaningful intellectual lives. Children like Bruce are confronted with the situation faced by Helen Cordero, a Cochiti Pueblo woman who:

> began making pottery twenty-five years ago, she turned her hands to figurines because her bowls and jars "were crooked and didn't look right." In so doing, she happened on what was to become a perfect embodiment of personal and cultural experience. All the "little people" she has shaped . . . are modeled selves, representing and recreating images of personal history and family life. . . . Through her ceramic creativity, Helen Cordero has made one of the oldest forms of native American self-representation her own, reinvented a long-standing but moribund Cochiti tradition of figurative pottery, engendered a revolution in Pueblo ceramics . . . and reshaped her own life as well as that of her family and her pueblo.[2]

Helen had to revise her understanding of what it meant to do pottery from the task initially set before her to one that allowed her to combine personal skill and cultural norms. Like students who have problems adjusting to school, Helen had to define a task that allowed one experience to give direction and meaning to another. In contrast to Helen, Bruce had difficulty putting the various parts of his school experience into satisfactory relation to one another and with other aspects of his life. In this respect, Bruce created internal barriers and external conflicts that could not be resolved in growth-enhancing ways.

This fractured experience was certainly evident when, a week before Thanksgiving, John began observing in Thyra's classroom. During the class announcements, Bruce drummed his pencil, yawned and drummed again, then waited, showing no interest in discerning the shape of the day Thyra had planned. After the announcements, Thyra asked Bruce, Tim, and Rick—slower students who often formed a group separate from the rest of the class—to go to the table at the back of the room in preparation for reading. Sitting there, Bruce tapped his face with a ruler and flicked his pencil, happily waiting, steadily stimulating himself. The readiness to wait idly and the associated self-stimulation proved typical of Bruce. Bruce's inattention continued later in the day while the school social worker led a discussion and the students ate snacks. Bruce's attention was on his food, not on the discussion. Oblivious to those around him, Bruce carefully sucked a large pretzel away until there was a pointed sliver that, smiling, he finally relished out of existence.

A science project was next—testing various materials to see if they were magnetic. Groups of children were given magnets, a collection of small objects, and a worksheet to record specific predictions and findings about which objects would be attracted by the magnet.

Bruce's group quickly figured out that the magnet would not pick up aluminum foil. Eager to help, John Nicholls deviated from the worksheet and showed the boys how the foil could be picked up if they put a paper clip under it. Immediately John wondered if he should have intervened because Bruce proceeded to adopt the manner of someone engaged in an illicit activity. Although John hoped only to foster interest, he inadvertently fostered something else.

"Wow! Mark!" declared Bruce, showing the effect to his friend.

Bruce would briefly approach the assigned task, but repeatedly return to the foil trick, moving around the room with a slightly conspiratorial air, to show his classmates. Like a devious magician, Bruce carefully positioned the magnet to hide the paper clip that made his trick work. Bruce knew enough not to call his discovery to the attention of Thyra. Instead, he shared his discovery with others in a slightly surreptitious fashion that seemed to imply and sustain the idea that what is interesting to him is not legitimate school knowledge.

Embarrassed, John could see how easy it was to encourage Bruce to become distracted from the intellectual aspects of how magnets work. One unassigned trick was to see how many paper clips could be hung in a line below the magnet. When Thyra noticed that one student invented this, she encouraged other students to try. Instead of finishing the assignment, Bruce began doing the trick and then created his own variation—hanging a string of clips from both ends of the magnet.

The other students in Bruce's group expeditiously and accurately completed their assignments before inventing exercises in ingenuity, some of which were later endorsed by Thyra. Bruce neither worked on the assigned task nor persisted on extension activities that Thyra appropriated from other students. Instead, he invented his own spin-off activity, one that might be credited either as an ingenious variation or as an example of his sometimes-disruptive tendency to break loose from instructions. Were these behaviors indicative of the inattention attributed to students with learning disabilities or did they reflect a calculated display of autonomy? Bruce's reasons for such behavior are not as easy to identify as the behavior itself.

Thyra, surveying the busy students, passed Bruce working on his variation and commented amiably, "You can't do it like that. I have to watch you every minute Bruce." Consistent with later observations, her comment implied that it was common for Bruce to deviate from whatever was assigned. This time, Thyra conveyed only a gentle condemnation because Bruce's activities were not that far away from the assigned task and his behavior was not interfering with others' ability to learn.

Bruce, on the other hand, may have interpreted Thyra's off-handed comment as implying that he was not constructing legitimate school knowledge. If he could reflect on his own behavior, Bruce would discover that he completed only exercises in ingenuity, and at least one of those exercises was gently classed as deviant. Unlike the other students, Bruce had not managed to coordinate his talents and interests with the approved school agenda. His initiative was preserved, but the gap between legitimate forms of school knowledge and his "illicit" forms of personal knowledge might have been widened slightly.

Inattention and work-avoidant behavior remained relatively common for Bruce. When the class went to the rug for a story, for example, Bruce sat at the back, against the wall, with Chris. Rather than listen to the story, Bruce twisted the drawstring on his jogging pants around his fingers in complex ways. He attended to the legitimate classroom activity only when overactive Helen interrupted the proceedings. Bruce scowled at Helen, bared his teeth, and shook his head in condemnation of her behavior. Then, Bruce returned his attention to twisting his fingers into different arrangements, grinned, and showed them to Matt. As Thyra discussed the next assignment, Bruce continued to play with his fingers before leaving to get a drink.

When the class moved to a discussion of the Plains Indians, Thyra called on Bruce. Her attention, combined with the topic of how Native Americans used the different parts of buffalo, seemed to capture Bruce's interest. Bruce stopped his finger play and, later in the discussion, waved his hand vigorously, indicating that he wanted to contribute. When the discussion turned away from the use of buffalo as food, Bruce returned to experimenting with his hand, folding his thumb and fingers in diverse arrangements. The stimulation of food, fingers, and face seemed more compelling than the discussion Thyra was leading.

As instructions for the next assignment were given, Bruce again attended only intermittently. As with the science project, Bruce was not dependent enough on Thyra's encouragement to listen to, much less follow, her instructions. This behavior reduced Bruce's opportunities for legitimate independent action. Like any caring teacher, Thyra would help Bruce, but he would inevitably be in the position of starting the assignment about the time other students were almost finished.

Soon other students would be working alone, in pairs, and in larger groups, sitting cozily in self-chosen places, reading self-selected books or writing personal stories. Such students would develop tastes and talents that defined their individual intellectual identities, while Bruce would avoid his work or languish on material that offered less scope for the development and expression of identity. As a result, Bruce's identity as a slow learner would be reinforced.

Bruce's enthusiasm when called on to answer questions about buffalo and Native American life, and his ability to recite facts suggested that he could do more intellectual work than he often did. John found another hint of this when he followed the class to spend time with a specialist in the computer lab. Bruce shared a keyboard with Chris, and the two boys played a word game in which they had to compete to solve multiple choice vocabulary items. When Chris, an able reader, got stuck, John asked Bruce, who was not paying attention, to help. Bruce perked up and twice managed to assist Chris. Though this helping violated the competitive nature of the task, neither boy objected. Bruce found ways to eliminate alternatives and made good guesses, even when he could not read all the words. Nevertheless, Bruce's attention to the task was constantly in a state of flux: He participated eagerly only when John nudged him to do so.

For most of the game, Bruce remained ahead of Chris. But, the game ended with a tied score. The display on the screen was not programmed for a tie and declared Bruce the winner. Bruce announced, "I won, but we were equal."

To those of us who study moral reasoning and achievement motivation, this sequence of events holds many levels of meaning. Like the computer, Bruce seemed confused about how to interpret this tie score. This same kind of confusion is found among young children who typically have trouble distinguishing between testing and learning situations. Many second graders seem captured by the test score itself and rely on scores as the "correct" indicator of competence. They do not see that collaboration undermines the validity of test scores. Most children of that age will ignore the amount of coaching that goes into obtaining a particular score. They assert that equal attainment is the criterion for establishing fair testing and that peer tutoring is a fair way to have a test as long as everyone scores equally high.

Confusion about the interpretation of test scores manifests itself in a larger confusion about when helping is a means for fostering learning and when it is a form of cheating. Second graders find it difficult to determine whether worksheets offer opportunities for copying to learn or whether copying is cheating. Even when teachers offer direct instruction on this issue, students are not always able to use that information effectively. It would be problematic, therefore, to assume that Bruce revealed a form of confusion found only among second graders with learning disabilities.

On the other hand, Bruce's confusion over who won the game could also be seen as a form of egotistical thinking. Researchers have been speculating about a possible causal relationship between the development of an understanding of ability as current capacity—the idea that one's capacity will limit the effect of effort on task performance—and the ability to become fully ego-involved. Second grade is a period during which most children do not fully differentiate ability from effort and so, theoretically speaking, could not be ego-involved in the same way as adults. With this in mind, Bruce's comment about who won seems to be ecological validation for the idea that, like many second graders, he could not sustain the adultlike ego involvement implied by his preoccupation with winning the game.

Here, regardless of the reasons why Bruce made his comment, it seems appropriate to emphasize that Bruce was not optimally motivated. Missing the essential purpose of the word game, Bruce did not walk away preoccupied with the new words he might have learned. Comments such as those Bruce made about his standing relative to his peers reflected ego-involvement rather than task-involvement.

At the time, John concluded that Bruce's divided intellectual experience manifested itself in a preoccupation with being smart relative to his peers rather than in a preoccupation with the particular information he might have gained. Yet, Bruce did not entirely reject the kinds of knowledge fostered in school. At the end of John's second day observing, for example, a worksheet had been assigned. Bruce was waiting for help from Thyra before doing each item. When a nearby classmate announced he was finished, Bruce focused and, unassisted, made steady progress. Bruce continued to work hard until Thyra announced, "There are five minutes to go [until school ends]."

"I'll bring this home and do it," said Bruce, sounding eager. But after saying this, Bruce stopped immediately. His puzzled look suggested a gap between his words and feelings. Then, instead of taking his work home, Bruce put the unfinished paper in his desk and left for the day. Although Bruce acknowledged the importance of school knowledge, he was not ready to act in accordance with this acknowledgment.

Bruce did not seem to see the contradiction between his thoughts and deeds. This was evident the next day when students filled out a report for upcoming parent conferences. The sheet read, "My favorite subject is . . ." Bruce wrote, "*math*."

"This is how I think I'm doing in reading," the sheet continued. Bruce wrote nothing.

Thyra asked Bruce, "How do you think you are doing in reading?"

"I'm doing good."

"OK. Write, 'I am doing good,' and then tell me why," suggested Thyra.

Bruce's body went floppy. Next, he took a bathroom trip. Zipping back to his desk, he finished his sheet, eliciting occasional advice from Thyra. Bruce's completed report read:

> Reading: *I am deg* [doing] *gud* [at reading] *becus I am working.*
> Math: *gud I pist* [passed] *math pakit* [packet] *better.*
> printing: *I cat* [can't] *rit* [write] *gud.*
> What Mrs. DeBolt should tell my parents about me: *I like school.*

Bruce's sense that he was "doing good" and the poor qualities of this writing do not match well with the competence that John noticed. John wondered if the gap between Bruce's words and action, between the experience of school and the speaking and writing about it, was too large for Bruce. John also wondered if Bruce's positive talk would create personal interest and deeply satisfying learning, or if it would stop Bruce from analyzing his experience constructively. Bruce's personal desires and academic performance seemed not to be in constructive relation with one another: Either Bruce could not recognize or could not speak honestly about the different aspect of his experience.

The contradictions that were evident in the first three days of observing were also apparent when John initially met and interviewed Bruce about becoming a participant in this research. John asked Bruce to describe his feelings about schoolwork, homework, and personal learning projects. When Bruce was asked to describe a really good day in school, the following conversation took place.

"OK. What days make you feel good? When is it a neat day for you?"

"No work." Bruce made a rather blunt assertion of his lack of love for learning that contradicted an opening declaration that a good day is when he does good things. The divided nature of Bruce's approach to schooling is evident when he says that schoolwork is not inherently satisfying for him, but he wants to do well.

"OK. What would you do if you had no work? What sort of things?"

"Play."

"OK. You'd play. What sort of playing do you like?"

"Computer."

"Oh really. So what do you have? Computer games?"

"Computer games."

"So what are your favorites?"

"Munchers." Later, John noticed that this word game was popular in the classroom. In contradiction to this claim of favoritism, however, John saw Bruce try the game only once, and then Bruce revealed no mastery. In his haste to press buttons, Bruce learned nothing from a nearby classmate who tried to coach him. Bruce was ready to mislead John, and perhaps himself, about the nature of his experience.

"Do you have some times . . . when your schoolwork's like you'd like it to be?"

"When it's hard."

"When it's hard? Can you give me some examples?"

"Math."

"Ah ha."

"Science. . . ." Bruce continually directed John's attention to areas in which he felt competent. Bruce did not call for hard reading even though reading was the subject he had the most difficulty learning.

"Ah. . . . Can you explain a bit?"

"All right. I do something hard because I like it. It's fun."

In some students, the desire to do hard things, although not in reading, might indicate a desire to learn and a preference for substantive content areas. Yet, to focus only on the difficulty of school tasks suggests a thin vision of the value of schooling and is often an indicator of motivational difficulties. Saying that a task is hard reveals no sense of someone's intellectual interests and does not, in itself, reveal a critique.

Additional evidence that Bruce's critiques of his educational experience were quite thin emerged when John brought up the topic of homework. John asked if Bruce could think of a new kind of homework that would be good to have, Bruce said, "Math. Math packet." This was homework that had been assigned previously. Although Bruce did not love homework, he offered no ideas for improving it.

"OK. So what if you were the big boss in school, like the principal. . . . You could say homework, or no homework."

"Yeah!" Bruce was excited about the prospect of no homework.

"You'd say no homework, eh!"

"Yes. . . ."

"OK, why is that a good idea? I think I can guess. . . ."

"They [his classmates] wouldn't get mad."

"OK. You'd be everybody's friend if you did that, eh!"

Bruce nodded as if confirming a law of nature.

"In a lot of schools," John continued, "the homework that boys and girls have is the work they don't finish in school. . . . Do you think that's a good idea?"

"Yeah, so they don't have it the next morning."

"Ha! Would it be a good idea if you didn't have to take it home *and* you didn't have to do it the next morning?"

"Yep!"

"Better still would it?"

"Yeah 'cause you finished it."

Schoolwork here is defined as fixed in amount—not part of a never-ending flow of learning or a series of tasks that help Bruce articulate his questions or concerns. Bruce assumed that if schoolwork was not finished immediately, it must be finished later: He was not lazy. Yet despite a professed desire to learn, Bruce's goal was merely to be expedient in completing his assignments.

"OK, if you don't have homework and you're at home, are there some things you like finding out about. . . ?"

"All kinds of birds. . . . I look at books with birds in them, different kinds of birds and look at birds outside." This was a good sign—Bruce did have some intellectual interests.

"Are there any other things?"

"Yep. Dinosaurs."

"Anything else you like to find out about?"

"Flowers, 'cause my next door neighbor has a lot of flowers and trees. I walk around and look at them." These interests seemed real—Bruce's relaxed gestures, words, and personal experience seemed in tune with one another.

"OK," John continued, "Are there some things you can learn about better at home than you can at school?"

"Some things."

"Like what things?" Bruce became silent. "Anything you can learn better at home?" More silence.

When comparing Bruce's experience with schoolwork, homework, and personal tasks to that of other second graders, Bruce appeared to fall between two categories representing different alienated visions about the importance of school learning.[3] Comments made about his interests outside of school suggest that Bruce agreed with children who had life-expanding personal intellectual projects, but did not find such personal expansion in schoolwork or homework. Yet, when Bruce talked and behaved like a work-avoidant student, he seemed to agree more with the children who saw sharp separations between personal experience and learning of any kind. Bruce was constrained by a narrow view of school knowledge as a collection of facts to be memorized, and preoccupied with the difficulty rather than the meaning of that knowledge.

This interview could be seen as evidence that Bruce lacked a clear sense of direction or set of reasons for learning. Bruce did not or could not intelligently frame purposes and act on purposes so framed. By avoiding as much schoolwork as possible and failing to define his own purposes for learning, Bruce resisted opportunities to define his intellectual identity. In this respect, Bruce made it difficult for the educators in his life to secure his active collaboration in the formation of useful intellectual pursuits. To facilitate the development of a less fractured experience, teachers are obliged to try enticing students like Bruce into acknowledging their areas of interest. Yet, Bruce actively resisted such encouragement toward autonomy and self-efficacy.

With this vision of self-determination, John interviewed Bruce for a second time in the library. John tried to elicit Bruce's interests and evaluations of his experience. "You remember last time I asked you to see if you had any ideas about things that could make schoolwork or homework better for you?"

"More harder work," repeated the tough guy.

After John asked Bruce why he wanted harder work, Bruce said, "It would make me know more and be smarter."

"OK, what about in reading stuff? What would make that better?"

"Easier."

Bruce's pattern of answers revealed an emphasis on being smart in the global sense of the term. Bruce wanted hard math, a subject he declared himself to be competent at doing, and easy reading, a subject he more readily acknowledged was difficult for him. These beliefs offered rather strong evidence that Bruce was preoccupied with how smart he was rather than with the aesthetics of things or whether his ideas made sense.

John turned to the subject of dinosaurs, declared to be one of Bruce's favorite topics. "What do you think would be most interesting if you were going to study dinosaurs?"

"Finding bones. Then you could bring them in and get money."

"Be hard to arrange wouldn't it? What if you could study and try to think about how they died out? Have you thought about that? Why they've all gone now?" asked John.

Many children recognize the unsettled nature of the dinosaur story and of much scientific knowledge. In Susan Hazzard's second grade class, for example, a student said, "Nobody really knows the answer [to why the dinosaurs became extinct]. But it would be a good [question] to study," and his classmates agreed.[4] Bruce, by way of contrast, had difficulty moving off the topic of gaining wealth and on to this or other more substantive issues that led many other second graders to find dinosaurs interesting to study. Bruce's mother assured John that Bruce had recently seen a TV program that had emphasized the continuing controversy about why the dinosaurs died out. However, Bruce did not respond to the substantive nature of John's question or offer any other information about the dinosaur program.

"They think that they died from starvation, because when it got so hot they didn't have any more food or water," Bruce told John, inventing his own answer.

"Do you think everybody thinks that or is that something the scientists are really not sure about?"

"That's what all them think."

"They do? Are there some things the scientists don't know?"

"Ah no. They know everything they can know."

"Scientists do, do they?"

"Mmm. Hmm."

Did Bruce think all knowledge of importance is factual and noncontroversial? Or, could he recognize the controversial nature of some topics even though he did not do so with dinosaurs? Most second graders can easily distinguish these two forms of knowledge. Yet, Bruce's preoccupation with the difficulty of schoolwork suggested either that he might not make this distinction, or that he might not be using his ability to do so. Only settled knowledge can be judged precisely hard or easy. In this respect, Bruce's concern to "be smart" and master hard tasks matched the view of knowledge that constitutes the aptly named game, Trivial Pursuit.

Such unsettled questions as why the dinosaurs died out, in contrast to factual information, are impossibly hard in that no one can, for the moment at least, come up with a definitive answer. In another respect, unsettled questions are very easy in that anyone can adopt a position without fear of being judged wrong or stupid. Controversies could provide students like Bruce, who are concerned about their competence, with a measure of protection from appearing incompetent. Unfortunately, Bruce, who remained preoccupied with a world of discrete facts and truths, did not seem to see this possibility.

Despite Bruce's hesitancy to do so, many second graders make school learning personally meaningful. Second graders generally do not believe that they must learn facts before they can be allowed to think about controversial matters. Typically, students in Bruce's class and school were not confined to a world of noncontroversial knowledge and moved easily from one form of knowledge to another.

When Bruce's peers finished their assignments, they made their own experiments, asked their own questions, chose their own books, and found favorite authors and topics. If Bruce made a choice at all, it was more often to avoid finishing assignments. His choice of tasks seemed more like distractions than legitimate opportunities to learn. As long as

Bruce was preoccupied with his ability, he would have to constantly deal with the fact that he did not measure up to his peers. And, if Bruce confined himself to knowledge on which he could be judged either right or wrong, he could hardly develop the voice or initiative central to self-determination. Bruce could not put his personal and academic experience into satisfactory relationship with one another if his competence needs interfered with his sense of self-determination.

Bruce's ambivalence about academic achievement was also apparent at home. Talking with Bruce's parents, John noticed that they also recognized the conflicted sense of priorities John observed in their son. Bruce's parents had been recently coming out of hard financial times, had just finished getting their house sound and comfortable, and were busy trying to meet the needs of eleven children. Yet, Mr. and Mrs. Johnson quickly made time to meet John and were eager to talk about Bruce's progress. Bruce's parents were pleasant, direct, and open about Bruce and the difficulties the family had encountered.

"Personally," said Mrs. Johnson, "We're a Christian family and we try to encourage the right morals and actually that is more important. . . . What if you're an intellect and you don't care about being kind to someone? But then again, you want [your children] to reach their potential."

"Yeah," John agreed. "You know talking with Bruce . . . he's a good soldier, but it is hard for him to keep the interest there. It's like he's trying to make himself learn."

"He'd rather be fishing," his mother chuckled.

"Well, we had a book on owling," said Mr. Johnson. ". . . I read him the book and Bruce said, 'I'm going to learn this book.' He wanted to practice. He was going to spend hours reading that book."

"Soon we couldn't find the book," added Mrs. Johnson.

"He looked for the book though."

"We're going to have to buy another one, 'cause he wanted to learn the whole book, word for word."

"That might help him. It might snowball," noted Mrs. Johnson.

"[In the book, Bruce read] the word *disappointed,* and I said it's a long word. 'But I read it didn't I,' [Bruce] said. He gets so excited about it because of the subject."

". . . So I wondered," stammered John, "if asking him—putting him more in charge of deciding what he could do that would be interesting and would help him learn. . . . Explicitly, asking him. . . ."

"You know," interrupted Mrs. Johnson, "that's another thing. Our [younger] kids haven't had a lot of opportunity to make a lot of decisions. A lot of kids will get an allowance and they can spend it. They go to the library and pick out the books they want. We're starting to again, but we just haven't been in that position for three years."

"I think that generating and maintaining interest would be the thing. That would be my bias," suggested John.

"Just the way he clung to that owling book, that was his. It was his, you know," said Mr. Johnson, thoughtfully.

"That's the thing about home schooling, where they say it actually motivates the kids more, because they start applying things more."

Mrs. Johnson was to return to the theme of home schooling several times over the course of the year. She had noticed an emerging phenomenon among a growing number of parents who believe that *where* one learns is essential to *what* one learns. To learn only at home rather than accept school as an alternative place for intellectual inquiry could be interpreted as an extreme way in which to fracture one's educational experience by overlooking self-determination and affiliation needs. Bruce's parents were concerned about Bruce's tendency to ignore some of his academic needs at school.

"Generally school focuses too much on the type of knowledge that everyone agrees on. You know—how you spell this or that whereas most of the things we do are controversial. Like what church you choose to go to." John introduced his bias.

"Yes, right."

"You're right," agreed Mr. Johnson, ". . . like building a bridge, one engineer might build one way and another would do it differently and they might both be right."

"Somehow you forget the perspective of teaching kids to think. To really think!" added Mrs. Johnson. Bruce certainly did not acquire his rigid definition of knowledge as noncontroversial from his parents.

John ended his session with Bruce's parents by looking through the photographs of the recent major renovation of their house to accommodate the large family. A major piece of work, now virtually complete. "Look, see how happy they are," commented Mr. Johnson. Bruce and the others were smiling at the camera, clearly happy and actively roaming the house in progress. These pictures of Bruce and his relaxed siblings emphasized the strain of school for Bruce.

It was clear that Bruce was often so busy at school, working to impress adults, that he paid less attention to the task at hand. His energies were devoted to sustaining an ego orientation that undermined his ability to meet self-determination and affiliation needs. Is it fruitful to ask whether the causes of Bruce's difficulties were at home or at school? Should school be more welcoming to students who, after but seven years in the world, find that their classmates have been off and running several years before they realized there was a race? Should parents be pushing their children to love learning as much as they love their family members? What of homes, unlike Bruce's, that somehow encourage children to see, as lesser beings, peers who take longer to finish an assignment? And how was Bruce, who played a small but active role in the construction of his life, responsible for his

Challenges and Controversies

- What does fractured experience look like?
- How can teachers encourage students who are avoiding schoolwork to identify reasons for learning?
- Is it always important for students to have reasons for doing schoolwork?
- Should teachers alter the curriculum to include respect for students' areas of interest?
- When students do not notice that some topics are open to multiple interpretations, how can teachers encourage them to do so?
- Should teachers introduce both controversial and noncontroversial topics in school? Would this help students, like Bruce, who hold narrow definitions of knowledge?

situation? John hoped that, by talking with everyone about all these questions, they would learn how to help Bruce move his need for competence into a more satisfactory relation with other parts of his experience.

Helpful Coaching or Facilitated Laziness?

When John began observing Bruce, he noticed that Bruce was very dependent on receiving special attention from Thyra. During John's first visit, for example, when math assignments were introduced, Bruce paid no attention as Thyra gave instructions. As the other students started work, Bruce called, "Hey, Mizz DeBolt. Hey, Mizz DeBolt," then waited while Thyra attended to others.

Bruce looked briefly at the instructions, and then walked over to ask Thyra for help. Thyra proceeded to take Bruce and Rick to the back table for special instruction. Under Thyra's attentive eye, Bruce looked positively cozy. Some of the sensuality of his pretzel eating showed, as if he was snuggling into a smooth, warm bed on a cold night to be told a story. Bruce clearly trusted and appreciated his teacher. Unfortunately, whereas most of the other students were well into the assignment, Bruce had not begun.

On John's second day, Bruce walked into class smiling, and Thyra commented quietly to John, "That smile!" John could see why Bruce appeared comfortable with Thyra. Although not specially trained to be particularly sensitive to the needs of students with learning disabilities, Thyra made a special effort to ensure that Bruce had a snack each morning, and her manner toward him was naturally warm and caring.

Bruce continued to start assignments slowly and elicited special help from Thyra. He applied energy to maintaining his dependency on Thyra, but not toward defining the shape of independent literary or numerical activities. Concerned with fairness, Thyra made a habit of giving special treatment to students with learning disabilities, hoping to reinforce the value of everyone's ideas. During a discussion of maps and compass directions, for example, Thyra called on Bruce when she thought he would know an answer. Bruce did. When another student repeated Bruce's information later in the discussion, Thyra said, "That's what Bruce said too, and he was right." Bruce smiled broadly and looked around. Such public affirmation of Bruce's ideas seemed to help his sense of competence.

Thyra was clearly in Bruce's corner, and went out of her way to support him. Rather than ignore him or imply that he could not contribute, Thyra constantly called on Bruce when she thought he would be unlikely to embarrass himself. Nevertheless, Thyra's approach involved taking the risk that Bruce might publicly prove himself foolish. It was easier to take this risk with questions that required relatively little interpretation. Yet, because Thyra's questions were factual, the simple relaying of information could have reinforced Bruce's commitment to the belief that school knowledge should consist of "hard truths."

For teachers like Thyra, who empathize with slower learners, trying to guess when students might be able to succeed can be stressful. Thyra saw Bruce as performing lower in reading than almost anyone she had taught in the past, but she also saw Bruce as more able than many students with learning disabilities at keeping track of assignments. And,

"He's not a behavior problem. He can be a bully once in a while, [but] he can hold his own."

"I think of him as a good soldier," John agreed. "He wants to do his best—his duty."

"I think he does. When he knows an answer you can tell it makes him feel good. He gets a smile on his face. He gets a smile on his face when he's being a little devil, too."

"That doesn't seem very often," John wondered out loud.

"No, but he knows I've got his number. He's really good. I thought, when I saw his name on the class list, 'This child is going to be trouble.' But, he isn't." Nevertheless, Thyra sought positive ways to enhance Bruce's achievement that inevitably necessitated special treatment.

Later in the year, John sat by Thyra facing Bruce as Thyra worked with the slower learners. At the start of the first reading worksheet, Thyra repeatedly pointed to words, directing Bruce's attention to them. Bruce did not look at the words, but stared intently into Thyra's face as if to extract the words from her head. When Bruce did glance hastily at the paper, he misread the question. Bruce's whole body conveyed a powerful single-minded focus on Thyra's face rather than on the task at hand. Thyra's prompts eventually led Bruce to focus on the words. With Thyra at his side, Bruce steadily became more attentive to the words and read alone. "Any more?" Bruce asked as he finished.

Thyra produced a sheet requiring more reading than was necessary on the first two assignments. By then, Bruce had momentum. He focused on words by pointing with his pencil. Bruce did not daydream and finished well before Tim and Rick. At the beginning, Bruce's efforts were considerable, but wholly directed toward extracting answers from Thyra. Once sure of the questions, and focused on them, Bruce could perform competently. This was an amazingly difficult transformation from his initial preoccupation with social interaction.

As the class prepared to research an animal of their choice, each student had a sheet asking for a name and what students want to know about their chosen animal. Bruce started, then changed his mind. He looked, as he often did, in the beautiful, large animal book that Thyra had bought for the class. New animals kept distracting Bruce from settling on a single animal of interest. Bruce was carried away, turning pages, peering in fascination at the photographs in Thyra's book.

Eventually, Bruce settled on studying leopards. Thyra told him to write that down, helping him to the first step. Bruce then read the rest of the question sheet with a little help from John. One question was "What do you want to know about this animal?"

To nudge Bruce, John eventually suggested, "What they eat? How fast they run?" Thus Bruce trapped John, like Thyra, into taking away his need for initiative in the name of help. Lamely realizing, after the fact, that Bruce had trapped him, John rushed to expand his list of suggestions so Bruce would have to take at least some initiative by choosing.

With assistance, Bruce found a book with a page on panthers—temporarily declared to be his topic. Bruce read first with Thyra's help and then with John's. Several times, Bruce turned and looked right into John's face with an appeal for help. The force of Bruce's flirting was more compelling to John when Bruce directed his attention toward John than when John watched Bruce make the same gestures toward Thyra. Bruce was a significant presence, hard to resist partly because too much resistance might have led Bruce to opt out of the task.

John waited a bit longer than Thyra typically did for Bruce to figure out words, saying "You can do it" or "You got that one!" John tried neither to take over nor to let Bruce drown in the difficulty of the task, but Bruce left little middle ground, and John read an occasional word. At one point, when Bruce was stalled on a word that John thought Bruce was about to read, Thyra, who was watching nearby, could not resist helping him. At the end, John was not sure if he had pushed Bruce too hard. Although Bruce remembered and understood the half page he read, John could not tell if Bruce felt coerced into learning. Had John killed what interest Bruce had in learning about panthers? With Bruce, the balance between encouragement and coercion was very hard to find, but self-determination hinges on sustaining a balance between offering informational feedback and encouraging initiative.

One weekend in March, John was ready to share his writing with Bruce's parents and, in the process, made a suggestion about how Bruce's family might help him move out of this dependent approach to learning. John explained that he thought it might be helpful to find ways to encourage Bruce to take initiative in figuring out what to do on his assignments. To help Mr. and Mrs. Johnson understand why, John gave them a brief summary of research on the value of telling children that they are doing the things that they should be doing.[5] The findings of this suggest that children will improve their performance if adults label the things they actually *do* rather than tell children what they *should be doing,* and John thought this information might be helpful. John's nervousness about placing more burdens on a family that seemed overwhelmed with other, more pressing concerns was quickly dispelled when Mr. Johnson announced that the research summary was interesting and the project was proving interesting for him as well as helpful for Bruce.

Despite this new kind of encouragement, Bruce continued to set himself up for embarrassment, undermining his initiative: It was sometimes difficult to find forms of intellectual inquiry to label positively. One afternoon, for example, the topic was fish, one of Bruce's favorites. Bruce had drawn a hammerhead shark and was supposed to label its parts. When Thyra reminded him, Bruce said, "Do I *have* to? Do I *have* to?"

Thyra insisted, so he wrote, "*Fin Fin Sc[ale] and Mo[uth]*" in small print and handed it to Thyra for inspection.

Next, a "Fish Facts" sheet followed a filmstrip. Bruce looked at the sheet and burst, "Why do we do this? It's so easy!" He looked at Lucy and Jean, who sat across from him, and repeated, "It's so easy!" The girls just looked at him seeming to know that Bruce had not had enough time to assess the difficulty of this task.

As one of his classmates read a passage from this fact sheet Bruce did not pay attention, but when Thyra asked a question, Bruce's hand shot up. Because he had not listened, Bruce was uncertain about distinctions between gills, gill slits, and mouth and barely avoided making a public mess-up.

When the students began writing labels on a fish diagram, Bruce asked, "Are you supposed to do them on these or these?" He failed to understand the very task he had just declared easy.

Soon, Bruce had the location of scales and gill cover transposed, Thyra came to help and, across the desk, Jean sniggered at his mistake.

"He'll get it," said Thyra, who did not hear Bruce bragging about the "easy" work.

Later, John handed Thyra his roughly typed notes for this section of the day, including details about Bruce's bragging. John hoped to illuminate the difficulties Bruce faced when coordinating issues of pride and embarrassment when he added a note describing his own reactions to the events:

> As I see it, this [behavior] puts you in a tough spot—defending Bruce when he probably seems [like] an egotistical male buffoon to Jean. He loudly declared the material easy and then proved, in several ways, that it was hard for him. He and you are in a tough place and Jean makes it hard for both of you. Bruce's egotism adds to the problem. I wonder if, somehow, you rather than Jean might go on the offensive. It seems to me, she has you on the defensive a little on this occasion. Does this make sense?
>
> Pressing to make tasks cooperatively done might be the only way out of it. . . . People like Jean might have to be told, perhaps directly, that the big mistake in class is not to make a mistake, but to laugh or snort when someone makes a mistake. Bruce somehow has to learn not to say things are easy. . . . You are [already] on Bruce's side in this, so assertively undermining the sort of impulse Jean displays would be consistent with that.

Despite everyone's best attempts to avoid undermining Bruce's initiative, Bruce continued to respond only to the help of adults. He never really worked independently or accepted help from his peers for more than a few short bursts during a school day. Late in the year, for example, when students were given the task of finding a good part in their novel to read out loud, Bruce said his novel had all bad parts. Thyra found herself sitting by him saying, "Do you remember a part you liked?"

Bruce shook his drooping head. He did not look at Thyra. Suddenly, Bruce popped up in his seat, and screwed up his face in anticipation of Thyra's next comment. "Well, maybe you can find something," Thyra suggested and moved on, resisting the temptation to solve this dilemma for Bruce.

Brucc yawned, put his face in his book, stretched, and scratched. John proceeded to read a bit for Bruce, but Bruce was not following along. The book was not easy: There was no way Bruce could get much from it. Fortunately, Bruce drifted off and looked at another book. The second book was a little easier, and Bruce smiled as he zipped back to his seat with it. It was difficult for adults to demand self-determination from Bruce but Bruce needed such restraint if he was ever to set tasks for himself that were of an appropriate difficulty level.

By May, Bruce seemed to be holding his own more often and sometimes worked in a constructive fashion. But the old themes appeared again and again. In math, for example, the work seemed well within his grasp. Some of it involved only counting, which was easy for Bruce. Yet, Bruce did not try to read the simple directions or ask a classmate. Instead, he stole looks at Lucy's work or asked Thyra for help.

It was frustrating to see Bruce seek adult help without seeking independence. Bruce's declarations that difficult tasks were easy coincided with inattentive and work-avoidant behavior. When drawn to a task, either out of interest or by his teacher, Bruce exhibited low levels of self-efficacy when confronted with challenge. Not quite helpless, Bruce was very skilled at eliciting advice from adults while ignoring the expertise of his peers. Students like Bruce put quite a burden on teachers who rely on principles of care

Challenges and Controversies

- Can adults identify children's motivational needs? What behaviors reflect self-determination, competence, and affiliation needs?
- Should teachers monitor their responses to particular students? How can teachers become aware of the ways in which they reinforce dependency?
- How can teachers encourage students with low self-efficacy to become aware of their talents and interests?
- Are there easy ways for adults to identify themes in the tasks children approach and avoid?
- How are patterns of helpless behavior different from patterns of egotistical behavior?
- What can teachers do to help students become aware of egotistical behavior?
- What is the nature of interpersonal relationships in school? What levels of intimacy and exchange are appropriate?
- How can teachers convey affection and still encourage autonomy?

and equality of outcome to organize their classrooms. Ensuring that such students learn to read, write, calculate, and speak as well as their peers is an admirable—but sometimes unattainable—goal. Finding ways to help them become constructive members of the community and identify value in their work may be the more practical alternative. Toward that end, it is worthwhile to revive the teaching adage, "catch them being good" and label those behaviors.

Flashes of Connected Experience

Thyra was committed to labeling positive behavior and was undaunted by debates over the cause of Bruce's overly dependent and egotistical behavior. She was sustained by occasional glimpses of Bruce working in a comfortable state of task-involvement. Early in the year when Thyra asked, "How do migrating salmon find their way back to the place they hatched?" Bruce's hand was up quickly. He answered confidently and adequately and soon put his hand up to ask, "Do they turn red because they were in the ocean?" Thyra called on Bruce when she judged he would not embarrass himself, and she was delighted to find him engaged for much of this discussion about salmon.

As he and his parents pointed out, fish were of special interest to Bruce. The work-avoidant boy could become comfortably task-involved when the topic of fish came up. Bruce had plenty of fish stories and said, "I got a book in my locker about fish."

On John's third visit, when half the class was in the learning center with a specialist teacher, the students wrote wishes related to peace to be put on posters. "*I wih [wish] me dad wud stoq smok*," wrote Bruce.

The learning specialist suggested other ideas, "How about stop polluting water? Stop killing certain animals?"

"Yeah!" said Bruce, reacting to animals. He wrote, "*I wih pepl wad stoq kileg unmils*." Bruce's spelling was hardly standard, but he expressed and shaped his interest in animals. His involvement during this session was intermittent, but Bruce could voice his interests in school.

Later in the year, when Thyra read to the class about Harriet Tubman, Bruce was a different person. At the front of the rug, he was alert and answered questions thoughtfully—wholly part of the class. Bruce was not required to read, and seemed to experience no worry that his oral contributions would be judged foolish.

Once we pulled these kinds of behaviors out of the routine observations made each day, it became possible to see a theme in the kinds of activities that sustained Bruce's attention. Bruce consistently became interested in activities that involved nature and prototypically masculine forms of risk-taking.

When the class moved to writing about a favorite object, for example, Bruce chose "fishing rod." But, despite his interest in fishing, he sat without writing, playing with his earring, and ignored John's attempt to talk of fishing. His behavior seemed like that of a man-of-the-world who wanted his personal interests kept private.

Formerly a pioneering mountaineer,[6] John showed color slides of his adventures and Bruce answered a question that wholly stumped his more bookish classmates. Bruce might not have known the classics of children's literature and he might deny his experience of mathematics, but he was distinctively knowledgeable about the world of "manly" action.

Later, when Thyra read a story, Bruce was alert and competent. In the story, the characters traveled across the country in 27 cars and trucks. Thyra asked how that could happen. There was confusion and uncertainty among the other students, but Bruce's hand shot up, "Oh! Oh! Hitching."

Near the end of the year, Thyra was pleasantly surprised by how well Bruce had persisted on the time-consuming standardized comprehension test. Bruce persisted even though everyone knew that many items were probably too difficult for him.

Knowing that Bruce had difficulty learning from his peers, probably the most exciting moment in John's observations was the day when Bruce took a self-selected novel, sat near the window beside Rob, and read. He came across the room to ask John for a little help once, but went back, mouthing words as he read. John's eyes widened in delight as Bruce occasionally asked Rob rather than an adult to tell him words. Bruce then drifted off briefly, but was soon back to mouthing words, as he read largely unassisted. Was Bruce becoming a more self-determined learner?

Controversies abound over whether students' motivational orientations are best characterized as stable aspects of their personalities or induced by situational variability. Like many intellectual dichotomies, such conversations serve to highlight important features of individuals' motivation, but offer oversimplified explanations of a particular person's experience. Over the course of the academic year, for example, Bruce began to show more task-involved behavior, making it possible for him to concentrate more fully on the task at hand. Nevertheless, he exhibited behavior consistent with all three of the competence orientations evident in the research and did so in unpredictable ways. When Bruce managed a state of task-involvement, he became free to explore the kinds of activities that would promote greater self-determination. When he could not maintain such a state, his competence concerns undermined his ability to attend to self-determination and affiliation needs. The contradictions in Bruce's behavior exemplify why researchers hesitate to encourage teachers to classify students in terms of their motivational orientations.

Challenges and Controversies

- How much energy should teachers put toward labeling students' self-determination, competence, and affiliation needs?
- Is it helpful to talk with children about maintaining optimal motivation?
- How can teachers convey expectations without undermining children's motivation?

Classifying some students as task-oriented, others as ego-oriented, and still others as work-avoidant serves only to highlight some aspects of their experience to the exclusion of others.

Coaching at Home

As is common among many large families, Bruce's parents classified their children into age cohorts whose experience differed in the kinds of advantages the family could provide. In this respect, Mr. and Mrs. Johnson seemed most comfortable adopting a sociological approach to describing the difficulties Bruce faced and sought systemic reasons rather than psychological ones to explain his behavior. Listening to them describe their family and Bruce's role in it, affiliation seemed to occupy their thoughts. They were aware of difficulties that life in a large family posed for Bruce's sense of self-determination. They also noticed his sense of competence decline as early as kindergarten. By emphasizing intimacy and exchange issues, Bruce's parents identified a positive role for him and critiqued the family system rather than individual members.

The Johnsons were confident in their ability to communicate with one another, and happiness pervaded their household. Bruce and his siblings benefited from their parents' self-critical approach to providing for the family. "I can see the difference between our older kids and the younger ones," said Mrs. Johnson. "You know, we didn't have a TV for the first 16 years we were married. . . . Later we started to use the TV as a baby sitter, so the little kids [including Bruce] haven't read so much. Being with a lot of kids, the younger ones don't have a lot of things of their own. Their personal identity doesn't get developed as much. . . . Even if they get a book for a gift, right away everyone will use it, then it's lost or hard to find. I don't think that's been real helpful. You should see the differences in the eleven of them. But Bruce has always been a real questioner."

"How do you feel about how the school impacts [Bruce's life]?" John asked.

"I get a bit frustrated," responded Mrs. Johnson. "We've always encouraged our kids to be kids. I find it a little frustrating to have [children] planning to be a doctor when they are two and reading when they are three. You know, get their degree when they are five." Mrs. Johnson laughed amiably, but was serious. "A lot of those kids have had three years of preschool and our kids never had it. . . . The next school district [over], where we used to live, is very mixed culturally and financially. . . . They didn't seem to pressure the kids. There was more of a variety."

"Moving here," said Mr. Johnson, "all of a sudden [Bruce is] one of a few. . . . He started kindergarten here and was expected to read and write. He was backward almost from then. Halfway through the year he was supposed to be able to know the alphabet . . . I think his self-esteem dropped. . . . That wouldn't happen in the other school district. Well, I don't know, maybe with Bruce it would have.

"I remember [when I was] in the first grade, I could not understand how it was that all these other kids could read. . . . The principal came in and we would read for her. I remember I made all kinds of mistakes . . . I just remember being corrected for it, four or five times while I was reading. Terribly embarrassing." Mr. Johnson detailed how he went on to do well in school.

"What I take out of that," John said, "is the importance of keeping interest. The fact that you're behind a bit at this point is not in itself a big deal. It becomes a big deal if it undermines him, which is really what you're saying isn't it?"

"We're more concerned about the way he behaves you know," said Mr. Johnson. "I think the rest he'll recover."

"That's what bothered me about labeling him," said Mrs. Johnson.

"Like getting him called LD?"

"Yes," she continued. "The label can do more harm than being behind. It's a good thing depending on what the true picture is . . . I believe all kids have talents. They're certainly not all geniuses. They have things they are good at, and you want to encourage them. You don't like it?" Mrs. Johnson interrupted herself, seeing John distracted.

Far from disapproving, John was surprised that Mr. and Mrs. Johnson had so quickly put their finger on what John presumed was a major cultural cause of Bruce's difficulties—the social definition of school as a competition for grades, test scores, colleges, and socioeconomic status. John was surprised because although Mr. and Mrs. Johnson put this critique so eloquently, he had great difficulty helping members of research communities understand his critique of schooling as a competition. John was wondering if his critique was more obvious to parents whose children fall behind and tried to explain his distracted look.

"I think that the focus on competition undermines a great deal in our society. Not that we shouldn't be [in favor of] quality, but that's different from wanting to be better than other people. . . . It becomes hard for a teacher to make the classroom like a family where everyone is respected."

"Yes, you'd expect kids to have weaknesses and strengths. In a family you learn that, you know, you help and share strengths . . ." asserted Mr. Johnson, emphasizing the value of exchange relationships.

After the initial visit to Bruce's home, Mr. Johnson began reading Hardy Boys mysteries to his children. For Mr. Johnson, this activity reminded him of listening to radio plays as a child. Bruce, Mr. Johnson said, had several times said that he could really imagine things in the stories. Bruce looked forward to the reading sessions and reminded his father if he forgot. At school, behavior that may be characterized as meeting Bruce's affiliation needs seemed to undermine his self-determination. At home, however, the two parts of Bruce's experience were no longer in conflict. Perhaps at home, boy and reading were more organically related. Certainly, Bruce's interest in and ability to answer questions when Thyra read to the group emerged at about the same time in the year and remained evident until the end.

Bruce's concern with affiliation at home raised, in John's mind, questions of similar concerns in school. During the month of February, John became more or less continually concerned that his presence in the classroom was making Bruce feel stigmatized. John spent plenty of time observing, talking with, and helping other students. Yet, because Bruce remained somewhat self-conscious and a bit of a show-off in school, John could not discern whether his involvement with Bruce made Bruce uncomfortable or if this was Bruce's natural approach toward schooling. John began to think that, to Bruce, his physical presence served as a constant reminder that Bruce was academically behind his peers.

At the end of February, John called Bruce's parents to tell them that he had some partially edited writing to show them. Mr. and Mrs. Johnson relieved some of John's nervousness about Bruce's comfort when they warmly welcomed John to join the family in a meal. This offered the Johnsons time to read and discuss John's writing without the usual time lag and interruptions.

Arriving at the house, John was even more relieved when Bruce comfortably greeted him at the door, very obviously at home—relaxed and smiling. Bruce made John feel like an old friend. Would John play snooker on the table they just bought for the basement? John did not know the game, but Bruce explained it well. Then, John and Bruce played table tennis, with older siblings taking turns as well. Later, at John's suggestion, they used the table and ball to play blow soccer. Bruce and his siblings did not know this game, and at times Bruce could not blow for giggling. Meanwhile, Mr. Johnson read what John had written, and Mrs. Johnson prepared dinner.

After dinner, Mr. Johnson and John were talking when Bruce came over with a new computerized spelling game. Mr. Johnson observed as Bruce and John played. Words with letters missing were displayed along with pictures to provide clues. Bruce displayed his typical fluctuating attention and competence, looking to Mr. Johnson instead of at the problems for answers. Mr. Johnson who whispered to John, "That was a convincing demonstration," of how Bruce depended on his teacher for answers.

Mr. Johnson knew, he later said, that Bruce was not perfect but that the family values him as much as any of his kids. John's writing confirmed that Thyra also liked Bruce a lot, and Mr. Johnson appreciated that Thyra had let John observe and write about Bruce.

Mrs. Johnson wondered about sending Bruce to Catholic school and discussed home schooling again. She was still bothered about the LD label. Mr. Johnson, however, was more committed to leaving Bruce where he was.

As John left, Mr. Johnson said he was pleased that Bruce seemed only to have a motivational problem. This bothered John because he did not want to leave the impression that Bruce's difficulties were *only* a matter of motivation. John wanted only to convey that motivation was a large and real part of things that they could explore and perhaps alter. John was also aware that to see "*only* motivation" made Bruce's difficulties sound easy to change. Yet, Bruce's motivation was a function of his personality and of an interaction between that and various spheres of his life. Bruce's well-established responses to his experience kept people treating him as they did, almost forcing people to help him maintain his dependent status. To change that motivation would be a considerable task, involving changes in the person as well as changes in the environment.

Driving home, John thought about how important it was to see Bruce so relaxed. The Johnson's expertise as parents was illuminated when they readily identified Bruce's self-determination, competence, and affiliation needs. This accentuated the fact that Bruce

Challenges and Controversies

- How important is it for parents to identify their children's self-determination, competence, and affiliation needs?
- Do children find ways to show parents what they need?
- Is it helpful for parents to talk with their children about motivation issues?
- What activities can parents plan at home that could help children identify their needs?
- How can parents convey expectations without undermining children's motivation?

---

was generally uncomfortable at school. Thyra remained in Bruce's corner. But, why the boxing metaphor "in his corner" should come to John when he thought about this young boy was a puzzle. He was a tough, fighting manly-man who had to fight the sometimes aggressive power of his peers. Like a soldier, Bruce seemed involved in a fight where people got hurt. But, he also spent a lot of energy dancing around the ring, looking for an ideal place for his punch to land. Was Bruce bringing to school the same behavior that he used to construct an autonomous identity in his large family? Bruce's parents certainly avoided the propensity to expect all their children to follow the same developmental trajectory. Yet, Bruce had ample opportunity to compare his competence with that of his siblings and may have become preoccupied with such comparisons out of habit.

Co-Constructing an Unsafe Place

School is a culture in which competence is more highly valued than self-determination or affiliation, even though all three parts of an individual's experience are affected by academic activities. Social comparison is essential to determining one's level of competence, yet knowledge of one's standing relative to others also affects self-determination and the desire to interact with others. When one performs at the bottom end of the academic distribution, social comparison can be quite painful.

From the first day John observed Bruce in the classroom, John noticed that Bruce did not get along well with his classmates, a problem commonly observed among students with learning disabilities. The little snorts children made when someone stumbled and their casual declarations that the work was easy were blows that hurt this boy who could not learn quickly. Such comments also bothered Thyra and John, and they decided that Bruce's adaptation to school could not be changed without changing this aspect of the classroom.

That first day began with announcements. Thyra, who had been replaced by a substitute teacher the previous day, asked the class how that day went. Bruce's hand shot up:

"OK," Bruce said. "But Helen got in trouble."

Bruce's concern with the misconduct of his classmates continued to surface throughout the year. Bruce was no angel, but he could be intensely judgmental about other's small deviations from classroom norms even though he intermittently imposed these strictures on himself. Within an hour, for example, Bruce, Tim, and Rick—the three weakest readers in the class—were sent to the library to make up a story about *Anno's USA,* a book with detailed drawings but no text.[7] This was an opportunity to exercise imagination and initiative, but Bruce was seriously concerned about correct procedures for turn taking. And, when the others did not tell a linear story, something the book did not demand, Bruce burst, "You messed up again." Assuming there was one right way to tell a story, Bruce squelched his classmates' initial playfulness and imagination.

During another work session, when Rick said, "I know!" in response to a question from Thyra, Bruce looked at Rick's work, compelling Thyra to use a book to shield Rick's work. As Thyra helped Rick, Bruce briefly played at peeking over the book. For each problem, Bruce waited for Thyra to define it. When Thyra helped Rick, Bruce stopped and waited without looking at the problems or at Rick's work, even though he could have competently counted his way through the subtraction problems.

When Rick asked, "Are you all done?" Bruce turned his page over to conceal his work. Bruce had no intention of collaborating even though collaboration was permitted. Elsewhere in the class, students who were far ahead of Bruce comfortably discussed their interpretations of questions and solutions.

Bruce's preoccupation with comparison also revealed itself the next day. Doing math on a table at the back of the room, the three slower boys propped up books, hiding their work from one another. The ethic of this group was that the teacher should help, but no one must give or receive help from his peers. Bruce, Tim, and Rick were preoccupied with more competitive forms of solitary work and the practice of absorbing facts that could easily pass into a form of selfishness. Yet, in Bruce's case, preoccupation with absorbing facts could not be linked to Thyra's classroom practices. Bruce brought this vision to school with him.

As the class got ready to go to the library, Thyra urged Bruce and a few others to complete an assignment most had finished. As the others began to leave, Daniel, sitting in front of Bruce, finished, stood up, and looked back. "I beat you. You still have to finish. I just finished. Finished!" Daniel taunted, leaving to line up. Bruce did not react visibly, but this teasing could have diminished his preoccupation with doing high-quality work and helped him sustain a macho commitment to showing he was just as competent as his peers.

Thyra wanted to protect Bruce, who she saw as further behind in reading than almost any student she had encountered at this school, from failure on the sorts of tasks he might face in the third grade. At the same time, Thyra tried to prevent Bruce from being demolished by pressure to measure up to the advanced students who were the norm in this school. She and John began to explore ways of helping students focus on talents rather than on superiority.

When John raised the question of pressure, Thyra said, "At one time we had stickers and stars on charts to show how everyone was progressing. We've gotten away from that, and I think that's good. Well if kids say, 'I'm done,' I say 'It's not a race here.'" Thyra was aware of the negative effects of public forms of comparison.

Ability groups, while based on individual differences in talent, can present another problem for students like Bruce. Groups have long been standard in elementary school classrooms, but have been going out of favor because, in many ways, teachers have been observed to convey low expectations to less able students. Whereas three and four groups used to be the norm, Thyra's two-group classroom was a reluctant concession to the distance that Bruce, Rick, and Tim were behind. Even if Thyra did not promote it, and John did not see such promotion, Bruce could become stigmatized when associated with the lower group. Early in the year at least, Bruce was eager to go to his group. Nevertheless, like his mother, his teachers were aware that comments like those made by Daniel eventually could do real damage.

"I'm wondering," John said to Thyra later, "whether LD students generally don't get chances to exercise initiative and voice that others do." John was trying to imagine how students like Bruce could display their talents.

"Well, I think it depends on how you set up your classroom. If everyone does the same thing all the time it's a problem. If they are doing things where they have choices, it is better. I also encourage them to do what they are able to [on assignments] and then go on [to something else]."

"What about times when some take much longer to do something?"

"Well, I think a teacher needs to alter it, like with the spelling."

"So you shorten that task?"

"Yes."

"Is there a potential other side to that one, too? . . . It makes it real obvious who are the slow guys."

"It's obvious anyhow, whether they have less or get the same. The kids can tell. They might always have to have their work altered. . . . So they can be successful."

"The meaning of 'successful' is tricky, isn't it?" asserted John.

"Right. . . . According to the rest of the class, he's behind, but for what his ability is, he's doing very well. . . . I think they should compete with themselves. They try to win all the time, but at school it should be different and it's hard for kids to understand that."

"Yes. What's your sense of how much competition pressure comes from home?"

"The biggest question [most parents have] is, 'Where is he in relation to the rest of the class?' What reading group are they in? When I first started teaching, I tried to gloss over it. Now I tell [parents], 'He's one of the best readers or whatever.'" Yet, it is difficult for teachers to be honest about progress without demolishing students who progress slowly.

In contrast to his academic struggles, Bruce was very skilled in athletics. Thyra was confident that Bruce did not have difficulties in gym class or on the playground. When John observed in these places, he agreed. In gym, Bruce had no trouble following instructions and did so vigorously and in an agile fashion. Bruce's physical competence also served him well on the playground, and he seemed relaxed when engaged in physical activity.

Bruce's preoccupation with his standing relative to his peers was limited to academic tasks. His cocky style of learning was evident when Thyra introduced the greater than and less than symbols. Thyra wrote 606, 732, and ___ > ___ on the chalkboard. The students were to write one number on each line. Bruce stood up waving his hand to be called on before Thyra even finished posing the question. Turning to seek volunteers, Thyra chose Bruce. But, Bruce had not been listening carefully and misunderstood, thinking that one digit should go on each line. Thyra whispered in his ear, but he was still in too much haste to listen. His clumsy attempts got a loud snigger from Jackie, who sat with him at the back of the room in a cluster of four desks. When Thyra said, "Let's line up for art," Bruce flashed across the room to be first at the door. He could be first to the door, but the impulse to be first served him poorly in mathematics.

In the afternoon, when the class went over math homework, Bruce did not have his sheet of problems. In the middle of the session, Bruce walked to the pencil sharpener, picking Daniel's pencil off his desk as he passed. "Would this be yours?" Bruce teased, and whipped the pencil away as Daniel reached out. Sauntering back from the pencil sharpener, Bruce returned the pencil, patting Daniel on the back as he passed. While the others were engaged in math, Bruce practiced the role of casual trickster, working to slow down the progress of his more able peers.

Tim returned to class and needed his math paper, which Bruce had been using. Thyra was out of spares, but Bruce would not share with Tim. Thyra asked Bruce to sit by Tim, but Bruce resisted. Bruce brimmed with sullen social confidence—looking as if he was Mr. Cool. "I don't want to," he said. When Thyra persisted, Bruce moved over, but declared, "I won't look at the paper though." Bruce stopped attending to the task, played with his pencil, wiggled in his seat, and put his hands on his face.

Later, John asked Bruce why he stopped working. "I thought you liked math?" Bruce mumbled inaudibly. John then asked if Bruce quit because he did not want to sit with Tim. Bruce agreed, but could or would not say why. He smirked and seemed pleased with his defiant attitude toward Thyra's request. Here was initiative, but Bruce's initiative was maintained at the expense of his capacity to do the hard math that, in his interviews with John, Bruce had claimed he wanted to do.

During afternoon math, Rick, Bruce's group member, worked a problem at the board. Rick came up with an unusual procedure for obtaining the correct answer. A couple of classmates said, "What!" in a tone of loud surprise and scorn.

"He knows what he's doing," said Thyra, backing him up.

Thyra then asked Bruce, "Want to try?"

"No."

"Why?"

"I don't want to do it." Perhaps Bruce feared that, like Rick, he would face sneers from his classmates. Bruce's preoccupation with his ability seemed sustained by students like Jackie, who derogated peers who were slower to catch on. Despite Thyra's attempts to label students' talents, the students themselves resisted imitating such talk.

Bruce's discomfort with appearing less competent than his peers became more apparent later in the year when he began to resist attending his special education sessions. When Alice Kay, Bruce's special education teacher, arrived to take Bruce to the resource room, Bruce became stubborn and slightly surly, "I don't want to." Alice patiently encouraged Bruce to write in his journal a little, and to show Thyra his work. Only then did Bruce agree to leave.

Later in the day, Bruce, Tim, and Rick were to make sock puppets and produce a version of *The Three Billy Goats Gruff.*[8] Thyra hoped that drama would engage them more fully than did the more cut and dried literacy tasks. Bruce smiled broadly when the assignment was announced. John worked with the boys at the back of the room. However, the boys took no initiative with this project: They had difficulty imagining how it might come out in the end and so could not visualize how to proceed.

John nudged the boys to start making puppets. Bruce moved around the table, waving socks about with no apparent sense of where to begin. Volunteered to help with needle threading, John began with Bruce. When John turned to help Rick and Tim, Bruce became overly silly. He put a needle through the calluses on his hands, impaling bigger and bigger areas—more inquiry into the human body.

After finishing his puppet, Bruce put snaps on his ear. At first Bruce played with the possibility of piercing his ear using a snap to make an earring. Bruce soon discovered he could get the same effect by clipping the edge of the snap to a small piece of skin on the end of his ear. His experiments with the human body showed ingenuity, but they were remote from the established task.

Once again, when Alice came for Bruce, he resisted going to the resource room. Likewise, Thyra agreed with John's suspicion that Bruce resisted the notion that he needed help and tried to avoid the label of slow learner. A clear pattern in Bruce's behavior was becoming evident to the educators who sought to support him.

This suspicion was confirmed when, in mid-February, Bruce joined Tim and Rick to read with Thyra. Bruce wanted to sit up on a heating unit, slightly removed from the rest. Bruce's expression again said, "Mr. Cool." Thyra allowed his choice of seat on the condition that Bruce agreed to follow the story. Bruce agreed but did not follow along very well. Bruce banged his heels loudly enough to be slightly annoying, although he did not intend to disrupt the group.

The story the group was reading was about a boy with a teddy bear who visited a friend. Thyra asked, "If you had a teddy bear and you were going to a friend's house, would you take it with you?"

Tim and Rick said brightly, "Yes," declaring that the friend might also have a teddy bear.

With his man-of-the-world air, Bruce said what Thyra and John both expected, "No." Bruce's desire to be grown up and smart probably made him uncomfortable when hearing about the adventures of teddy bears with this group of low-ability readers.

Soon, when Thyra announced, "We are going to see a videotape of *The Bremen-Town Musicians,*" Bruce called, "Yeah!" If anyone led the class in enthusiasm for this play, which they had already read, it was Bruce. He placed himself right at the front below the TV, and was wholly engrossed with this version of the story.

At the end, Thyra asked how the video and the version they read were alike. Bruce had his hand up right away and kept it up as others contributed. When Thyra turned to differences, Bruce still had his hand up. "The robbers."

"How were they different?"

"They were animals." Other students contributed, but Bruce still waved his hand vigorously long after everyone else ran out of ideas. "What the rooster said."

"What was that?" asked Thyra.

"One crowed, then said, 'Cock a doodle do,' and the other said, 'Cock a doodle do.'" Here was an activity that did not make Bruce feel self-conscious. He had legitimate points, although he did not fully elaborate them. Did Bruce not see a need for precise communication? Was he speaking in macho minimalism or was this an indication that he had deficits in vocabulary and syntactic structure? After the session was over, Bruce recalled another point and told Thyra that the rooster was to be cooked by the farmer's wife in one version, and by a cook in the other. Bruce was at the top of the class during this activity.

The class next door joined Bruce's class for a second showing of the video. Bruce was again engrossed. Jean turned to talk to him but, before she could, Bruce used both hands to turn her back and kept watching. For Bruce, this repetition did not seem to suggest low ability.

Of course, the plot of Ilse Plume's *The Bremen-Town Musicians* involved imagination, tension, humor, and action.[9] No doubt the story helped Bruce remain sufficiently engaged to make contributions as intelligent as those of anyone else. Although his points were more factual than interpretive, the musicians captured Bruce's imagination.

At the end of this day, John visited the resource room after Bruce had been working there with Alice for about 10 minutes. Bruce was reading four blocks of words on the chalkboard. Bruce read the first two blocks well, needing no real help. He stalled on the third block and looked to Alice's face for the answers. As he had done with Thyra and John, Bruce's hangdog look made a powerful demand for help. "Look at the word," said Alice, not about to be drawn into this.

"Right on!" John thought. Bruce stumbled through the third group then sailed through the last. This exchange supported John's belief that when Bruce was not self-conscious about his ability, he was capable of performing well. In the privacy of Alice's room, perhaps Bruce could concentrate more fully than was possible in front of a larger group.

Back in class, John sat by Bruce's group of four as they worked on math. "This is easy stuff. Easy stuff!" said Mark. Students were adding and subtracting without regrouping (carrying) in preparation for a new lesson on regrouping. Mark was not a bragger and generally supported Bruce, but that comment could not have helped Bruce's sense of well-being.

Proud of himself, Bruce announced, "Now I know times!" Sitting across from him, Jackie upped the ante, "I knew times in first grade." Jackie's tone was pinched and righteous, as if she intended to sting Bruce. This was not the first time John had seen her putting down Bruce. This game of asserting competence was not one Bruce could win, yet it might be said that he helped keep it going. Thyra worked to encourage constructive forms of social comparison by minimizing public forms of praise and prizes. She also tried to eliminate ability groups while ensuring that students got the help they needed. Calling attention to the good things students said and did, regardless of their social position, and encouraging teamwork should also have helped Bruce find comfortable ways to coordinate his needs for self-determination, competence, and affiliation.

Mrs. Johnson continued to say that she felt bad that Bruce did not have the support with reading that her older children had, and accepted this label to some degree. John disagreed. At home, Bruce seemed well respected as an individual and as a person with unique interests and needs. Bruce seemed to agree with John's assessment when at school, for Mother's Day, he wrote:

Challenges and Controversies

- Can children benefit when teachers encourage them to reflect on their motivational needs?
- What activities can teachers plan to help children identify their needs?
- Is it appropriate to talk with children about problems with their motivation?
- What can educators do to help children engage in constructive forms of social comparison?
- What might educators do when they notice that students are insulting one another?
- How can teachers and students sustain conversations about matters of substance and minimize personal attacks?

My mom works hard for us.
My mom si nice
My mom maces the Bast coces [cookies]
My mom is a house cleaner.

On this occasion, Bruce's writing seemed to reflect what was genuinely in his heart. The message did not seem at all alien to the experience John saw and Bruce sought to communicate.

Seeking Friendship: A Means to an End or an End in Itself?

Later in the year, Thyra began to incorporate more elements of whole language instruction into the curriculum, a move she had been considering for a while. The readers designed for particular grade levels were put aside and, with them, the separate ability-based reading groups. Thyra also took up John's suggestion of directly encouraging students to collaborate, telling them of the importance of listening to and helping one another, hoping to reduce the invidious comparisons. These changes enhanced John's ability to observe how Bruce met self-determination, competence, and affiliation needs with his peers.

In groups of three, charged to collaborate, the whole class began reading children's literature. They began with a variety of William Steig's engaging books. Bruce, Matt, and Jimmy read one book and were lying under a table with a sheet of questions to answer. "Don't copy," said Matt to Bruce.

Matt had become Bruce's occasional, slightly nervy, edgy conspirator in second grade macho horsing around. Matt's reading was low to middling in the class, and Matt had given several signs that he was conscious of Bruce's lower status. "This isn't a race." John said. "You can talk and get ideas, can't you?"

Relaxed, easy, and agreeable, Jimmy agreed with John. Tenser, Matt and Bruce went along as well. Bruce soon drifted to the fringe of the group. Everyone finished, but Bruce wrote only short, one-word answers.

Later in the day, this group began another Steig book. Jimmy helped Bruce steadily. They became uncomfortable lying under the low table, and when they moved out, Bruce wanted to sit far from the others. John more or less insisted that Bruce join the group.

Bruce compliantly came closer, trapping John in the role of enforcer rather than helper, friend, or observer.

The next day, the group continued reading Steig's, *The Amazing Bone*.[10] Matt was impatient with Bruce's slow reading and looked away, saying he knew what was about to happen. "I read this in first grade," Matt claimed, though the book was not especially easy for him.

Matt's pressure probably did not help Bruce relax. When anyone stalled, John would ask if one of the other boys could help. Bruce helped twice, in one case reading "determined" for Jimmy. More often, Jimmy tactfully helped Bruce, whose involvement always seemed touch and go, on the point of drifting from the circle.

Back working where he normally sat—with Jackie, Mark, and Ruth—Bruce abruptly dragged his desk away from them. Soon Bruce asked Thyra if he could be put in a different group because his classmates said he copied. John had seen Bruce taking a sneaky look, although the occasion would have allowed collaboration. Thyra asked Bruce whom he would like to work with, but Bruce was not sure, so the conversation ended with Bruce agreeing to think more about the move.

Early in March, Thyra made a more direct assault on the competition and put-downs among the children. "Yesterday," she told John, "before we talked about who they'd like to work with in the reading group, I said, 'Do all second grade kids read the same? Are there some kids who can read better than others?' They said, 'Sure.' I said, 'Well, are there some people who are better at math than other people?' Well, they agreed that was true. I said, 'Then everybody agrees and you realize that's the way life is.' I used myself as an example. When I was in school, I was always better in reading and worse in math, and I knew that. So I said, 'If this is true, is it OK if people help each other on their work?' [The class] seemed to think that was OK, and I said, 'Well, what if you can help each other and you can work together like you have on the William Steig books?' They really worked together and came up with answers they could all live with, which is all cooperative. I said, 'Is that cheating?' and [the class] said, 'No. That is working together.' And I said, 'Can we do that if we are working in groups?' They seemed to think that was OK. I said, 'Really what cheating is, if we are doing a spelling test and you are looking at your neighbor's paper when you are not supposed to. That's cheating, but when you work together and you come up with answers that you agree on, you are helping each other out.' I tried to lay the ground rules for more cooperative work. For so many years it was all competitive. . . ."

"I also asked, 'Is everybody in here going to third grade next year?' Most said yes, but some weren't sure. Well I asked [Tim, Bruce, and Rick] and some others, and they weren't sure. I said, 'I want everybody to know right now. Everybody in this classroom is going to third grade.' So I hope that gets it off their mind. . . . I do think some of them worry about that."

Hoping to reinforce the value of community, Thyra had the children write down possible partners for the group work that they were about to begin. Sadly, no one chose Bruce, and he chose Tim and Rick—his old group members. For Bruce, there seemed to be no real place for change in a world that was not especially happy for him.

When Bruce arrived the next day, he was a relaxed man-of-the-world, talking with Matt and Jimmy before class. When class started, however, Bruce's desk remained apart from his group. Bruce started work very slowly. The other students were well into work, and Bruce was wiping his mouth after getting a drink. Bruce examined the staple-remover on Thyra's desk before returning to pull out the assigned sheet. But Bruce did nothing with the sheet. Nearby, Peter, Rob, and Robert were amiably comparing interpretations, enjoying one another's company, and sweeping along to completion. Bruce, who needed this kind of friendly collaboration, isolated himself and was ignored.

Next, Thyra recapped yesterday's theme of cooperation, but Bruce—who should have been a major beneficiary—seemed not to listen. Bruce pulled his shirt up with his teeth, chewed, and sucked intently.

"Is it OK for someone to say, 'I don't have a clue?'"

"Yes!" was the consensus.

"Is it OK if two people write the same answer?"

"Yes!" said several students.

Robert called, "No!" Then Robert quickly declared, "I'm joking."

It became clearer over the subsequent weeks that Robert was not joking. Robert wanted a contest and would put other students down by declaring the work that he could do "easy" in a way that seemed like bragging. Robert's parents told Thyra that they were bothered by his tendencies, and pleased that she was encouraging a more communal climate in which Robert might flourish. Yet, despite Thyra's best efforts, Robert had a mind of his own and a strong need to demonstrate superiority over his peers. He perpetuated a spirit of competition in which only a few individuals can feel competent. Such a world encourages students to hide their vulnerabilities out of fear of being undermined by their classmates.

Despite high ideals, responsibility for classroom climate cannot reside entirely with the teacher. Teachers must work with the students they have, and can hardly be expected to entirely change behavior that parents cannot. To allow children like Robert, Bruce, and their classmates to attain their potential requires a level of responsiveness that makes it imperative for teachers to accept even the most annoying personality characteristics. Working to effect positive growth in their students, many teachers satisfy themselves with subtle indications of progress and small declines in the kind of disruptive behavior that undermines healthy community life.

Later in the week, for example, Thyra repeated the discussion of differences between learning and cheating. Bruce paid attention intermittently. When the class moved into new cooperative groups, Bruce avoided starting. John nudged him: "They can help you."

Mark said pleasantly, with no hint of derogation, "Bruce and Tim are going to need a little help. Me and you [Jeff] can do it faster."

Bruce began writing without imagining the task. The students were to find a word to finish a sentence and match that word with its Spanish translation. It was not long before Bruce lost direction and drifted into himself on an invisible tide.

"You guys," said Mark amiably. "Bruce has to catch up." Mark and Jeff then helped Bruce through the first task.

"OK," said Mark, taking the teacher's role, and gently trying to focus Bruce's attention on the second task. "We are on page 19." Jeff was not sure about this, so Mark and Jeff went to check with Thyra. Following to show Thyra his completed first task, Bruce did not value learning, but he wanted to be done and to show off his efforts.

When Thyra announced the next day that these groups would again work together, Mark called, "Yes! Yes!"

Bruce had no reaction. He looked downcast, drawing on the cover of his folder then erasing it, making little squealing, singing sounds. Bruce went happily enough to the group, but seemed not to follow instructions. He closed his book as if done with it, opened it with a sigh, and left for the bathroom. In high animation, Mark and Jeff discussed the task, and Tim plodded along alone. When Bruce returned, Thyra helped him, but Bruce was not very engaged. Quickly he was off to the bathroom again. When Bruce returned, Tim hid his work from Bruce who then left the group completely. Alone at a large table, Bruce started work, then waved his hand about, wrote a little, got another book, flicked pages, put the book back, got another, and returned to the task.

Meanwhile, Mark and Jeff finished the first task and asked to keep working together on the next assignment. Thyra told the boys to work alone, but they returned to collaborate anyway, sweeping each other along and exploring the world of words while Bruce maintained his dependent style.

John asked Tim to explain why he covered his work from Bruce.

"I don't like him copying."

"Didn't Mrs. DeBolt say learning from each other is OK?"

"I don't like him."

"Why?"

"He bothers people." John could not get Tim to explain more.

That afternoon, Thyra again emphasized the value of cooperation. "Yesterday," she concluded, "some of you did a better job than today. I think what I will do tomorrow is put you in pairs."

After lunch, Bruce left math to go to the bathroom: He was not settled. While waiting for Bruce to return, John noticed that Robert had a mass production method for doing the assigned problems quickly. When Mark adopted this method, Robert said Mark was cheating. John suggested otherwise, but Robert was adamant. One of several signs to come that Robert resisted the new ethic of cooperation. This was a sign also of the confusion, common among second graders, between the value of copying to learn and copying to cheat.

When the class worked with buddies, Mark helped Bruce. Bruce declared, "We're done," before they were finished. When the boys did finish, Bruce declared, "We're done before they are." At least that time it was *we,* and not just *he* who won. Yet, it was sad to see Bruce, right at the bottom of the class curve, sustain the competition that oppressed him and sever his experience into domains that worked against one another. Bruce would stand a better chance of feeling competent if he could assess his progress in terms of personal improvement relative to past performance rather than by comparing his performance to others around him. In this respect, it would be possible for him to allow one form of meaning to shape the development of another.

On a day when Bruce started his schoolwork a little quicker than usual, he took a break and drifted over to Thyra's desk. Thyra helped him briefly until Tim came up. "Tim, do you and Bruce want to work on geography together?" asked Thyra.

"No."

"OK."

When Thyra left, Bruce looked at his sheet, then called, "Mrs. D. This answer is easy." Was Bruce trying to defend himself against Tim's insult?

"Then do it!" snapped Mark, Bruce's slightly exasperated but generally very patient helper.

Bruce was just a little boy trying to survive. But he could also be offensively egotistical and in danger of being cut off even from those who, like Mark, were disposed to help him. When it was time for gym, Bruce ran to be first in line.

Other assignments filled the rest of the day. At snack time, Bruce kept working on geography, a positive sign. A little later, Alan said, as he passed Rob, "This is easy,"

"What?" said Rob.

"This," said Alan, pointing to the geography Bruce was still struggling with, "is easy."

"I know," said Rob. Fortunately, Bruce did not hear him.

By the end of the first week in May, Bruce was more willing to ask classmates for help and perhaps, as Thyra suggested, better at choosing helpers. One day, while lying on the rug working, Mark joined Bruce. The two boys tried to go to the bathroom together, but Thyra insisted they take turns. When he returned, Bruce began floating away from the work.

"Bruce, come here," Mark called and told Bruce what to do. Bruce stretched out on the rug and continued. Then, he twice hunched up with his bottom in the air and farted. Each time, the two boys giggled. Jackie glanced at John with an expression that said, "Oh boys! Must we endure them?"

"Are you getting your stuff done back there?" asked Thyra.

"Yes," they answered and proceeded to work.

"Mark, do I do this one?" asked Bruce.

"Yeah."

Soon, Mark asked, "Who are you going to pick for your special friend [to write about for an assignment]? I'm picking Rob. Who are you putting down? Rick? Me?" Mark sounded hopeful, but not anxious or coercive.

"I don't know," said Bruce. Bruce did not have Mark's ease with academic or social tasks. Mark had been his consistent helper, showing no condescension. But, Mark asked (or almost asked) Bruce to choose him, while he announced his allegiance to another. Mark's manner was open and friendly, but Bruce said nothing. Did Bruce lack the ability to interpret Mark's rather blatant request for an affirmation of friendship? It would have probably been Bruce's best option to choose Mark, but instead Bruce left for the bathroom again.

After gym, Bruce and Mark continued on the rug. Bruce was relaxed and again asked for and received advice from Mark. Thyra and John exchanged a glance of relief at the continuation of this trend. The work was a little hard for Bruce, and he drifted away occasionally, but each time returned to the rug and kept at it.

Sadly, such harmony was short-lived. The week after Bruce and Mark worked so well together, Thyra said, "We are going to read some other Native American folk tales. I'm going to read one tale then [promoting cooperation in a different way] I'll ask you to pair up with someone you haven't worked with. There will be two kinds of grades—how well you work with your partner, and how well you answer questions. I want each boy to work with a girl."

The mention of grades elicited no visible reaction from the students: The children did not seem to see grades as placing limits on their autonomy. Instead, the announcement that boys and girls would be paired precipitated a general eruption of emotion, with the boys complaining especially loudly. Bruce pretended to vomit violently.

As Thyra read, the boys calmed down and Bruce became a competent contributor to the discussion. Then, "Before we go to the learning center, you have five minutes to pick partners. Come and tell me who your partner is, then pick a book," Thyra announced.

Suddenly boys and girls became creatures from different planets, afraid to approach one another. Bruce smirked, sniggered, and bobbed about at the back of the milling crowd of boys.

"You are not asking someone for their hand in marriage," Thyra quipped.

Matt and Bruce, behind the cluster of boys furthest from the girls, laughed, squirmed, and smirked. Bruce pretended to vomit again. Gradually pairs formed and settled to reading. Soon the only ones left were Helen, Matt, and Bruce. The two boys kept giggling and circling.

Avoiding Helen, Matt chose a book, and started reading. Bruce sat a little too far away to see Matt's book, but soon closed in and followed along with Matt. Helen was left to her own devices.

Despite everyone's hope for improvement in students' willingness to collaborate, Mrs. Johnson told John that recently Bruce cried when he came home from school, saying that he had been called "dumb." This was particularly sad to hear because as far as John and Thyra could tell, this sort of thing had dropped off considerably. The next morning, when John passed on the news, Thyra was obviously disappointed and hurt. Thyra wondered how Mrs. Johnson responded to Bruce and why Mrs. Johnson did not let Thyra know. The incident made everyone feel bad.

The day John told Thyra about Mrs. Johnson's comment, Bruce was very interested in a container of cookies that Thyra brought in. Bruce appeared about to slobber on them. "Who made these?" Bruce asked.

For most of the morning, Bruce's attention had been intermittent. Most students were measuring plants they had grown, but Bruce was on the loose with a ruler. Thyra gently drew him in. As the class worked together through a sheet on plants, Bruce drifted. Thyra asked, "Rob, can you help [Bruce]?"

"Oh sure! Flower. Here is flower." Rob walked Bruce through the task.

At snack time, Bruce got the largest share of Thyra's sugary cookies. He was the same comfort-seeking, slightly flirtatious boy John had seen when he first met Bruce.

John was not ready to conclude that Bruce's behavior was solely a result of his learning disabilities—not all children with learning disabilities have difficulty sticking to assigned tasks. John noticed that Rick, in contrast to Bruce, was typically engrossed in schoolwork and the associated discussions, despite his learning disabilities. Rick turned to John, seated right behind him, to point out things that interested him in the book he was reading. Later, Rick noticed *The Three Billy Goats Gruff* hand puppets on the wall and talked about how he, Bruce, and Tim never finished that project. Unlike Bruce, Rick seemed wholly himself, comfortable with his peers, and happy to be in school.

The elements with which Bruce was constructing his man-of-the-world identity were readily apparent in American society. Little boys like Bruce are continually told that they should become tough—that they should scorn nerds and geeks. Stallone, Van

Damme, and armies of cartoon characters and football players send the message that this is how "real men" get along in the world. Tough guys are intense. They fight back. In Bruce's world of right and wrong answers, where he too often had the wrong answers, Bruce sought to be right by any means possible. Bruce wanted to show that he was smarter than his classmates. He wanted to win. What could be more American and yet, for Bruce, what could be more destructive?

Bruce remained the edgy tough guy right through to the end of the school year. With the year almost gone, for example, John swept out of another boy's classroom to see Bruce and Matt in the corridor. Everything in their manner said, "bad boys on the loose." Bruce and Matt were facing down a corridor at right angles to the corridor John was on. Bruce was doing his intense, angry, palms out wide, "Drop dead you spasticated idiot!" gesture to someone John could not see. As John passed, he said, "Two bandits in the hallway?" Knowing John was joking, Matt sheepishly grinned. Bruce looked startled, as if caught in a serious crime.

The same week, Bruce turned up in the principal's office for starting a ruckus by insulting an extremely bright second grader who had imperfect muscular coordination and speech. At recess, Bruce called this boy a geek—distancing himself from an extraordinarily bright lad, who was himself cut off from most of his peers. Smitten, Bruce would smite back—cutting himself off from his own decency, becoming like those who oppressed him.

Bruce seemed most committed to the happiness of personal pleasure and enjoyment while less committed to the roles of citizen, thinker, or philosopher. Missing opportunities to exchange pleasantries with his peers, Bruce had great difficulty forming communal relationships. Because the degree to which he attained social acceptance was unstable, Bruce's peer interactions could not buffer him from the pain associated with his academic difficulties. The adults in Bruce's life worked to ease tensions between Bruce and his peers, but Bruce was committed to establishing his own kind of autonomy.

Bruce's macho tendencies made it hard for the different aspects of his experience to relate satisfactorily to one another. As John looked for ways to ease the social tensions in Bruce's life, it became clearer that Bruce, in many ways, also set himself up to live a divided intellectual life. Bruce, for example, wanted to develop his strengths and do hard math, but this desire obliterated any yearning for coherence or understanding. Bruce wanted to be able to read, but at times he almost as desperately wanted to avoid the entire

Challenges and Controversies

- In what ways do individual students prefer the intimacy and exchange features of their relationships?
- Can adults help students like Bruce form communal and exchange relationships with their peers?
- Will asking students with learning disabilities to exchange ideas help buffer the pain associated with social comparison?
- Will encouraging students with learning disabilities to find intimacy in friendship also help buffer the pain associated with social comparison?

business of learning to read. Thus, Bruce fell further behind in his world of right and wrong answers and lower in the hierarchies of competence that so preoccupied his attention.

Lessons from Bruce's Life

Bruce taught us that some children become so preoccupied with meeting their competence needs that they ignore their self-determination and affiliation needs. Unaware that over-reliance on assistance from adults undermines their ability to appear competent, such children can establish relationships that maintain cycles of unmet needs. Children who become preoccupied with their competence needs assume that their parents, teachers, and peers exclusively value outstanding performance. Without reflection, they will seek to comply with such unrealistic expectations. Lacking self-efficacy, such children cannot sustain task-involvement and are unable to achieve rewarding forms of ego-involvement, but will persistently seek to demonstrate skill. The ability to sustain satisfying relationships is undermined when these children ignore others or behave as if others are equally preoccupied with their competence.

To address the struggles associated with unmet needs, Thyra and John taught us about four types of interventions. First, identifying patterns in children's behavior can help caregivers notice how they reinforce children's inconsistencies and maintain cycles of unmet needs. Caregivers can then minimize their involvement in such patterns of behavior. Second, encouraging children to express their needs, compare their beliefs with those of others, and imagine other life concerns can also undermine self-destructive cycles. Third, establishing environments that sanction those who ridicule peers of lesser ability and encourage interest-focused forms of social comparison can help buffer the pain associated with ability-based comparisons. Fourth, organizing curriculum so that only some forms of knowledge can be judged right or wrong, self-expression is encouraged, and controversial topics are welcome, can help children learn about the ambiguity of competence judgments. Of course, such interventions are likely to take time and teamwork. Even under ideal conditions, children can remain so persistent in their preoccupation with competence that they will cheat or become inattentive before altering their assessment of the world.

ENDNOTES

1. See Gresham & MacMillan (1997), Kavale & Reese (1992), McLeskey (1992), and Pearl & Bay (1999).
2. See Babcock (1986, pp. 316–317).
3. This coding scheme was designed by Nicholls, McKenzie, & Shufro (1994) to measure children's theories of education.
4. See Nicholls & Hazzard (1993, p. 130).
5. These were obtained by Miller, Brickman, & Bolen (1975). See also studies by Schunk (1982) and Butler (1987), who found the same things using different dependent variables.
6. See Nicholls (1960, 1962).
7. See Anno (1992).
8. This classic folk tale, told widely among Norwegian people, was first published in 1837 by Peter Asbjörnsen and Jörgen Moe (Griffith & Frey, 1981).
9. See Plume (1980).
10. See Steig (1976).

CHAPTER

3 Quiet Bird*

Fractured experience can take at least one of two forms. Like Bruce, individuals can focus on some needs more than others, fracturing their experience by failing to balance their needs for self-determination, competence, and affiliation. Bruce seemed obsessed with his need for competence, fracturing his experience by overlooking his needs for self-determination and affiliation. His sometimes rough-and-tumble behavior contrasted with flashes of task involvement to accentuate these internal divisions. Children can construct different gaps in their experience with the same net effect—relationships become unstable and learning declines.

Details of David Richardson's life exemplify a second kind of fractured experience: behaving like a different person in different settings. David had little difficulty coordinating his motivational needs but fractured his experience by behaving like one person in school and another person at home. It was only by listening patiently and observing David at home and at school that John was able to see how David was an imaginative, creative thinker at home and a quiet, impulsive thinker at school. David had comfortable relationships with people in both spheres of his life, yet he had difficulty attending to tasks that he could not find personally meaningful.

In John's opening interview, David's unwillingness to speak in school made John nervous and Bruce seem loquacious. As with Bruce, John hoped to explore the ways in which aspects of David's school and personal experience enlightened, stimulated, and complemented one another. Yet, John's excitement and confidence in his ability to help David were undermined by his inability to engage David in a comfortable conversation.

"So. I want to see what you think about school. Is there anything special that comes to mind . . . that you think about school and you want to tell me about first?" Small, pixielike David did not seem anxious, but gave no answer. Neither tense nor defensive, David was hard to read. Self-contained, perhaps? He was definitely cute and a touch winsome. "I've got some questions, but I thought maybe you could just give me your first ideas. What do you think about school?" John paused. David showed no embarrassment, yet stayed silent. "Maybe if I ask you this one? Can you think about a time when you had a really good day in school? Was there ever a day like that, that was really good in school?"

*Portions of the material in this chapter previously appeared in Pollard, Thiessen, & Filer's *Children and their curriculum: The perspectives of primary and elementary school children* (Nicholls & Thorkildsen, with Bates, 1997); published by The Falmer Press, Bristol, PA. The author is grateful for Dennis Thiessen's patient editorial advice.

"Mmmnn. No."

Most children can think of good times in school, so John continued hopefully, "Not really? Not a really good day, eh?" David did not flicker. "Was there any time when you had a good hour or good few minutes, a minute that was really good?"

"Sometimes."

"OK. What was happening in those times when you had a few good minutes? What were you doing?"

Silence. Then, "Forgot."

John asked about bad times and again encountered silence. On they went, with John awkwardly doing most of the talking. John asked about homework, and David had nothing to say.

"OK," John babbled. "Suppose there wasn't any homework. When you go home, you can choose anything you want to do. What would you choose?" Silence. "You can choose. When you are free, do you have some things you like to do?" David gave no answer. "Do you sit there and look, or do you run around?"

"Run around."

"Yeah! What sort of places do you run." Ha! "What do you look for?"

"Lots of things."

"Oh. OK. What things? I don't live here so maybe there's a lot of different things you can look for that I don't know."

"Rocks."

"Rocks. Oh yes! Are there neat rocks here?" David nodded. "Good. So you're interested in nature are you?" David nodded. "Rocks. Any other things are there? Are there a lot of animals there?" John was leading—many children brought up animals in his interviews.

"Some."

"OK. So you look at things outside. Any other things? Anything else?" Silence. "OK. How about TV? Watch that?"

"Mmmm."

"OK," John proceeded, "what about reading? Are there some books you like to read at home or pictures you like to look at in books?" Again, David gave no answer. "Do you like books at all, or not much?"

"Not much."

"OK. Um, did you ever like looking at books? When you were littler, did you like it more?"

"Yes."

"You did? That's interesting. What sort of books did you used to like looking at?" Silence. "Animal books or anything?"

"Yeah."

"That's interesting David, that you liked looking at books a bit more than you do now. Can you tell me why? That happened to one of my boys. He used to like it, then he sort of changed. Why did that happen to you?" Silence. "Hard to tell? When do you think it happened? This year or. . . ."

"Last year." David interrupted, suddenly surprisingly decisive.

"Oh. So, before you got into first grade you liked books, is that right?"

"Mmm. Hmm."

"And in first grade you didn't?"

"Mmm," David nodded.

"Well, tell me something about first grade. That would really help me. Could you tell me some stuff about first grade? What happened in first grade? What was it?"

"Bored." David left little doubt about these feelings. This sentiment was as clear as anything he had said and seemed to come with a tiny sparkle in his eyes.

"Got bored did you? Hey, that's no good." John could not get more detail, so changed his tack.

"What if you were the teacher? What would you think of that would help make it fun again? Would just looking at pictures make it fun again?" Silence. "Can't think of anything? Maybe we can think about that again? Maybe I can try and think of things, eh?"

"Nah." David gave a trace of scorn here.

"Don't think so?"

"Nah."

John came home after this initial interview quite discouraged. After a lengthy discussion of why some children choose not to talk, even to adults who see themselves as caring and easy to talk with, we concluded that David's belief that reading could never again be fun revealed a faint hint of a devil-may-care tough guy. David did not relish school, visualized no reform, and left his attentive listener stammering. Yet, he did not give an articulate critique of school.

What did David think about the kinds of knowledge he was asked to acquire? Did his life in school lead to personal discovery? Or, did he see school learning as simply something the adults in his life made him do? John assumed that David had no critique of schooling and sought to help him establish such values. Assumptions such as John's are common among parents and teachers who presume that it is possible to know the experiences of children without questioning them directly. Like most teachers, John made inferences from the little things that David said and did in unstructured contexts and sought ways to help him value school knowledge. Unlike most teachers, but consistent with Ann Bates's agenda for the year, John sought to do this by helping David discover the delight that can come from integrating school knowledge and personal interests and passions.

My own sense of school led me to assume differently. Perhaps David was silent because he knew adults would only dismiss or seek to change his views once he asserted them. There is no integrity in essentially being called a liar for asserting a critique. Yet, adults often do that, in gesture if not words, to children who tell them things they do not want to hear. In this respect, children are not free to address their need for power. Children receive few opportunities to influence others and can rarely do so without guidance from adults. Children can reveal thoughts about adults' agendas and establish personal agendas when at play. But, for the most part, children can simply express forms of self-determination within the boundaries that adults establish for them. In his interview with John, David showed difficulty expressing any form of self-determination, yet he gave hints of another side of his life when talking about what he did after school.

Listening to David, it is easy to assume that his silence and alienation from reading occurred because he had learning disabilities that prevented him from tuning into the intellectual world that other second graders took for granted. Yet, if David had not been in a public environment wherein his abilities could be compared to those of his classmates, we might look for other explanations. It is conceivable, for example, that David disliked

Challenges and Controversies

- How can caregivers determine whether a child is behaving one way at home and another way at school?
- How can caregivers determine whether quiet, well-behaved children are ignoring some of their needs?
- How can caregivers tell the difference between behavior that reflects a fracturing of needs or behavior that reflects a fracturing of responsibility to others?

reading because it forced him to engage with a medium for self-expression that he found unfulfilling—a stance that would also lead him to erect barriers to separate his school and personal lives.

During the six-month study of David's home and school lives, John discovered evidence to support all of these possibilities. David did not have Bruce's egotistical tendencies, but he did have difficulty reading with the fluency and comprehension his peers took for granted and exhibited different symptoms of a divided intellectual life. David camouflaged his artistic nature, social conscience, and vivid imagination, hiding important dimensions of his identity from those in school. He seemed to accept the traditional view that personal impulse and desire were illegitimate concerns in school, yet he could not always resist the temptations of these impulses.

Meet Quiet Bird

The day after the initial interview, all the second graders in the school sat on the clean, polished floor of the gymnasium to hear from Singing Bird, a Chippewa visitor from Michigan. Singing Bird explained that, just as the children did not come to school on horses or in buggies as their ancestors might have, so she lives like a modern American. She went on to help the children experience some of the cultural rituals her people retained from their past.

John was on the floor, too. He was an outlier near the back of the large island of occasionally squirming but generally attentive children, just behind David who had placed himself on the flank.

Well into her program, Singing Bird said, "You all have a special gift. How many of you believe that? How many believe you have a very special gift to give?" A sea of hands went up, but David's was not one of them. David's thoughts were well hidden.

Singing Bird's "Song of Children" highlighted the fact that children can teach many things to adults who take time to listen. Listening to David, a boy who would not speak, required ingenuity and posed an interesting challenge for John.

A minute after claiming to have no special gifts, David pulled some food from his bag and twice successfully teased the girl next to him—pretending to offer her the sandwich, then pulling it away. His twinkle helped John see that perhaps it is through gesture and not words that David revealed his identity.

Singing Bird's performance capped the second graders' projects on the Indians of North America. John remembered that earlier that day, when David's class completed sentences, David had found another way to assert himself. The first sentence read, "My Indian name is. . . ." David wrote, "Quiet Bird." This seemed like a revealing caption for David's approach to schooling.

The next sentence to be completed was, "I chose it because . . ." and David simply wrote, "it's a good one." Even though Ann Bates, David's teacher, encouraged students to give and justify their views on matters that are open to interpretation, Quiet Bird kept secret his thoughts. Was David unable or unwilling to articulate the source of this imaginative name? It was difficult to know if David chose Quiet Bird on an impulse that was hard for him to explain, or if this was an example of a carefully crafted camouflage stemming from the belief that school was no place for personal revelation.

Ann showed John another example of David's lack of voice. On a sheet where she asked students to evaluate their work on Indians, David simply listed what he did. *My legends, Red Deer packet, little Deer packet, My dream catcher.*

Like Bruce, David's attention often wandered when he was listening to instructions from his teacher. As Ann went over directions for a phonics assignment, for example, David's attention drifted. When Ann finished, David asked and was given permission to go to the bathroom. Upon returning, David waited in his seat, presumably for Ann to come and assist him. David put his hand up to attract Ann's attention, took it down, stole a look at an active group on the rug, then came to ask Ann about the instructions. George and Tanya, sharing a cluster of desks with David, were well underway on the task before David began.

Early on the day of Singing Bird's visit, David joined a group of seven, most of them girls, who were working on booklets. Instead of working, David sniffed the fruit-scented felt tip pens and offered them for others to smell. David chattered happily enough to the other students, fooling around in a not-too-disruptive way. Monique explained to Ann, who came over to the group, "He's trying to make us laugh."

"What are we doing?" asked Ann.

"We are getting ready to read out loud." David was not put on the spot by Ann's reprimand, but calmed down and worked reasonably steadily.

At break, Ann told John, "That sort of joking is common for him. If he thinks he can be funny or get someone to laugh, he'll always go for it. It's irresistible to him. He likes the role of being a little bit silly and cute and having people laugh at him. Some of the girls who enjoy him . . . treat him like a funny little brother. They can play about and still get everything done, but he can't. When he gets with them, he gets a little bit overwhelmed and gets silly."

After his first few days observing, John concluded that David seemed to easily meet most of his needs in Ann's classroom. He blended in reasonably well with his classmates and usually seemed engaged in some form of learning. From time to time, however, lack of voice, avoidance of assigned tasks, and impishness suggested that David had difficulty meeting his competence needs. With limited ego-involvement, David actively refused to participate in activities in which his personal interests might be revealed to others. This sometimes affected his ability to become fully task-involved, resorting instead to work avoidance when self-expression was encouraged.

Typically, Ann started some students reading different books in pairs while other students, sitting on the rug, worked with her on a different task. Ann often varied the distribution of assignments in this way to avoid the stigma associated with constant membership in a low reading group. The net result was a classroom of busy children, each with his or her own teacher-directed agenda.

Even in this multi-task classroom David exhibited the same motivational difficulties that were evident for Bruce and are common among students with learning disabilities. David's behavior suggested why, regardless of how they started and which form the behavior takes, motivational problems can persist. Like Bruce, David was inattentive and sought diversions at the outset.

One day, for example, David became distracted from his own work by listening to Eleanor, who was sitting behind him reading aloud. He started again, then talked with Liz, who was next to him reading an attractively illustrated book. Nearby, Ann was busy helping others and did not notice David becoming engaged in Liz's book. David caught himself, stretched and exclaimed, "Oh!" before forcing himself back to the phonics sheet he should have been doing. Whereas Bruce tried to avoid schoolwork altogether, David seemed to find the assignments of his peers more interesting than his own.

Around David, other students were reading and occasionally talking about what they were doing. "I found a crossword puzzle!" announced Valerie. David's classmates occasionally deviated from what they were doing, but David remained busy with anything but the assigned task. Unlike Bruce, David valued the drills enough to persist. Nevertheless, David seemed driven by impulse and desire rather than by a serious commitment to finishing. Consequently, like Bruce, David was strapped with less interesting work.

David might easily infer his own incompetence or laziness if he compared his progress to others. Yet, he showed no sign of laziness or of Bruce's egotism. Even David's "off-task" time was spent in other intellectual pursuits, looking over the shoulders of his classmates or eavesdropping on discussions that Ann was holding with other students. Nevertheless, David's habit of forcing his attention back to his own work, even though he could not apply himself suggests he might have gained some satisfaction in completing assigned tasks. David's implicit acceptance that authority resided with Ann and not with his own imagination was also evident when he expressed guilt or embarrassment about his limited progress and inability to adhere to her wishes. Because David did not finish, his diversions could hardly afford the sense of virtue and competence promoted by successful accomplishment.

Ann explained her strategies for addressing David's restricted view of schoolwork by saying, "The reason I sent them to do different things is, when those extra [more interpretive] things were offered as choices after other things were completed, it was a reward for people who worked quickly. It encouraged slapdash work. So, I'm trying to remove this whole time pressure thing, but at the same time, and this is difficult to do, to encourage productivity. . . .

"The fact of the matter is, we have a curriculum to be gotten through and certain things that I am accountable for. . . ."

"And they are getting that, too?" asked John. "David, in a way, shares this work ethic thing . . . that feeling he should get through the cut and dried part of the curriculum?"

"Yes, he does."

"It's not as if you're imposing this upon him," John agreed.

"No, not at all. He feels that he should."

John was committed to the belief that "the things they have to get through" were part of what divided David's experience—preventing David from making schoolwork his personal work. John thought that the curriculum that Ann felt pressure to get through consisted of factual knowledge and skills. Ann valued the more unsettled and controversial matters as well as discussions where nothing was written down or checked off. But, she also felt the obligation to spend time on the cut and dried matters that comprise most standardized achievement tests.

Ann continued, "But, [the more interpretive activities] are not taking them from their work. This is their work, too. When I called some people up this morning, and they all wanted to come—that's very different than it was two months ago. They used to be disappointed at leaving this stack of stuff to get through, as if they were afraid they weren't going to finish . . . I didn't want all of their learning to be that."

Talking with David's mother, John found confirmation for his emerging hunch that David assumed that legitimate schoolwork must be cut and dried, and divorced from one's personal experience. Mrs. Richardson gave vivid descriptions of David's stubborn adherence to a dichotomy between schoolwork and the rest of his life, and his concern with obtaining correct answers.

"David doesn't really say a lot about school," Mrs. Richardson told John. "He's generally here, like ten minutes before I get home. He's usually like he is now, out the door. If it's daylight, he'll be outside. I have him come in for dinner and then he has spelling words. . . . It's scheduled after dinner. . . . He's had his time to play and he's full of food so now he can stretch his little brain.

"So, we do spelling words on Monday. I'll give him the words and find out which ones he's got wrong. Then, Tuesday, Wednesday, and Thursday we practice all the words he's gotten wrong. . . . If he's got six wrong, we do like two a day. Then, Thursday night we do all of them just to make sure he hasn't forgotten. . . . Math and stuff, I don't have time. I really don't. I wish I did.

"Mrs. Bates, she said just to work with what I can get him to do right now without putting extra pressure on him."

"Sure." John commented empathetically.

"So, I do . . . I spend most of the time with David because my husband is exhausted when he gets home from work, and then, generally, the older kids need his assistance. We have our hands full. It's job sharing, but it's not always that easy. David relies on me. I have more patience with him."

"OK."

"I don't know what else. David never really pulls out papers from school," continued Mrs. Richardson. "I mean, unless he gets 100 on his spelling tests. Then it's right in my face and it's up on the refrigerator. And, he's very proud and I'm proud, too. He gets rewards when he's done well. A special treat of some sort. . . ." Here is another indication that David is more preoccupied with cut and dried forms of learning.

"We found at kindergarten, he just wanted to play. He didn't want to settle down. And we felt that was all right, but then in first grade, we didn't hear about any of his problems." This is a theme that Ann had also mentioned.

"It's my impression, in observing, that school's not a lot of fun. Is that right?" said John to David who was suddenly pretending to hide behind a chair. David did not respond so John continued talking to his mother, noting that this seemed another occasion where personal fun and conventional behavior did not seem to easily coexist for David. "But, [David] also has some fun, like he is now. He fits it in around things. But, I think it's hard to make a lot of schoolwork fun. . . . He's trying to do the work, but it's not his."

"Expertise."

"Maybe that's part of it," said John. "I'm wondering if it's like his life is divided up, like there's schoolwork and there's fun, and you can't do both at once?"

"Well, we do reading. When I read to my little ones, he'll be there. Now he'll help with reading. I'll read a page and he'll read a page. . . . He enjoys it, if it has something to do with trucks, fire trucks, firemen." David had disappeared and returned bringing an attractive toy truck made by his grandfather, and a larger fire truck.

"You know," said John looking at the way David handled his toys, "Ann has been thinking of ways to connect that [imagination] to schoolwork."

"Well, he does things. He has a farm downstairs. It's usually set up on our pool table. . . ."

John continued, "The impression I get watching in school, and Ann does too, is that there's a rich something going on in there that doesn't come out in school."

"True," agreed Mrs. Richardson.

". . . We maybe need to find ways to get schoolwork to use that imagination that he has. . . . Is there anything else you think the school could do better in the way of adapting?" asked John.

"David is really stubborn compared to my other kids . . . and he didn't have preschool and the older boys had preschool. . . . Being as stubborn as he is, there are times when I want him to do his spelling words, he'll just have a fit. A total fit. . . . He will cry. He will cry for fifteen minutes. And I'll go 'David, I know you want to go do this with somebody, but you know this is the time, and your crying is wasting your time,' and then he'll stop and then think about it. And he'll do it and he's done. And he's fine." The theme was consistent: Even though David wanted to do schoolwork, it was not his. He or someone else must make him do it.

At this point in the year, David was caught between approach and avoidance motivation. His behavior was not quite consistent with any one dimension of the intrinsic/extrinsic continuum currently fashionable in some theories of motivation.[1] It was rare, for example, to see David in an amotivated state and he was not particularly stimulated by rewards or punishments. Consistent with what researchers are introducing as introjection—compliance to gain approval—David sometimes approached tasks as if it were his duty as a citizen in Ann's classroom to complete them. Consistent with the definition of identification—endorsing particular goals—David approached the tasks his peers worked on while avoiding the task in front of him. And, at home, David exhibited high levels of intrinsic motivation on tasks he and his family members invented. Looking at John's field notes, it is relatively easy to classify David's behaviors along the intrinsic/extrinsic continuum. Nevertheless, such knowledge made it difficult to imagine how to help David connect aspects of his personal and school experience more fully.

"I don't know what the school can do to help," said Mrs. Richardson.

Ann confirmed John's conclusion that David's "lack of voice" represented a separation of school and personal knowledge when she told John that, for David, going to school must be almost like being a victim. "Like going to the doctor. Not that going to the doctor is oppressive for some people either: Some can take charge even there. But, it's like he lacks entitlement. Some [students] . . . see good schooling as a sort of right."

John and Ann returned to this topic the next day. "It's sometimes said," John began, "that learning disabled students aren't very verbal. Well it seems to me a different thing to say they don't have voice."

"Very different. Yes! . . . I have some who are not very verbal, or talkative, but who have a great deal of voice." Ann commented.

"In that they know what their values are?"

"They know their rights. And they know. . . ."

"They will draw the line?"

"Yes. David's disenfranchised at some level."

Although David hid from opportunities to publicly reveal his identity, he was not at odds with classroom life. David had many friends and often participated in whatever activities were planned, but contributed in a playful or mischievous way that sometimes suggested he was alienated from schoolwork.

This was apparent when Ann called the class to join her on the rug and discuss the Indian legends they had read. David arrived quickly and sat away from the group, against the wall. Ann urged him to move so he could see and thus participate. David moved, but not enough to make himself included. The class discussed factual and interpretive, potentially controversial questions. There was a lively discussion of whether one legend involved trickery or whether it involved clever action and planning. David seemed not to follow the conversation and did not contribute. We saw, in David's behavior, support for John Dewey's assertion that some students can assume it is the responsibility of the teacher to keep order because order is in the teacher and not in the shared work being done.

Later, Ann observed that with legends David "is working very much at the literal level. I work to get him to understand what happened in the story. He stays on task pretty well then. I think it's when he feels a little inadequate or he feels the conversation is going in a way he doesn't understand. He might get silly. . . . Now, in his skill group, I'll ask a question or one comes up, and he'll say an answer under his breath, as though he's testing the water. Then, I'll encourage him to say it to the group. But, raising his hand and saying I have something to say that I know is right—that I am confident it is something that is going to contribute and people are not going to laugh or think I'm silly. . . . He'd like that, laughing [with his peers], too."

"That's a bit different. . . ?" asked John.

"Yes, [David] wants them to laugh, but not think he's stupid. He did the funniest thing when he was "Star of the Week.". . . [The "Stars"] give an oral presentation where they tell about themselves and they show photos and different things they've brought in. Then on Friday, the students write a letter to the Star of the Week responding to the things that were said in the discussion. For whatever reason, [the children] began to ask whether you're a vegetarian. They ask this each week. When they asked David, he said, 'No I'm an American.' [The class] laughed and laughed: They thought he was being witty. And,

[David] realized they thought it was a wonderful answer, so he was pleased, but surprised. He managed to get out of it."

"That week, from Wednesday when he gave his talk, to Friday when he got the bag of letters to take home, he had a difficult time staying on task and being serious. . . ."

"He got too excited?"

"Yes. He got sillier than I had ever seen him. . . . And, I think it's true he likes things to be made a game, but . . . it's very difficult for him to not just play with the material. So, I feel he needs structure. It has to be interesting and fun, second grade appropriate, and he has to reach a little bit, too. . . .

"He has not felt success in reading. Not enough to . . . give him pleasure or reward. . . . He loved to have things read to him, but I think he's beginning to feel the pressure [to keep up]. How can he not?"

"It kills the interest?" John asked.

"How can it not?"

John began groping to construe David's world: "I'm very intrigued by the occasional goofing off—like the "Star of the Week" incident. Does it show a disconnection between school and his personal life? Like school is this thing that's important, serious, but you have another life that is yours and more exciting, and somehow the two don't fit together. You said there are some girls who can do everything at once. Maybe that could be just their more multi-track minds. But, it could also be partly that those parts of their lives. . . ."

David suddenly signaled the end of lunch break and prompted John to shut off the tape recorder by appearing at Ann's elbow, flushed from running. Here was another sign of life, but life outside the classroom.

Perhaps it was only describing part of the difference between David and the girls who adopted him as a little brother to say that the girls could do more things at once, joke and complete schoolwork, read at the literal as well as more interpretive levels. It might be that the girls were able to live their personal and academic lives more or less simultaneously whereas David had two different worlds. In the world of school, David was disenfranchised from intellectual tasks even though he exhibited flashes of autonomy and self-efficacy. David had fun at times and seemed to easily be able to find intimacy and exchange relationships, but this was at the expense of schoolwork, not as part of it.

Challenges and Controversies

- What does it mean to say that a student lacks a sense of entitlement?
- How do students with limited verbal skills use gesture to communicate?
- How can educators help students like David learn about their rights in a classroom?
- Is it fair to assume that students who are cheerful, funny, and cute are also appropriately engaged in academic activities?
- What can we learn by categorizing students' behavior using a taxonomy ranging from amotivation to intrinsic motivation?

After much speculation, John and Ann decided that it would be premature to assume these and other similar incidents could help them understand the roots of David's alienation from reading. They could have spent months or years wondering if he disliked reading because he lacked competence or because he could not connect the teacher-structured drills emphasized in school with the imaginative world evident in visits to David's home. Rather than become preoccupied with why David was alienated from reading, John and Ann responded as if his lack of competence and failure to connect his personal and school lives were both true. They designed activities to help David learn to appreciate books with the hope that he would also integrate his school life and personal life.

Learning to Love Books

In the early months of this project, Ann's informal sort of ability grouping had an individualistic quality wherein students read stories of their choice on a theme addressed by the whole class. The students then completed Reading Response sheets, consistent with their particular level of skill, wherein they wrote or drew reactions to the book and mapped the plot of the story. From day to day, Ann varied the way in which she distributed other more structured tasks, limiting opportunities for social comparison and the ability of students to compete with one another. Eventually Ann came to see that she also limited the extent to which children collaborated when learning. Without opportunities to collaborate, students like David find themselves in the frustrating predicament of not being able to expand their current abilities. Rather than work on the tasks in front of them, such children invent their own forms of entertainment.

Bruce avoided schoolwork when inventing his own tasks. David, however, seemed to prefer the academic tasks of his peers. When Ann began to call a group to the rug, for example, many hands waved and David's was one of them. Not chosen, David avoided his own work by reading Liz's book. Liz pointed out aspects of pictures that the two of them then discussed. As David turned to completing the last four pages of his writing assignment, Mark finished and found time to read for pleasure. David was not the only student with work to finish, but instead of working to keep up with Mark and his other classmates, David slowed down. When Liz, who had a different assignment, finished her book and filled out a Reading Response sheet, David, not impelled to compete with his peers, trapped his pencil under the lid of his desk and held it there.

On the rug with Ann, a lively group of students discussed Robert Frost's use of repetition and rhyming and, on the initiative of some of the students, the poet's intentions. Not included in that conversation, David discussed George's book instead. David seemed happy, but woke himself up from this distraction with a little jolt and returned to his assigned task. Almost immediately, however, David's attention lagged and he began watching the discussion Ann was leading.

Such impulsive, off-task behavior was not David's whole life in the classroom and seemed easy to change when compared to Bruce's similarly work-avoidant behavior. David's off-task behavior changed as soon as Ann, hoping that students could learn from one another, asked the class to read a variety of books in pairs while she taught structured drills to smaller groups of students. David easily became more engaged in such collaborative learning, helping us to see that David benefited from opportunities for exchange rather than solitary work.

"Bob could you possibly buddy-read with David?" Bob grinned across at David who reciprocated, maintaining eye contact while Ann arranged other pairs. David and Bob chose a book, then, very deliberately, looked for space. Finally, the boys put two chairs in the center of the rug that was normally clear of furniture. They took turns, reading continuously until recess. Ignoring all around them, David took his fair share of pages with Bob, a more fluent reader, helping judiciously.

The next day, the boys finished the book. With Bob's assistance decoding difficult words, David read with some expression. As they finished, Ann knelt to look into their eyes.

"Sixty-three pages!" commented David.

"David. Which part did you enjoy most?" Ann encouraged. "So, did you find some funny things?"

"She stuffed the stocking," David finally piped up. "That's my favorite part."

"David and Bob, can you turn to the favorite page and read it to me?" David found a page and read. Ann provoked more discussion then, "David and Bob, you need to do your Reading Response sheet."

After a couple of minutes John checked on the boys' progress. Bob showed John that he fit the long title on the top line of the sheet. David's larger letters made his title overflow the line. Bob appeared to be expressing pride in his own accomplishment rather than trying to insult David. John responded with, "As long as you get the name, that's probably the important thing, don't you think?"

"What does it mean, 'Response to the book'?" David asked Bob. David clearly did not seem insulted by Bob's burst of pride.

"Tell what you think about the book," responded Bob.

David nodded and then wrote, "It is good. I think the author is a good writer."

David collaborated much more easily than did Bruce. Working with a partner and helped by Ann's encouragement, David's involvement in reading and writing had been clear and strong. David was no longer bogged down in the way he had been with solitary work.

Later, assembled on the rug, Ann asked the class about "the fables you worked out with your fable friends on Friday." She then asked children to read a fable and plan a new version. The children could change characters and the setting, and add humor. David sat with Bob, busily illustrating their new fable, occasionally chatting with other students. David and Bob had changed only one character, but seemed to be enjoying their project. Bob, Ann told John later, was not a risk taker and David seemed comfortable following Bob's lead.

To coordinate the conflicting visions of skill development and imaginative forms of collaborative learning, Ann gave out work folders and asked David which task he wanted to do first. Ann hoped that, by allowing David to choose when to do various tasks, she could provide him with some of the benefits obtained by the children who did not become overwhelmed by reading comprehension tasks and other drills. Ann told David he need not do all the work immediately and encouraged him to schedule his learning—not to become bogged down on any one assignment.

David seemed pleased, started on a phonics task, then went to read with Matt. The two boys formed a good team. They chose a book that was about the right challenge for them both, and each boy could read words the other could not. David played briefly with an eraser, but was soon back to reading the book that he and Matt then finished. After reading, David worked a little on phonics. Encouraging David not to become bogged down seemed to pay off.

Later, Ann showed John a Reading Response sheet that David had spontaneously decorated with a delicate sketch. The doodling looked like an act of affection for the book, a solid attempt, albeit nonverbal, at expressing his personal reaction. By encouraging David to "buddy-read" and allowing him some control over when to do what, his appreciation for books gradually began to return. Unlike Bruce, David gained strength from interacting with his peers.

When the class moved to the rug for show and tell, David was relaxed and self-contained, affectionately twisting a signet ring on his little finger. Ann began to ask each child who had not volunteered if he or she would like to contribute news. David bobbed up and down playfully behind a desk. When Ann asked David if he had any news, he popped up and said, "No." David was not yet willing to share his personal stories.

In February, Ann had put up a message board intended to encourage students to write about issues of importance. One day, George tacked a message for David to the board. While waiting for his work folder, David did not notice George's note because he was busy looking through the attractive display of fable books Ann had arranged by the rug. David pulled out two books, and poured over them like a serious book lover.

David was one of the lower-skill clusters of students who were to read Arnold Lobel's story "The Letter."[2] David took the book with the first page turned as if it had already been read. "Read the first page," said Ann. "I'm on the second."

"You already read the first?" David queried.

"Yes," Ann replied, but David was already reading the first page while Ann finished giving directions to the other students. David needed no kick-start that day. He waved his Reading Response sheet through the air as he continued to his seat.

When David finished reading the story, he looked at the front cover of the book, savoring it. Then he looked at the back cover and flipped the book back and forth, comparing the pictures on both sides. Next, David turned to the questions on his Reading Response sheet: Why was the toad sad? *No one sent him a letter;* What did frog do for Toad? *sent him a letter;* and How do you feel when you get mail? *good.*

David then went to ask Ann for help with a question that was difficult for most of his classmates. On his way, David saw the note from George, "George, you wrote that?" David grinned broadly, wrote an answer, put it up, and then briskly walked back to his seat.

What better way to convince a boy that school and personal life can be connected? No adult had to tell David about the possible connection between these two aspects of his experience. He proceeded to the display of fable books, picked one, looked at it, chose another, sat, and read contentedly. Was David wondering what hidden messages were possible in the new fable? David certainly began treating books like powerful, but sacred, objects, exactly what Ann had been hoping for, but did not want to impose on David. Engrossed in his book, David read with his head resting on his arm, lost in his book, and moved immediately on to answering the response questions.

Later, on the rug, the group took turns reading "The Letter" to the class. The more able readers, who had not read the story, also wanted to take turns. "I can tell these are popular stories," said Ann to the group. Ann was pleased that the more able readers' interest was conveyed to the slower readers, and everyone could see that this was real literature. David followed the class reading, but did not volunteer. At the conclusion of the book, the class spontaneously clapped. Next, Ann went over the response questions, David raised his hand, was called on, and effectively answered his assigned question.

When John and Ann talked about David's progress in reading, they noticed that his imagination was stimulated with the work he had been reading. "Like that story today ["The Letter"]," commented John.

"He loved that story," said Ann. "He does like fantasy. That's why we did the Arnold Lobel stories. Fables led us into that fable book."

"So . . . he can start to connect," noted John.

George's note dealt with problems at recess. John went outside to see what the boys were up to, but could not find David in the sea of children. When the bell rang, John finally saw David near the entrance of the building, far from where the children should have lined up. David was trying to enter the building without lining up and John could now see how David had consistently managed to be the first to return from recess each day. David still tried to form a life around and in spite of social conventions like spelling and lining up, avoiding the rest of his class who lined up at the bottom of the stairs. This was certainly one kind of self-determination that might be useful to explore.

As John arrived to the line, David ran to find a place in line, apparently turned back in his attempt to thwart the system. "Hi, Speedy," John said to see if David would acknowledge that he had been observed. David flashed by John without comment. Later, as the line passed John in the hallway, John put out his hand, not sure how well he had gauged David's nonverbal behavior. David reassured John by giving him a healthy slap as he walked by.

A week later, on February 9, the class had been reading William Steig's books. Everyone knew Steig was the featured author because his books were on display next to a sign that said, "William Steig, author and illustrator."

To the students on the rug, this display offered a clue when Ann showed them a small gray cloth bag and said, "What is it?"

"Sylvester's in there I bet."

"It's a magic pebble."

Finally, Ann opened the bag to reveal a stuffed toy version of Sylvester, a mule in Steig's book, *Sylvester and the Magic Pebble.*[3] In the book, Sylvester found a colored pebble that granted wishes, and, changing into a rock, was unable to return to his original form. The second graders' interest in Ann's bag and the hidden toy suggested that this story had meaning to them.

After discussing the details of the story and Sylvester's options, students' attention was directed to the board. "Phonics is there for the week, but I don't want you to worry about it today. What is the most important thing?" [Work hard.] "Why?" [So you can learn.] The students were ready with answers because Ann often asked them to describe how they scheduled their work.

The discussion was intended to help David and a group of students who had difficulty reading to find meaning in this challenging book. David held his own even though the story was difficult for him and a number of the other students. To keep the story flowing, Ann would occasionally read some pages and asked the group to read a few additional pages in unison. When the students who were reading would stumble, other students would gently chime in with the correct word. A gentle cooperative ethos prevailed.

Ann also called students' attention to the language. "Listen to how William Steig said that, 'Flowers showed their young faces.'" Ann's message was that words were to be savored because magic could be done with them. She talked to students using language they could imitate. Encouraging students to become philosophers and thinkers and to share their pleasure and enjoyment with reading took precedence in Ann's classroom.

At the end of this session, students went to their seats to answer questions about the story. Soon, the class was back on the rug and Ann discussed the difference between fantasy and reality. "Could a fantasy story be real if the character in it was not an animal? Could Sylvester be a real story if Sylvester was a person?"

"No." chimed the class.

As the group went through the questions about the story together, David methodically filled in his answers. Ann prodded a few of the students who were less engaged, but did not need to prod David.

For the first question, students were to describe the magic pebble. David's hand was up to share his answer. Afterward, Ann solicited other answers from the class. After hearing a variety of descriptions, Ann said, "You notice they are all good answers and they are all different." Ann was establishing the legitimacy of personal interpretation, converting the questions into an exercise in imagination rather than in detailing factual information. David followed comfortably and participated several more times before the call for lunch.

Over the next few days, the whole class worked on *Doctor DeSoto,* another of Steig's stories.[4] David was diligent and his report describing the book was filled with cute little drawings. All the children made drawings for the cover of their reports. Jenny and some of her peers traced pictures from the book, whereas David and a few of his peers made freehand, childlike drawings. David certainly had no difficulty displaying his reactions to the book, even though he was less competent at writing about those feelings.

Several "advanced" children had almost copied the drawings of adults. John wondered if this sort of copying was what children had to do to be labeled "advanced." Conceding that David and Bruce had difficulty bridging the gap between the worlds of childhood and adult culture, John also wondered if those who copied adults were molding themselves too hastily. Leaving David and Bruce behind, did some of these "advanced" children lose potential to frame strong, coherent identities? Ann's style of encouraging multiple forms of self-expression may well help those who prefer the written word over drawing as much as it helps students like David who prefer drawing to writing.

As the year progressed, such early signs of appreciation for the printed word blossomed into full-blown reverence. David began to treat books like powerful, but sacred objects—exactly what Ann had hoped. One day, for example, David came in as school was about to start, went directly to his desk, and sat reading a report that he had written the day before. Meanwhile, Ann gently announced the date and the rest of the morning routine. She almost whispered, maintaining calm without obliging everyone to attend to her. David remained engrossed in reading, with his head on his hand. This gesture, along with Ann's quiet manner and the hushed tones of the other children, made John feel like he was in a cathedral—a small, square cathedral, with yellow walls and a flat, low roof. David's sense of competence was apparent and his choice of books was at an appropriate difficulty level.

Ann had a knack for encouraging all the children to participate in reading activities. When she began poetry readings, for example, she first asked for volunteers. Some students never volunteered to read poetry and Ann gently encouraged them to participate. Poetry readings seemed a noncontrived way of publicly celebrating the magic of words—a natural form of oral reading. The slower readers could learn words from the public repetition, rhythm, and rhyme without making the repetition seem boring. Ann's practices culminated in a well-rehearsed and thus safe, pleasurable public performance.

John was frustrated with the fact that David still worked so hard on spelling, a task that seemed to lack meaning in its own right. John was aware that, if students become too preoccupied with the conventions of writing, they could avoid using their imagination. Visits to David's home revealed evidence of his rich imagination, and John wanted to encourage him to bring that talent to school.

Wanting to be helpful, Mrs. Richardson continued to talk with John about the ways in which she was able to invent new and better strategies to help David learn to spell. When John told Ann about these new strategies, Ann hit on John's concern that frequent testing teaches children about their mistakes rather than offers opportunities to learn. Ann noticed that David did particularly poorly on a spelling test that was, for the first time, marked by his then current buddy, Jill. As Jill found David's many mistakes, she commented, "I'm just checking them."

"A bit embarrassing for him," said Ann who was ambivalent about having students check one another's work. John was impressed by the fact that Jill announced she was "just checking" and avoided the implication that she was judging the overall competence of her less able partner. Fortunately, less defensive than Bruce, David reciprocated Jill's sensitivity and thereby moved more deeply into the evolving community by establishing more intimate relationships with peers who were eager to help.

Near the end of the year, after discussing fairy tales, David approached Ann to say, "I have not read very many fairy tales because I'm so busy." He was "busy" on language drills and did not want to miss reading fairy tales. Reading fairy tales might mean, by implication, not being busy. John wondered if there could be a time when David says, "I couldn't get busy reading fairy tales because I was buried in details of worksheets." That

Challenges and Controversies

- How can teachers model the intellectual activities they would like to see in their students?
- Given that learners benefit as much from acting out their feelings as they do from writing about them, are there ways to connect action and words in the curriculum?
- How can teachers structure their classrooms to permit surprises like those David received when finding his own letter after reading about one?
- What can teachers do to coach students who do not appreciate books as easily as David? How can teachers pique students' curiosity?

would be asking for a more elaborate critique, perhaps necessary before David could find himself too busy reading fairy tales to do the drills. David was no longer losing momentum in carrying out tasks. When David accepted the freedom and guidance that Ann offered him, he became a more self-determined, competent, and socially connected member of the school community. David's progress might become less dependent on Ann's guidance if Ann and John could elicit more personal information from David and help him see the value of integrating these parts of his experience.

Making Room for the Personal Awakens the Intellectual

John's view that David seemed to have difficulty connecting his school and personal lives was supported by David's behavior in gym as well as the early classroom observations. Because David had difficulty with literacy, gym was a place where his particular learning disabilities should not have affected his performance. Yet, David exhibited the same impulsive behaviors and attempts to stay on the edge of the group that he did for reading. These were observations that clued John into the fact that David's approach to school differed considerably from his approach to personal forms of learning. Whereas Bruce easily fit into gym class but could not embrace literacy activities, David seemed to reject all assigned tasks and invented his own agendas.

One day, for example, watched by an instructor and two assistants, the children began by running around the gym to music. David ran slowly, then quickly. He slid along the wall, then waited for Mark. Whereas most students ran at a steady pace, David and Mark cavorted and played tag briefly before David ran off again. Most students ran around a track marked by dayglow plastic traffic control cones at a pace they could sustain. David exercised, but he zigzagged and was not always part of the general flow. Nevertheless, his small deviations were no threat to the general order.

When the students were instructed to each get a basketball, David was lying on the floor, apparently daydreaming, quite relaxed. He was last to get a ball. When the group was given instructions for ball-handling exercises, David was lying on his back. When the music started, the others began and, after a pause, David tried to imitate them. David then tried the newly described skill, but gave up quickly and bounced his ball until the instructor stopped him. Then, he began to nudge the ball like a bull and to crawl after it.

Next, David decided to change his ball, another activity that was not assigned. As he passed the instructor, she patted his head—neither a gesture of approval nor a demand to stop his unofficial enterprise. David dribbled his new ball while others did the prescribed exercise. The dribbling briefly turned into a flailing of the ball. Then, David lay on the floor, chin on the ball, listening to new instructions. David briefly tried the assigned exercise, but seemed not to have understood the instructions. Given that this exercise extended earlier ones, David's previous lack of attentiveness could not have helped. However, he remained active, trying to balance the ball on the point of a plastic traffic cone and simultaneously held the ball under his chin and on the point of the cone. This began to look like a slapstick routine. Though impish, David's manner offered no challenge to the general authority of the instructor, and the other students were not distracted.

Next, with his ball on the floor, David picked up a cone and jammed it on top of the ball. Noticing that the ball was stuck, David picked up the cone, quite satisfied with his new discovery. When the instructor demonstrated a duck walk while dribbling the ball round and round between her legs, David dribbled his ball over to get a new one instead of trying this task that the other students were finding difficult.

Over the weeks, John noticed that the gym instructor allowed David more latitude than most students were permitted. David had trouble making the official activities of gym class his own and learning the lessons taught. The instructor told John that she liked David, and that David had difficulty with some activities, yet he tried and kept active. Whereas the gym teacher saw incompetence in David, John saw initiative and self-determination.

John gained more insight when telling Mrs. Richardson about David's behavior in gym. "He's always played by himself. Until recently, all the other kids were older, and he didn't have play partners. So it was just always David in the sandbox. We have a huge sandbox, and he'll spend hours building roads, using his imagination beyond anything you can believe. I mean this guy has built golf courses, and a construction area. Everything in a sandbox. . . . He's always been that way."

"You know, maybe that's a thing the school needs to find a way to use?" suggested John.

"I think they are a little bit with their writing, because he's written papers about Dad's work . . . then about grandpa being a fireman. And he loves to draw trucks."

"Ann certainly encourages that," commented John.

Mrs. Richardson continued, "She uses his interests . . . but he can't do that through everything. He'll do animals, because he loves animals. His grandfather is very good guidance. They spend the summer up there, and there are deer in the backyard, raccoons, birds. . . . If they can work with him with nature stuff, he'd do a great job."

"Yeah," reflected John, "School is just like —this mental wall there."

John changed the direction of this conversation, moving to one of his favorite topics, "What about thinking about what is good for his own education. Not many children get asked about that. I think it might help if, rather than thinking that education is something that people do to you, that you can exercise some judgment about what it should be."

"When he was littler, [David] said, 'I'm going to drive big trucks.' Now that his grandfather's a fireman, he wants to be a fireman."

"Yes. Yes." coaxed John. This was just the kind of information he wanted to know.

"My other two sons, they never really said what they wanted to be, but David's very confirmed in what he wants to be."

"Which might make a lot of school seem irrelevant, like I don't have to do this stuff to be a fireman?" John probed.

"But, his grandfather said, 'You think, like, "I don't have to read," so how are you going to learn how to do anything if you don't know how to read?' 'Oh,' said [David's] grandpa, 'but those reports that you have to make when you are a fireman. You have to be able to spell.' And then [David will] spend the time."

"That turned him around?" asked John.

"Right. Exactly!" answered Mrs. Richardson.

"That's very interesting. That suggests the complexity of young children, that we don't recognize." John found support for our belief that educators have to take students' reasons for learning or not learning more seriously—to respect their ethics for achievement.

Mrs. Richardson also confirmed that David's seemingly impulsive behavior was not due to an inability to delay gratification when she told John that David's allowance, "never burns a hole in his pocket. He'll save up because he wants something. He'll ask me, 'Do I have enough, yet?' . . . He always gets what he wants."

"That testifies to the sort of toughness you were talking of."

"Exactly. . . . He knows what he wants and he'll go after it."

In addition to hiding his imagination, David was also reluctant to discuss personal matters. One day, for example, John asked David how he got a scratch on his eye. Rather than answer, he teased Elliot, saying Elliot did it. Then David asked Bob if he liked lemonade, challenging, "Answer yes or no!" David's methods for distracting John's attention seemed to be a polite way of saying, "mind your own business."

After Christmas, Ann had asked David about his presents, but he had nothing to say about them. John knew that David had received plenty of toys for Christmas. Yet, David's silence fit with the observation that he rarely spoke of personal matters in school. This might suggest the separateness of his worlds, but it might also reflect David's emphasis on nonverbal forms of communication, especially of emotion. David attended to people and indicated his feelings, but often without words.

The next afternoon, John was surprised to see David in Alice Kay's resource room. John calculated whether he could give David a playful pat on the back as he walked behind him to sit down, and decided to take the risk. David's need to shelter his personal side made John reflect on what might otherwise be a natural gesture.

But during this session, David surprised John by directly challenging Alice. In giving directions, Alice referred to the children as students. David piped up: "We're not students."

"What are you?" Alice was surprised, too.

"We're pigs," said David.

"Why?" Alice looked a little worried. Could this be an expression of low self-esteem, commonly expected among students with learning disabilities?

"We ate a lot."

John was not sure, but David's comment seemed like a joke. Yet, Alice did not take it that way. "Not in here. In here, I'm a teacher and you're a student. You are not pigs. You are students," said Alice earnestly.

Perhaps teachers' reactions to David's sense of humor had something to do with his unwillingness to share his personal thoughts. Yet, David did send ambivalent messages when he politely rebuked them for inquiring into his personal affairs. John and Ann decided to try to help David see that, at least in this school, personal and academic themes were equally valued. To do so, they had to work hard to decode David's ambivalent messages.

Still unsure about his interpretation of David's comment, John later drove to David's house. When John arrived, David was outside with his sister. He flopped excitedly on his back in the soft snow as John walked up. Again, not sure how it would come off, John said, "Hello. I wonder what that is over there? Is it a boy or is it a pig?" To John's relief, David's grin suggested the joke hit its mark.

As John talked with Mrs. Richardson, David darted across the room to hide behind John's chair. "You know what I learned today in school?" said John with a wink.

"What?"

"That he might look like a boy. He might look like a student. But what he really is is a pig."

"David you are a pig? Are you? Now you are supposed to be a cheetah [in the school play]." The adults chuckled.

Mrs. Richardson interpreted David's interest in pigs, " One of my girlfriends at work, Lisa, they are pen pals. So, when [David] does good in school, I'll let her know and she'll write a note and he'll write back to her. This all came out of getting him to use his spelling words in writing. . . ."

"He's pretty clever isn't he!" John's interruption reflected his awareness that David was hiding behind the furniture. "He moves around this room and you don't see him. Is he a spy?"

"Well, my girlfriend Lisa loves pigs."

"Oh, yes. That's why he's a pig."

"I think so. That's her favorite. He owes her a letter right now so she won't write to him 'till he writes back."

"And what about books?" continued John.

"We buy books about fire engines. Yes, and we just had the book club. He picked out two and I picked out one. David's got them in his room. They're downstairs, everywhere. So we never lose sight of them, we just keep rotating them, having so many kids."

"It would be really nice to use that imagination. That liveliness, because there is this liveliness." Quiet Bird appeared a tougher bird than John first thought, enduring school and protecting his personal world of animals and imagination.

This knowledge reinforced Ann and John's resolution to encourage David to share his personal thoughts, and they became more assertive. One day, for example, Ann was talking to George about his weekend when David arrived. David stood beside George and Ann turned to him, "How about you David? What kind of weekend did you have?" David smiled and shrugged. Ann asked again and he said, "OK." David was clearly pleased to be recognized by Ann, but this was apparent in expression, not words.

Later in the year, David began to be more consistent in his willingness to share his feelings. One day, for example, when lunch was announced David ran to his locker and to line up first at the door. Waiting for his classmates, he pretended to kick and punch the doorway. John pointed to a chip in the paint near where David almost hit the doorway, with an expression hinting that David had done it. David grinned gently and asked if John would come out to recess.

The work Ann was undertaking with respect to David's learning reflected an aspect of her major agenda for the year—to make everyone's learning personal, positive, and comfortable. Ann could see that David was becoming more secure as he came to understand that she accepted him as he was. Ann recalled when thinking about her goals for the year, "I don't want to be center stage. I want their responses to be important. . . . The literary response is a personal response. . . .

"I think," continued Ann, "students like David have become accustomed to things in school not making sense to them. I think they sense that it makes more sense to others. But

. . . they don't question when it doesn't. . . . They don't come to me and say this isn't making any sense to me. They'll say, 'I've read this.' The whole reason you read is for meaning. [The children] don't demand that in what they do here [in school]. It must be their experience in school from the beginning—that things don't make sense. But, you just carry on. . . .

"As much as we try to say that the phonics paper wasn't as important as the [imaginative] writing, to some it was more important because you can finish and check it off. . . ." Ann was aware that some students need the structure that comes with controlling types of feedback.

"When I talked with David's mother," John said, "the first thing that came up was spelling. Only later, we got on to David's imagination. . . ." Preoccupation with drills was not surprising given that spelling was what came home for homework. As in most elementary classrooms, students regularly had tests and got numerical scores on spelling, not on imaginative work. "I wonder if it's worth saying, 'Forget spelling. Absolutely forget it and do something else, like more reading'. . ." continued John.

"If perhaps we wanted to modify the list," said Ann. "We could cut the list. I just do think he has to have some responsibility for a certain number. . . . This is not going away in his life." Here Ann's concerns seemed similar to those of Mrs. Richardson. Both women saw and valued David's imagination but felt he had to get through the cut-and-dried stuff.

"No, I see that," said John, "but there is the problem of that other thing—his awareness that things have got to make sense. School is not all a matter of stuff like spelling that you don't really make sense of. . . ."

". . . If she felt that lightening the list would help," wondered Ann.

"She didn't," John asserted.

"She would never raise that."

"No," coached John, "but thinking of the dilemma we are talking of, could something be modified?"

"One thing, better for him than learning [spelling words] and then forgetting them," suggested Ann, "would be . . . if he would dictate sentences to his mother, and she would write them down and he would read the sentence back to her."

"He'd learn spelling in the process," John mused.

"I'd rather that they learn to read. . . . I'm so frustrated with the spelling books. The exercises are so silly."

To ensure that a literary response remained a personal response, Ann accepted Singing Bird's advice and listened carefully to what her students said. Listening to David, Ann learned that he attended to people and indicated his feelings, but often through art and gesture rather than words. If Ann could expand David's comfort zone, maybe she could teach him that responding through reading and writing offered additional means by which to attend to people and express feelings. Maybe David could learn to find pleasure and enjoyment in becoming a philosopher and thinker as well as a free and responsible citizen.

John joined in Ann's agenda. At recess, when John saw David, David scampered off playfully and peered at John, like a spy, from behind a climbing apparatus. John pointed his finger at David and shot. David ran to the next piece of equipment and the two repeated their game. John was a personal friend as well as an authority figure interested in making sure David learned to read.

That evening, John called Mrs. Richardson to tell her about Ann's suggestion for spelling homework—to involve more imagination and make it more engaging. But, John explained the process poorly. Mrs. Richardson assumed that John meant that David should write out sentences in the way that more "old-fashioned" teachers used to punish students. John could not tell if he was also competing with the children in the background, or with Mrs. Richardson's preoccupation with getting through spelling assignments in a way that might also teach David that learning time is not play time. Mrs. Richardson reminded John in this phone conversation that she wanted to teach David to be a more disciplined student, but John wanted David to bring some of his free spirit from home to school.

As the year progressed, David began to accept the agenda of linking personal and intellectual tasks. In his journal, for example, David wrote:

My day was bad it
Killed me i am
gowen to Bed.

Here was grim emotion, leavened by wry wit. What could be more personal? Yet, David was not ready to share the source of this emotion. When Ann responded in his journal by asking why David's day was bad, Quiet Bird wrote no answer. Later, Ann asked her question orally, but David became coy and shrugged. The next day, however, David again framed pain poetically.

The sun
the sun had a
bad day it was dark
and cloude it strarted to rand.

David's poems revealed the rich sensitivity to emotion and artistic nature that John witnessed when visiting David at home and that his mother took for granted. With Ann's encouragement, these isolated forms of self-expression gradually became more common.

A day after David wrote about the sun, Ann read to the class two versions of a fable about the North Wind and the sun. David listened avidly, but faded off when instructions for morning work were given at the end. David's attention waned when art and imagination were not the topic of conversation. When the students were encouraged to write their own version of the fable, David asked to go to the bathroom. Yet, when he came back, he began writing reasonably quickly and showed that he had followed the story:

the sun and the cluod
one day the cloud and the
sun war in a fight thay
whill see which one can
blowe the mans coat the cloued
went first he blowe and
blowe the man wirapped his coak
around hisself. now it's my turn
and the suf first he shone a little
on the man and the loosened

his coak. then the smild warmly
on him the end

David was particularly attracted to cleverly illustrated books. When he went in search of a fable book, for example, he was drawn to a difficult one by its illustrations. Ann had to suggest a book closer to his reading level, but she understood the spirit of David's first choice. By encouraging David to make decisions about what he should learn and when, Ann could see his interests more vividly and gently challenged decisions that seemed inappropriate.

With Ann's encouragement, David's contributions to class discussions became more consistent, but only when he found the work meaningful. As the months passed, David was no longer the boy at the back of the group. He inched forward to the center and once in a while to the front. Through gesture and metaphor, David accepted Ann's suggestions, offering her flashes of artistic integrity and symbolic insight into his personal life.

David and his classmates had coaching on how to invent a personal response to literacy. Ann and the other second grade teachers arranged opportunities to help the children make such links. Shortly after the Christmas holiday, for example, Laurie Lawlor, an author of such children's books as *The Worm Club* and *How to Survive Third Grade,*[5] spoke to the whole second grade about how she got ideas and how she wrote her books. A small woman, Laurie spoke in a quiet manner that was similar to Ann's teaching style. Laurie had the children riveted as she described how simple everyday things like a pet dog or the appearance of a person on the street could start adventures in fiction.

Laurie introduced one story by showing a box and asking what might be in it. Then, she revealed a tiny delicate doll. Laurie told how she initially found a small, old porcelain doll's head on her family farm. She fixed up the doll and constructed a story based on her experience.

The next day, Laurie visited each class to help the children get ideas for their own writing. The children discussed how particular objects could be starting points for stories, and everyone decided to bring objects to stimulate their writing. David's object was a treasured ring that he had been given by someone in his family.

"Have you read the story [David was working on]?" Ann asked John at the end of the next day.

"No, I haven't. I've got it here," John answered.

"I haven't either. He was going to share it yesterday . . . then Alice came to get him. I let him go [to the resource room] but it would have been a great time to stay with the group," Ann suggested. "A lot of them had trouble taking an object that was meaningful to them and not just writing about the object. But, David did not have the need to tell about his object. . . . He showed it and said it was a ring, and really dove right into this writing."

> Once upon a time a boy named George was walking. He stepped on something and turned into a deer and ran away at night. A hunter came in the woods shot at George's friend. George looked up at his sharp horns and he ran as fast as his little legs can go. [He] poked the hunter in the butt. The hunter went, 'Ahhhhhh.' He jumped up tree. George was scared that he would never

> see his friend and family. The next day George woke up. He looked down. He wished I [was] a hewman. He walked home. He did not make it home. He stepped on something again, but he found what he stepped on. It was a ring.

"Quite something," John responded. "The kid is taking off. He's doing with words what he has been doing with drawing, and his sandpit and stuff at home. Presumably he's doing that with reading, like that story today."

"He loved that story," said Ann. "He does like fantasy. That's why we did the Arnold Lobel stories. Fables led us into that fable book."

"Those little things in David's journal are also quite poetic," John announced.

"The sun had a bad day."

"So . . . he can start to connect."

"Well, his voice . . . I think he's starting to have one. . . . And he has a nice way of putting things." John and Ann suggested that David's intentions had changed, but perhaps they had simply taken this long to see that David often expressed himself and was hardly a passive victim in school.

"He's an artist." John reflected. "That 'sun had a bad day' thing, I was wondering if it is a thing you could read out and discuss as a sensitive expression. Showcase his talent without making him have to do a pile of stuff."

"Right. I could ask him if I could share that when we are talking about figurative language. . . . We are going to start a new author next week and I think this is one he will like. It's all fantasy and transformation . . . so it will fit in well . . . I'm just thrilled to see them all reading so much. Even David." Having the benefit of hindsight, we can see that Ann had a very perceptive understanding of David's needs and values. Yet, Ann was also willing to let it be David who ultimately determined what materials were most interesting to him.

"I was thinking about what you said the other day," said John, "your vision of your ideal class. . . . Could you get those words back, because they connect to David."

"Well, I wanted personal response to be a big part of what we do in school. . . . Then you can get away from who's where in terms of skill and ability because personal response is not something that can be measured that way."

"Right. And you said that means respecting David and the others as individual people?"

"Yes, because he has as much of an opportunity to get just as good an evaluation on his fable packet as Jan."

"Yes, even the way you talked just then is a slightly different way to when you spoke of wanting David and the others to know that they were valued as persons. Like his imagination, whatever it turns out to be is interesting and should be seen as so."

"Yes. And his work is more imaginative than [Jan's] is for example. And there's many a day he works harder. And those are the things we really have to take into account. It's individualizing, but I hate that word in a way because it's such an old word."

Near the end of January, almost a month after Laurie Lawlor's visit, David asked Ann when Laurie would be coming back. David's comment paid high tribute to Laurie's connection in helping him see that personal and school knowledge can be intimately connected.

Ann was giving up separating the class into skill groups. With Steig's fantasy and the fables, everyone read the same books. There were times when the students would choose their own reading material, but Ann increasingly aimed at making everyone feel included in reading and discussing common works. It was sometimes a struggle for David, but with Ann's support and that of his peers, David stretched without getting separated from himself, the stories, or the rest of the class.

"You can individualize by having worksheets at their own level," John probed. "That wouldn't be what you are talking about."

"No, not at all. It's responding to the material in a genuine way, in a way that shows that you've thought about it, gained some insight, responded—that is really the only way I can say it. . . . I want to think that it's personal."

"For each one."

"For each one, and there's a place for them here. But, it's expecting a lot, too. It's expecting—"

"A lot of you," interrupted John. "You have to find a way to see each of them."

"Yes! It's draining. It's a more emotional way to teach and that's hard sometimes . . . the downside is that you take a bad day a lot more personally. . . . I think the rewards are great. You find them invading your thoughts a lot. And knowing that, as well as . . . I think I am serving them, educationally, emotionally, and all those ways—[yet,] you know you're not really preparing them for what's ahead in some ways. . . . Is it going to make it harder for them next year?"

"That's one that keeps coming up. The third grade [curriculum demands]."

"I worry about that," admitted Ann.

"I think everyone has that in common [including David's mother], and I don't want to take you off it if you want to stick to it, but what is intriguing to me is this, something like reverential feeling emerging in your class. . . . It's almost like we are in church here."

"Ha. Ha," laughed Ann.

"But it's not solemn . . ." stammered John, "and it fits for David. This sensitive, quietly artistic kid who can't connect, but he's starting to connect."

"I value the artistic part."

"I wonder if the quietness that you have—"

"I hope it's quiet, is it quiet?"

"Yes. You're quiet. . . . But it doesn't mean they are repressed. I don't see that. . . . It's particularly interesting in terms of David who had not much voice, but who seems to be getting it. And, getting it quietly in his little world of imagination. It's sort of like magic." John was clearly impressed with Ann's teaching style.

"Well, yes. Valuing the artistic and the aesthetic is important to me. . . . And, it's a thing we don't measure in school. . . . If you are an artistic person, that is a huge part of who you are.

"I'm from a family where that was valued and celebrated. A couple of my brothers and sisters are in the fine arts and my father was a wonderful writer himself—wrote journals all his life. Wonderful poetry. He encouraged it in me. Literature and stories . . . all kinds of things. And I do value it, and I remember my mother or father telling us, 'Other people aren't going to understand you. . . .' I really do think I have a sensitivity to it. . . . I bring that here, I hope." Ann's own response to literacy is a personal response.

Challenges and Controversies

- Why is it important for students to connect their school and personal lives?
- In the hectic pace of a busy classroom, how likely is it for teachers to misinterpret children's intentions?
- How can children challenge adults while remaining respectful of their authority?
- What kinds of public activities can educators design to stimulate children's imaginations and encourage rich thought?
- Is it too much to ask students to reflect on the educational aspects of their experience?
- To respond to academic material in a genuine, personal way requires the ability to coordinate self-determination, competence, and affiliation needs. Is that too much to ask from children?
- How can teachers cope with the inevitable emotional drain that occurs when trying to help students coordinate all aspects of their experience?

Perhaps that is why she has so many ideas about how to stimulate the imaginations of her students.

"I think I sensed that the very first time you talked with me about David. I wished I'd had my recorder on," John affirmed.

In advocating a personal response to literacy, it would be unfair to encourage educators to imagine that all children with learning disabilities will fracture their needs for self-determination, competence, and affiliation by behaving egotistically. After all, learning disabilities are not descriptions of social relationships. David's social skills and willingness to learn from the feedback he received offer a testament to the value of using caution when labeling students' behaviors. While acting out frustrations may be prevalent among some students with learning disabilities, other students are as likely to turn their frustrations inward. When students are fortunate enough to have teachers who are sensitive to such individual differences, they are more likely to examine their frustrations rather than fracture their experiences.

Quiet Bird Shares His Social Conscience

Interesting surprises emerge in classrooms where there is a match between students' needs and teachers' responses to those needs. David, for example, had areas of expertise that he respected, but was unwilling to share with others. David never needed reassurance about his art: In this domain he respected his own voice. As he revealed his sensitivity to emotions and artistic nature, David gained security from knowing that his art was also respected in school. By connecting his drawings with literature, David's writing voice gradually gained similar integrity. David's limited assertiveness began to seem a strength. David was quiet when unsure of his place, but also seemed to be quietly protecting his world. His stubbornness suggested a grip on his own experience. His impishness and imagination found expression in clever thought, writing and drawing, and conventionally acceptable forms of wit.

David's newfound security in the classroom was never accompanied by a tendency toward dominance. As Ann told John, "He is never mean. There are some [students] I get a lot of complaints about. Some do have a mean streak. Never have I heard anything like that about him." When Quiet Bird was quiet, it sometimes reflected an ethical stance, not mere shyness. And, when confronted with potentially oppressive acts, David could initiate a strong ethical critique.

"David is calling me mean," Nate told Ann one day. David did not explain himself clearly. Ann kept them both talking to glean that David was reacting to the egotism suggested by Nate having written "Nate the great" on a name card in the computer room. In the discussion, after discovering that this is also the title of Sharmat's book, David revised his charge from meanness to rudeness.[6]

David's behavior reminded John of another very quiet second grade girl who seemed "merely shy," but who wrote in her journal that she was not a bragger. Such an impulse, in other settings, can inhibit a student's academic growth: To be concerned about fairness and equality does not often lead to personal advantage in an environment infected by a competitive spirit. Nevertheless, this incident fit with David's other expressions of support for the underdogs. It seemed as though acknowledging this parallel might help David put his personal and academic lives into satisfactory relation.

In December, for example, when in the Learning Center, the class was asked to draw peace symbols and write two self-chosen slogans on them. David wrote, "Homes for the poor," and "Save the Indians." David did this work as quickly as any in the small group and drew teepees when his teacher asked, "What would be a good symbol for those [slogans]?" David drew quickly, brightly, and schematically, obviously enjoying his work. When the learning specialist asked David to notice the time, David said, "Oh no! Time to go!"

"We're not going to have time to finish," said the specialist.

"No. No. I will!" responded David and pressed on.

When Ann came to pick up her class from the center, she commented on David's slogans. The learning specialist said, "He's the only one who came up with that." David's peers, by way of contrast, drew hearts and wrote about universal symbols rather than calls to eradicate particular forms of oppression.

Ann confirmed the legitimacy of David's unique ideas when, after asking him to read his slogans, she said, "I agree with all of those."

Likewise, completed in honor of Martin Luther King's birthday, David's story and the corresponding drawing about his own dreams for the country contained unusually vivid detail on the nature of racial inequality in the United States and a plan for rectifying this. Ann called this to John's attention with, "His art was interesting from day one. Those little detailed drawings. They had so much life. . . . I don't know if you saw his finished dream story, but he did a great thing." David's final copy said:

I have a dream that
for black and white people will
get along and that everybody

can sit on the bus together.
And to build more homes for the
poor.

The detailed drawing above this writing was of buildings under construction. Homes for the poor? "And see the arrows," said Ann. "Don't forget to turn this. [Hidden behind the writing] he showed the world as it's going to be. Everybody's on the bus. You see the black and white people and here they are together. And here are the houses they've built." The dream is realized. The drawings were a metaphor for David himself: On the outside he is a learner under construction, but concealed underneath are a rich imagination and a commitment to social justice.

Jenny's work was next in the pile—a pastel-shaded sheet with three hearts and "Peace!" in large letters. She had written:

My dream is to stop people from murdering.
My dream is to see on the news that
people aren't but I can't do anything,
it's really up to the murders.

"She'd be considered an absolutely top second grader," said Ann. "But when you look at artistic integrity. . . ."

"And, indeed, complexity . . ." added John.

"Yes. Yes. There's a lot of thought," and, as John and Ann later added, ethical responsibility in David's work.

Ann and John concluded that, as David got more expressive in his approach to schoolwork, he revealed a much more developed social conscience than did most of his peers. When one understands that the competitive ethos promoted in American schools makes it difficult for students to respond to their altruistic impulses, David's attempts to camouflage this part of himself seems rational. A concern for equality and fairness often does not lead students to seek personal advantage or to demonstrate pride in their work. Yet, it seems as though David needed to express his ethical concerns in order to put his personal and school experience together.

At the end of February, for example, David came in smiling and relaxed, with new shoes. When Ann called his name to go to the rug, he spoke firmly and moved sharply. "Let's look over the choices for today . . ." said Ann. One activity on the list was to do a page for a class alphabet book to be written in the style of William Steig. "Those who had trouble with your letter, you might go to someone who has done theirs. I'm going to be doing some important work with a group, so if you have a problem, what are you going to do?"

As Ann talked, David picked up a Steig book and looked through it, showing Joe some of the pictures. "David," asked Ann, "Do you have a letter yet?" By then, many letters were already claimed. "Look at the ones that people don't have and see what you want to do. David, do you want to take *O*?"

"I'm thinking," said David. He gave every impression of not wanting to make a hasty, aesthetically inept decision. Earlier, this would have appeared as a lack of confidence, voice, or a failure to accept that stating preferences is a legitimate part of school.

By the time this event occurred, however, Ann and John could see that deliberate and sensitive decision making was David's way.

Finishing questions about Steig stories later in the day, David had two interpretive questions to answer. Ann helped Rose with the first one; "Do you like the character?"

"Yes"

"Why?"

"He is weird." David listened coyly and later put these same ideas down.

"The remaining question was, "What would you do if you had Sylvester's magic pebble?" David wrote, "I would give it to my brother." Here was another of the many signs of altruistic behavior John began to notice in David.

John noticed that David's concern for the underdog seemed stronger than the need to assert a competent self. Whereas most children sought to please their teachers and show off newly acquired skills, David sought reassurance only while he was working. If David felt like an underdog, he might be able to easily observe instances of oppression without differentiating his feelings and the feelings of others. Yet, there was a toughness in David that seemed to reflect a determination to retain his integrity while struggling to imagine a better world—a toughness that suggested he could step outside his own experience to imagine the experiences of others.

John asked for Ann's opinion on this, "Do you wonder if [David] doesn't feel like [an underdog] a bit himself? A bit cut off?"

"Yes, he could identify with it probably. . . . He expressed a lot more understanding [than did Jenny] . . ." reflected Ann.

"Yes. Talk about moral responsibility!" John agreed.

"And artistic integrity," Ann continued. "I think he knows that. I hope he knows that he has that. I hope he gets that sense."

". . . You know it seems like earlier on, he sort of valued this, but he sort of decided it couldn't come out. You know, the tough guy was going to hang in there and survive. But now this is connecting. The division is going," said John with excitement.

". . . He's gonna find his own way. He's starting to find his way, and I have to say I'm happy to see his skills are coming along, too." Here, Ann seemed to echo themes brought up by Mrs. Richardson about David's stubbornness and the fact that he generally got what he wanted. David's toughness seemed to reflect a determination to retain his own integrity.

Another way in which David asserted himself was to seek Ann's validation of his ideas. Ann did not encourage such dependency in all students, but David seemed to be checking trust and seeking human connection rather than merely checking answers. David was not manipulating Ann so that she would solve his problems for him. He was just sharing his thoughts and checking that all was well—perhaps checking that he really had a place and that his judgment worked.

Ann affirmed David's ideas in many simple ways that probably required only minimal thought once such responsiveness became her habit. When the students were matching words from Steig books to letters of the alphabet, for example, David asked Ann, "Is it OK to use Steig for *S*?"

"I was hoping someone would put Steig for *S*," Ann affirmed. Later during that same session, Ann announced, "Boys and girls! David has thought of a word for *X* that we hadn't thought of. X ray. Who took X rays of patients?"

"Doctor DeSoto," the class chanted as David worked on.

David's way of checking to see if he was really a member of the classroom community was evident when he asked Ann for help on a cut-and-dried question. "That's a good answer," Ann told him.

"But, what should I write?" David responded.

"Let's write down what you just said." Why the lack of confidence, even when the answer was good? Ann remained warmly encouraging, despite the fact that David's reaction was difficult to understand at times.

Late in March, on a day when he generally held his own even though most tasks were routine and teacher-directed, David handed Ann a note:

> Miss Bats I like you You our a good teacher
> from
> David.

With this encouragement, David also exhibited more of his playfulness. On a day when Ann discussed the records students made about their research with mealworms, Ann returned reports the students had made. David did a spider-walk to collect his report. Then, David and Jill began an experiment in which they taped two colored paper squares to a desk. David lined up three mealworms on the border between the squares to see which square the worms would prefer. When Jill moved the worms away from David's imaginary starting line, David did not protest her attempt to return to the assignment. Yet, listening to the two scholars, John also noticed that the worms were named Mrs. Bates, Mr. Bates, and Mr. Best. The two researchers got along amiably, with David doing the more systematic observations and Jill busily writing.

Later that morning, the children were asked to read a poem and write a note to Tanya, who was Star of the Week. After 20 minutes, Ann prodded David to write his note. With relaxed concentration, David wrote, *"Tanya. I liked your picture and your star of the week,"* then added color. Perfect spelling. The previous day, David had asked Ann how to spell "picture." When writing his note, therefore, he was able to fish into his desk for the card with "picture" written on it. Had David been thinking about what to write in his note to Tanya as long ago as the day before it was due?

Challenges and Controversies

- Is it realistic to assume that children as young as second grade can have an active social conscience?
- Can teachers nurture concerns about social justice without becoming overly dogmatic?
- In what ways would it be problematic to introduce societal dilemmas into the curriculum?
- Are some students more sensitive to social justice themes than others?

With patience, teachers can draw out interests that students are hesitant to share with their teachers. It is rare for adults to explore children's conversations about issues of social justice. Children can be so surprised at being asked to think about situations of social justice that they imitate the language of adults in their social worlds or become tongue-tied. Yet, once students are convinced about the seriousness of the question, they can offer wise insight into the value of schooling.

Living an Integrated Life

About the middle of March, David's behavior suggested that he was fully integrating his school and personal lives. As Ann and John began asking David and the other students to talk about their fairness beliefs, David seemed to find more obvious ways to verbalize his critiques of the learning process. David's peers also encouraged his initiative in a way that Bruce's peers would not.

After spring break, for example, groups of students read summaries about parts of Gertrude Chandler Warner's *The Boxcar Children.*[7] The audience evaluated each group's presentation, and Ann had directed the students on how to grade the group's treatment of the main point, the setting, and so on. Ann asked children to critique this grading system based on their experiences from the day before.

Tanya objected, "It's like giving yourself the grade you want."

"It is a very fair way to do things," Tom said, and his view was closer to the predominant view. The class, therefore, proceeded to use the same grading system again.

When David's group went up, he was a little self-conscious. Jill read the group report. "We need another reading," said Ann.

"David." "David." "David." "Give it to David," said playful voices from the floor. David grinned, slightly embarrassed and impish.

"One more reading?" said Ann. "David?"

Though he had been standing in the front preparing to speak, David said, "No," clearly but gently.

"If we need one more, it will be your turn," coaxed Ann. Ann then asked Elliot, who was next in line, to read. David followed and prepared himself in case he should have to go next. After some discussion, there was still time for another reading.

"David, what is the title of your chapter?" asked Ann.

"A big meal from little. . . ." David stalled briefly and a voice from the floor quietly prompted, "Onions." There were friendly chuckles, and David, seeming to take this as encouragement, proceeded easily. Some of David's invented spelling also made his text difficult to read. When he finished and group discussion took over the floor, David silently reread some of his text, standing comfortably between his partners.

Next, David slid his tee shirt sleeves up to his shoulder, and shot a finger-gun at Nate. In a clear burst of pride, David leaned back with his elbows on the bookcase, as if waiting for more muscle and a cigarette pack to put in his rolled sleeve. But, David inadvertently knocked over the books behind him. Jill, his work-buddy, adjusted the books with a silent, firm expression of criticism. David pretended to push the books over again, challenging Jill's cleanup with a grin. Jill eyed David firmly, but with a twinkle. All this took but an instant while the class discussion continued.

"They are actually a very good team," said Ann later. "It's like [Jill acknowledges] this is the way guys are—spilling things, doing a messy job, and I'll just fix it up. But the class, I think, is supportive of [David]."

"That's what I thought . . ." reflected John. "The laughing didn't have a nasty edge to it."

"They do enjoy him, and he enjoyed it. . . . There's a whole side of him I don't see. Recess. The bus. The gym. Other things go on that make [the other students] appreciate him. And [David] is never mean. There are some I get a lot of complaints about. Some do have a mean streak. Never have I heard anything like that about him."

"Which is consistent with his writing."

"Yes." continued Ann. "He's a very gentle character. And he very much wants to know when we are having writer's workshop. That has become his favorite thing. . . . The whole philosophy of writers' workshop is to do with choice. . . . He definitely does better when he has a choice in what he's going to read and write. David has some feelings about that. And I think it is more important for him, because often he will come up against something that's hard. So [in the workshop], he can easily select a book or topic he can get started on. And I've seen him help other people get started.

"Now with things that are not connected, like faulty sentences, [or spelling], I have to get him started. That's different."

Is it not a society at risk when it judges a child at risk if he has trouble engaging in discrete tasks with right-wrong answers and no story, moral theme, imaginative journey, or artistic motif? Yet, David was still David, and the classroom steadily became more his world. The gap between the personal and academic appeared and disappeared, but grew steadily weaker. David's voice became clearer, and he became more a part of the community.

A day later, David worked with three students who were doing a new activity called *Daily News for the Week.* David wrote less than the other reporters, but was determined to write his own story: "Today we read the story called *Heckedy Pig.*" [This story was in actuality Audrey Wood's *The Heckedy Peg.*[8] David's love for animals seemed to have distorted his perception a little here.] David also added drawings to complement his story, and his idea caught on. Soon, other students added drawings to their stories.

On the rug, while the news was being discussed, Joe quietly tied David's loose shoelace. David seemed to appreciate the attention, but when Joe finished, David quietly undid the other shoelace. David did not undo Joe's work, but was determined to remain the waif just off the boat. "David is David," commented Ann.

For the day's assignments, Ann suggested that the children start reading before doing faulty sentences—sentences on the board that students must write out while correcting punctuation and spelling. David started on the sentences, working at top speed—looking up at the board then snapping his head back to write quickly. This level of concentration had become common. Concentrating on putting in speech marks, David forgot to capitalize names, but sustained focused attention to an activity that was cut and dried.

When he moved to reading a chapter about *The Boxcar Children,* David followed Ann's instructions to sit at the big table and became fully engrossed. When Ryan stopped to talk to him, David listened, before turning straight back to the book. The four girls at the table were also silently absorbed in reading.

After reading, pairs of children were given questions to answer about their particular chapters. David was happy working with Rose. They collaborated well, and both contributed when the class later discussed the questions.

The class then discussed whether students should work with people Ann chose or with friends. Given Bruce's difficulty in getting support from his peers, John wondered if this question would also provoke interesting discussion among Ann's happy second graders. Although students in Ann's class collaborated well, these second graders did not seem to see the complex issues of trust and reciprocity raised by the fourth and fifth graders. The children deferred to Ann's authority about how collaboration should be organized. Nevertheless, John could see the benefits students gained from the wide range of collaborative experiences Ann arranged for them.

Rose said, "I was with David and I wanted to be with a girl. But [I was surprised that] I didn't care." Rose smiles with pride in her new discovery.

At this point, the class was reading fairy tales. Various versions of *Puss in Boots* were being read.[9] Ann wrote on the board several questions and included, "Fat question: Was Puss wrong to lie in order to improve his master's life?"

Ann gave David and two other students a clipboard and asked them to poll the class on the "fat question." The pollsters had a bit of trouble deciding how to record their classmate's answers, but learned that Bob was the only person who definitely endorsed Puss's lying. The survey was a prelude to a lively class discussion of the question. Toward the end Tanya summed up, "All these questions have been going back and forth, back and forth, and I'm going to go from 'no' to [undecided]." Public discussion of controversial topics had become a well-established part of classroom life, and David followed thoughtfully.

The next question for discussion was "Who were the good and bad characters in *Puss and Boots*?" "I think there weren't any good characters," came the first announcement. This idea was met with some agreement, but others disagreed.

"This isn't going to be so simple," said Ann, looking at John. Ann and John were both pleasantly surprised at the ease with which students openly disagreed with one another. When inquiry about unsettled matters is established as legitimate, students can later discover that matters that seemed settled are not. Discussion of good and bad characters became a discussion of the nature of good and evil. Students defined personal positions that helped them put their previous knowledge, the experience of the story, and the views of their classmates into satisfactory relation with one another. Yet, to call this problem *solving* would be to debase it—the children were beginning the process of problem *defining*.

At the end of the discussion, Ann read a third version of *Puss in Boots*. David was riveted. He perked up on his haunches, and shuffled close to the book. At the end, Ann asked if students had preferences among the various versions of the story that they had seen. David's hand shot up. He preferred the last version, "Because it has more colors." Ever the artist, David looked at the deep, richly colored pictures of this latest version while still following and adding to the discussion.

Ann found other ways to scaffold the task of helping students see the controversial nature of interpreting literature. Aware that students learn best through constructive activities, Ann encouraged dramatic readings and invented concrete ways of helping children represent their positions in a debate. Near the end of April, for example, David was in a group reading a dramatic script of *Rumpelstiltzkin.*[10] David's delivery was a touch flat—he could barely cope with the words and did not change his voice to match those of the characters in the story. However, when Ann asked for the class's opinion, the group agreed that David had the right expression for Rumpelstiltzkin. "You read with expression," said Ann, encouraging David and reinforcing the opinions of his peers.

Referring to the scene where Rumpelstiltzkin stamps himself through the floor, David bantered gently, "All we need is the floor breaking."

The children took turns reading through the play once more with expression. Rhonda Newman, the assistant principal who was working with the group, encouraged the children to improvise, but the class had trouble letting go of the script. David, no longer the center of attention, was once again relaxed and read the book as others spoke.

Ann returned and asked David, how the play was going. "OK," David told her.

"You got a big part?" Ann probed.

"He did well," said Ms. Newman.

"[Rumpelstiltzkin], that's the part he wanted," said Ann. David was set on this part, as soon it was clear that he would be in the play. "And that's the part he got."

With play practice over, David went back to his desk and, again, was all business working on faulty sentences. His eyes snapped back and forth between the board and his paper. Getting what he wanted did not distract David from his other responsibilities as a student.

The day before, Ann told John that David had told her, "Bob said I read like a robot."

"How did you feel?" Ann had asked David.

"Bad."

"The others said you did well." Ann continued to encourage David, and he was not completely discouraged by the feedback he received. Opportunities to practice reading prior to public performances offered David concrete feedback about his understanding of the story.

Subsequent class discussions offered an even greater opportunity to reflect and critique. To make such discussions concrete, Ann had the class on the rug sitting around two large hoops. One hoop was for names of characters who were good, the other hoop for those of characters who were bad. The class, however, decided that the hoops should overlap for characters who were both good and evil.

"I'm going to give out the names of characters [on cards] and you are going to decide. . . ." David's hand was up straight away. He put Rumpelstiltzkin in the evil area. "Why?" challenged Ann.

"He was going to take the baby," David asserted.

"Brian, what do you say?"

"The middle because he gave her something, and he made a deal with her. But taking a baby is not good." David argued his case undeterred, and was supported by Matt.

The class moved on to the Big Bad Wolf and other characters. By the time they came to the Pied Piper, not a single character had been placed in the good circle. Jackie put the Pied Piper there. David disagreed and argued his case assertively. "Somebody has to be good," declared Jackie, which seemed, more or less, a concession to David's position.

After more lively discussion, everyone was charged to draw a personal Venn diagram and categorize all the characters they wanted to remember. David concentrated with his tongue in the corner of his mouth and left his seat only to check correct spellings. At the end, David had written as many or more names than most of his peers. When Ann called the class to the rug, David continued working and was last to come. Late, he placed himself right in the middle of the group, a gesture that suggested he was clearly a member of the class.

In the computer lab, with a specialist teacher, the class was introduced to a Safari Search program. There was a 5×5 grid and the task was to "intuit [where in the grid] the iguana [is placed]." Most students were eager to guess, but not David. The teacher asked, "You haven't picked a place yet." David shook his head indicating that he did not want to guess.

On the next task, David's buddy Jill noticed, "David hasn't had a turn." Again David shook his head, indicating that he did not want a turn. David's behavior really looked like a choice rather than pure shyness.

When the teacher tried to help the children distinguish between guessing and systematic elimination of alternatives, David did not follow closely. In the next task, children were offered clues that made it possible to conduct a systematic elimination of alternatives. Yet, David did not follow along with this sort of guessing game.

In another incident, David did not correctly load the intended game into his computer and was soon lost. When David corrected his mistake, he just guessed when a more systematic line of inquiry would have helped. David watched the teacher work with Mark, then tried to imitate him. "Come on!" David said to the computer as he struggled happily. David playfully put his hand over his disc to stop the teacher from taking it out for a new program, but accepted the new disk when the specialist persisted.

"I don't get this," David said of the new disk, unembarrassed.

"Either do I," said Rose beside him, working on the same game. David and Rose were persistent in their happy blundering.

When the specialist turned out the light to signal the end of the session, David said, "No!"

"Sorry, David," she said, casually joking.

A bit of his occasional compulsion to follow instructions might have helped David, but his "failure" looked more like a moral choice. David was not defensive, and easily admitted to not knowing when necessary. He would become involved, but in his own way. David's own way was not very effective in the computer room, where the very specific but arbitrary conventions of particular programs were paramount. Yet, his approach worked well enough in imaginative writing and art.

The warmth with which David and his classmates treated one another was frequently in evidence, and David was rewarded with comfortable peer interactions. "We'll be learning [cursive] capital *M* today," said Ann. There were murmurs of approval. The class moved to the rug and, while waiting, David arm-wrestled briefly with Bob. Then, David and Joe started a spontaneous spelling game. Challenged to spell "panda," David closed his eyes because he knew the word was on the wall.

"P-a-n-d-a," spelled David.

"No." said Joe, startling David.

"P-a-n-d-a," spelled Joe with a grin. David accepted this second grade wit, and the boys continued to play with words.

Endangered species was the topic of discussion. Three girls captured the class with a brief improvised play using stuffed animals. When the discussion turned to nocturnal animals, David contributed a story about the raccoon that his family feeds. The raccoon repeatedly carried off plates of dry cat food, and a stack of plates has accumulated under the deck. Soon he had another story. David's contributions were all relevant, clear, and sometimes even personal, quite unlike those of the Quiet Bird whom John first met.

John checked on David's progress after four minutes of library time. David and Jill had found two books with information on dolphins. Jill asked for John's help with the passage she and David were studying, after which the two of them wrote busily.

"I'm going to ask Mrs. Bates how long [we have]," interrupted David.

"Won't she send someone to tell you?" John asked.

"I want to go." As Mrs. Richardson said, David was stubborn. Strange how instructions were sometimes sought and at other times ignored. John wondered if his inability to sort out when David was interested in instruction and when he was not indicated that John still remained quite a distance away from understanding David's experience. John's criticisms of his own knowledge could also be appropriately leveled at all teachers who are presumptuous enough to think that they fully understand the experiences of their students.

When they returned to class, Ann said, "Look at all the facts you got, David. You can work on saying what you want to, and make a picture of a dolphin."

David got a large sheet of paper and a book with pictures of dolphins. He drew a curvaceous and powerful dolphin, looking back at the book without lifting his pencil. "Look, it's got an eye," he said pointing at an accidental dot near enough to the correct spot. David moved the dot commenting, "About the right place." After looking at the book, David then erased his round eye and did a more oval shaped one. David continued drawing the bottom of the fish and formed a tail that, like the rest of the animal was appropriately curvaceous, but small and not well balanced. "I don't like the tail," David critiqued his work as soon as it was done. He was right: The tail did not complete the creature. He erased the tail and tried to repair it.

Nate came by and said, "It looks good, David," referring to the whole dolphin. Nate was right. It did look good.

Rose passed and said, "I like the face." Not the tail, John noticed.

David puzzled over the tail and told Ann, when she passed, that he did not like it. Ann suggested that Jill might help. No-nonsense Jill took the pencil and quickly drew flippers like a walrus tail—a real step backward. David said nothing, but when Jill left, he erased her work and tried again. David was interrupted when it was time for gym. "Oh well," he said lightly. "I give up." Yet, he took time later to finish.

It was exciting to see this child who once behaved one way at home and another way at school openly critique his own work and share that critique with his teacher and peers.

Challenges and Controversies

- What can educators learn from watching children's choice of tasks?
- Describe other ways to help students form a personal response to literacy.
- How can teachers balance activities designed to stimulate interest with opportunities for students to reveal their own interests?
- How can teachers differentiate students' need for validation as a trust-building exercise from validation as a sign of low self-efficacy?
- What behaviors suggest that students are integrating various aspects of their experience?
- How can collaboration help students meet their motivational needs? How can collaboration go awry?
- How can discussion of controversial topics be made concrete enough to assist children in integrating the features of their experience?
- How can students learn to define important problems and still cover the essential curriculum?

The integrated quality of events in Ann's classroom suggests that most students, including David, were optimally motivated. David and his classmates received spontaneous encouragement and help from their classmates. Without diminishing those who sought to help him, David accepted the help even though it was sometimes unhelpful. David recognized that he had models from which to learn, but his own judgment also remained intact. David's behavior suggested that he knew as well as anyone when he had fallen short, and gently and firmly worked to improve his own work. Such rewarding days can be few and far between for students, like Bruce, who fracture their motivation by ignoring some of their needs. Students like David, who fracture their experience by rejecting one sphere (e.g., school) and preferring another (e.g., home), may more easily be enticed into rethinking their evaluations.

The subtle changes in a boy who initially fractured his experience by rejecting school are difficult to identify without using particular events to exemplify this development. John found it challenging to communicate his insights about David to the people who loved him most—people who cherished the snapshots of David's experience that John was able to capture in words. Like many busy adults, David's parents and grandparents sought to label features of his character and assumed that his character was stable and unchangeable. If it was difficult for David's loved ones to notice subtleties about his motivation, imagine how difficult it must be for those with only fleeting interest in a child to notice such development.

Lessons from David's Life

David taught us that not all children come to school believing that they are entitled to personal needs, interests, and expectations. Behaving as if identity-enhancing growth is inappropriate in school, such children will fracture their experience by behaving one way at home and another at school. Their needs may be well coordinated in both spheres of their life, but will be valued in one place and not in the other. When categorizing children's behavior along a continuum of amotivation to intrinsic motivation and monitoring their choice of tasks, it becomes easy to identify when a child's reasons for learning in school are teacher-determined and his or her reasons for learning at home are self-determined. Task-orientation is likely to be stronger than ego-orientation at home, whereas ego-orientation at school takes the form of pleasing others. Such children can become so preoccupied with living up to others' expectations at school that they avoid even the most basic forms of communication, ensuring that relationships involve exchange but not intimacy. The needs of such children become easy to overlook because, when these children are noticed, they are generally compliant. Educators will be surprised to learn that children who fracture their beliefs about others' expectations have a wide array of intellectual projects and identity-enhancing interests that they keep private.

Ann and John taught us about five interventions that can help children who fracture their understanding of others' expectations. First, offering children opportunities to share their identities in school while identifying similarities between their interests and ideas in the curriculum can legitimize the importance of consolidating knowledge in identity-enhancing ways. Second, requiring children to give reasons for the things they do encourages them to theorize about their intentions and evaluate their experience. Third, offering a rich array of tasks and labeling gestures, speech, writing, and art as acceptable forms of communication introduces such children to a range of methods for sharing their knowledge with others. Fourth, offering opportunities for collaboration that require initiative and associations between word and deed can legitimize the relevance of private thoughts in public interactions. Fifth, and most importantly, labeling positive features of a child's character and incremental changes in behavior as signs of growth can enhance trust. Fortunately, many children, whose needs are coordinated differently at home and at school because of misguided assumptions about others' expectations, can easily respond to persistent, concrete requests to integrate aspects of their experience.

ENDNOTES

1. See Ryan & Deci (2000). It is interesting to note how similar this motivational continuum is to the progression of stages in Kohlberg's theory of moral development (e.g., Colby, Kohlberg, Gibbs, & Lieberman, 1983). Whereas theorists working in moral development assume that this continuum reflects global approaches to solving moral problems, researchers in motivation generally disagree. Motivation, it is commonly assumed, is rarely so stable and is definitely affected by the demands of the situation and the nature of the tasks under consideration.
2. See Lobel (1970).
3. See Steig (1969).
4. See Steig (1982).
5. See Lawlor (1988, 1994).
6. See Sharmat (1972).
7. Warner's work has been reprinted in many forms since it was originally published in 1942 (Ellsworth, 1997). The series continues to be developed by other authors, despite Warner's death in 1979. The children John observed seemed to be focusing on her original story by name, but read the sequels as well.
8. See Wood (1987).
9. This story was originally told by Pierre Perrault and published in 1697, but many versions have been published since that time. Opie & Opie (1974) and Sale (1978) offer brief histories of this work.
10. This story was first published in English by Grimm in 1823, and that was influenced by work published as long ago as 1709 (Opie & Opie, 1974; Sale, 1978).

CHAPTER 4 Coordinating Needs and Expectations

We began this project by asking, "What if equal educational opportunity required the establishment of a level motivational playing field rather than the simple equality of test scores?" Finding children who would have difficulty in such a world, we explored the boys' attempts to consolidate the events in their lives so that ideas from one experience could give direction and meaning to other parts of their experience. We discovered that these children fractured their experience at two levels, by failing to respond to all of their needs and/or by becoming different people in different contexts. When experience is integrated it is possible to attain a sense of equilibrium that promotes happiness. When experience is fractured, children and those around them feel uncomfortable.

Fractured experience fosters discomfort because it leads individuals to undermine their ability to live in communion with others. To live in communion with others, individuals must coordinate their own needs and others' expectations, establishing identity-enhancing interests that are of value to society. This chapter offers a review of research related to children's ability to achieve such ideal forms of happiness. Coordinating children's need for self-determination, competence, and affiliation in family, school, and peer groups, it should become possible to imagine just how challenging it is to integrate various aspects of experience in identity-enhancing ways.

Self-Determination in a World Where Obedience Is Easier

Politicians are best known for acting out their need for power, yet most individuals need to experience some level of prestige, agency, and independence. Preoccupation with self-determination is central to theories that characterize motivation as falling along an extrinsic/intrinsic continuum.[1] Coordinating individuals' interests and feelings of control, researchers define *amotivation* as a state in which individuals are not stimulated, *introjection* as involving compliance in order to gain approval, *identification* as the endorsement of particular goals, and *intrinsic motivation* as pleasure in working for its own sake. While such states are easy to imagine, it is difficult for caregivers to identify them simply by watching the behavior of children.

In adults, self-determination is most obvious when individuals try to control others by influencing, aggressing against, or helping them. Individuals are asserting their sense of agency and seeking prestige and/or independence. When self-restraint or situational factors inhibit a person's expression of his/her power needs, physical illness and difficulties relating to others can increase.[2]

As is evident when reading about the lives of Bruce, David, Jack, and Earl, children are so dependent on adults that it can be difficult to differentiate their need for self-determination from other needs. When adults are preoccupied with gaining children's compliance, it can be expedient for children to passively comply with others' requests and ignore opportunities for self-determination. Distinctions between self-efficacy and autonomy are currently under investigation. As they become better understood, perhaps it will become easier to understand how children explore the limits of whatever freedoms they are permitted. In the meantime there are a few lessons apparent in research findings.

Family Contexts

Some of the contradictory behaviors of Bruce, David, Jack, and Earl were similar to contradictions in research on power relations within families that emerge when motivation is less than optimal. Unfortunately, contradictory research findings make it difficult to offer clear directions for parents looking for ideal family practices. Adults who are highly creative, for example, are more likely to come from families that stressed independence or from sometimes hostile environments that fostered an exaggerated need for power.[3] Families that stress the need for independence are probably more likely to help children sustain happiness in becoming free and responsible citizens than families that foster a hostile environment, yet research does not support the value of one family structure over another.

Bruce, David, Jack, and Earl were like most children who voluntarily act in accordance with their family's values and spontaneously come to "own them." Once in a while, however, adults use harmful strategies that interfere with children's internalization of such norms.[4] Such interference can take the form of proffered rewards, abusive punishments, or reinforced beliefs connected with a fragile self-esteem or the wrongful assumption that a particular act is essential for health or well-being. These events can undermine some children's sense of self-efficacy by confronting them with values they do not understand. Similarly, overreliance on others' expectations undermines the autonomous ownership of identity-enhancing values.

To become free and responsible citizens, children need to understand the rules that govern their lives and can benefit from extrinsic structures while learning about such rules. In addition to meeting the expectations of family members, however, children's self-determination needs are met when they are free to influence family dynamics. Children can influence their family's achievement expectations, ability to participate in communal and recreational activities, and sense of harmony.[5] Ideally children influence their parents' expectations as often as they respond to them. As found with other children, when the Johnsons, Richardsons, Davises, and Nortons allowed their children's needs to affect family practices, school achievement was enhanced.[6]

Bruce, David, Jack, and Earl were comfortable at home in ways that were not always apparent in school. Yet, children who fracture their needs for self-determination at home may be reacting to messages of domination and subordination implicit in their interactions with other family members, or may be refusing to embrace opportunities to contribute to discussions about family goals. When autonomy and intimacy orientations conflict, for example, children may find it more rewarding to maintain their dependency on caregivers whose affection they crave. When family values conflict with school values, children are likely to coordinate their needs differently in the two social spheres. Children need convincing forms of permission to assert a comfortable sense of self-determination in a world largely governed by adults. There is little research validating specific parenting practices for promoting self-determination in second graders.[7] Fortunately, the Johnsons, Richardsons, Davises, and Nortons found many of the practices used in school to be beneficial at home.

School Contexts

In the classroom, as at home, adults regulate much of children's activity. Therefore, self-efficacy—the sense that applying effort will lead to success—is a more common indication of self-determination than are less structured forms of autonomy.[8] There is a solid body of experimental research on methods for influencing students' sense of self-efficacy in school that can be applied in other contexts as well. For example, we know that the nature of the task and the content of whatever feedback children are given about their performance have powerful effects on children's efficacy beliefs. Moderately difficult tasks are more appropriate than easy or hard tasks. Children also need opportunities to make choices whenever it is practical to do so. They will, if optimally motivated, choose esteem-enhancing tasks that are moderately challenging. When their lives are unbalanced, children reveal their discomfort by choosing excessively easy or impossibly difficult tasks.[9]

When task-choice is not a practical alternative, self-efficacy can be maximized by giving students either consistent task-focused feedback or task- followed by effort-focused feedback.[10] Self-efficacy is also enhanced when children are able to participate in setting goals, to evaluate their own progress, or to follow learning-focused rather than performance-focused guidelines.[11] Similarly, many students thrive when they receive verbal guidance from others, information on the appropriateness of their choice of strategies, and substantive feedback on how well they are doing.[12] In short, teachers can do a wide range of things to ensure that children feel powerful in school and parents can modify such activities for use at home.

Children who fracture their experience tend to resist opportunities to choose identity-enhancing activities and/or do not understand the messages in the feedback they receive. As with family life, children may elicit feedback that encourages them to remain dependent on adult guidance. They may also fail to understand when it is appropriate to choose their own agendas and when it is better to comply with more communal goals. Bruce and Earl were more assertive than David and Jack, but all four children were like those second graders who had difficulty exhibiting appropriate forms of self-efficacy and autonomy in school.

Peer Contexts

Self-determination is also a factor in how children negotiate with their peers, and in what they expect from close friendships and casual relationships. Young children are more

Challenges and Controversies

- What can caregivers do to encourage children's self-determination while also maintaining the compliance needed to respond to the rest of life's demands?
- Can caregivers encourage children's self-efficacy without encouraging their autonomy?
- As children grow, hopefully they will need less guidance from caregivers. How can caregivers learn when to stand aside and let children experience their own triumphs and failures?

---

likely to have satisfying peer relationships when their parents help them select friends and activities.[13] By second grade, however, most children need less direction because they are better able to coordinate their own goals and those of their peers.[14] Children become the agents who decide whether they will facilitate close ties or casual exchanges with their peers.[15] Personal values rather than chance tend to influence children's decisions about who should be friends and how their relationships should be managed.[16] Typically, adults intervene only when individual children seem to be having difficulties.[17]

Children who fracture their experience are likely to rely on inappropriate strategies for seeking and developing friendship. They may have difficulty understanding how to approach potential friends and/or what to do with the excitement of discovering that interest is reciprocated. Children may not notice or understand the expectations of their peers clearly enough to sustain comfortable levels of reciprocity, or they may feel so unworthy that they fail to follow through on the gestures that keep friendships intact. Such difficulties are quite common among children with learning disabilities. Like other children, Bruce, David, Jack, and Earl required some intervention on the part of caregivers to help them understand the boundaries of friendship.[18]

As the boys sought to address their needs for self-determination, their caregivers used all the recommended techniques to help them do so. Caregivers tactfully intervened to nurture the boys' self-determination needs while offering clear rules and guidelines. At home as well as at school, the boys were encouraged to set personal goals and evaluate their progress while offering detailed information on their choice of strategies and self-evaluations. The boys' teachers, with assistance from the their parents and from John, encouraged them to label their interests and offered leadership opportunities in areas that were most likely to enhance growth. Caregivers encouraged the boys to choose tasks that interested them and to explain their choices. When it was impractical for the boys to choose tasks, caregivers offered detailed feedback emphasizing particular features of a task and strategies for completing the work. Caregivers intervened to help the boys find friends when they were struggling, but stood aside while children determined whether intimacy or exchange would be the basis for reciprocity. Despite the subtle ways in which family members, educators, and peers conveyed their expectations and offered ways of responding to their requests, the boys were not always able to successfully coordinate those expectations and still meet their needs for self-determination.

Competence in the Face of Continual Challenge

Whereas researchers have used a variety of means for exploring self-determination needs, they have captured the essence of competence in relatively stable ways. To offer a simple summary of the vast body of research in this area would perpetuate serious injustice to the range and sophistication of research questions related to competence that have been explored. For example, findings addressing individual differences in absolute levels of achievement have made it possible to identify precisely how children like Bruce, David, Jack, and Earl fail to learn in the same way as their peers.[19] Quite a bit is also known about how individuals' perceptions of their competence influence their performance and mental health.[20] And, we can take it for granted that all children enter school with a basic sense of right and wrong, but their use of this knowledge is likely to vary in accordance with their needs.[21] These directions did not offer much insight into how children construct fractured lives. Nevertheless, it is helpful to review common assertions about how children with learning disabilities construe others' expectations of their competence and how their assumptions differ from those of their peers without learning disabilities.

Family Contexts

Normative research on how family life affects school achievement can be quite discouraging to those who work with children like Bruce, David, Jack, and Earl. We learn that parents have a strong influence over children's achievement expectations, community and recreational participation, and expressiveness.[22] Children classified as scholastic achievers tend to come from child-centered families in which achievement is valued and young people strongly identify with the goals and values of their parents.[23] Yet, many children with learning disabilities also come from such environments and have not become high achievers.

The Johnsons, Richardsons, Davises, and Nortons, for example, seemed to know that, normatively speaking, children who grow up in environments that are rich in intellectual material and offer stimulating activities that are developmentally appropriate are more likely to attain high test scores. Yet, irregularities in family income and work demands place limits on parents' abilities to provide material and intellectual stimulation. The positive benefits of such stimulation are most marked when parents consistently provide intellectually engaging activities rather than limit such stimulation to infancy. Nevertheless, as most conscientious parents will confess, practicalities of life place restrictions on opportunities for intellectual stimulation and are difficult to ignore.

There is strong evidence that structured family schedules help children meet their competence needs. This has led researchers to speculate on whether working mothers place limits on children's achievement by establishing irregular schedules at home. Results are inconclusive, but the issue can still elicit high levels of guilt among conscientious parents whose children have learning disabilities.[24] Although girls with working mothers seem to benefit or remain unaffected by the kinds of altered family lives that emerge, boys do not benefit from relevant maternal modeling.[25] Children from moderate-income families generally receive more sensitive care than children from low-income families, but many parents require two salaries to generate opportunities for their children.[26] When children have opportunities to interact with museums, churches, art galleries, and theaters, for example, they are encouraged to step outside their own subjective experience and consider other worlds.

To organize opportunities for children outside the home fosters tension because it involves a complex coordination of demands from work and family life. It is worth noting that such tensions have not been linked to parents' marital relationships or their parenting styles.[27] Yet, children need adult guidance, and those who are not watched carefully can exhibit poor ego control, work habits, and diligence. Fortunately, mothers are not the only caregivers who help children understand society's expectations, and most children accommodate to expectations from multiple caregivers quite easily.

Despite children's flexibility, structured routines and regular interactions among family members seem to have a stronger influence on children's ability to meet competence needs than to meet self-determination or affiliation needs. Achievement motivation is higher, for example, in families where moms report structured schedules and assert that children have relatively low levels of autonomy and a stronger than average internal locus of control.[28] In a 10-year longitudinal study of the relationships among family environments and achievement, children's task orientation was associated with family member's participation in academic activities.[29] Task orientation was not associated with the opportunities for self-determination available in children's early environment or with other styles of interaction that might fulfill affiliation needs. Parents have the ability to help their children focus on essential features of academic tasks well enough to fulfill their competence needs.

Children who fracture their experience are likely to feel an imbalance when coordinating the happiness that comes from pleasure and enjoyment and the happiness that comes from deep, complex thought while learning. Like Bruce, David, Jack, and Earl, such children are likely to avoid tasks they cannot comprehend rather than invent strategies for approaching them. Structured activities can support those who are committed to particular competence agendas, but can become stifling to children who are confused about what is expected of them. Finding ways to help such children imagine alternatives and/or take delight in their accomplishments will require flexibility in how family members set competence expectations for particular children.

Some family interactions are more beneficial than others for helping children meet their competence needs and take pleasure in scholastic achievement.[30] Children benefit when parents use language in a playful, but complex manner. They also benefit when parents promote imitation, expose them to different life-roles, and offer regular motivational feedback. Children with learning disabilities, more than their peers, benefit from shared reading activities, family libraries, fun and frequent contact with print, and exposure to reading as a form of entertainment rather than as a series of skills to be acquired. Parents have also found it useful to seek out alternatives to traditional forms of instruction, evoke their own folk wisdom, and/or build networks of support with other families who face similar issues.

School Contexts

In school, many children with learning disabilities are preoccupied with issues of competence in ways that encourage them to fracture their intellectual lives.[31] Although children with learning disabilities see themselves as less competent than their peers, they rarely adopt "helpless" or "antischool" attitudes.[32] Such children have genuine processing limitations and less complex knowledge of how to go about learning.[33] But, when a task is interesting or complex, children with learning disabilities can sustain a strong desire to learn.[34] In this respect, children with learning disabilities can exhibit a strong task orientation and love for learning even when they do not attain normatively high levels of achievement.

Like most people, children with learning disabilities can also be highly ego-oriented. There are numerous studies of children's attributions for their success and failure and findings are overwhelmingly consistent. Many children with learning disabilities, while they may work hard, have little faith that their effort will pay off in the long run.[35] The roots of this paradox have been convincingly linked to children's relatively limited meta-cognitive knowledge of how to apply specific learning strategies and about the learning process itself.[36]

Whereas children's needs for self-efficacy and autonomy have led researchers to advocate offering them choices whenever possible, children's need for competence has led researchers to promote highly structured methods for facilitating task-engagement. Most children learn well when material is presented in a meaningful and appealing context because the promotion of interest can increase the depth of engagement, amount of material learned, and perceived competence. Encouraging children to focus more completely on the task at hand and to learn procedures for regulating their own study habits has also been beneficial.[37] When adults continuously talk about how children can do their work, children who have difficulty sustaining attention are likely to persist on difficult tasks. Strategy instruction in combination with effort-focused feedback can be especially helpful for children with learning disabilities, but could prove useful to all children who are undermining their competence needs. Children also benefit when adults help them select learning-oriented rather than performance-oriented goals and offer feedback on the effectiveness of their choice of strategies.

When caregivers set expectations by exclusively relying on absolute levels of achievement, they maintain cycles of fractured experience because the need for pleasure and enjoyment in learning is overlooked. Similarly, offering children highly structured activities may improve their chances of completing the task successfully, but could undermine their emerging sense of self-determination in the process.[38] Children who fracture their competence needs are often wise to these contradictory messages about schooling and are confused about how to respond. Children like Bruce and Earl respond by becoming overly preoccupied with demonstrating superiority over others. Children like David and Jack work equally hard to avoid letting others know what they are thinking so as to avoid appearing incompetent. Nevertheless, most children can exhibit a love for learning and high levels of achievement that are obvious to anyone observing their behavior.

Peer Contexts

Children's needs for academic competence have been associated with their needs for social competence. Fortunately for boys like Bruce, David, Jack, and Earl, stable social acceptance can buffer children from the pain associated with early academic difficulties.[39] But, children who are rated low in achievement and have low social status have been rated significantly less competent by their teachers than have children who rate low either in achievement or social status.[40] Not surprisingly, then, children who are victimized or who otherwise have unsupportive peers tend to dislike school and eventually find ways to avoid it.[41]

Caregivers who notice children "showing off" to impress their peers might want to remember that merely gaining short-term compliance or peer approval will not offer fulfilling ways to meet competence needs. Interpersonal competition, when taken to an extreme, lowers rather than enhances children's social status. Whereas competition can lead children to view learning as a means to the end of achieving superiority over their peers, children who compete with their peers in egotistical ways are less popular than children who compete with their peers while remaining task-oriented.[42]

For these and many other reasons, children's competence when establishing peer relations has been closely scrutinized.[43] Many studies have been conducted to validate popular, rejected, neglected, controversial, and average social status categories used to classify children's casual relationships.[44] Much of this research is correlational, but these social preference classifications have led to the discovery that children's status in any given year can be significantly related to their status in previous years and that the underlying skills that led to such status can be stable unless otherwise challenged.[45] While such stability may be beneficial for children who are classified as popular or average, stability can be another discouraging aspect of life if children face social as well as learning difficulties.[46] Because of their unpredictable behavior, children with learning disabilities often hold controversial, rejected, or neglected social status and so are likely to have difficulty establishing casual relationships.[47]

To help children gain more opportunities for companionship, it is natural to want to identify particular social skills in need of improvement. A few themes are apparent in such research. Children need to be able to engage in and notice prosocial behavior and correctly interpret forms of rejection. They need to be able to sustain levels of involvement, even when in conflict situations, without withdrawing or responding aggressively. Surprisingly, children's ability to accurately read the emotions of others is strongly related to their social status, but their ability to read their own emotions is not.[48] Similarly, children's conduct problems affect their social status, but are not related to their moral reasoning.[49]

Children like Bruce, David, Jack, and Earl with rejected, neglected, or controversial social status commonly exhibit aggression and withdrawal. Low social status leads to negative social self-perceptions,[50] but there are marked individual differences in the nature of those perceptions. Researchers have identified four kinds of socially withdrawn clusters—active-isolates, unsociable, passive-anxious, and sad-depressed— that represent varying degrees of involvement in casual relationships.[51] Bruce, a rejected child, actively isolated himself from peers but frequently sought teacher approval. David, socially neglected, fluctuated between exhibiting unsociable and passive-anxious behaviors. Jack was sometimes rejected and sometimes neglected by his peers and exhibited sad-depressed behaviors. Noticing such patterns makes it easy to see why children undermine their competence needs when they withdraw from peer interactions.

Sadly, the kinds of nonassertive behavior exhibited by children who are socially neglected sometimes leads to chronic victimization.[52] Yet, some neglected children exhibit positive academic profiles. The lives of Jack and David offer examples of both extremes. Jack faced chronic victimization in that his peers generally ignored or teased him, maintaining his unpredictable, controversial social status. Perpetuating this cycle, Jack usually submitted to his peers' social initiatives and rarely attempted persuasion or initiated conversations. David, on the other hand, was not victimized by his peers. He seemed easily motivated, self-regulated, prosocial, and compliant. Although he was ignored by his peers, David was well-liked by his teachers and had little difficulty in social situations. He seemed successful in his attempts to remain unnoticed.

Children who are rejected by their peers can also be rejected for different reasons. The lives of Bruce and Earl suggest at least two such differences. Bruce was a kindly aggressor who saw himself as upholding important social norms. Earl, on the other hand, seemed unaware of the needs of others when acting out his emotions. The boys' teachers and parents worked hard to help them identify and alter their aggressive behavior. Nevertheless, like other rejected children, Bruce and Earl spent more time in antagonistic and unoccupied behaviors and less time engaging in prosocial interactions.[53] They participated in both verbal and physical aggression, and when they could establish friendships, their friends were similarly drawn into such hostilities. Naturally, these events caused stress and influenced the children's ability to meet their competence needs.

Like Bruce and Earl, many rejected children have difficulty identifying and understanding their peers' emotions, discovering the underlying reasons for their peers' behavior, and interpreting forms of rejection.[54] Adopting hostile social goals, such children maintain cycles of conflict when they respond aggressively to provocation.[55] They are also more likely than their peers to engage in verbally competitive behavior that undermines any benefits of peer collaboration.[56] They are not alone, however, in failing to imagine the needs of others sufficiently well enough to respond appropriately. Many children have difficulty monitoring their position in relation to others, influencing the quality of their casual relationships.[57] Such children can consider the perspectives of some of their peers some of the time. But, like most second graders, they also apply rules, imagine the motives of their peers, and consider task-relevant details when allocating resources, inconsistently.[58] It is possible that these unintentional acts influence children's social status, but second graders seem to be relatively forgiving of such transgressions.

Fortunately for children with low social status, although social status is often stable, friendships are often less so.[59] Children establish close friendships with peers in many ways. When seeking information, for example, peers' knowledge of a specific social or nonsocial situation is more highly valued than their general social status.[60] Children also find friendship when they communicate with clarity and exhibit a desire to connect with others. Such communication often takes the form of exchanging information, finding common-ground activities, exploring similarities and differences, and discovering ways to engage in constructive forms of reciprocity.[61]

Second graders are particularly generous when responding to clumsy attempts to initiate friendship. They seem to know that good friendships can serve as a buffer in conflict situations because they hinge on loyalty, trust, commitment, and honesty.[62] These are particularly strong characteristics of mutual friends—pairs of individuals who choose one another as friends. Mutual friends are often more alike than are unilateral friends (pairs in which one child sees a friendship while the other does not), and demonstrate reciprocal awareness of one another's differences.[63] Moral reasoning and prosocial behavior are enhanced by both kinds of interactions, yet mutual friends offer one another warm, close, communicative relationships that are not apparent in unilateral friendships.[64]

At some point during the school year, Bruce, David, Jack, and Earl were able to find satisfying relationships with their peers. This was the case even though, like other children with learning disabilities, they often had difficulty collaborating, engaging in shared decision making, and participating in cooperative play and shared laughter. The boys sometimes had such difficulty identifying the needs of others that the result was an asymmetrical, hierarchical division of roles rather than companionship or intimacy.[65] Like other unpopular children, these boys did not always have even one mutual friendship. In a few cases, close friendships flourished. More often, like most children, the boys found at least one unilateral friend with whom exchange rather than intimacy formed the basis of the relationship.[66] As all four boys were able to show us, children with low acceptance can have a best friend and be satisfied with that friendship: Having a friend, friendship quality, and group membership offer separate contributions to the prediction of loneliness.[67]

To help boys like Bruce, David, Jack, and Earl alter their social status, caregivers found gentle ways to coach them in social skills. Although academic skills training facilitated improved social preference scores as well as higher achievement scores, direct social skills training also improved the boys' quality of life.[68] Some basic suggestions taken from systematic classroom studies were used to covertly target areas in need of coaching.[69] Peer acceptance was improved, for example, when the boys were encouraged to ask questions, given leadership opportunities, and encouraged to support their peers.[70] As part of this movement, it became helpful to encourage the boys to stop focusing on the consequences of people's social transgressions and focus on the underlying intentions instead.[71] Victimization was also reduced when the boys had friends help them with peer-related problems rather than when they aggressively fought back.[72] Yet, rough-and-tumble play allowed at least some of the boys to exercise their newly developing social skills.[73] Furthermore, the boys learned that well-accepted children were neither aggressive nor particularly prosocial in conflict situations, whereas poorly accepted children often relied on adult intervention.[74]

Like researchers who disagree with the idea that problems with peer relations lie solely within the child, caregivers looked for ways to alter peer group dynamics that affected the lives of Bruce, David, Jack, and Earl.[75] In school, peer collaboration improved the children's choice and use of learning strategies. Collaboration also offered opportunities to promote positive motivational orientations and moral agency, ensuring that the children were included in classroom activities. For social skills to develop more fully, the children needed informal opportunities to play with peers outside of school. With the help of their parents, the boys were able to make the necessary contacts to maintain emerging relationships. Bruce, David, Jack, and Earl needed more help in these situations than most second graders because they had difficulty in accurately perceiving social cues and were more likely to associate with peers who had a negative influence on their social growth.[76]

Responding to the competence needs of Bruce, David, Jack, and Earl, caregivers looked for subtle ways to offer encouragement and structure that did not undermine the boys' self-determination. They were also careful to establish expectations that were based on clear goals and did not withdraw affection when children disappointed them. At home, family members spent time reading with the boys, improving their family libraries, and constructing activities that highlighted the fun of reading. They promoted imitation, exposure to different life-roles, playful and complex use of language, and more casual forms of instruction. At school, teachers encouraged the happiness that comes from deep, complex

Challenges and Controversies

- How can caregivers establish interventions to help children meet their competence needs without undermining children's self-determination?
- How do children's competence needs differ at home, at school, and with peers?
- Is it too much to ask children to understand the difference between close and casual relationships and to use that information to develop appropriate social skills?

thought by labeling children's task-involvement. Teachers also found ways to celebrate the happiness that comes from entertaining others and through artistic expression by offering opportunities for children to reveal pleasure in learning. When children were overly ego-involved, teachers offered structured tasks, encouraged attention to the details of the tasks, and asked the boys to reflect on when and how they learned best. Teachers also organized a rich array of activities to permit children to learn with their whole bodies, find meaning in the tasks before them, and develop new interests. The boys were involved in peer groups that helped them consider the emotions of others, sustain levels of involvement rather than withdraw or become overly aggressive, correctly interpret forms of rejection, and otherwise adopt prosocial behavior. Although the boys were rarely able to coordinate all of these expectations, by the end of second grade, the possibility of doing so was significantly less daunting.

Sustaining Strong Relationships

Work on the development of the need for affiliation focuses primarily on children's basic attachments to parents. Nevertheless, existing research with adults made it possible to speculate on how Bruce, David, Jack, and Earl fulfilled their relatedness needs. Generally speaking, affiliation takes the form of social comparison, emotional support, positive stimulation, and attention.[77] In close friendships these needs are fulfilled in ways that hinge on warm, close communication, whereas in casual relationships it might be enough to establish and maintain engaging interactions. Research on children's friendships seems to capture an intimacy orientation, whereas research on peer relations seems to reflect more of the exchange orientation that comes with companionship.

Types of social comparison that facilitate affiliation permit children to determine how their own expectations correspond to the expectations of their peers. Such comparisons are distinct from comparisons that facilitate an ego orientation toward competence.[78] Intimacy and exchange orientations involve social comparison for the purpose of connecting with others. Ego-orientation involves social comparison for the purpose of demonstrating competence and establishing intellectual superiority.

Recently, researchers have begun to speculate on whether affiliation and competence orientations might be theoretically integrated. They have assumed that children formulate more global prosocial, individualistic, or competitive orientations by coordinating social comparison, emotional support, positive stimulation, and attention.[79] Integrating constructs associated with affiliation and competence needs might facilitate parsimony, and when children consolidate aspects of their experience, they may simultaneously meet both types of needs. Nevertheless, we would have difficulty describing how children like Bruce, David, Jack, and Earl fracture their experiences if we failed to differentiate affiliation and competence needs. On any given day, such children may successfully meet either their competence needs or their affiliation needs, but are usually unable to integrate both types of concerns.

It is also tempting, but problematic, to conflate the need for affiliation with the personality construct of agreeableness or with prosocial behavior.[80] Individuals can become agreeable in ways that undermine their affiliation needs. Children who are agreeable, for example, may engage in aggressive behavior to comply with the expectations of others even though that behavior undermines their affiliation needs. Similarly, children may engage in prosocial behavior because they are expected to do so rather than because such behavior is a useful strategy for developing comfortable relationships. Compliance with moral values does not necessarily facilitate meaningful forms of intimacy or exchange.

To fulfill affiliation needs, children need to be able to coordinate their sense of being cared for with their willingness to reciprocate such care. These two dimensions of affiliation, if left unconnected, sustain fractured experience and involve distinct psychological concerns. Individual differences in the extent to which people feel cared for have sometimes been linked to self esteem and attachment.[81] Children's willingness to care about others, on the other hand, has been linked to the attributions they make about their peers' behavior and to empathy.[82] When children recognize these distinctions, they could well use that knowledge to construct stronger close and casual ties with others, fostering comfortable levels of intimacy and exchange.

Family, school, and peer contexts serve different purposes in helping children fulfill their affiliation needs.[83] Parent support has been linked positively to school-related interests and competence orientations. Teacher support has been linked to school and class-related interests as well as children's willingness to be socially responsible. Peer support has been linked to prosocial goals. Hopefully, if children are able to meet their affiliation needs in each of these contexts, they will also be able to consolidate rather than fracture their life experiences.

Family Contexts

It is encouraging to know that family stability, regardless of whether children live in nonconventional, conventional, or single-parent households, has been associated with high grades in school.[84] All four boys were lucky enough to live in intact, stable families. Both attachment theorists and socialization theorists perpetuate a view that children's needs for affiliation are fulfilled either through their attachments to significant caregivers or through a meticulous process of mutual reinforcement among family members.[85] Looking only at the boys' behavior in second grade, it was impossible to verify attachment theorists' view that children need to be securely attached to their mothers to achieve the benefits of a stable environment. But, socialization theorists' claim that mutual reinforcement and reciprocity influence children's development is supported when we look carefully at these boys' lives. Understanding the lives of Bruce, David, Jack, and Earl becomes easier when research on attachment is linked to questions of intimacy and friendship, while research on socialization is linked to questions of exchange and companionship.

Intimacy requires the formation of strong attachment bonds between individuals. Children's earliest attachment bonds occur, of course, with primary caregivers. These attachments to primary caregivers have been strongly associated with children's later behavior toward their environment.[86] Longitudinal studies of how children interact with their mothers when confronted by a strange situation and subsequent behavior in other contexts have led to the identification of three types of attachment. Secure attachments are the most beneficial and enable children to see themselves as effective agents when interacting with the world. Such attachments are associated with children's cooperative, prosocial behavior.[87] They can also provide the starting point for intimacy, a developing capacity for healthy protest, and autonomy promoting forms of detachment.[88]

Not all children are fortunate enough to feel the ease and comfort of secure attachments. Insecure attachments have been associated with a range of children's rejecting or aggressive behaviors and are likely to be one of two kinds, anxious/avoidant and anxious/ambivalent.[89] When reading books, for example, mothers who have had anxious/avoidant relationships with their children might be more likely to read the verbal text and less inclined to initiate interactions about the pictures in a book.[90] Similarly, anxious/avoidant children would be less inclined to respond to the book while their mothers read. In anxious/ambivalent relationships, mothers are likely to be overcontrolling and exhibit overstimulating behavior, whereas children are likely to offer intermittent attention to the book. Such insecure attachments, while sometimes uncomfortable, do not generally involve hostile forms of parental rejection or neglect.

A painful aspect of looking at these psychological patterns emerges when people overzealously blame caregivers for their children's difficulties. This occurs whenever causal statements are used to defend the existence of correlational patterns. Patterns of correlations are important to notice because they enable us to imagine ways to formulate interesting questions and respond to important social issues. Yet, it is a mistake to rely heavily on them when working to predict and control the behavior of individual children. For example, logic might dictate that children's attachments to their mothers influence their ability to form intimate relationships with others. However, mother-child relationships do not exist in isolation.[91] Most children also have warm, close relationships with their fathers, siblings, and/or other relatives. Infants' physical needs delay their ability to reach out to others, yet, by second grade, most children have a wide range of intimate relationships. Despite their fractured experience, for example, Bruce, David, Jack, and Earl were each fortunate enough to find reciprocity and intimacy in relationships with their primary caregivers as well as other family members.

Attachment theorists have also been aware of the fact that children's behavior affects that of their caregivers as well as the reverse.[92] Intimacy within the family is characterized by reciprocal forms of warmth, responsiveness, unconditional acceptance, noncontingent positive reinforcement, and involvement. Like other children, Bruce, David, Jack, and Earl worked to balance intimacy issues. They also had to cope with exchange-related matters of direct confrontation, monitoring, intrusive-directiveness, and firm consistent demands for social growth.[93] At home, then, the boys had to coordinate both intimacy and exchange orientations in order to function comfortably within the family unit.

We did not systematically explore how the boys' parents assisted them in learning to coordinate their intimacy and exchange orientations. Nevertheless, we know that parents teach children about their physical growth, language, and views of themselves and others. They also teach children about their impulsivity, meta-cognitive forms of reasoning, autonomy, and conscience. To nurture children's growth in these areas, most parents use one of several forms of control, socializing children into understanding their family's moral and cultural beliefs.[94] Ideally, parents strive to adhere to authoritative parenting styles that involve clear, firm structuring and limit setting while sustaining warm levels of responsiveness.[95] In contrast, the kinds of authoritarian parenting behavior that is characterized by harsh control without warmth has been linked to many kinds of negative acting-out behaviors in children.[96] Permissive parenting behavior involves an unstructured, child-centered approach to regulating children's behavior that also has negative correlates. Affiliation rather than self-determination or competence needs are met by these patterns of parental control because they lead more directly to variation in how children trust their parents more often than to autonomy or expertise.[97]

Trust, of course, is essential for the formation of intimate relationships but often involves a process of exchange as well.[98] Correlations between mothers' fulfillment of promises and children's trust in adult caregivers have been strong and positive.[99] Children who trust their mothers have been more likely to trust their teachers as well. It is also important to remember that fathers as well as mothers influence children's trust in adults. Although mothers might shape their children's trusting beliefs, fathers are more likely to shape their children's trusting behavior.

The variety and forms of agreements that take place in families also have an important influence on how children establish trusting relationships.[100] Mothers, for example, help their children imagine solutions to daily problems. Mothers who adopt a problem-focused reaction to their children's negative emotions typically have children with well-developed social functioning and coping skills.[101] Unlike girls, however, boys benefit when their mothers also encourage them to express emotions. Boys exhibit more comforting behavior when mothers combine emotion-focused and problem-focused reactions to their sons' negative emotions. All four boys—even Earl, who chose to strike out at his parents to gain additional adult attention—seemed quite comfortable with the rituals and norms that dominated their family life.

When establishing friendships, children often imitate the kinds of relationships that occur in their families.[102] The relatively short duration of our involvement in the lives of Bruce, David, Jack, and Earl made it difficult to know exactly what this imitation might have looked like. Yet, in more general studies, families highest in relatedness tended to be outerdirected and focus on relationships with the community at large. Such families have relied on children's self-help skills as well as parenting practices that foster social adjustment, motivation, and competence at communal living.[103] Children with accepting mothers and siblings have been more likely to exhibit prosocial behavior with their peers.[104] Likewise, aggressive children who are victimized by their peers have been more likely to experience punitive, hostile, or abusive family treatment than children who are not victimized by their peers.[105] These general trends can help struggling parents formulate important questions, but it should be noted that these conclusions are largely drawn on the basis of group norms rather than detailed case studies.

Children who fracture their needs for affiliation at home are likely to mistrust family members and/or are unable to understand adults' expectations. Family members can contribute to children's confusion by establishing irregular schedules, behaving in unpredictable ways, or withdrawing affection when children disappoint them. Nevertheless, children's own feelings of unworthiness and/or inability to step outside their own subjective experience can also facilitate insecurity and mistrust.

In addition to helping children learn to relate to others, families can also have a strong influence on how children adjust to school.[106] As noted earlier, children's social skills and adaptation to school have been linked to their attachments with parents. Parents can serve as coaches who interpret essential academic rituals as well as provide support when children need comfort. Furthermore, by becoming directly involved in school activities, parents gain valuable knowledge and mediate difficult transitions that can offer additional levels of social support. Because of differences in their family structures, Bruce, David, Jack, and Earl offer distinct examples of how children express their affiliation needs in ways that reflected their understanding of family members' expectations.

School Contexts

Work on early attachments might encourage conscientious parents to assume that children's relationships with their mothers have a major influence on their school achievement. Yet, from carefully constructed longitudinal research, we learn that, in school, teacher-child attachments can be more important than maternal attachments.[107] For example, when researchers looked at how children represent attachments rather than at how they behave when separated from their mothers, children's general attachment beliefs were linked to their attention to and participation in school activities, to feelings about the self, and to grades. Predictably, children with secure representations of their attachments showed the most beneficial outcomes.[108]

Not only do we know that secure attachments with teachers have been more beneficial in school than secure attachments with primary caregivers, secure attachments to teachers are more beneficial than secure attachments to siblings and peers.[109] For example, attachments with teachers have been related to children's communicative competence, school and class-related interest, and feelings of responsibility.[110] Children have also been more aware of rules for determining teachers' anger than for peers' anger.[111] In other words, supportive teachers can stimulate students' enjoyment and commitment to school.

As is evident in the literary and artistic experiences of Bruce, David, Jack, and Earl, teachers can facilitate enjoyment by finding ways to represent curriculum as personally relevant to their students.[112] To do so requires high levels of sensitivity to children's needs, a sensitivity that is also necessary for maintaining comfortable attachments. If children can become securely attached, they are more likely to engage in prosocial behavior and comfortable levels of task-involvement.[113] Yet, as Bruce's behavior taught Thyra and John, teachers need to remember that too much attachment can foster dependence rather than autonomy.[114]

Children who fracture their affiliation needs in school are likely to mistrust their teachers, misunderstand their teachers' expectations, and/or fail to differentiate parent and teacher expectations. Children can easily bring enough feelings of insecurity or unworthiness with them to school, perpetuating a general mistrust of school and anyone affiliated with it. They can misunderstand the degree of intimacy and exchange that individual teachers are willing to nurture in their students. And, some children imagine that their teachers and parents are omnipotent and hold identical expectations. Regardless of their reasons, children who fracture their experience come to school ready to act out their hostilities or transfer levels of intimacy that may be unrealistic or inappropriate.

Fortunately, teachers and students who engage in dialogue about curriculum and the fairness of educational practices can negotiate a balance between attachment and dependence.[115] Most second graders are eager learners who want to learn all forms of knowledge, and have complex views about the types of knowledge they value.[116] Typically, they have not yet understood all the reasons adults have for organizing school around testing, learning, and contests, but their emerging knowledge is linked to the definition of the situation at hand and they can be insightful critics of schooling.[117] Second graders are quite capable of engaging in moral dialogue about how schooling ought to be organized when teachers want to be fair to everyone. Thyra, Ann, Nancy, and their students demonstrated how such conversations can help children imagine satisfying ways of forming intimacy and exchange relationships within a community that is larger than their family.

Peer Contexts

Children's relationships with their family members and with their teachers are generally asymmetrical in that differences in age and social status are stable features. Their peer relationships, however, can be either symmetrical or asymmetrical.[118] The degree to which children fracture their affiliation needs with peers can be linked to the degree of symmetry in their relationships. The extent to which children have popular, average, rejected, neglected, or controversial social status, for example, places them in more and less symmetrical relationship to one another. When children are not particularly popular, they are likely to find themselves in uncomfortably subordinate positions, unable to find common interests with their peers.

Common interests and agendas foster symmetry that can lead to strong moral and intellectual growth.[119] Issues of domination and subordination are absent from symmetrical relationships. This makes it easier for children to identify with their peers and find common ground from which to experience happiness in life as free and responsible citizens, thinkers and philosophers, and entertainers and artists without fear of ridicule.

Exchange issues such as group acceptance, behavioral reputations, social competence, and behavioral problems can be differentiated from the process of forming friendships.[120] Casual relationships tend to be less symmetrical than close friendships and social status is dependent on children's ability to negotiate positive forms of companionship. Children find it easier to adopt an exchange orientation when they are able to collaborate with peers who are facing similar challenges.[121] Despite their potential asymmetry, casual relationships offer children rudimentary exposure to the kind of reciprocity and trust necessary to establish comfortable friendships.[122] By second grade, for example, boys are more likely to establish trusting relationships with other boys than they are with girls. Similarly, girls are also more trusting in same-sex friendships.[123] These patterns may be maintained because children involved in same-sex relationships tend to look to one another for common definitions of happiness.

Children benefit from casual relationships, but affiliation needs are better met in mutual friendships. At the very least, mutual friends have developed rudimentary levels of intimacy on which stable forms of trust can evolve into a more personal sharing of ideas and values.[124] When working to join a group, for example, friends are willing to admit "guest friends" more often than they are willing to admit nonfriends. Friendship also prescribes a kind of self-sacrifice that is not evident in less intimate relationships. Friends who collaborate on school tasks also say they collaborate on more academic and nonacademic activities outside the experimental setting than do pairs of other classmates.[125] It becomes easier to nurture common interests when relationships involve close ties than when relationships are informal.

Like Bruce, Jack, and Earl, children with learning disabilities are often less well-liked and more frequently rejected than other children, creating an uncomfortable form of asymmetry that is likely to nurture fractured experience. Low social status can foster loneliness and lack of stimulation, which in turn affect children's social self-evaluations, a cycle that is difficult to break without some form of intervention.[126] Relationally aggressive friendships, for example, are high in intimacy, exclusivity/jealousy, and aggression between friends.[127] Similarly, loneliness has been linked to low self-esteem and perceived social competence in a way that has also been linked to high levels of defensive forms of ego-involvement.[128] Because asymmetrical relationships offer more negative consequences than positive ones, once children are caught in a cycle of low social status, they have difficulty altering those cycles.

Learning more about the nature of children's close friendships provides clues about how children fulfill their need for symmetrical relationships. Researchers continue to look for ways to encourage children to describe the emotions associated with a strong friendship. Yet, preoccupation with evaluating competence has misled some researchers into representing children as incapable of describing the qualities of a warm, close relationship. Certainly Bruce, David, Jack, and Earl had great difficulty talking about their relationships with friends, but they found ways of communicating through gesture, art, and writing.

As researchers accept new ways of exploring children's perceptions of their intimate friendships, it will become easier to compare symmetrical and asymmetrical relationships.

Challenges and Controversies

- Is it wise for caregivers to assume that children's early attachments with their parents are likely to guide their ability to form later attachments?
- Are there subtle ways for caregivers to help children understand how to negotiate appropriate intimacy and exchange relationships with their teachers?
- What can children do to construct and maintain symmetrical relationships with their peers?

Readers can speculate about the nature of friendship among the second graders at Sprague, but concrete evidence is hard to generate without stronger research tools. Perhaps asymmetrical relationships are a function of low social status that perpetuates uncomfortable patterns of domination and subordination. Yet, there may be positive kinds of asymmetrical relationships that can assist children who currently fracture their needs and other's expectations. Until we know more about the details of such relationships, children are advised to work toward building symmetrical rather than asymmetrical relationships with their peers, and caregivers will probably need to intervene when children become overwhelmed.

Bruce, David, Jack, and Earl revealed unique sets of unmet affiliation needs. To assist these boys, caregivers examined the ways in which their own behavior conveyed unclear or contradictory expectations. At home, parents looked at how they taught the boys appropriate ways of responding to their physical growth, impulsivity, and emerging interests. They evaluated their ability to maintain predictable schedules, their attitudes about schooling, and the techniques they used to interpret academic rituals when their children were confused. At school, teachers examined the quality of their relationships with each student, nurtured trust, and negotiated comfortable boundaries. Teachers also looked for small ways of noticing children's interests and personalities. In peer groups, potential friends worked to create symmetry by sharing interests, permitting the boys to join activities, and responding to the boys' attempts to share their emerging identities. All the children benefited from participating in reading teams, group activities, drama, class discussions, and after-school activities. This combination of good will, realistic feedback, and flexibility helped the boys minimize their loneliness, anger, and frustration enough to also alter their social status. Casual relationships that nurtured the boys' exchange orientations sometimes blossomed into mutual friendships that facilitated intimacy. Nevertheless, each boy differed in his ability to consistently address his affiliation needs while coordinating the expectations of others.

Fracturing Experience in Multiple Contexts

It is much easier to identify the habits of students who fracture only some parts of their experience than those of students who fracture both their needs and relationships. Jack Davis and Earl Norton, the two boys who are the focus of the following chapters, took the challenge of fractured experience to a more intense level than did Bruce or David. Jack and Earl ignored some of their motivational needs and found others' expectations overwhelming. Jack and Earl also received more services from school and privately funded sources than is common for children with learning disabilities. In comparison to Bruce and David, who exhibited annoying habits and showed problems that were relatively common, easy to identify, and changeable, Jack and Earl were much more complex personalities who resisted labels and just about all offers of help.

The boys' own inconsistencies combined with confounding expectations from family, school, and professional sources made these children more difficult to understand than all the children we had worked with over the years. These inconsistencies led me, as narrator, to turn to more detailed clinical language to illustrate the subtlety of the boys' behavior. Jack and Earl were lucky enough to have teachers who respected their individuality, were not afraid to challenge their views, and remained delightfully explicit and honest with them. Their parents also faced bravely the challenges these children put forth. Nevertheless, in entirely different respects, Jack and Earl teach us why it should not be surprising to hear teachers complain about inclusion movements in special education. These boys made it difficult to promote the kind of education that serves self-determination and affiliation needs as well as competence needs. "Majority rules" forms of decision making would always leave students like this wanting. Likewise, the "tough love" tactics that are common in militaristic models of education could exacerbate the problem: Children who overlook some of their needs and others' expectations cannot pull themselves up by their own bootstraps.

The boys posed a challenge to the way we conduct business in most schools because offers of help sometimes undermined their will and sense that they should be held responsible for their own growth. To ensure that the boys complied with normative standards of success, their caregivers put strong limits on their initiative. Those restrictions, while necessary, sometimes sent the implicit message that the boys were too incompetent to sustain the levels of self-determination necessary for meaningful accomplishment. This, of course, was not the caregivers' intent. Nevertheless, both boys responded to this implicit criticism from time to time and in ways that were very frustrating to their peers and adult guardians. Everyone felt misunderstood at some time during the process of negotiating the curriculum and establishing fair and effective classroom practices.

ENDNOTES

1. See Deci & Ryan (1985), Hidi & Harackiewicz (2000), Ryan & Deci (2000), McClelland (1985), and Wiggins (1991).
2. See Emmons (1997) and Wiebe & Smith (1997).
3. See Freeman (1993).
4. See Piaget (1965). Grolnick, Deci, & Ryan (1997) and MacDonald (1997) review current research.
5. See Mink & Nihira (1986).
6. See, for example, Grolnick, Deci, & Ryan (1997) and Scheinfeld (1983).
7. L. Walker (1991), Walker & Hennig (1997), and Walker & Taylor (1991) have begun an initial line of inquiry focusing on promoting self-determination in children's moral development. See also Ladd & Golter (1988), Ladd & Price (1986), and Ladd, Profilet & Hart (1992) for an emphasis on children's social skills.
8. See Schunk (1989a, 1995), Schunk & Zimmerman (1996), and Wigfield & Guthrie (1997).
9. See Nicholls (1984).
10. See, for example, Newman & Wick (1987) and Schunk (1982, 1984).
11. See Gagne (1975), Schunk (1985, 1996), and Schunk & Cox (1986).
12. See Schunk (1989b), Schunk & Rice (1993), and Schunk & Swartz (1993).
13. See Dunn, Brown, & Maguire (1995), Howes (1983, 1997), Jones & Nelson-LeGall (1995), and Rosen, Furman, & Hartup (1988).
14. See Garner (1996), Howes (1983), Jones & Nelson-LeGall (1995), Ladd (1988), Ladd & Golter (1988), Lollis, Ross, & Tate (1992), McGillicuddy-DeLisi, Watkins, & Vinchur (1994), Miller, Eisenberg, Fabes, & Shell (1996), and Sigelman & Waitzman (1991).
15. See Clark & Mills (1993) and Laursen, Hartup, & Koplas (1996).
16. See Bigelow & LaGaipa (1995).
17. See Damon & Phelps (1989), Epstein (1989), Nicholls & Hazzard (1993), Selman & Schultz (1989), and Thorkildsen & Jordan (1995).
18. See Gresham & MacMillan (1997), Lincoln & Chazan (1979), Pearl & Bay (1999), Saunders & Chambers (1996), and Siperstein et al. (1997).
19. See Farnham-Diggory (1992).
20. Bandura, Barbaranelli, Caprara, & Pastorelli (1996), Sternberg & Kolligian (1990), or Weiner (1994) offer current formulations.

21. See Colby, Kohlberg, Gibbs, & Lieberman (1983), Damon (1977), Eisenberg & Mussen (1989), and Turiel (1983).

22. See, for example, Bradley, Caldwell, & Rock (1988), and Mink & Nihira (1986).

23. See Olszewski, Kulieke, & Buescher (1987).

24. Evidence by Beyer (1995), Bowes & Goodnow (1996), Goodnow (1995), Greenberger & Goldberg (1989), Howes, Sakai, Shinn, Phillips, Galinsky, & Whitebook (1995) and Melton (1995) support this assertion.

25. See Goldberg, Greenberger, & Nagel (1996), and Poresky & Whitsitt (1985).

26. See Kontos, Howes, Shinn, & Galinsky (1997).

27. See Poresky & Whitsitt (1985).

28. See Fontaine (1994).

29. See Bradley, Caldwell, & Rock (1988).

30. See, for example, Baker, Scher, & Mackler (1997), Freeman (1993), Morrow & Young (1997), and Rosier & Corsaro (1993).

31. See, for example, Deci et al. (1992), Gresham & MacMillan (1997), Grolnick & Ryan (1990), Lincoln & Chazan (1979), Pearl & Bay (1999), Sabatino (1982), and Short (1992).

32. See, for example, Friedman & Medway (1987) and Pintrich et al. (1994).

33. See Farnham-Diggory (1992), Hagen, Barclay, & Newman (1982), Newman & Hagen (1981), and Törgesen (1982).

34. See Cordova & Lepper (1996), Nicholls (1989), and Weiner (1994).

35. See reviews by Licht (1993) and Stipek (1997) as well as case studies by Skaalvik (1993).

36. See Hagen, Barclay, & Newman (1982) and Pintrich et al. (1994).

37. See, for example, Butler & Neuman (1995), Chen (1990), Fuchs, Fuchs, Karns, Hamlett, Katzaroff, & Dutka (1997), Schunk & Cox (1986), Schunk & Rice (1993), and Schunk & Swartz (1993).

38. Children's understanding of and reliance on the beliefs of authority figures can place limits on their curiosity (e.g., Damon, 1977; DeVries, 1970; Laupa, 1995). Despite the effects of a curriculum designed to promote moral growth (e.g., Selman & Demorest, 1984; Selman & Lieberman, 1975), children also tend to confound issues of morality and intelligence (Leahy & Hunt, 1983).

39. See Adalbjarnardottir & Selman (1989), Butler & Neuman (1995), Gresham & MacMillan (1997), O'Neil, Welsh, Parke, Wang, & Strand (1997), and Plummer & Graziano (1987).

40. See Bursuck & Asher (1986).

41. See Kochenderfer & Ladd (1996), Ladd (1990), and Ladd & Coleman (1997).

42. See Tassi & Schneider (1997).

43. See Selman (1980) for an initial review and subsequent research on social status for more detailed analysis of children's social competence.

44. Newcomb, Bukowski, & Pattee (1993) offered a meta-analytic review of the research validating this social status typology. Crick & Dodge (1994) offered a reformulation of the social information-processing mechanism that underlies these categories of adjustment.

45. See Coie & Dodge (1983) and Howes (1988).

46. See Youniss (1994).

47. See Gresham & MacMillan (1997) and Pearl & Bay (1999).

48. See Asher & Rose (1997), Bierman & Welsh (1997) have summarized such work. See also Eisenberg, Guthrie, Fabes, Reiser, Murphy, Holgren, Maszk, & Losoya (1997) and Hubbard & Coie (1994).

49. See Richards, Bear, Stewart, & Norman (1992).

50. See Arsenio & Fleiss (1996), Astor (1994), and Boivin & Hymel (1997).

51. See Harrist, Zaia, Bates, Dodge, & Pettit (1997).

52. See Schwartz, Dodge, & Coie (1993) and Wentzel & Asher (1995).

53. See Ladd (1983), Ray, Cohen, Secrist, & Duncan (1997) and Zakriski, Jacobs, & Coie (1997).

54. See Arsenio & Cooperman (1996), Erdley (1996), Selman (1981), Selman & Demorest (1984), and Zakriski & Coie (1996).

55. See Dodge, Price, Coie, & Christopoulos (1990) and Erdley & Asher (1996).

56. See Zarbatany & Pepper (1996).

57. See DeVries (1970) and Graziano, Leone, Musser, & Lautenschlager (1987).

58. See Damon (1977), Graziano (1978), Graziano, Brody, & Bernstein (1980), and Graziano, Musser, Rosen, & Shaffer (1982).

59. See Howes (1987, 1990).

60. See Damon (1984), Phelps & Damon (1991), Selman (1989), Selman & Lieberman (1975), Selman, Schorin, Stone, & Phelps (1983), and Stremmel & Ladd (1985).

61. See Gottman (1983).

62. See Bukowski & Sippola (1996) and Musser, Graziano, & Moore (1987).

63. See Ladd & Emerson (1984).

64. See, for example, Garner (1996), Kruger (1992), and Miller et al. (1996).

65. See Guralnick, Gottman, & Hammond (1996), Siperstein et al. (1997), and von Salisch (1996).

66. See George & Hartmann (1996), and Ladd (1988).

67. See Parker & Asher (1993).

68. See Coie & Krehbiel (1984), Ladd & Mize (1983), and Malik & Furman (1993).

69. See Damon & Killen (1982), Harrell, Doelling, & Sasso (1997), Ladd & Profilet (1990) and Yeates & Selman (1980).

70. See Ladd (1981).

71. See Glassco, Milgram, & Youniss (1970), Selman & Lieberman (1975), and Sternlieb & Youniss (1975).

72. See Kochenderfer & Ladd (1997).

73. See Smith & Boulton (1990).

74. See Hopmeyer & Asher (1997).

75. See, for example, Ackerman & Howes (1986), Banerji & Dailey (1995), Coie & Kupersmidt (1983), Evans, Salisbury, Palombaro, & Goldberg (1994), Gottman, Guralnick, Wilson, Swanson, & Murray (1997), Kindermann (1996), Manion & Alexander (1997), Neckerman (1996), and Putnam, Markovchick, Johnson, & Johnson (1996).

76. See Farmer, Pearl, & VanAcker (1996).

77. See Eisenberg (1992), Eisenberg & Mussen (1989), and Hill (1987).

78. See Juvonen & Wentzel (1996).

79. See Butler & Neuman (1995), Nelson-LeGall & Glor-Scheib (1986), Newman (1990), and Van Lange, DeBruin, Otten, & Joireman (1997).

80. See Graziano (1994) and Graziano & Eisenberg (1997).

81. See Freitag, Belsky, Grossmann, Grossmann, & Scheuerer-Englisch (1996), MacKinnon-Lewis, Starnes, Volling, & Johnson (1997), and Van Lange et al. (1997).

82. See Collins & DiPaula (1997).

83. See, for example, Wentzel (1998).

84. See Weisner & Garnier (1992).

85. See, for example, current critiques by Cowan (1997) and DeWolff & van IJzendoorn (1997).

86. See Ainsworth (1979, 1985), Ainsworth & Marvin (1995), Freitag et al. (1996), Furman & Buhrmester (1992), Koski & Shaver (1997), MacKinnon-Lewis et al. (1997), Robinson, Zahn-Waxler, & Emde (1994), and Van Lange et al. (1997).

87. See Bretherton, Golby, & Cho (1997), Burnett & Demnar (1996), and Meins (1997).

88. See, for example, Holmes (1997).

89. See, for example, Ainsworth (1985), Dunn & Brown (1994), Dunn et al. (1995), Dunn, Creps, & Brown (1996), Dunn & Herrera (1997).

90. See Bus, Belsky, van IJzendoorn, & Crnic (1997).

91. See Fox, Kimmerly, & Schafer (1991).

92. See, for example, Patterson (1980).

93. See Baumrind (1989), Grusec, Goodnow, & Cohen (1996), and Warton & Goodnow (1991).

94. See Maccoby (1984, 1992).

95. See Baumrind (1966, 1971), Goodnow (1997), Grusec & Goodnow (1994), Maccoby & Martin (1983), and Smetana (1994).

96. See Hetherington & Martin (1986) and Hinshaw, Zupan, Simmel, Nigg, & Melnick (1997).

97. See Erikson (1963).

98. See Gambetta (1988) and Hinde & Groebel (1991).

99. See Rotenberg (1995).

100. See Cashmore & Goodnow (1985).

101. See Eisenberg, Fabes, & Murphy (1996).

102. See Leve & Fagot (1997).

103. See Mink & Nihira (1986).

104. See Hinshaw et al. (1997) and MacKinnon-Lewis et al. (1997).

105. See Schwartz, Dodge, Pettit, & Bates (1997).

106. See Stevenson & Newman (1986).

107. See Howes, Matheson, & Hamilton (1994).

108. See Jacobsen & Hofmann (1997).

109. See Imber (1973), Newman & Goldin (1990), and Stipek (1997).

110. See Klann-Delius & Hofmeister (1997).

111. See Underwood, Coie, & Herbsman (1992).

112. See Cordova & Lepper (1996).

113. See Howes, Hamilton, & Matheson (1994).

114. See Nadler (1997) and Weiner (1996).

115. See Thorkildsen (1994) and Thorkildsen & Nicholls (1991).

116. See Nicholls & Hazzard (1993), Nicholls & Nelson (1992), Nicholls, Nelson, & Gleaves (1995), and Nicholls & Thorkildsen (1988, 1989).

117. See Thorkildsen (1989a, 1989b, 1991, 2000) and Thorkildsen, Nolen, & Fournier (1994).

118. See von Salisch (1996).

119. See, for example, Brown, Donelan-McCall, & Dunn (1996), Loehlin (1997), Piaget (1965), Volling, Youngblade, & Belsky (1997), and Youniss (1980).

120. See Parker & Seal (1996).

121. See Asher & Coie (1990), Berndt & Ladd (1989), Damon & Killen (1982), Eisenberg & Mussen (1989), Hinde & Groebel (1991), and Laursen, Hartup, & Koplas (1996).

122. See Rotenberg & Morgan (1995) and Rotenberg & Pilipenko (1983-84).

123. See Rotenberg (1984).

124. See Zarbatany, Van Brunschot, Meadows, & Pepper (1996).

125. See Berndt & Perry (1986) and Berndt, Perry, & Miller (1988).

126. See Gresham & MacMillan (1997), Pearl (1992), Pearl & Bay (1999), Sabatino (1982), and Vaughn, Elbaum, & Schumm (1996).

127. See Grotpeter & Crick (1996).

128. See Sletta, Valas, Skaalvik, & Sobstad (1996).

CHAPTER

5 Enlightened Egocentrism

Jack, the quieter of the two students with learning disabilities in Nancy Brankis's class, had also been diagnosed as having *attention deficit disorders.* Whereas Bruce looked for opportunities to cajole others into doing his work for him and David kept his intellectual pursuits private, Jack seemed unaware of others around him. In this respect, Jack's behavior was consistent with the type of egocentrism that Piaget called heteronomy and others have defined as a limited ability to take social and intellectual perspectives. Jack was a complex person to understand because, while he showed many signs of holding an egocentric perspective, he also revealed signs of a concrete, individualistic perspective and an awareness of himself in relation to others that reflected more advanced kinds of sociomoral and intellectual growth. Jack's approach to life served as a baffling sort of protection from any potential ridicule he might face by not keeping up with his peers, but also kept him unaware of why others around him behaved as they did.

Jack's withdrawn and insecure demeanor was evident when looking at his silly sentences the first day John observed in Nancy's class. He wrote in large shaky script on paper with extra wide spaces between the lines. After the class had gone over the work, Nancy announced, "Jack will come and pick them up."

Jack looked happy with this responsibility and buzzed around the room, but missed five papers. Sitting across from him, Jean twice mentioned in a matter-of-fact manner that several papers were not picked up. Jack looked around after Jean's comments, but took no action until Nancy also prompted him. Jack seemed unable to see the children whose papers he had missed despite hearing Jean's coaching.

In gym, Jack, a head shorter than most of his peers, sat waiting. He said nothing to anyone and barely moved. After students heard instructions about various activities they might choose, Jack spent most of the session waiting in line for the most popular of three climbing ropes.

The rope was popular because it had knots that made it easier to climb. The bottom of the rope was also a long way from the ceiling. Many second graders could climb all the way to the top, but it was a challenging achievement.

For the entire class period there was a line for this particular rope, but Jack never reached the front. Instead, he unobtrusively let others ahead of him. Reaching second place at one point, with only two girls behind him, Jack walked off decisively, as if headed to another activity. Twenty feet away from the rope, he stopped and returned to the end of the line. Jack's behavior was strikingly different from that of students who needed to be first in everything.

Back in the classroom, after a lively group discussion of freedom, Jack responded to the question, "What does freedom mean to me?" by writing:

> *What does freedom*
> *mean to me?*
> *turn on the teve*
> *turn on my super*
> *Netla.*
> *I get to help my mom.*

Looking at the social vision of Jack's poem, he seemed to define freedom as relief from oppression. Imagining a life of rules that are determined by authorities external to him (in this case his mother), Jack defined freedom as compliance with or an absence of such rules. On a more personal level, however, Jack's poem indicates that he was oblivious to the larger social vision valued by Fromm, the psychologist who coined the phrase "freedom from" oppression to explain this heteronomous vision of freedom.[1] Instead, like Piaget, Jack seemed "not really interested in individuals . . . analysis of individual situations, individual problems, and so forth."[2] Unfortunately, Jack did not have Piaget's fascination for the study of knowledge that also served a valued social function.

Jack behaved in ways that were consistent with Piaget's description of an egocentric approach to social interaction. Egocentrism in this view:

> Begins at the moment when the child receives from outside [him or herself] the example of codified rules. . . . But though the child imitates this example, he continues to play either by himself without bothering to find play-fellows, or with others, but without trying to win, and therefore without attempting to unify the different ways of playing. . . . Children of this stage, even when they are playing together, play each one "on his own" (everyone can win at once). . . . This dual character, combining imitation of others with a purely individual use of examples received, we have designated egocentrism.[3]

Jack's form of egocentrism manifested itself in striking contrast to Bruce's egotism. Jack's lack of awareness was not a form of selfishness, as was sometimes the case for Bruce. Instead, Jack seemed to adopt avoidant attachment behaviors toward adults. He displaced anger and distress by displacing attention away from adults and toward the inanimate environment. His respect for rules involved an attempt at blind obedience to rules established by others—rules that did not always make sense to Jack himself.

As might be expected of a child who is not interested in individuals and has no other obvious passions, Jack's social position in the class seemed to be that of a neglected or socially isolated person who was not about to take over the world. On "The Child Behavior Scale," for example, Jack would score about average on all the subscales and, to accurately measure his behavior, we would have to look at particular items.[4] Jack would score highest on items like, "is worried," "appears miserable and distressed," "prefers to play alone," and "withdraws from peer activities." Jack was also excluded by his peers (e.g., not chosen as a playmate, ignored by peers, and excluded from peers' activities), yet he was not actively rejected in the way that some items on the exclusion measure would suggest.

During a snowy recess, for example, Jack drifted alone, as if practicing how to be invisible, and never joined his classmates' ice-breaking activity. During snack time, Jack looked at the computer screen over the shoulders of two classmates: He commented quietly, pointed at the screen, and was wholly ignored.

When Nancy announced that part of the class would go to the learning center, Jack was first to the door. He did not lack all initiative, but sometimes avoided it.

At the learning center, Miss Stevens took a Styrofoam cup, held it over her nose, and asked, "What is it?"

"Nose," someone called. Miss Stevens put the cup on her ear. "Big ear." This game continued, with many of the children generating ideas. Each person, Miss Stevens eventually told the class, would have a plastic cup, toothpicks, a spoon, paper plate, string, and more to create with.

"Are your minds thinking here?" asked Miss Stevens.

"Yes," the children called, eager to start. At the back of the room, Jack shook his head decisively, but did not protest publicly. "No! He is not thinking!" said his gesture.

When Jack reached his assigned space, he declared, "I don't have any ideas," and began to drift toward Miss Stevens.

John pulled him back, asking "What does it look like?"

"Flowerpot," said Jack.

"Hey, you have ideas! It does look like that," encouraged John. But, Jack moved to leave again. John stopped him by asking how Jack could make this cup into a better flowerpot before saying, "What else might it look like?" Jack turned the cup on its side and said, "Spider."

"See! You do have ideas," said John with delight.

Yet, Jack rejected the spider idea, stuck the spoon into the base of the overturned cup, put toothpicks beside it, and wrapped string around the whole thing. John could not tell what Jack was making, but Jack had done something that would not be embarrassing. John had the impression that they had both dodged a bullet.

Another bullet, however, was on its way. Miss Stevens called the class together and said they would take turns thinking aloud about objects of different colors. First, yellow. Ideas flowed easily. Yet, at his turn, the only one to do so, Jack said, "Pass."

Later that same day, it was Jack's turn to be interviewed by John. Walking with Jack, John wondered if Jack would enjoy the interview. Jack's quiet nature and John's experience with "Quiet Bird" made John wonder if Jack would be open to conversation or embarrassed by the extra attention. John was comforted when, after a few yards, as soon as John stopped chattering nervously, Jack asked if John had talked with his father. John had talked with Mr. Davis to explain his project and ask permission to include Jack. Jack seemed calm and pleased when John confirmed this.

Beginning the formal interview, Jack had no general comments on school. John asked, "Do you have a favorite subject?"

"No," said Jack definitively.

"No? Do you have one you don't like mostly?"

"I like all them," Jack corrected John.

"All of them! OK, I see that when you come in the morning, you sit down and get right to work, don't you."

"Mmhu."

". . . Can you think about a time when school was really good for you?" said John.

"No." Jack spoke more than David had, but did not have Quiet Bird's underground impishness. John felt as if forthright eye contact was an assault for Jack, but never for David. The fact that a simple, friendly approach from John could be received as an assault suggested a pervasive fear of committing errors. Jack seemed self-conscious about how he appeared to others and whether he could pass their imaginary evaluations.

"Can't think of any special time when it was good. Can you think of any special time when it was really bad?"

"No." So far, the interview reflected the same emotional flatness suggested by the gestures that John had observed. Jack said he liked to learn, but there was no hint of affection for such adventures.

John moved on to discuss grades and report cards. "What do you think about that stuff? Is that good or bad or sort of. . . ?"

"Good," Jack cut in.

"Grades are good to have?"

"Mmhm."

"Why's that?"

"I listen."

Jack's sense that grades are good is consistent with a heteronomous morality, an orientation to school that involves obedience for its own sake and a search for evidence that rules have been enforced. On the global ruler used to assess sociomoral development, this reflects the least complex understanding of morality. Grades are a sign of being good, and being good is valuable in its own right.

"I see. Can you explain a bit more about that?" John was familiar with this global ruler and wanted to determine if Jack would show evidence of more complex sociomoral reasoning if encouraged.

"I listen to the teacher and stuff."

"OK, and that's good?"

"Mmhu."

"OK. Um, well, that's interesting. And what's the grades got to do with listening?"

"You get smart." Jack offered a more complex reason for his interest in grades, describing an instrumental preoccupation with doing good in order to get something in return. This involves slightly more complex coordination of his own and others' perspectives than the more heteronomous approach evident earlier in the conversation. Jack may have missed important aspects of some situations, but he understood the personal benefits of complying with the requests of adults.

"I see," said John. "OK. . . . Any other ways you learn besides listening?"

"Concentrating." In the classroom, Jack listened and concentrated. The threat of grades would make Jack listen, and that was how he would learn. This impression of dogged uncritical learning was sustained when John asked, "How do you tell when you are doing good in school?"

"I don't know."

"It's hard to tell that, is it?"

"Mmhm." Further probing from John revealed no more insight here.

John returned to the topic of report cards. "OK. So some schools don't give report cards to children. Most do. But, do you think it would be a good idea to have a school where they don't give out report cards?"

"No."

"Why would that not be good?"

"Mother and dad wouldn't know whether you'd been good or not."

"OK, they wouldn't know if the boys and girls had been good. That right?"

"Mmhhu." Jack seemed to be defining the process of learning as a moral issue in which interpersonal expectations guided decision making. Regardless of his reasons for being good, Jack did not seem to strengthen his identity by exploring interesting topics or becoming more articulate about his likes and dislikes.

When discussing the topic of homework, Jack's position seemed like that of his peers who saw school learning as an imposition. He asserted that homework should be avoided, but he had no clear justification for this stance. Most second graders tend to justify their positions by inventing forms of social action, altering the ongoing decisions of others and thereby attaining the freedom to pursue personal goals. Jack did not seem to imagine such action. "What if you could decide whether or not boys and girls in the school had homework. Like you can be Mr. Best. . . ?"

"I don't know," Jack spoke quickly and abruptly. He seemed to want to avoid this topic.

"Would you not be sure what to do?" challenged John.

"Yeah."

"But we are going to make you the principal and you have to decide," John prompted. After a bit more prompting, John asked, "Would you give them a bit more or a bit less than they get now?"

"Less."

"Less, eh. OK, why would you do that?"

"Cause they'd go and play." Jack could certainly offer alternative things to do with the time that he normally spent doing homework.

"OK, and what if your school did that? What if they said that all this week there's not going to be any homework at all?"

"I don't know." Jack seemed unwilling to imagine an alternative world in which there were new rules. He refused to examine his conflicting desires to play rather than do schoolwork, and his earlier assertion that he enjoyed all school subjects.

After more nudging, Jack conceded that he might play video games if he did not have to do homework. John continued, "Are there some things you like finding out about when you have free time at home?"

"No." Jack's initial declaration that he liked school would have been more convincing if he had listed some activities here. Like Bruce and David, even children who fracture their intellectual experience can usually list authors and topics they like, or describe reasons for being absorbed with reading.

"OK." John drew a deep breath. "Are there any sort of books you like to read when you aren't in school? When it's not a school book."

"Chapter book."

"Chapter books! OK, what's good about chapter books?" For second graders, a chapter book is a book for big people and good readers. This seemed like evidence that Jack wanted to prove he was not incompetent, and perhaps even to make John think he was perfect.

"I don't know." Jack's logic seemed similar to Bruce's assertion that he wanted hard work. Jack displayed no intrinsic desire to read, and to teach him that reading can be pleasurable would be a hard sell. Additional interview questions confirmed that Jack shared the now familiar discontinuity between personal and school learning evident in many of the students with learning disabilities. Jack's lack of voice and the grayness with which he talked of the in-school and out-of-school curriculum was discouraging to think about. To close the interview, John thanked Jack and said hopefully, "You've been thinking about school quite a bit, haven't you?"

"Yeah." John was relieved to hear Jack's enthusiastic agreement.

Hindsight makes it possible to organize the aspects of Jack's experience to help you see how he undermined his ability to meet his motivational needs, and the conflicting agendas he established with his peers, at school, and at home. Jack described himself as experiencing every kind of fractured experience we could imagine. He was one confused little boy and the adults who cared for him were doing everything they could to understand the cause and cure of that confusion.

While still working to identify the ways in which Jack fractured his own experience and his interests, for example, Nancy told John, "His mother says he plays with young children in the neighborhood, and that's the only way he can find a friend. . . . You think of him as being the oldest child in this room. You see how significantly behind he is, and he's just drowning."

"Really. Drowning?" said John with surprise.

"And then I have the dilemma . . ." continued Nancy. "Is academic skill level that important? [Is that] more important than the psyche? And I say no! It's not! I care more about how he feels about himself because I feel once he starts feeling good about himself and can take control that, [he'll say,] 'Yeah, I've got some difficulties, but I can do things and learn.'

"Oh, I never told you this. Up until about a month ago, this child has been given Ritalin—since last spring—and they never told him what he was taking. They were giving him a pill each day and didn't tell him what it was for. . . . I said, 'Why are you doing this? What do you think? He thinks it's a vitamin?'" Jack continued to take Ritalin, but learned more about why from Nancy rather than his parents or the doctor who prescribed the drug.

"Yeah," John prompted with a little embarrassment and confusion.

"He has a right to know," asserted Nancy.

"Really." John knew he was not informed enough about this issue to assert an opinion.

"You have a right to validate his thinking that he has a struggle. But there . . . was no permission given to him to feel that it was a struggle and to have frustration."

Nancy presumed that Jack must have felt that he was different from others in his class and needed to have such awareness validated. She was also conscious of one of the most difficult ethical issues faced by educators—how far a teacher should take the idea that students need to be informed about the expert diagnosis of their troubles. Nancy was not about to give up her responsibility as an adult, but she presumed that her young students could face tough issues from which they are often sheltered. Nancy seemed to agree with those who labeled Jack's problem in terms of a need for affiliation rather than for enhanced self-esteem, and saw honest communication as essential for meeting that need.

"But . . . now the boy will say, 'I have to take my medicine,'" Nancy continued. Jack's sense of autonomy was preserved in at least one part of his experience.

"He takes it himself?" asked John.

"He goes to the nurse. That's another thing. He doesn't want to be pulled out of class. So it's one thing he remembers, so he's not called out." Nancy's commitment to establishing rituals that her students would think are fair meant that she noticed, and took seriously, their unique feelings. She also encouraged everyone to develop personal habits, facilitating a sense of control and voice within the collective.

To help John understand this concern, Nancy reached for the self-evaluation Jack wrote at report card time. "I don't know if you can read this writing. 'I need something. . . . More help in math.' I've been away from this," said Nancy, struggling to decipher Jack's writing. "'I need more help in geography. I don't have any friends. I need help on writing. I need more help on reading. I need help working with others. Nobody likes me in the classroom.'" What a sad vision of life in school—Jack certainly knew he was different from his peers.

"Oh boy," said John, sadly.

"'I need help following directions. I need more help on listening. I need help on. . . .' I don't know what that one is. Is that a cry or what?" said Nancy.

Two days later, Jack came up to Nancy and chattered in a much more open and personal fashion than usual. John and Nancy were puzzled about the change. Jack talked about how he did not like where he lived, and wanted to move back to Oregon, where he used to live. Jack's feelings were not happy, but he named and communicated his feelings to people who were not members of his immediate family. This was an important step away from being so preoccupied with his experience that it was impossible to see the perspectives of others.

In the second week of John's observations, during a reading comprehension assignment about worry, Nancy asked Jack, "Do you worry?"

"No," he claimed, trying to be perfect again. Nancy suggested that everyone had worries. Only then did Jack admit that he was like everyone else. John and Nancy learned that Jack worried about mixing up things in his locker, and that his brother would fall down the stairs.

"Did you say, 'I don't know,' a lot to John?" asked Nancy.

"Yes," said Jack.

"Is that a way to get out of saying anything? When you say 'I don't know,' in class, is it a way of getting out of saying your ideas?" Nancy bluntly asked Jack, in a language he could understand, if he would label his approach to life as one who seeks to avoid the solution to problems. Nancy wondered if, rather than struggle with a problem, Jack sought to "side-step" it in order to avoid defeat. Nancy sure was direct with her students, but Jack seemed to welcome that directness and appreciate the concern implied in it.

"Yes," he agreed.

Challenges and Controversies

- How far should teachers go in helping students understand their disabilities?
- When teachers receive the kind of cry for help evident in Jack's self-evaluation, what should they do with such information?
- It is common for most children in elementary school to be preoccupied with obeying rules, sometimes confusing authority's perspectives with their own. What things can caregivers do to encourage them to develop more independent reasons for being good?
- When children become preoccupied with following rules only if it is in their immediate self-interest to do so, what can caregivers do to encourage them to consider other reasons for being good?
- When children become preoccupied with impressing adults, what can caregivers do to encourage them to consider other reasons for being good?
- Establishing rituals that promote self-determination requires listening thoughtfully to students' concerns. Should teachers be explicit about such agendas?
- What can parents do to help a fearful child explore his/her impulses and concerns?
- What can teachers do to help a child who is fearful learn to relax?

"Why do you do that?" said Nancy.

"I worry I won't know anything." Jack's response had a strong ring of honesty to it. He did not seem to be trying to guess what Nancy wanted him to say.

Nancy encouraged him. "You have a brain with ideas of your own."

"I'm afraid I will forget things," admitted Jack. Jack's worry that he would forget things suggested to John that the things he was trying to learn were not his. He was not constructing ideas or opinions, but things that could be lost. After more encouragement, Jack returned to his seat and finished his assignment more competently than usual.

Jack showed evidence, albeit fleetingly, of three kinds of reasoning reflecting different levels of social and intellectual growth. At the least differentiated level, Jack could not step outside his own immediate experience well enough to imagine the perspectives of those around him. This was most evident when he collected papers and failed to see some of his peers. At a slightly more differentiated level, Jack sometimes endorsed rules as a means to the end of serving his own self-interest. Getting smart was the reason for complying with teachers' requests, for example. And, occasionally, Jack seemed concerned with the welfare of those around him, being good to please his parents and to ensure that his little brother did not fall down the stairs. In conversations with adults, Jack seemed preoccupied with deciding how to earn the most praise and/or face the least amount of challenge. He did not seem to trust that people outside his family could be genuinely interested in knowing what he thought.

Searching for Interests

It was very difficult to find themes in Jack's work that might reflect particular interests. Instead, we learned more about what made Jack fearful. When the class read *Penny-Wise,*

Fun-Foolish,[5] for example, Jack said nothing in the introductory class discussion, but when the students were sent to read the story, Jack told Nancy, "I can read this. I know a lot of answers." His comments were encouraging signs of confidence, even if Jack was simply confident that he could remember answers instead of framing questions. Something sparked his interest, and Nancy wanted to encourage that initiative.

"Jack, I want you to read these two pages and then come back and tell me what it is about." coached Nancy, who then told Derek to read with Jack. Jack was almost chirping while reading with Derek.

Nancy whispered to John that Jack's understanding was poor. John sat on the hall floor beside the two boys. Derek misread a word, and blundered on in confusion. John asked if Jack could read the word. Jack read it, but not in a tone that might help Derek. Jack also missed or ignored John's nudge to try helping next time Derek was in need. Taking a turn, Jack read blandly, more to finish the page than comprehend or savor the story.

Before Derek, Jack, and Earl finished, others moved on to self-chosen tasks. Jean read a book on Martin Luther King, Jr. Ted recorded his version of King's life. Jill and Beth drew and wrote a booklet titled *Our Pets.* Beth had propped her journal up on her desk, with her troll doll inside it: Inside this cozy enclosure, she drew a portrait of her doll.

Nancy shortened the boys' assignment to help them find time for similar pleasurable tasks by asking them to choose only one question to write about. Checking progress, she encouraged, "Hey, you chose the hard question." The change allowed the three slower students to finish at about the same time as the last clump of students who were not given extra assistance.

Nancy's sensitivity to students' need for free time, regardless of their abilities, meant that she monitored students' progress more closely than John would have imagined when he wondered about whether to give students easier work or to expect them to keep up with others. All of Nancy's students did normatively difficult work, even if they did not all do the same quantity. Nancy also had an easy-going tone to her voice that comforted rather than embarrassed students who needed their assignment modified.

When the class became critics of the book, Jack initially joined the group with positive reviews. Then, as others crossed over into the group with negative reviews, Jack followed. When asked for his review, Jack simply said, "Boring." Given his monotonous reading style, it was not surprising that Jack could find no delight in this story. But, at least Jack asserted his opinion.

After the critiques, when Nancy asked students about their photo album topics, Jack's topic was "My dog."

"What things about it?" prodded Nancy.

"Taking it for a walk."

"Anything else?" encouraged Nancy.

"Playing. Throwing balls." Jack painted a vision of himself and his dog, comfortably playing in a park.

Jack's desire for a relatively quiet, comfortable life was also evident when something in the discussion prompted him to talk of a shark's head in a friend's basement. "There are rats and mousetraps in the basement. That's why you can't go in there." Jack spoke with more than his usual intensity—a spark of daring. Was Jack ready for an adventurous visit to the dark side of life? Sharing this vision of where "you can't go," Jack's

Challenges and Controversies

- How can caregivers help children who claim to have no intellectual interests discover meaningful topics to think about?
- How can teachers identify students' interests?
- Is it necessary to modify the curriculum to help students like Jack, who do not engage in social comparison, identify new interests?
- When adults notice themes in the activities that attract children's attention, is it useful to encourage children to notice those themes?
- How can caregivers help children connect their reasons for being good with their intellectual interests?
- Can caregivers teach children to look for interests by comparing their ideas with the ideas of others? Should they?

excitement seemed out of character, but his cautious choice of avoiding action was not. John hoped that this story offered early evidence of underground currents in Jack's sense of adventure. This impression was reinforced nine weeks later when Nancy asked what kinds of books students wanted to read. Jack said, "Mysteries."

"What kind Jack?" asked Nancy.

"Scary ones," asserted Jack. Typically withdrawn, Jack was not entirely disinterested in experiencing a thrill of adventure.

During the math and spelling tests, Jack revealed a rather methodical approach to the task. After everyone had their booklets, Nancy called out page numbers for students to find. Working to keep himself pointed at the target, Jack circled each page number as it was announced. When Nancy was finished, John asked Jack, "I saw you put circles. . . ."

"Oh, oh," Jack muttered, as if caught doing evil.

"Around the page numbers. Did someone give you that idea?"

"No," said Jack, timidly.

"That's a real good idea," encouraged John. "Did you think of it yourself?"

"Yes," Jack responded. John could not tell if Jack was being truthful or if he was merely trying to be agreeable. Jack's assumption that he had done wrong again suggested that, in the dualistic world of good and bad, Jack wanted to be judged good.

Discovering Jack's interests was an inordinately difficult task. His assumption that adults engaged in a form of ridicule by asking questions established boundaries that were very difficult to penetrate. Despite the variety of ways in which the adults in Jack's life sought to encourage him, Jack did not grant himself permission to imagine topics of interest.

Searching for Meaningful Friendships

Jack's defensive stance and unwillingness to reveal his intellectual interests made it difficult to develop the kind of comfortable peer relationships that he coveted. Nevertheless,

Nancy looked for opportunities to encourage Jack to interact with his classmates. One day early in the year, for example, Nancy suggested that two students who asked her for help on an assignment should ask Jack. The students were surprised, but went to him. Jack looked paralyzed and held his paper to his chest. With Nancy encouraging, Jack gingerly peeled the paper off his chest and showed what he did. Jack's sense of egocentrism worked two ways: He did not notice the needs or expectations of his classmates and assumed that, likewise, they did not notice him.

On January 21, Nancy heard that Jack had a new friend. It was Arleigh's mother who called to arrange for the two boys to play. Arleigh was socially and academically competent and assured. This was an exciting breakthrough in helping Jack achieve his goal of finding friends. The boys were often together, and Jack was obviously happy.

The topic of manners came up during one class discussion and Nancy asked, "Why are they important?"

In turn, Jack suggested, "If someone burps out, they are disturbing someone," a comment that certainly reflected an awareness of other people's needs. After lunch, during show and tell, Nancy asked if more people had things to share. As children volunteered, Jack called "Arleigh. Arleigh," pointing to his new friend.

Encouraging as these events seem, it would be unrealistic to assume that this new social interest replaced Jack's tendency toward egocentrism. Later that day, for example, Nancy held up symbols students had made to represent their country. There was much ingenuity, and most of the children explained their symbols well. Jack's symbol, however, was a fuzzy spectrum of colors with no discernible form. When asked to explain, he said, "Red, white, and blue." Nancy might have asked for more, but did not want to put Jack on the spot. She let Jack's turn pass without comment, ignoring Jack's inability to consider his audience when speaking.

At the end of this second week, Jack's Ritalin dose was increased, and Nancy was asked to monitor his behavior. The effects were not obvious to Nancy, but Jack's behavior was in marked contrast to that of Shane, a gregarious and lively newcomer to the class who was also on Ritalin. Shane had moved to a house near Jack's. The adults in Jack's life hoped that Jack's tree fort would help him gain Shane's friendship and sought ways to encourage the boys' interest in one another.

Shortly after this introduction the class moved into math groups, and Jack and Shane raced across the room to the last chair at their table. They arrived together. Jack held his own, and finally won the chair. Nancy and John exchanged hopeful glances—not the manners Jack spoke of earlier, but some spunky initiative.

Later, Nancy said that if Jack really came out of his shell, we should expect to see some inappropriate behavior before he found ways to be himself *and* fit in with his peers. But, for every sign that Jack's social self was emerging there was one that he was in retreat.

During a class discussion with the social worker on friendship, Jack said nothing. The social worker had brought the results of a survey that Nancy's students had taken and lead a lively discussion on increasing friendship and reducing conflict. The discussion moved on, completely missing the plight of the neglected, invisible Jack whose friendship with Arleigh by then had floundered. John asked students to voluntarily reach out to people whom no one wanted to have for a buddy. As John spoke, Jack suddenly looked squarely at him. Jack's unusually direct, intense gaze was startling to see. It was as if he was about to be saved from a permanent state of torment.

As the group broke for snacks, the social worker suggested that they might look for buddies, and there were sounds of agreement. Earl, Derek, Fred, and a few other boys played music and bounced around loudly. Most of the children were busy, but Jack was flotsam—looking lost and as if he were waiting for a friend to materialize. Jack kept glancing toward Nancy and John, as they struggled to imagine who might rescue him. Jack drifted to his accustomed place, invisible behind those at the computer.

Nancy asked quiet, sweet Tom—a newcomer to the class—to make a friend of Jack. Tom approached and exhausted his few words speaking to the unresponsive Jack. Tom stood there awkwardly, beside Jack who stood glancing at the computer screen and around the room. Tom did not concede the rebuff, but seemed stumped about what to do next.

Nancy swept over toward the boys. She grabbed a bag of blocks and then the uncomfortable pair. "You want to play with these!" Nancy's approach worked. The boys played with the blocks on the rug. Jack looked over his shoulder in our direction twice, then got into the blocks as others joined.

After gym, Nancy asked the class to write about what they thought of the discussion with the social worker and of what came of it. Tom wrote, "*It was fun playen with Jack. me and Jack were board at first but then we got blocks and had fun*!"

Later, Nancy showed Jack what Tom had written. Jack did not want to look, but Nancy persisted until Jack saw and acknowledged that someone enjoyed being with him.

Arleigh had written, "*My friend Jack tells others that I said bad things about them.*" Arleigh had also raised this frustration in the discussion, and Jack had squirmed and tried to silence Arleigh.

In the corridor, John found a way to ask Arleigh if he knew why Jack did this, and Arleigh admitted that he did not. John suggested that Jack had no friends and might have been trying to keep Arleigh for himself. Arleigh nodded but said, "That won't work. Jack has to realize that I'm still his friend even if I have other friends." John suggested that Jack had difficulty understanding this. Arleigh was most agreeable, but seemed not to comprehend Jack's possessiveness. John complimented Arleigh on his understanding nature and mentioned how he helped Jack.

At recess, Jack hung on the rail of the steps while most of the boys zoomed around playing football. He had a part-time friend from another class who also hung there, but the two boys did not talk much.

Despite changes in Jack's relationships with his peers, he still avoided adults whenever possible. Hanging around at the end of the day, for example, John said to Jack, "Garfield!" referring to pictures on his lunch box. "No," Jack corrected John. Jack turned the box around and completely killed off John's attempt to connect, making John feel uncomfortable. Nancy mentioned that she found it more difficult to make a connection with Jack than almost anyone she had ever taught. Jack's first grade teacher had also said that it was almost as if he had forgotten being in her classroom: She had difficulty obtaining eye contact or any friendly acknowledgment when she saw Jack. Adults were to be obeyed, but not welcomed.

Two days later, at the beginning of the day, Jack came in with *The Guinness Book of Records.*[6] He flipped through, obviously interested. "Derek! Derek!" Jack called, but Derek shook his head and turned away. Ignored as usual, Jack turned and talked with the amiable Shane. Whereas Quiet Bird had an artistic imagination that helped him determine what was important, Jack had no comparable perspective. If Jack came up with something others did not like, he assumed that he had done something wrong.

Jack's emerging social networks remained tenuous. This was obvious when Nancy asked students to organize themselves into groups while studying rain forests. Specializing in different levels of the rain forest, students decorated the walls, reaching almost to the ceiling. Jack hoped to work with Fred and Shane, but they said, "Go away!" when he sat beside them. Such meanness was typical of Fred, but Shane usually accepted Jack. As Jack moved off, John suggested to Fred and Shane that Jack needed encouragement from them. It was encouraging to see Jack return, push up beside them, and persist.

Later, John approached Jack and Shane in the hall. Jack said, "We don't need help. We don't need help." None of the other children ever said anything like this when John approached them. Was Jack doing unto others as had been done unto him? Did he think that John's presence had something to do with the fact that his peers rejected him? Or, was Jack aware that John had intervened and hoped to regain a bit more autonomy in how he related to his friends?

Not long after this exchange, Jack drifted away from Shane and Fred, keeping invisible. Unfortunately, John saw no way to encourage Jack without seeming to violate Jack's request not to intrude in his silent, isolated world. John was encouraged when during gym, Jack was more active than the first time John had watched him. Nevertheless, Jack's activities were still rarely connected to the activities of others.

Following gym, students worked in groups to prepare plays. Shane appealed to the formerly rejected Jack, "Jack you can be in it right now."

"I don't want to," Jack said defiantly before drifting off.

When Jack did try for inclusion, his attempts were generally not very effective. One day before school began, when football cards were the focus of discussion, Jack came up to a little group clustered around a deck. Jack burbled something that was barely acknowledged by the others. Because Jack started talking before he had anyone's attention, it was hard to tell what he was saying. Jack looked quizzical, and moved to the margin of the group.

Jack's behavior was in stark contrast to the larger, bull-in-a-china-shop Fred who joined the group shortly after Jack moved. Fred barreled up to the group calling, "Hey guys!" as he approached and gained everyone's attention by the time he arrived at the group. Yet, even if Jack had gained the boys' attention, he would not have been able to do much with it. Too often Jack's only message was "I want to be included." To join a conversation, one must have something to contribute.

Jack's egocentrism in relating to his peers was also evident later, when he chattered to John and the very open and accepting Fiona. Jack spoke of having play-fights with Shane at home—throwing soft toy animals between top and bottom bunks. Jack's story was triggered by the toy animals brought in to help populate the forest, not from anything said by those who were listening to him: He showed no interest in hearing from John or Fiona. Fiona, who often told John things about her life and asked about his life, was happy to listen to Jack, but did not challenge his fundamentally disconnected chatter.

As Jack began to establish relationships with his peers, moving out of his typically withdrawn state, his behavior was not entirely constructive. As Nancy put it, coming out of his shell, Jack was likely to become a bit wild for a while. "Cleaning out his locker, I found some of my papers, and one of my books," explained Nancy. "The other day, I found him hiding one of my books under his shirt. His mother told me she found a rock with a label on it [which Nancy had been looking for]. Now he is coming out and being a bit more active. . . . He might take things to have a piece of someone—a piece of the classroom. His mother saw it as bad—it could harm him socially." No doubt, at the very least, this could have adverse effects on Jack's ability to make and sustain friends.

Nancy also found Jack carrying off a novel she was reading to the class. "I'll never do it again in my whole life"; Jack delivered, what became for him, a common line when caught. Jack behaved as if absolute evil, in the form of all of his own impulses, must be absolutely stamped out. Nancy said she'd find a copy of the novel for Jack to have. Why didn't he simply ask?

Jack's expression when he stole things from his peers suggested that he enjoyed being bad. Yet, when he played with objects belonging to other students, he had a tone of playing at being bad rather than wholly being evil. To Jack, adults rather than his peers were the custodians of good and of evil. His peers were the feared arbiters of social and intellectual competence. They could become accomplices, but could not offer satisfactory responses to his "bad" impulses.

In a contradictory way of seeking intimacy, Jack expressed himself by misbehaving and doing mean things, but spent a lot of energy hiding many of these impulses. No teacher could help Jack gain what he wanted, because Jack knew that teachers did not promote the evil that interested him. Acting on impulse, the book had to be stolen from the teacher rather than borrowed. Nancy's patience with this emerging sense of identity eventually led Jack to begin publicly acknowledging his "evil" impulses, including his dislike of schoolwork.

Sadly, the emergence of Jack's identity in class came about slowly and was not fully resolved by the end of the school year. As May progressed, Jack often came in first thing in the morning, sat down, and chattered with Shane, Arleigh, or Ben. But when Allan said to other children sitting nearby, "Want to go to a party at my place?" Jack was not included. Jack kept himself busy at his desk and was soon discussing basketball and the virtues of B. J. Armstrong (of the Chicago Bulls) with Ben. It was difficult to tell if Jack had heard about the party that he was not invited to attend.

When Nancy asked, "Let's see. What topic should we write about [to practice paragraphs for a State test]?"

"Rain forest," called Jack, first with his suggestion—a sign of legitimate initiative. Later discussions, and the fact that a week earlier Jack had brought a book to school on the topic, confirmed that this was a topic he enjoyed. Jack's paragraph was not indented, but his printing was unusually clear. If he had heard Allan's insult, Jack did not let it interfere with his work on rain forests, as would likely have happened earlier in the school year.

Coming back from music, however, Jack asked Allan, "Am I coming to your party?" He had heard the conversation.

"No," said Allan and walked on without glancing at Jack.

Rather than sulk or withdraw as he might have done, Jack sought opportunities to help Allan get to know him better. In free time, for example, Jack moved to sit by Allan and others in a small group. Jack persisted, reasonably comfortable on the fringe of the group, and was not willing to allow his peers to exclude him. Jack was no social star, but he showed some competence and initiative.

Other indications of greater connections between Jack's relationships were evident when Jack began to tell classmates that John visited his house. It took most of the year for Jack to let others see connections between his personal and school lives without feeling strange or incompetent. Arleigh, who talked easily with John throughout the year, often telling John which of the second graders' ideas should be recorded, wanted to know why John could not visit *his* house. What better way to alleviate some of Jack's self-consciousness?

Jack's greater ease with and acceptance by classmates was also evident in Jack's writing about his experience in second grade. As an end-of-year activity, Nancy suggested headings for organizing a collection of statements about what students gained and the advice they would give to others. One heading was friendship. Not many of the students listed particular friends, but Derek wrote, "*I have lots of friends lik Shane, Earl, Arleigh, Allan, Jack.*" Furthermore, Fred, who was initially ready to scorn the weak, listed nine of the twelve boys in the class, including Jack, as friends.

Jack remained far from troublesome, but his "evil" impulses were more openly displayed. Shane, who was warned twice not to interrupt a discussion, again loudly interrupted. Jack nudged children who were sitting by him and conveyed a look to Shane of conspiratorial glee. Rejecting Jack's "bad boy" conspiracy, Shane ignored him and was the more genuine free spirit, unable to contain his excitement about schoolwork.

When unable to find boys who enjoyed being bad, Jack usually coped with his problems by withdrawing. In his withdrawn state, Jack made it difficult for others to determine his interests, preferences, and feelings about himself. When that was his only approach to relationships, Jack made it difficult for his peers to get to know him. Jack's angry and sometimes coercive tactics (e.g., stealing and lying) undermined opportunities to attain the intimacy that he seemed to long for when complaining to Nancy that he didn't have any friends.

Challenges and Controversies

- Children are more comfortable in classrooms where they feel they have friends. How far should teachers go in helping children find friends and learn how to sustain friendship?
- Sustaining friendships requires individuals to assert a consistent identity. How can caregivers help children who are impulsive see the confusion they cause by behaving unpredictably?
- How can caregivers help children see that future exchanges with peers are affected by their responses in immediate situations?
- Should caregivers help children see the value of exchange in friendship before responding to their intimacy orientations?
- When teachers notice children stealing and lying, at what point does it become important to intervene?
- Drawing out impulses in a child who is withdrawn may lead to the discovery of mean ideas as often as gentle ones. What parameters should teachers place on such forms of self-expression?

By the end of the year, Jack's behavior was impulsive and unpredictable, but easy to see. Jack often found it easier to speak to adults rather than a classroom audience of his peers. Adults established rules and consistently enforced them in ways that Jack could understand. It was a sign of progress to notice that Jack was responding to his peers rather than withdrawing from them, yet he still remained unaware of how his immediate behavior affected the quality of future exchanges. However, Jack's responsiveness was inconsistent. In one situation, Jack would stand tall in the face of overt rejection. In the next, he would crumble and withdraw into an isolated world. This instability made it difficult for his peers to recognize who Jack was, essential for imagining how to sustain a satisfying exchange relationship with him.

Adults can overlook inconsistent behavior more easily than children. Nevertheless, children like Jack cannot rely solely on the acceptance of adults. They eventually have to find similar acceptance from their peers.

Connected Experience in Competition with Discrete Skills

Jack's difficulty in considering the perspectives of his peers and helping them to imagine his identity required some of the same skills necessary for doing his schoolwork. Aware of this parallel, John and Nancy looked for ways to assist Jack in seeing the entire task before him. They challenged his tendency to remain fixated on only one facet of an assignment. They hoped that by helping Jack meet his need for affiliation, he might also develop greater competence. For this agenda to work, however, Jack also had to show greater levels of self-determination than he often exhibited in class.

The following sequence of events, narrated by Nancy into an audiotape recorder immediately after it happened, illustrates the kind of egocentric thinking that is common among children like Jack who have difficulty giving up a heteronomous orientation to inquiry.

> They were able to choose any [animal] they wanted [for the rain forest]. Shane [an elephant fanatic] wanted to do an elephant. Jack, next to him, wants to do an elephant. . . . Jack made something that had no semblance of an elephant, and asked, "Does this look like an elephant?" I said, "Well maybe it needs some legs."
>
> Shane's was a very simple . . . good representation of an elephant. So . . . I said, "Shane is going to teach you and me." Jack immediately did one little circle. I stopped him and I said, "Lets turn the paper over and look at how big his circle is, and look where it is placed on the paper." Shane had to hold his hand, and he made one circle. Shane said, 'Great. That does look like my elephant. Now it needs some eyes.' Jack put two eyes, whereas Shane's had one. Shane explained. Jack didn't get it, so Shane took the pencil and made the thing one-eyed. Then instead of looking at Shane's drawing, he made an ear that stuck up on top of the elephant. Shane said, no the ear doesn't stick up.

> [When, after more of this, they had a recognizable drawing] Shane said, "Now you sit down and cut it out." He was able to cut out the tail, but totally separated the head from the body: Didn't realize what he did. Shane is saying, "Look what you did." I don't know whether he doesn't focus enough to realize what he is doing or had no idea how the parts connect.
>
> Now I'm coming back into the room. I want to see what Jack is doing. He's hiding behind a chair. He has his elephant . . . taped back together, and it does resemble an elephant.
>
> I told Jack he had to make something else so we decide on a snake. I put him beside Fiona. He said, "I know how to do my own." I said, "No, I want you to sit down and look at something in a book." And so he sat next to her and looked at hers. . . . Drew his own snake. Not a great drawing, but it does resemble something. And he came to me and said, "I did it. Snakes are easy to do." He seemed pleased with something that he is able to handle. Maybe that's the problem. Maybe it is just getting it to the level of what he can handle.

Jack's lack of focus should not be attributed to a lack of effort. Typically, Jack came to school in a cheerful mood and went right to work, but his reasons for learning seemed to be someone else's. When others talked about Friday at school, Jack reminded them that there was no school on Friday. He knew what page he was on. He knew when there were five minutes left before he went to the resource room, speech teacher, or social worker. His schedule was complicated, and in following that schedule he seemed to exhibit none of the difficulties commonly found among children with ADD. Yet, all Jack's powers of concentration seemed to be caught up in adhering to this schedule. Sadly, Jack rarely had his own reasons for doing the "right" thing in any of these places.

After a series of conversations between the specialists who worked with Jack, his parents, Nancy, and John, the adults agreed that it might be best for Jack if some of the special services he needed were suspended until he could build comfortable relationships in Nancy's classroom. The adults also looked for opportunities to help Jack overcome his fear of talking in front of his peers.

Jack's peers seemed willing to go along with this invisible action plan. Students worked on autobiographies that they later presented to the class. When it was Jack's turn, he went up easily enough. "This is a book when I was a baby. This is my family tree. These are places I visited." Jack had a map with names of states and cities. "Homes I have lived in. Foods I like. What I want to be when I grow up—a computer salesman. There are pictures when I was a baby. That's all."

"You have lots of writing stuff in the back," Nancy added. "Did you do all the drawing?"

"Yes."

"It's quite nice."

"What I want to know," said Arleigh, "is why you put a lot of pictures in there?" Jack did not respond.

"To decorate it," said Shane, speaking for his shy friend.

"Like, I didn't ask you," said Arleigh. "I wanted to know what he thought."

"To decorate it," repeated Jack.

With Shane's help, Jack's fear of questions disappeared and he fielded others in a relaxed fashion. Jack seemed to feel a high degree of private self-consciousness wherein his sense of competence in testlike situations was easily undermined and his nervous affective state dictated his response to his peers. When he felt uncomfortable, he behaved in an awkward manner, but when he felt confident, he could field questions as easily as any of his peers.

John was sitting at the table where students put their autobiographies after they presented them to the class. Jack came over to put his book away. "You can read it," Jack told John proudly. He clearly hoped that John would take extra time to look at this work. Jack chatted with John in fine style, similar to his posture in the photos of a younger him, smiling with cousins and playing with his now grown puppy. These moods highlighted the sadness of Jack's more recent struggles with life in the second grade. Jack had written seven and a half pages of text in his large printing, in answer to questions, proposed by Nancy and put to his Mom and other family members, about what he was like when he was little. Jack's readiness to show and talk of his past suggested that he was learning to feel comfortable as a peer group member. Here was another indication that Jack's personal experience was becoming more legitimate in his own eyes and less alien to life in school.

Several days later, Mrs. Davis told John that she had asked Jack to tell her what he wanted to write. She wrote it, and then Jack copied her writing. "That seems to be easier for him than trying to think of it and write it at the same time. . . . He's real proud of it. Even last night he brought it out. That was a fun thing." Although this structure would ultimately have to be replaced with one that required an integration of thought and writing, everyone was delighted with Jack's ability to find meaning in a school project.

But, Jack had difficulty moving beyond this interest in his personal history and connecting with other activities. During the trip to Shedd Aquarium, for example, Jack did not get absorbed in anything except, briefly, the videotape on great white sharks that entranced many of his peers: moving pictures of fish rather than real fish. He zipped from place to place without settling on one thing long enough to get absorbed. Others busily talked to one another about their discoveries, but Jack rarely showed or was shown anything. During the sit-down-and-listen lesson on fish, Jack looked back toward Nancy, John, and the other adults so regularly that he could hardly have followed a thing.

A few days later, sitting across from Allan, Jack did seat work very slowly. He slyly pulled off a paper that Allan had taped to his desk. Reading intently, Allan did not notice, but Jack noticed John and gave an impish grin.

Nancy said, "I'm coming around to see if your word list is done."

"I'm not. I'm not," called Jack, but rather than work, he talked to Shane who was finished. Jack was not his usual, extrinsically driven self, and showed no desire for schoolwork. He adopted an occasional "bad boy" guise and moved from messing with Allan's desk to his folder. In return, Allan showed Jack a clawed fist.

As the class corrected the assignment, Jack did not follow. When Nancy called on him he managed to give correct answers, but Jack was more interested in Allan's eraser that dropped to the floor. With a big stretch, Jack pulled the eraser toward his own desk. Jack left the eraser under his seat for a moment, then picked it up, and put it on the table behind him.

"I found it," Jack whispered, when he noticed John watching. Jack's spunkiness was encouraging. Yet, as Nancy had suggested earlier, Jack would probably be on the wild side for a little while before he fully came out of his shell.

That same day, the class began reading a story on a family called the Littles, who were mouse-sized. Earl and Jack were asked to work together thinking and drawing a house they might own or where they might live. Jack suggested a tree house, but when Nancy asked if termites would present a problem, he replaced the tree house with a cave. Earl drew a mouse hole.

"You need to think of more ideas," suggested Nancy.

"I can help, I can help," said Earl. "I'm gonna help someone else."

"You come up with an idea; then help someone else," said Nancy, encouraging Jack and Earl to discuss their ideas. Jack asked how Earl's little people would get in the refrigerator.

"Maybe there's a crack," said Earl, confidently.

"What will you do if there's a cat?" challenged Jack. He challenged Earl in the same way Nancy had challenged him.

"Cats are dumb," said Earl.

"What if you were in the hole and the cat came in there?" Jack would not be put off.

"You could frighten the cat away with fire."

Jack was surprisingly talkative, and Nancy encouraged him. It became surprisingly easy to make eye contact with Jack, and he looked right into Earl's eyes as he spoke to him.

Unfortunately, this surge in self-assurance was not consistent. The social worker told John and Nancy that, when talking to her, Jack was full of information about a visit to Yellowstone. However, when Catherine suggested that Jack share the details in show-and-tell, Jack declared he was confused, and that it was his father who went to Yellowstone. Jack's mother confirmed that Jack had not lied about his visit to Yellowstone, and agreed to send Jack to school with a prop that could make talking easier. Nothing came of this, however. Mrs. Davis made several attempts to send Jack to school with props, but the objects disappeared or failed to emerge from Jack's bag.

Nancy also found ways to encourage Jack. When the class tried problems in a new math book the school was reviewing for possible adoption the next year, Nancy looked at Jack's progress. "Ring the one that's larger. Very good! Now which is larger? Atta boy! Now keep going." Jack enticed adults into coaching and nudging to help him keep up, but it was rare to find occasions to tell Jack, "You are really figuring things out, really thinking."

Two days later, Jack came up to Nancy. "I have a question. I don't understand how this page works." Nancy explained and Jack was ready to rush off. Holding Jack back, Nancy questioned Jack to see if he understood her explanation and discovered that he had not understood a word. Nancy described the task again and Jack responded, "OK. Now I see." Fortunately, after the second explanation, Jack understood.

Nancy became more assertive, but affectionate, when encouraging Jack. During an experiment on seed growing, she kept trying to focus Jack's attention to keep him drifting around the room. "Have you watered it?" Nancy asked. Jack started writing, stopped, erased, and then started over.

"What are you going to write?" asked Nancy.

"I planted seeds," Jack said as he wrote it.

"Did you put water in?" probed Nancy.

"No," said Jack.

"What are you going to write?" cued Nancy.

"I didn't put water in?" Jack wrote that. Nancy left and Jack started erasing what he had written. John asked Jack to explain his behavior. Jack did not answer. John suggested that Jack just add more to his narrative if he wanted to change things. Only after John's suggestion did Jack copy over the writing he had erased, resurrecting his ideas.

Nancy reappeared. "Why did you go back and erase this? What else did you have to write?"

Jack was silent. Then, he quietly said, "I forgot."

"No. I don't accept 'I forgot,'" coached Nancy.

Nancy knew that Jack had gained confidence in his own judgment, but here it fluctuated. Jack could be quite assertive when he understood his work. When the class was looking at a math page requiring a choice of figures to illustrate the concept of half, for example, Nancy asked, "Jack, did you circle the second one?"

"Yes"

"Why?"

"It's the same as the picture," Jack said confidently.

"How?" Nancy challenged.

"Its [halves are] equal [as in the standard]." Jack was quite self-assured in this exchange.

"You know what he did?" Nancy addressed the class. "He looked at the example to see how it's done. Some kids don't think to do that. Good thinking."

A major turning point in this rather frustrating cycle of explanation and misunderstanding seemed to occur when the class began reading Patricia Reilly Giff's novel, *The Beast in Ms. Rooney's Room.*[7] Ironically, the hero was called Richard Best, sharing the same name as the school's principal.

"Can you think of one interesting thing about Richard Best?" Nancy asked the class. She called on Jack.

"He doesn't listen," said the boy who declared listening important and a valuable way to learn. Breaking the rules appeared to make Richard Best seem interesting to Jack. Did finding a storybook character who felt as he did help Jack acknowledge some of his "evil" impulses? No observer can really know, but the change in Jack's behavior certainly suggests this possibility.

"How do you think that affects his schoolwork?" asked Nancy.

"He doesn't do it," said Jack quickly.

In the book, Richard faced the prospect of being held back. Knowing that this might be a concern for her students, Nancy asked, "How do you think he'd feel?"

"Upset," said Jack.

"Why?"

"He wouldn't know anyone in the class."

"What else would he feel?"

"I can't think of any more."

Nancy persisted, and Jack said, "Sad."

"Why?"

"Because maybe they mixed him up [got him in the wrong grade.]" Jack focused on forces outside himself in a way that suggested that he felt helpless and avoided issues of personal responsibility. With Nancy's prodding, however, Jack spoke of his own experience as well as that of Richard.

Working to help Jack differentiate his feelings with those of story characters, Nancy suggested to Jack that he take home his journal and write about the coming visit of his cousin that he talked about so eagerly.

"They aren't coming till Friday," he said.

"You can still think and write about it."

"OK." But, the next day Jack was sick and that topic got lost. Jack was not ready to fully share his own emotions. He did not entirely avoid talk about feelings, but Nancy had to be satisfied with the progress evident in his class participation. In the next class discussion on the continuing exploits of Richard Best, Jack had his hand up to contribute.

"Jack, why do you think he doesn't like school?"

"He always gets in trouble."

"That's a good observation," said Nancy, still trying to find constructive ways to draw out Jack's feelings.

Talking about feelings rather than avoiding them seemed to be getting easier for Jack. A week earlier, for example, as the class left to attend a show put on by first graders, Nancy asked about appropriate behavior for members of an audience. First off the mark, Jack said, "Not laugh at them."

The book discussion turned to special services. Fortunately, most second graders are not fully aware of the fact that extra effort on tasks reflects limited ability. They reveal little embarrassment when admitting a need for special help and can sustain higher levels of task involvement than older students. Erica started this tangent by saying, "Me and Colleen and Derek go to reading and we don't get teased. Even if we did, I'd still want to go."

"Why?" asked Nancy.

"I want to read. It helps me read new words. We help each other, and she helps us." Erica seemed to have a pretty strong task orientation.

"I get teached my ABCs," added Earl. "I don't know why. And she [the reading specialist] helps me with math."

Derek added more details about special reading sessions that he shared with Erica.

"Gee, you guys are lucky," said Fred who, earlier in the year, would have denigrated any sign of weakness.

As Nancy read more about Richard Best's adventures, Jack moved close and followed intently. Closing the session, Nancy asked, "How many of you think reading is fun, that there's an adventure in books?" Jack looked around and saw many hands up before raising his.

Over the next few weeks, the class continued to read the series about Richard Best and his trials in school. Sometimes Nancy read, but more often, pairs of students read and then wrote in their journals. "Take out your journals," said Nancy. "You will be sharing one book. Two chapters . . . Richard Best again. *Lazy Lions, Lucky Lambs.*"[8]

Jack happily worked with Kate, taking turns reading. Before asking the class to write in their journals, Nancy went to Allan, Earl, Jack, and Kate reading at the back of the room. "Tell me how things are for Richard Best now. Jack?"

"He didn't get in too much trouble." Jack's theme of trouble was emerging again.

Nancy sought to clarify Jack's meaning by discussing school rules. She wondered if horsing around in the snow the way Richard and his friend did would be against Sprague's rules. "I wrote that he made a friend," said Earl.

"If you want to show me you have an understanding of this story what would you write?" asked Nancy.

Jack wrote something and then erased it.

"He had made a friend," said Earl. "He went to the principal."

Jack wrote, "*He mad a friend.*"

While the discussion moved to the topic of siblings, Jack stole a pencil out of Ben's desk. Ted nudged Ben to indicate that something was up. Ben looked in his desk, then at Jack who, with a smile, offered up the pencil. Jack's conduct was hardly conducive to making a friend, but suggested levels of disengagement that were parallel to those evident in the stories about Richard Best. Despite his greater involvement in the prosocial dimensions of class discussions, Jack had not given up his "bad boy" tricks and seemed delighted to read about a child with similar interests. Jack probably knew that stealing was wrong and was capable of the kind of empathy necessary for understanding the harm he caused. Yet, stealing and lying offered evidence that Jack had difficulty regulating his emotional life. He found physical ways of showing us that he rejected rules.

In the story, Richard Best did not ask questions. "Why might a kid not want to ask questions? Jack?"

"They [students] might make fun of him." Jack's themes were persistent. His competence needs could be met by impressing his peers, not teachers. Unlike individuals who expressed ego-involvement by acting superior, Jack's version involved avoiding the appearance of incompetence.

"I think you have a good point there," said Nancy. She described how even teachers might have such feelings.

"Everyone needs help," commented Shane, but Jack had already been distracted by another book.

Later, Jack wrote in his journal, "I like that part when he got . . ." and stalled, whereas Derek wrote a whole paragraph. Hearing about Richard Best's exploits seemed to give Jack a voice for expressing his feelings, but Jack's voice still lacked strength.

Two days later, the Richard Best book was finished and everyone was making journal entries. Nancy talked with Jack. "I like to read about kids that get in trouble," said the boy who was learning how to be bad.

"Why is that?" asked Nancy.

"I don't know," Jack hesitated. "I can't think."

"Yes you can. Why is it?"

"'Cause I learn words," said the boy-who-must-be-good.

"You could read about worms and learn words doing that. Is this different?" Nancy hoped she could help Jack admit his interest in being bad.

"Because it is interesting," Jack said, ignoring the request to consider worms.

"What is interesting about it?" said Nancy.

"It is funny."

"Get that down." Nancy coached Jack to write these thoughts in his journal.

Eagerly Jack wrote more fluently and with greater clarity than usual—the underground bad boy began to appear on paper: "*I like the part when He got in tribol . . . I like when he snak ut of reading class [to go to the bathroom] Because he Dosnt like to read. I Like kids hou get in triodel [trouble]. . . .*" This sneaky, devilish side of Jack was coming out in public as legitimate.

"Look how much I have," Jack told Shane, showing his journal. This kind of pride was new, but began a pattern that continued for the rest of the academic year. Jack often showed his work in an amiable rather than a competitive way to Arleigh, Shane, and sometimes others, even when he had done relatively little.

Perhaps emboldened by the stories of Richard Best, in the last ten days of the year, Jack twice told John that he would rather not do particular school tasks. Jack's open defiance was not the best possible news, but it was perhaps better than his initially dutiful, but empty declarations that all school tasks were valuable. As Nancy had said, Jack was a child who needed to emerge. "Then, we are going to see what Jack Davis is about." When Jack accepted a feeling that the "stuff" he had been making himself finish was not what he wanted to do, there would have to be new groundwork constructed to help him see the value of schoolwork. Unfortunately, the year was ending and the negotiation of comfortable relationships would have to begin all over again in the third grade.

When responding to Nancy's request for advice to the next year's second graders, Jack drew a surprisingly forceful looking jet plane, but then stalled. When Nancy asked Jack to explain his drawing, it seemed that he had drawn a plane because the idea of a flying schoolroom had come up in discussion. Jack had no clear idea of how his school would function. In response to Nancy's more detailed search for greater clarification, Jack said, "You learn a lot of stuff, like math. A teacher teaches you. The principal helps you not to get in trouble." Jack's commitments, to a considerable degree, are still this vision of trouble.

On May 13, the school personnel who worked with Jack met to discuss Jack's future. Lisa Fredrick, the school psychologist, seemed to have forgotten the results of a March meeting where the team of specialists working with Jack decided to simplify his schedule. They eliminated some of the services Jack received to help him build more comfortable relationships with peers.

"We did this for social reasons," Nancy reminded her, and summarized that decision process. "He is more relaxed and easier to teach. He is still a follower. He rarely brings things to discuss. He tries to make friends, but is still manipulative, and still steals."

Nancy did not have time to outline details of Jack's devious behavior. Times like the week before, when Shane, who was supposed to stay at school, went home on the bus because Jack said, "If you don't, I won't be your friend." Shane's mother, who had to leave work early to collect her son, was ready to "scotch the whole relationship." Nancy understood, but explained how serious a loss this would be for Jack, and the friendship remained preserved.

Earlier, Shane's mother had told Nancy how upset she was when the two boys thrashed a new bed of flowers to the ground. Of course, this thrashing was probably a lot of fun for the boys, but evil fun. Helping Mrs. Corrigan calm down, Nancy had reflected on the problem that Shane and Jack must have finding adventurous activity in a scrupulously neat and tidy new subdivision. But, everyone knew that Jack had a problem understanding how to be powerful, expressive, and legitimate. When Jack was powerful, his behavior was not legitimate. When he was legitimate, he behaved like a peon, withdrawn and easily bullied. In the conference, John and Nancy simply tried to convey how this problem affected Jack's learning.

"I don't know," Marty Kremer, Jack's speech teacher, told the group, "if his parents realize that he has a language problem. . . . He does have a language deficit."

"Jack's mother," said Nancy, "worries [about the fact] that he is not learning [what he could] from Alice, but sees him as more at ease in schoolwork."

"He is low in his language approach," said Miss Kremer. "I'm not sure the parents understand how low he is." Any parent, of course, would feel guilt hearing this plea for special services. Yet, as many critics of pull-out programs claim, it was sometimes difficult to discern who actually benefits from such special services. There was no concrete evidence that Jack could not learn how to approach language from Nancy just as easily as from Miss Kremer, herself.

Rather than take this stance, however, Nancy spoke about Jack's fractured personal and emotional life and how that might affect Jack's speech. And, although Nancy had previously been ambivalent about this issue, she said, "I don't see him in [separate] special education."

Nancy was referring to a proposal to create a separate, full-time special education classroom in the school. The conversation went off into discussion about the merits and drawbacks of such a plan. Alice Kay visualized herself and a group of four buddies in this separate class, with the boys spending part of each day in a regular third grade room.

"I still see him needing speech and language," said Miss Kremer.

Challenges and Controversies

- How likely is it that children with learning disabilities overlook central features of the tasks they are working on?
- How can teachers and peers assist children who overlook central features of the task without undermining their self-determination?
- Most children find it interesting to talk about their own histories. How can teachers use that interest to enhance intellectual growth?
- What can teachers do to help students whose reasons for doing schoolwork are completely extrinsic sustain commitment to tasks that offer no extrinsic rewards?
- Compare the affection Thyra offered Bruce with the affection Nancy offered Jack. How can teachers determine how much encouragement is enough?
- How can teachers monitor children's need for plain, assertive language and more subtle kinds of encouragement?
- Is it more important for children to feel comfortable in school or to ensure that they perform at grade level in all subjects?
- How can adults respond to the dualistic nature of the choice between children's need for affiliation and their need for competence? How do these responses affect children's need for self-determination?

Catherine Jamison mentioned that Jack's mother talked about how "extra-special good" Jack had become. Jack was getting up early and making his bed, dressing himself quickly, and organizing himself for school, then waiting patiently until it was time to leave. This was certainly no substitute for the thrill of whacking down flowers, John muttered to himself.

"There will have to be a lot of collaboration among the kids in the new classroom," said Nancy, persisting on the importance of affiliation. "It will have to be a group."

Later in the day, John mentioned to Nancy that she seemed to be the only person in the discussion about how to place Jack who focused on the person and his fears.

"Right," Nancy agreed.

"None of which comes up in the specialist evaluations." John was trying to help Nancy see how problematic it was to have specialists "just doing their jobs" when a boy's future was at stake. John was keenly aware of the banality of evil associated with failing to think deeply about the people affected by one's action.

"No. It's all skills," Nancy elaborated, knowingly. "We are teaching skills. It's like a workbook approach instead of a whole language approach to a kid. . . . These kids have trouble with part-whole relationships, and this is what we do to their lives."

Special services are intended to enhance a child's capacity for growth rather than reinforce feelings of incompetence. Attention-deficit disorder disrupted Jack's ability to connect the various parts of his experience, and special services sometimes offered supportive bridges. Unfortunately, because Jack fractured so many parts of his life, the number of services he received seemed to compound rather than limit his confusion. As you will see, even the adults in Jack's life had difficulty coordinating all of the issues that Jack confronted them with.

Managing Anxiety among Caregivers

The next two sections of this chapter offer a very courageous account of some typical struggles faced by parents and teachers of children with complex learning disabilities. This sequence of events reveals tension as adults struggle admirably to understand a very complex boy whose behavior was often so inconsistent that the people who cared for him most did not always see the same boy. The caregivers involved kept the welfare of Jack foremost in their minds, but Jack's inability to sustain a consistent identity at home and at school kept the adults guessing about which Jack they were imagining. No one could easily describe a Jack whom everyone knew. This made it unusually difficult for the adults in Jack's life to identify the common ground that adults in Bruce and David's lives could easily establish. The confusions in these conversations, while they are represented using the details of Jack's life, reflect confusions commonly instigated by children with attention-deficit disorder.

Tension among Jack's caregivers surfaced in the middle of March, when John was finally able to find time to meet with Jack's parents. Mr. Davis wanted to meet without Jack, limiting available times. John and the Davises had set up several meetings, but other things kept coming up. All that, combined with John's general ambivalence about picking up phones, finally led John to mail his writing to Mr. and Mrs. Davis. Receiving this writing, the Davises called the school to arrange a meeting, at about normal conference time, with everyone who worked with Jack, including John and the principal.

John called again and suggested to Mrs. Davis that he might talk with them before the meeting, with Jack there. John mentioned that Jack had said that it was uncomfortable knowing that adults were talking about him behind his back and that he worried about what things were being said. Respecting Jack's feelings, Mrs. Davis suggested the Sunday before Wednesday's conference.

Then, John and Mrs. Davis found themselves in a long, interesting phone conversation. Jack's parents had often sought expert advice at a substantial financial cost. It appeared as though they had encountered only behaviorist perspectives on how to help Jack—perspectives that had little place for such notions as voice or identity. John emphasized the controversial nature of the learning disabilities field and gently hinted that behaviorism was not the only available approach to helping Jack find more success in school.

Mrs. Davis also mentioned that she was bothered that, in John's account, Nancy asked if Jack thought his Ritalin pills were vitamins. John was not surprised by this anger and went on to note that, although Nancy spoke her mind, she also listened and could easily change her mind. The tense quality of this exchange revealed how tremendously difficult it can be to establish comfortable levels of communication between home and school for cases as complex as Jack's.

When John arrived on Sunday evening, he was relieved to find Jack perky and excited about his visit. Jack, his parents, and John talked easily. Jack contributed to the conversation in a reasonably appropriate manner and with a more pleasant demeanor than he often had at school. When John noted the difference, Mrs. Davis attributed it to the fact that Jack was on his home turf. She also noted that Jack went off Ritalin on weekends and wondered if this might also have had some effect on his mood.

Next, the adults watched Jack play a computer game. As Jack began, Mrs. Davis's stance reminded John of his own feelings when he observed Jack trying to invent something with a Styrofoam cup in the learning center: Jack made it easy for adults to cramp up with worry that he might embarrass himself. Here, he proceeded reasonably well, although when he got stuck, he ignored the relevant message on the screen, and elicited help from his father. Jack's behavior at home was similar to Bruce's general tendency to rely on adults for answers, but Jack was not as powerful an answer-extractor as Bruce had been.

Even though Jack was perky, when John asked him if things in school were fair or unfair, he did not assert an opinion. Jack was also noncommittal about going to the resource room. At home as well as at school, Jack had a limited vocabulary for describing his experience in school.

When Jack left the room, Mr. Davis wondered out loud why Jack should be more perky at home: Mr. Davis found ways to hint that perhaps Nancy was not doing something right. His suspicion and tendency to seek someone to blame paralleled Nancy's occasional concern that something strange might be happening at home. Yet, in John's role as a fly on the walls of both school and home, he saw that, despite occasional bits of mischief, Jack's behavior was generally appropriate. Jack was like boys who deliberately did things to make it hard for adults understand, almost forcing adults to react in ways that maintain the difficulties.

This fits with research findings on the development of social skills suggesting that children, as readily as adults, can be as much a part of the causal factors that maintain an uncomfortable relationship. The same adults who might have trouble relating to a child like Jack do not have this kind of trouble with other children: The parents have other children who thrived easily, and the teachers feel successful with most of their students. This success, therefore, almost inevitably leads adults to wonder if the problem is not, at least in part, caused by something in the *other* environment. Jack's withdrawn behavior presented greater challenges to everyone's understanding and patience, made suspicion and mistrust a rational response, and led his parents and teacher to continually wonder about his comfort in one another's environment. Yet, hints about where to place blame were not strong enough to warrant sustained attention, and John turned the conversation to possible directions for change.

"The one big difference we have seen," said Mr. Davis, "from first to second grade, he had a lot more friends in school. . . . He was more active, more energetic, put more into it, answered wrong, but at least he answered. . . . This year it seems like . . . it's more structured. We felt he needed more structure, but it doesn't seem like he's going to give a wrong answer, or. . . ."

"Or any answer," John agreed with Mr. Davis's hint that a sense of private self-consciousness had begun to dominate Jack's outlook on life.

"He seems very self-conscious, just overly self-conscious. Not at home," added Mrs. Davis.

"Well, you got a bit just now—he was asking you for answers on the computer," John reminded them.

"Right," agreed Mr. Davis. "He didn't want to make a mistake in front of us, I guess."

John described Nancy's efforts to encourage Jack to define his own tasks. Nancy recently gave Jack a book to draw in. When Jack indicated interest, he was allowed to stay in during recess to draw. Mrs. Davis approved, "if he is more comfortable doing that than going out to recess . . . I think that is wonderful."

"We are trying to deal with the thing from two different angles," Mr. Davis explained. "The education side and the social side. . . . And hopefully, out of that, you can get his motivation, his self-esteem, up. He will then become more part of the group . . . and once again be willing to answer. Right, wrong, or. . . ."

"That's right," said John. "Have an opinion."

"Right," agreed Mrs. Davis.

"He's very opinionated around the house. I mean, he's not at all introverted," said Mr. Davis, noting that Jack did not have a stable avoidant personality trait.

"No?" probed John.

"He never has been [introverted], even as a small child. So the thing we are seeing in school, I'm sure, is associated with both the self-esteem and the learning problem. . . .

"But, what do you feel? When we moved to Illinois two years ago, we wanted to get to Sprague school. It's an excellent school system. Everything we heard was wonderful. . . . Unfortunately, schools are rated by their test scores," Mrs. Davis mused.

John agreed with the "unfortunately" in her query.

"And I sometimes think testing gets in the way of education. . . . We've had families over. They'll say 'My kids are in third grade and they are doing this.' Teach them as much as they can in second and third grade. . . . A child that is having trouble, and an accelerated program combined, is a disaster."

All the parents John spoke with raised such concerns. Mr. Davis also noted that putting students in special education "gets them out of the average" of school test scores. Mr. Davis had done his homework before allowing the school to place Jack in various special programs.

"Well I think," said Mr. Davis, "the issue now is . . . the education that is right for Jack. . . . And what we've done is to try to mainstream him as much as possible. . . . Last year, right before he was diagnosed as ADD, they were ready to put him in special education. About the time school was over, they said, no he can go mainstream. This year, he seems to have social problems. It is interesting. He was in the top reading group in first grade. Well he had read all summer. He was in the top reading group, and now he's worst in class. What's the difference? Is this a reality?"

"Fair question," said John—Jack's parents had a range of conflicting information to put together.

"Generally, we've heard pretty positive things, except for the concerns in math and social problems. But, even gym—he's gotten rave reviews from the gym teacher. We are hearing lots of positive things back from school." John later noticed that music, gym, and art reports were favorable. He knew, however, that teachers who did not see this class often and are faced with students who were more demanding of their attention might not see much wrong with a lad whose school life was devoted to remaining invisible.

"That's interesting," said John, "because Nancy really encouraged me to send [you] the transcript of my first interview with him. She felt you should see that." John was hoping to help Mr. and Mrs. Davis understand what he had been doing with Jack. Worried that he had precipitated the Davis's demand for a special conference, John wanted them to know why he had mailed them the transcript of his interview with Jack and the written observations of Jack's behaviors.

"We had no problem seeing that," Mr. Davis reassured John.

"No. No," said John, wanting to help them see Nancy's position more clearly. "She thought it would indicate how serious his difficulties were. That was her thought."

"Right," noted Mr. Davis.

"What you didn't have was the comparison with other kids," Mrs. Davis explained. Only then did John understand how confusing the interview must have seemed to anyone who did not see Jack's difficulties as clearly as they appeared to Nancy and John—a form of egocentrism on John's part, to be sure.

"Right," said Mr. Davis with some relief that his point was finally hitting home. "For me, the question was, 'How much of this is social?' If he had a class of five friends, and he had the same things. . . . He went to that same class where he had to create something out of the cup. Would he be quite different?"

"Quite possibly." John had to agree.

"It is possible. I don't know John. I really don't." Unlike Jack, Mr. Davis assertively looked for answers. Yet, like Jack, he also often conceded that he did not know what to do.

"Right, OK," said John, retracing his initial steps, "Back to reading—he sounds words pretty well. There's a number of kids who can't do that well in the class. What he doesn't do well is read for meaning. . . . And, if it's a matter of writing something in his journal. . . . To have him in the top reading group in this class would be very strange."

Only after reviewing the transcript of this conversation could John see how badly he had failed to communicate how different Jack was from children who would be in the top reading group—if Nancy had had reading groups, of course. Jean, for example, read years ahead of her grade level, but her approach to reading was even more compelling. She read everything from books on nature to horror stories. Jean shared passages that she relished—showing John where someone's face melted off his skull in a horror story. During free time, Jean departed to other worlds through books, whereas Jack drifted in limbo.

To help Jack become less withdrawn, his teachers decided to foster what might emerge with encouragement. Knowing this, Jack's teachers looked for hope when teaching and when reporting to his parents. If teachers were to become preoccupied with Jack's standing relative to others, their tactic would increase Jack's self-conscious state and make things worse. As Thyra had put it, the challenge became one of communicating honestly without causing damage.

John noted, "[Jack's] worried about doing the wrong thing. . . . It's like he fears something's going to jump on him."

"Well," said Mr. Davis, "he's always concerned that something is being said about him—that something is going on behind his back." Of course, things were being said about Jack behind his back, and no one had planned to alter that method of operation

"Last year," Mrs. Davis continued, "when we had daily communication with his teacher, we found out that Jack had manipulated our intercom system from his bedroom. He listened into the conversations we were having on the telephone." This seemed consistent with Jack's statement to Nancy that kids should be in on conferences.

Rather than pursue this further, John returned to his favorite theme. "Do you think there are important areas where [Jack] doesn't know that we can have opinions? . . . Much of life is like that. I wonder if he doesn't sense that."

"I don't know, it is interesting 'cause we built a thing down in the basement, based on *The Boxcar Children.*[9] It had to be their ideas. . . . He pretty much told us how he wanted that to be put together. So, at times, he is really creative and at times he is not. And his drawings are getting so much better. He's finding that satisfying I think." Here, John noticed, Mr. Davis was looking at Jack's areas of growth, rather than his standing relative to classmates.

Mr. Davis went on to say that they had a clinical psychologist working with Jack. The psychologist would soon have a group "of six kids, all with ADD, working on social skills. That bothers him—how to make friends."

Mrs. Davis added, "He's got to feel good about himself. That's the key to this whole thing."

"I agree," said Mr. Davis.

Mrs. Davis continued. "Until he feels positive about himself, he is going to be afraid to answer." Jack's parents continually looked for ways to help him become more assertive in constructive, esteem-enhancing ways.

Hearing this prompted John to deliver part of his standard speech on self-esteem: "If you don't feel good about yourself, is it partly because you think the whole world is a collection of facts that you can only be right or wrong on? Boosting self-esteem or making him feel good about himself . . . might be hard to do if he is locked into the idea that this is a right-wrong world." A preoccupation with learned helplessness and self-esteem serves primarily to make students who were overly preoccupied with themselves and how they appear to others to become more ego-involved. It seems more fruitful, in cases like Jack's, to encourage students to look outside themselves to find ways to contribute to a community in meaningful ways.

"Yeah, you're right," said Mrs. Davis, respecting John's expertise, but not intent on changing her agenda for Jack.

"I'm not sure," said John, "'cause this hasn't really been worked out a lot. I have a strong sense that it is right, but I haven't seen anybody write about it."

"Well," continued Mr. Davis, "we are going to spend a lot of time, and money—tee hee—on self-esteem and social skills. I think if he can be more socially acceptable and feel OK . . . if we can do some of that over the summer, and continue to give him a structured environment, 'cause he needs to be in a structured environment."

"I'm not sure I agree about that," said John, without elaboration.

"Well, talk to me about that, 'cause last year he was in an unstructured environment."

"But," qualified Mrs. Davis, "he really was not in that environment while on medication for very long, so we don't really know how he would do."

"Well there are many forms of unstructured," said John. "The only thing that bothers me is, if you don't encourage the imagination. . . ."

"That's true," interrupted Mrs. Davis. "There's no choices."

"Hey," said Mrs. Davis as Jack appeared, "coming to say good night?"

Jack got plenty of kisses and hugs from both of his parents, and John received an exaggerated, friendly handshake. Jack was lively and relaxed, almost excited. After Jack went to bed, the rest of the conversation consisted of matters that came up in the subsequent conference at school and will be reported with the involvement of more players.

Upon leaving, John could not help but be overwhelmed by the complexity and ambiguity of the information Mr. and Mrs. Davis had to face in thinking about the best ways to help their son and his academic progress. Not only did Mr. and Mrs. Davis worry that their son might bring home good grades, they monitored the wide range of deficits that

Challenges and Controversies

- Is it possible for children with disabilities to receive too many special services?
- Jack's parents are professionals with research training that helped them monitor and make wise decisions about the complex range of services he received. How might more typical parents be assisted in finding the services for their children?
- How can parents who do not have resources to pay for special services obtain the information and support they need to respond to miscommunication?
- Why is it so easy for adults to assume that children's social difficulties reflect a lack of self-esteem rather than an inability to imagine the needs, expectations, and perspectives of others?
- Focusing on children's speech and gestures can offer insight into how they are feeling. Should caregivers respond to the literal messages children convey, or should they look at those messages as symptoms of a larger set of concerns?

were evident in Jack's academic performance relative to his peers, changes in his social status, and various doses of drugs used to treat his attention deficits. They developed expertise in the political aspects of labeling children, research on specific disabilities, challenges associated with finding appropriate services, how various specialists tended to focus only on their areas of expertise, and reconciling inconsistent advice about exactly what to do about the many challenges that Jack placed before them. They coordinated all these issues and still maintained a comfortable home, rich with interesting activities and affection for all their children.

Sustaining Honest Communication

The conversation that John began on Sunday continued the following Wednesday after school. In chairs designed for second graders that were placed around the large low table in Nancy's room, specialists of one stripe or another met to talk about Jack. All the adults were committed to helping Jack coordinate his motivational needs and develop a single identity that would be evident both at home and at school. Wednesday's meeting included Mr. and Mrs. Davis, Mr. Best, special education teacher Alice Kay, speech teacher Marty Kremer, social worker Catherine Jamison, school district psychologist Lisa Fredrick, Nancy, and John. Julia Smith, the psychologist hired in January by Mr. and Mrs. Davis to work with Jack on his social skills, joined the group midway through the discussion.

Putting his audiotape recorder on the table, John mused about the strangeness of meeting in Nancy's room—where so much relevant drama occurred between Jack, his peers, and Nancy. Few of the adults gathered to make decisions about Jack's future had ever seen these daily events. Some had read John's description of Jack's school behavior, but most of the experts who were about to make decisions on how to proceed could only go by their own intuitions and knowledge of Jack's reactions to them. Setting policies for how a particular child should be treated in school without actually seeing that child in action made John unusually nervous.

"We are gathered here," Nancy started, looking at Mr. and Mrs. Davis, "certainly a lot of people, here for one reason—your son. . . . Our mission is just sharing our concerns, our visions, and seeing what we can do as a group to help him. That is how I saw it [the meeting] going. Is that what you saw?"

"In the past," said Mr. Davis, diplomatically, "we met with each individual [who works with Jack] and I think that it's much easier to do it as a group." Interventions, like those Jack faced, make it impossible for anyone to obtain an overall picture of a child's life in school. The program, rather than the child, is the center of attention. The child becomes a pawn in a wider self-sustaining system that cannot be evaluated effectively. Parents who seek to find order in the inevitable confusion can easily appear ungrateful to the well-meaning educators who are working to help their child overcome his or her educational difficulties. Programs designed around notions of typical or common needs do not necessarily meet the needs of particular children. How, then, can someone tactfully critique the system without seeming ungrateful for its potential benefits?

Mr. Davis proceeded with his gentle critique. "My opinion is that you [Nancy] have the greatest exposure to what goes on. What I would like to start with is the individual specialists, but I would like to see your input on these."

Miss Kremer, Jack's speech teacher, began. Jack, she said, was "low on receptive and expressive language—vocabulary as well as articulation. I don't see a lot of carryover from session to session. . . . He has a tendency to rationalize a lot." Her language seemed frustratingly technical and difficult to follow.

Seeking to interpret this jargon, Nancy said, "What I don't find is that he is saying 'How do I make sense?' . . . When I ask comprehension questions, I find he just pulls any answer from the air."

Mr. Davis noted, with confusion, that he did not see these deficiencies when Jack read at home. "He reads a book before he goes to bed. On many nights, Cara [Mrs. Davis] and I will listen to him read a whole book. What I tend to do is, after five or six pages, ask him, what was the cousin's name. He'll know. What planet did they go to first? He'll know. He can go back four to six pages."

"What I am hearing," said Nancy, "is . . . that you are guiding his reading. I find that when I guide his reading, that's when he's OK. If he is left to his own devices, that is when it falls apart." John also noticed that the questions Mr. Davis reported asking required literal recall and not interpretation of the text.

Alice Kay, Jack's special education teacher, reported next. "Now, in anticipation, I gave him a test of academic skills." According to the results of Alice's tests, Jack had gained about a year in reading and slightly less in math since last year. Jack's scores were just under third grade level for reading and just under second grade for math. "Looking at the test results, I was quite pleased," said Alice without explaining these results.

"Alice," asked Mr. Best, "Could you comment on priorities?"

"I think we have to reach for a different level of skill—why do things happen? Things like that. [A level of interpretation that Mr. Davis did not mention and standardized tests do not measure.] He has always been cooperative with me. . . . I think he is coming along." John began to wonder if Jack might be exposed to activities that do not cohere because of his cooperative nature. Certainly, Jack's compliance in conjunction with an inability to describe his experience may fool his caregivers into thinking he was making progress.

Catherine Jamison, the social worker, spoke next. "Last year . . . in the classroom, Jack was very active, very social, but egocentric. We . . . worked on being more appropriate, less egocentric . . . anticipating others' needs. This year is a big change—he is on Ritalin. This year in the class—it's almost painful for him to reach out.

"I still see him being egocentric. . . . He's very social in the small group [I run]. . . . It's almost a guaranteed success situation. . . . It's not like the classroom where there are twenty-some kids."

"I have to interrupt," said Mr. Davis, trying to link the various trains of thought of these experts. "When John was over we had a discussion of his [Jack's] being afraid of saying the wrong answer, and not thinking for himself . . . as soon as he feels stress. So it almost seems, as his anxiety level goes up, he has a real problem.

"The learning problems, in my opinion, from what I've read, they seem to go in hand with [low] self-esteem, and ADD. Well, ADD and self-esteem definitely go hand in hand. And, LD and learning problems are definitely associated with ADD as well."

On several occasions, Mr. Davis cited summaries of research. Each time, John became nervous about the value of this type of generalization for parents who are trying to comprehend the needs of their particular child: Knowledge of the research literature certainly did not seem to help anyone see Jack's personality and needs more clearly. Unfortunately, however, these generalities seem to be the only types of information available to parents who seek expert opinion. Clinicians are expected to translate research findings into a form that can be used to better understand and assist individual children.

Mr. Davis continued, "I don't know what's different here. What happened in the summer? Why is he not as comfortable now in second grade as he was in first? You [Catherine] are right. John came around and said he's different from what he is in school. He's a different child in [Alice's] room than he is in the classroom. And when he sits and does his homework, I have a problem, because he'll . . . know the answer. It's not as much not knowing the answers, as it is not taking the time, rushing through, whatever. . . . It's not like I'm sitting there having to explain the fundamentals of things, though sometimes he does have trouble with instructions. . . . I get frustrated. . . . I get cross. My frustration is, if you know the answers at home, why don't you know them at school?"

After a somewhat stunned, but thoughtful silence, Dick spoke first. "There are two reactions. . . . I think last year was really traumatic for him. He was just beating his head against the wall. And when you beat your head against the wall a whole lot of times, your head's going to hurt. . . . He brings all of his baggage in here with him." Dick's comments avoided Mr. Davis' earlier implication that Jack had done well in first grade.

"The second thing is the setting," Dick continued. "Nancy has 20 people here. There are peer issues. He might look around, and think, 'Who cares if I get it right. I have an answer down. I've finished.'" Dick then added a comment about Jack's need for supervised performance.

To help, Julia Smith, the psychologist hired by the Davises added, "That's what you do at home—you guide him. . . . School is a very negative place for him. Also it's harder for him socially, because he is becoming more aware that he has more difficulties. . . .

"And another thing I noticed on Monday is how he misperceives others. I was joking with him. I have these two bubble timers in our office, and they disappeared. I joked that they had been stolen, and he went on for ten minutes, 'No, I didn't take them. Maybe they're somewhere else.'" More converging evidence that Jack saw his lack of skill as a sign that he was morally evil.

"Last year," said Dick, "he was not clued in to other's perceptions. Now he is, it's more of a struggle. . . . Last year there was a twinkle in his eye. You could see some of the struggle, but this was a boy who was excited about being here. That's gone. You can feel the cloud. Last year he was the class clown." Dick provided a thick description of a child who had been initially unable to see beyond his own direct experience. The younger Jack could not differentiate concepts of luck, skill, current ability, effort and long-term intelligence in a way that could facilitate the kind of social comparisons he was learning to make. Jack-the-second-grader was beginning to see that the academic world is much more complex than he had initially thought. Developmentally speaking, these discoveries are quite on target for any active second grader, but Jack seemed a little behind his peers in how well he understood this complexity. Unaware of these research findings, Dick was trying to help Mr. Davis see that Jack's reactions to those discoveries were what everyone was working to understand and to coordinate when helping Jack find school more comfortable.

"John and I just looked at each other," said Nancy, surprised with Dick's description of Jack. "It's so unlike what we see here."

"When I read John's report and it said he [Jack] was socially withdrawn, I was amazed," said Mrs. Davis, beginning to see the son she knew in Dick's description.

The group moved to a discussion of Ritalin as a possible causal element in this change. Jack was no longer the clown, disrupting the work of the group. But was he something worse? Did Ritalin help him or hinder his progress?

Dr. Smith commented, "I think his perception of others is that they are constantly looking for mistakes. . . . He's been corrected a lot. He's looking for people to be picking on him. I know you [parents] try to minimize problems. . . . That's what I work on. . . . The first step is admitting problems, and he can't say, 'Yeah I do have a problem.'"

Of course, it may be that Jack did not fully understand the nature of his problems because he had typically not been included in the conferences where adults talked about how to help him. Yet, his generally egocentric nature—that inability to really step outside of his own emotional life to fully see the complexity of the situation and respond appropriately rather than impulsively—may be what helped his parents decide not to include him. Here was another chicken and egg quandary that Jack posed to those who sought to help him.

"When we are talking about ADD and we are giving labels," said Nancy, "I have a concern that I think is outside of that, and it's the lack of voice, and the lack of interest in anything. . . ."

"The other day," said John, "Nancy got him drawing, and he started nicely. Then, because he was interested, she let him and Arleigh stay in for recess. I came in to check.

"Nancy and I were talking about trying to get some real interests, 'cause I think, part of the time, social relations depend on having something that you are knowledgeable about and have a genuine enthusiasm for—so someone wants to share. I think that's a thing he lacks. This is to reinforce Nancy. Anyway, we had hoped Jack might be having fun drawing. But, I find Arleigh sitting drawing, and Jack leaning over Arleigh's desk, almost on Arleigh's drawing, looking up into his face, and trying to talk to him. A powerful statement of his desperate need for friends, but that need was stopping him from developing his own intellectual agenda, about which someone else might get interested."

Nancy followed John's lead, "The other day we had sharing time on the rug. This can be totally nonacademic. It's up to them. Earl brought in this action figure. I said, 'How many of you have action figures?' And Jack is looking around. He's not going to put his hand up just to be accepted in the group.

"Today, however," Nancy continued, "he stuck up for himself. He said, 'Can I get a drink of water?' and I said, 'No.' He said, 'Why not?' and I said, 'I guess in that case you can go.' It was the first forceful thing I have heard. . . . He needs an interest, he needs his voice."

"But I don't see him like that," said Julia, "and you don't see that at home."

"He's got baseball cards, and there's lots of talk," said Mrs. Davis.

For many boys, baseball cards are serious business, but owning cards has little to do with establishing one's voice and intellectual identity. Trading cards can trap boys in a narrow world where questions are about power and price, not about connecting with their emotions and exploring community values. Knowing statistics about which athlete is currently popular reduces questions of identity to a matter of being comparatively able on a preestablished criterion rather than imagining a more realistic and meaningful contribution to society and direction for one's life.

"Then it all comes back to anxiety," said Mr. Davis.

Dr. Fredrick returned to the topic of Ritalin. "How much depression does [Jack's doctor] see?"

"My question too," said Mr. Davis, not quite clear on Dr. Fredrick's intent. "But we don't see him during that medicine time. We see him after drug time and before drug time. . . . We upped the afternoon dose, and it seems he started to do a little better in the afternoon. Dosage is one of those things you really have to work with."

At this point, the discussion has moved beyond the topic of establishing fair and effective classroom practices into the realm of medicine, leaving most of the adults who worked directly with Jack dependent on the conflicting testimonies of experts. Whereas some experts highlight the appropriate uses of Ritalin,[10] others dismiss the value of this drug entirely.[11] For adults who want to improve the quality of life for a particular child, this type of dependency on the edicts of "experts" is nothing short of frustrating and anger inducing—exacerbating the problems associated with sustaining open communication.

Changing tack, Nancy talked again of Jack's need for friends, voice, interests, and support. "What he really acts interested in," said Mr. Davis, "is planets, the solar system, asteroids, meteorites. He reads about that kind of stuff. He's into collecting cards. Shane is getting him interested in sports slowly but surely. Shane comes to me to talk about sports. But you're right, we've got to get him interested in school.

"And I just don't know why, all I can figure—and once again, my scientific brain," Mr. Davis poked fun at his professional training, breaking the tension. Yet, no one could possibly put all the contradictory information Mr. Davis had read, heard, and seen into a coherent framework.

"But," Mr. Davis continued, "it has got to do with the social skills. If he has interests at home, if he has interests in small groups but not large groups, is it because the anxiety is so high? He doesn't feel comfortable in that group? When he talks about having friends over, he'll talk about kids from his first grade class." Mr. Davis certainly was informed about current hot topics in the psychological world of research.

"He has kept in with friends from first grade," agreed Mrs. Davis. Cases like Jack teach us about the value of keeping friends together across grades. Students can learn from the cycles of conflict that emerge over time, modify their own behaviors accordingly, and see the results of that modification.

"[But]," Mrs. Davis continued, "last week I went through the list of the [present] class, and I called three boys, and they didn't want to come over. . . . It is really hard. Academics are a big concern, but right now I'm more concerned with the social and the self-esteem."

Mrs. Davis expressed her pain clearly and had no doubt spent time with a sad son who worried that something was wrong with him. Given Jack's continual lack of confidence, self-esteem was an obvious concern and Jack needed encouragement from supportive parents who see his need for affiliation with peers. Nevertheless, obvious "solutions" sometimes maintain existing problems.

"Last year," began Mr. Davis, "after we had analyzed the situation, with recommendations from the specialists at school, we went and had him tested for ADD. He tested incredibly high. We go to this parenting class and he was one of the highest there. . . .

Sometimes I feel I have problems, and I go there and I feel pretty good. Our big thing and the reason we are taking a parenting course, is for his self-esteem. Reinforcing the positive, not getting into the battles. How do you get him to be more compliant? 'Cause when he's not compliant, you get into the battles." Clearly these are not parents who are so preoccupied with their own identities that they are unwilling to do everything they can to help their struggling son. Perhaps they are doing so much for Jack that his sense of personal efficacy is undermined by his inability to live up to their expectations. In this respect, Jack had his parents trapped like Bruce had Thyra trapped into reinforcing dependency.

"And that's so funny," said Nancy, "because he is the most compliant at school."

"But he is on medication in here," Mrs. Davis reminded everyone.

"Then," said Nancy, "his medication is playing a big part, because he is overly compliant [here]."

"That indeed, is the problem. Isn't it?" asked John, hopefully.

"That is what *we* identify as the problem," agreed Nancy, turning toward John. John doubted that others at the table would agree, but no one was about to challenge her assertion.

"Nancy was pleased he argued with her today," said John.

"It goes back to the issue of voice," said Dick.

"Nancy," asked Mr. Davis, "do you want to see him for a week without [Ritalin]?"

"Might be interesting," said John with excitement. The audiotape suddenly filled with loud voices—some angry, others nervous.

"But is that cruel?" asked Mrs. Davis. It seemed impossible, in the midst of all this, to see how to reduce pain.

"I really think you want to consult with your doctor," said Dr. Fredrick.

"Can we think about this for a second," said Mr. Davis. "I hear about kids that are on Ritalin that are way depressed. I don't think of the social thing as being a side effect of depression."

"It's a thing we should check," said Dr. Fredrick. Jack's personal psychologist, Julia Smith, had left by this point and Dr. Fredrick was doing her best to fill in as the expert on such things.

"I wish that were the case, because that you can deal with," said Mr. Davis, again reflecting the uncertainty. It was ironic that Jack, the boy who presumed that the authorities who were remote from his personal experience decreed all good words and deeds, should himself constitute a question that resulted in no authoritative answer.

Dr. Fredrick asked, "How does he interact with his siblings?"

"Um," said Mrs. Davis. "Extreme jealousy with his younger sister. Not with his baby brother."

"They can play together," added Mr. Davis," but she knows where his buttons are. . . . It's not a violent situation. It was earlier in the year. We went to this parenting class . . . a special playtime they call it. Basically, one parent spends twenty minutes a day giving uninterrupted time."

"They do what they want to do, and you pay complete attention. You don't tell them what the rules are," added Mrs. Davis.

"It's Jack's rules for the twenty minutes. . . . That cut down on the aggression."

"It gave him voice," said John.

"It gave him that time," corrected Mrs. Davis.

"It gave him voice," repeated Nancy.

"This cuts down on the aggression," said Mr. Davis, not seeing the connection between lack of aggression and voice. "But once again, it's a slow battle on the self-esteem. . . ."

Nancy changed the topic. "The other thing I notice with Jack—You think of ADD as a disconnectedness, yet he knows exactly who he's going to see, and on what day." Nancy pointed out the contradiction in the fact that Jack was given this incredibly complex schedule compared to his peers because he was diagnosed as not being able to track information, yet he managed to track that schedule.

"But do you think that bothers him?" asked Mrs. Davis, not seeing Nancy's point.

"No he likes it. I think he likes to go out."

The conversation moved away from Nancy's point, but returned to it. "When Jack comes back," said Nancy, "he's conscious that the group is working on something different, and he doesn't like it. Image is so important to him. He sees what they are doing, and I say, 'Do you want to go and get the blocks for this?' 'No!' He doesn't have the comfort to work with me at the level he needs. He doesn't want to be different."

Everyone began looking for the positive, and there was a round of reminders that, "There is progress."

Mr. Davis recalled that Jack seemed more intellectually active in school during his friendship with Arleigh. "In Oregon," Mr. Davis elaborated, "he had a best friend. He associates Sprague with all these social problems. But the medicine might create some depression. . . .

"There's so many different things going on, and you are trying to pick them off one at a time, and we are all working on different things, ah, hopefully trying to get the ball around." Mr. Davis put his finger on why it is difficult to conduct research to help "experts" better understand children like Jack—there truly are so many confounding variables that it would be impossible to fully rule out alternative hypotheses.

Get the ball around. That, John hoped, would be the phrase to stick with. Help Jack get the different aspects of his experience into more satisfactory relation with one another. Eliminate the fragmented schedule he faced each day and try to imagine ways to help him stick with a topic of interest for a sustained period of time. Only then would Jack be able to experience a sense of task involvement.

"But you take the child," said Nancy. "This is a child with a good heart. This is a sensitive child. This is a handsome child. This is a child that just needs to evolve—emerge. And then we are going to see what Jack Davis is about. . . . We do not see that right now, and my concern is, something's got to happen."

"How would you feel about him not being on Ritalin?" Mrs. Davis repeated her husband's question, and again many voices erupted.

"Maybe they just need to adjust it," said Dr. Fredrick.

"We know he needs the medicine," said Mr. Davis.

"Are you asking me," said Nancy, "if the pediatrician decides to take him off, can I handle him being wild? I'll try anything." Frustrating though Jack's behavior could be, Nancy was ready to help him integrate his experience into a single identity by whatever means available.

"I'm asking you," said Mrs. Davis, "how would you feel having him off medication, to see if there is a social difference."

"I don't know if in one or two weeks you could tell," said Nancy, honestly.

"I don't want to decrease it," said Mr. Davis. "The dosage is required. Maybe we can change medicine. . . .

"We've been in the mind-set that the social problems are inherent to ADD, because you hear about it so much. And . . ." Mr. Davis pulled himself up short. "But Shane doesn't have that social problem. He is as social as a child goes!" Mr. Davis laughed. "Boy! He's ADD! But that child has no social problems." Mr. Davis nicely illustrated the dubious value of "scientific" generalizations when considering particular cases. No matter how safe the generalization about ADD and social problems, Jack had the social problems and Shane did not.

To support his hesitancy to take Jack off Ritalin, Mr. Davis recalled a visit to a restaurant with Shane and Jack. Mr. Davis had initially turned down the waiter's invitation to buy a drink. "Let me tell you, about 50 minutes into it, I said, 'I do want that drink!' Ha, ha, ha!"

"Medicate the parents," John laughed.

"When we left, I think people applauded," laughed Mr. Davis.

By this point many of the group members had left. Nancy asked, "Are there any unanswered questions—any things you want to know or want us to know?" It was hard to sum up all the things that had been discussed or to name specific plans that had been made. Yet, the conversation was valuable in that it offered everyone a chance to air their concerns and imagine possible solutions.

It did not come out immediately, but eventually Mrs. Davis tactfully explained her anger at Nancy. Mrs. Davis said, "I appreciate the fact that you've let [John] come in and do this. And, I appreciate your honesty, but there was a piece in this [writing] that really bothered me—your conversation about how Jack did not know why he was taking Ritalin. Although I appreciate your honesty and respect your opinion, I don't appreciate you judging my parental decisions. . . . When he started on Ritalin, I specifically asked my pediatrician. . . ."

"To put it in context," Nancy interrupted, "my conversation was with John."

"Right, but it was made public." Mrs. Davis pointed out an important ethical implication of putting such detailed information about any child into print for others to learn from. Although everyone's identities are masked, one cannot help but be self-conscious about how the details of these lives will appear to others.

"Well it's in the thing, I wrote," said John, knowing that if everyone was uncomfortable with this, he could easily delete the details.

"I'm hoping," Nancy continued, "through all this research, that you can say if you are upset. I would hate to suppress something. . . . I'd rather have the research be authentic."

"Right," agreed Mrs. Davis. Perhaps others with similar conflicts would feel more comfortable sharing their concerns if they knew they should speak out and that teachers could well learn from parents. Jack's parents' commitment to the greater social good rather than to matters of self-esteem was impressive. Everyone knew that it would be a challenge to help Jack see the value of commitments like those of his parents.

Jack arrived and was waiting outside the door, having finished visiting the 103 Club. His presence put some urgency into resolving the tensions amicably.

"You know what I'm saying?" asked Nancy, not wanting to let the issue die until it was settled.

"Right!" said Mrs. Davis. "I appreciate your honesty. . . . But, the way that I read it, and maybe I read it out of context, it just seemed very sarcastic. You know?"

"Mmhm."

"We were taken back a bit by it," explained Mr. Davis.

"I wish you would have called me," Mrs. Davis elaborated, "and said, 'Why doesn't he know?'"

"I did."

"I told you why. I told you the pediatrician had advised us not to."

"Right. OK. I'll be more careful. And I'm glad you said that because if we are going to be a group working together, you have got to be honest about your feelings."

"Right," said Mrs. Davis.

"And I guess this research, I haven't seen as a public document," said Nancy, revising her assumptions about the delicate nature of such conversations.

"It's not yet," said John, looking to see if anyone wanted him to revise the story.

"It's just the reality of what's going on," said Nancy. "And sometimes I do shoot from the hip with my mouth."

"I told you that," John told Nancy, and was relieved when everyone laughed. Turning to the Davises, John also asserted, "And I told you she can take it back."

"And that's fine," said Mrs. Davis. "And I appreciate the honesty. You know, Rod and I are doing everything above and beyond what we can do, and your criticism like that, just. . . ."

"Yeah. I know," said Nancy, sadly.

"Whose advice do you take?" Mrs. Davis elaborated. "The pediatrician? The psychologist? You have to do what you feel is best."

"Right," said Nancy. "And I know that as a person—a parent and a teacher—I function from a very realistic base. I'm very much into being very truthful with children. I'm very uncomfortable with him being out there [in the corridor right now] and not knowing. I think that's stressful. I think it's not fair. But, you know, I hope he knows why we are here.

"I'm sorry if—I didn't mean it to make any judgment of you as a parent. I don't know if I was in your situation, what I'd do. And when you look at what he goes through in his everyday life, just to cope with the situation, the boy certainly has a work ethic. Just to maneuver through this life." It seemed fortunate that Jack had so many people looking out for his welfare. It also seems as though people who care so much about a child need to tell one another how much they care. Leaving such trust implicit in cases as difficult to understand as Jack's could be harmful.

"Yes. He overcomes a lot," agreed Mr. Davis, leaving to go to Jack.

"I wonder," John said to Mrs. Davis, "if there's another thing you want to talk about later. Rob's question of trying to get the ball around, I thought that was very nicely put. Jack does go out to all these places and you are talking about establishing social relations. He keeps coming in when a thing is half way through. You are saying get the ball around.

There's different people chipping at the ball all the time. I wonder about that. Maybe talk with Nancy? Earl mentions it. He says, 'Sometimes I have trouble telling what's going on when I come back.'"

John wanted at least a few goals established before this opportunity passed, yet he was also aware that the adults who worked with Jack needed time to get to know one another better. John also knew that, in an earlier meeting with Alice Kay, the idea of leaving Jack in Nancy's class for a larger part of his day was introduced.

Nancy continued John's train of thought, "You go out. You come in. You go out. You come in. This is where I'm going today, this is where I'm going tomorrow. His mind's on that a lot." John and Nancy had often seen Jack checking the clock and occasionally preparing to leave well before the departure time.

"So it's. . . . Maybe we want to stop services for a while?" asked Nancy.

"I'm more concerned socially," Mrs. Davis agreed.

"But that's part of the social," encouraged John. "All the time you are there with these people who know what's going on, and you don't. You'd start to feel weird. . . ."

"Maybe he'd feel more a part of things," Mrs. Davis said, thoughtfully.

"I'm just wondering," said John. "Oh, I guess I'm in favor of it, or I wouldn't have raised it." John caught himself trying to be coy when he had just witnessed a wonderfully honest exchange between Mrs. Davis and Nancy. How embarrassing.

"Every day he is going somewhere?" clarified Mrs. Davis.

Challenges and Controversies

- How can caregivers untangle the many confounds apparent in the interventions used to help children meet their needs?
- How can caregivers find a common language for talking about particular children?
- Test scores are used to make many decisions in schools. How can specialists find ways to coordinate such empirical information with evidence of a child's daily performance?
- Can caregivers become overly preoccupied with a child's standing relative to his or her peers?
- When is it appropriate to use research findings to explain a particular child's experience?
- What criteria can parents use when deciding when and how to include children in conversations about their difficulties?
- How can parents find tactful ways to help educators see inconsistencies in a child's behavior at home and school?
- How can educators support parents in the struggle to help children, acknowledging the frustration that comes from trying everything possible and having relatively little success?
- What criteria can parents use when deciding when and how to include children in conversations about their difficulties?
- How can educators find tactful ways to see potential side effects of drug therapies?
- How does someone determine whether a drug is having side effects that are hampering a child's progress in establishing an integrated life?
- Can poor performance be caused, in part, by having too many caregivers?

"Yep," Nancy responded. "Some days, ah, you're looking at social work once a week, LD three times a week, speech twice [a week]. Six movements out of the class in a week."

"It's a lot," said Mrs. Davis.

Jack's voice interrupted the negotiations and he entered with his father. Jack was almost as perky as he had been when John visited home. Jack showed his parents his accomplishments, including each contribution to the colorful swathes of rain forest on the walls.

Obviously, the conference had been much longer and more complex than the usual. New possibilities eventually emerged, yet many uncertainties remained. The complexity of the conversation testified to the difficulty that everyone had in understanding Jack, one another, and their relationships with Jack. Home-school communication in such cases certainly involves a complex set of negotiations about educational values and about children who are hard to understand and explain.

Lessons from Jack's Life

Jack taught us that some children become so confused in the struggle to integrate their needs and others' expectations that they lose all sense of self. Because they do not fully grasp the events going on around them, such children overlook some of their needs and essential features of their relationships. Faced with persistent errors in judgment, they can become fearful, mistrusting others as well as their own intuitions. If asked to describe their needs, such children seek help on everything, refusing to label interests, demonstrate competence, or establish relationships. When asked to define their goals, such children will fish around looking for accepted definitions of what it means to be and do good. Missing sources of information necessary for defining tasks or situations, these children can essentially go on strike, expecting others to think and act for them. Such children become so locked into their internal perspectives that they appear helpless when asked to imagine needs and expectations outside themselves.

When children attain such a marked degree of helplessness, it is natural for caregivers to step in and seek professional support. Nancy, John, Jack's parents, and several specialists caution us that some children can receive so much help that they lose all benefits. Well-meaning experts can become so busy anticipating and responding to the particular behavior relevant to their discipline that they undermine one another and/or hamper children's ability to integrate the parts of their experience. It also becomes difficult to determine when particular services are no longer needed. Rather than add services, it can be wise to minimize them until these children demonstrate some form of self-determination.

The current multitude of available interventions makes decisions about which services are essential for children's health and safety inordinately complex. Drug therapies, for example, should be used and altered with care. Anxious caregivers can take comfort from knowing that children who need this much help can benefit from identifying one set of needs, grasping the complexity of those needs, and looking for ways to meet such needs before considering all of life's complexities at once. Being able to label a success, no matter how small, can be quite liberating when life becomes so confusing. As these children learn to identify their most pressing needs, caregivers should not be surprised to discover aversive ideas or behavior that children have tried to ignore or keep secret. When such children can examine ideas that scare them, with guidance from sensitive caregivers, it becomes easier to take another step toward managing life's challenges.

ENDNOTES

1. See Fromm (1942).
2. This was included in a series of conversations held with Piaget, published by Bringuier (1980, p. 86).
3. See Piaget (1965, p. 27).
4. See Ladd & Profilet (1996).
5. See Delton (1991).
6. See Young (1994).
7. See Giff (1984).
8. See Giff (1985).
9. See Warner (1992).
10. See Barkley (1997a, 1997b) and Swanson, Cantwell, Lerner, McBurnett, & Hanna (1991).
11. See Coles (1987). Henker & Whalen (1989) asserted that no type or extent of treatment has proven predictive of long-term outcomes. Nevertheless, it is not possible to determine whether these disappointing outcomes occurred because stimulants were not used well or because they were ineffective.

CHAPTER

6 A Fighting Spirit

Like Jack, Earl fractured his experience both by ignoring some of his motivational needs and by overlooking others' expectations at home and at school. In other respects, Jack and Earl were as different from one another as two boys could be. Earl's impulsive behavior involved jumping from one activity to another and focusing on one person or another rather than missing the details of particular tasks or situations. He displayed high levels of autonomy and a strong sense of self-efficacy, but sometimes did so to such an extreme that he undermined the efforts of others and missed opportunities to learn from them. Earl's competence needs were also unmet when he sought to show off his abilities without being able to offer a strong performance. And, Earl found it easy to interact with his peers, but did not often do so in ways that sustained close friendships.

Earl's impulsiveness was apparent both at school and at home, but took different forms. At home, Earl preferred physical activities to more academic pursuits, whereas at school he assumed that his interests in superheroes and Nintendo should remain covert. At home, Earl did not read for pleasure, but at school Earl read about interesting topics while completing cut and dried drills to improve his comprehension.

In the habit of taking what he wanted, Earl sought to be the center of attention. This was apparent when John first met Earl and followed the class to gym. As students sat waiting for the session to start, Earl made zooming noises with his mouth, flopped back and forth on the floor, waved his hands around, chanted, squealed, banged his head with his hands, and did the splits. Taller and heavier than his peers, he also appropriated more space than most.

On the signal to choose an activity, Earl barreled over to a thick rope intended for climbing. He bumped the child holding the rope, took the rope, swung briefly, and then rumbled off. Staying reasonably active, Earl skipped and alternately twirled another skipping rope, but did not sample the other activities.

At lunch recess, in the snow, Earl trundled and zoomed around. He threw a snowball, hitting his human target from a considerable distance. Earl then swung on the monkey bars before walking along a snow fence, vigorously kicking off the ice. He played by himself, but eventually joined a group of six children chipping away at a hardened pile of snow left by a snowplow. The group was busy breaking and tossing big lumps of icy snow and easily allowed Earl to join.

At snack time, the students had the freedom to choose their own activities. Earl sat at his desk going through a large book with his superheroes card collection. Derek and others followed Earl's actions and commented on particular cards. These proved to be common patterns: Although Earl was not particularly kind to his peers, he managed to join group enterprises and kept other children interested in his activities.

During an untimed test, Earl also adopted the familiar avoidance pattern of slowly sharpening his pencil for the second time. He looked offended when Nancy stopped him. Rather than go back to work, he came over to Nancy's table and looked to see what others were doing. Earl then began drifting, apparently looking for answers to the test. Back in his seat, Earl jumped around and went back to correct earlier sections of the test rather than get on with the present work. It was difficult to know if Earl was simply being disorganized, disrespecting his own achievements, or adopting strategies for looking good at the expense of learning.

Nancy called Earl over. "Is this hard for you?"

"I need some help." Like Bruce and Jack, Earl had no trouble asking adults for help. Earl was not dependent on adult guidance in the way Bruce had been. Instead, he worked impatiently and needed to be reminded that asking the teacher for help was an option.

Nancy read an example. "You just make yourself go through each one. You see how fast you did that? What could this be? Right. If you skip around, you're not going to remember which one you did. . . . If you have trouble, what are you going to do?"

"Ask the teacher," said Earl, sheepishly.

"Try and work it out, and if you can't, ask me. Is that a deal?"

"Yes."

Two days later, as class began, Nancy said, "Earl passed out assignments. That was nice of you." Then, in an aside to John, "He never sits and gets started."

Later in the day, John interviewed Earl about schoolwork and homework. When John asked about school, Earl talked easily. "First thing is, it's fun."

"Mmmh."

"They have great things to do. And one of the better things to do is write, and read."

"Mmh."

"And I like sports, and the gym. . . ."

When John asked about good days in school, unlike David and Jack, Earl had a lot to talk about.

"One was a gym day. We were playing a game, and I never got out. . . . I always have a good day in gym. And I never got out. I never got out, except for one game."

"So you were really playing for a long time?"

"First time I play every game, I get out once. And then, I get the hang of the game, and I start having never getting out. Then, one game that I first started playing, I really had no idea how to play it. But, do you know, the kids were running and I had no idea what to do, so I just ran with them. Then I never got tagged in the game."

". . . Neat."

"Although I do get out sometimes. Sometimes I do get out." Earl seemed to know that he was bragging about winning and worked to tip the balance in a more self-effacing direction. It was difficult to know if Earl recognized that bragging was a sign of bad manners, and therefore, socially inappropriate. Or, if this was a hint of a deeper struggle, linked to feelings of inadequacy.

Earl's combination of assertiveness and diffidence made it difficult to anticipate his reactions in this interview and his behavior unpredictable. He presented himself as the proverbial bull-in-a-china-shop in combination with a penitent sinner. On "The Child Behavior Scale," designed to assess children's aggressive, withdrawn, and prosocial behavior, Earl would score highest on the aggressive with peers, asocial with peers, and hyperactive-distractible scales.[1] Yet, he would also exhibit behaviors classified as prosocial with peers, excluded by peers, and anxious or fearful. It would be problematic, in other words, to assume that Earl's behavior could be used to infer stable personality traits. Instead, it is more accurate to label the general characteristics of the natural human state of egotism that dominated Earl's approach to schooling. Earl's form of egotism offered a public acting out of what Adler positively described as:

> the striving for superiority and the sense of inferiority [that] go together in every human being. We strive because we feel inferior, and we overcome our feelings of inferiority by successful striving. The sense of inferiority [becomes psychologically significant if] the mechanism of successful striving is obstructed or . . . it is increased beyond endurance by the psychological reaction to [organic] inferiority. Then we have an inferiority complex—an abnormal sentiment of inferiority which necessarily seeks easy compensation and specious satisfactions and which at the same time obstructs the road to successful accomplishment by magnifying the obstacles and decreasing the sully of courage.[2]

When John asked about "the learning parts" of school, Earl talked about art. "What made that fun more than other things?" said John.

"Well, I like drawing pictures, you know."

"What makes drawing good?"

"You can do things. Well drawing is a neat thing because it takes more time and you don't have to, ah, and there's no time [limit]. . . ." Earl explained.

"Umm. You don't run out of time on it?"

"Yeah. . . . In class, when you do it you have to have a certain time and they make you, so, rush a lot."

During this conversation, Earl changed topics often and as John attempted to probe more deeply into some themes, Earl resisted. This resistance was not limited to topics chosen by John. Earl seemed to interrupt his own train of thought as well. Given his streak of assertiveness, Earl was surprisingly hesitant to flush out his thoughts.

"OK," John said. "Let's see. These questions are about homework. . . . You can imagine you're Mr. Best [the principal], and you can say that all the boys and girls are going to have homework, or they are not going to have homework. . . ."

"Well, that's a hard question, 'cause some people wouldn't like homework and more people would like homework. Some wouldn't and some would."

"So you are saying if you were the principal, you'd try and do what the people wanted?"

"Yeah. More people don't [want homework]," continued Earl.

"Than do, eh?" probed John.

"But that would be a question that is hard to answer. But some people would like less." Earl lapsed into silence.

"So what would you do if you were the principal?" John prodded. "It's just a pretend."

"I would say, I can't really answer that. It's hard."

"Well fine. . . ." John changed his tack. "What if your school had a special week when there was no homework, what would you do?"

"I really like playing football. My favorite thing is football."

"What about finding out about things. Are there things you like to find out about when you are not in school and can choose? Things you like to find out about?"

"We get in a group and go in the woods and look around for any people." Earl talked in detail about friends. He highlighted where his friends lived and biked as well as how they organized meeting and cycling.

"So that's the sort of stuff you really like doing, eh?" John commented.

"Yes."

"So, what about books? Are there some sorts of books you like to read, or things you like to find out about?"

"Well, I like to, well, we don't do that in the summer we sometimes do that on Saturdays. . . . So on Saturdays, I don't really read on Saturdays. But I do like to read my library books. On Saturdays, I'm as busy as my friends. But on Fridays, when I'm by myself, I really like to just play with my football, but I do read more often and watch TV. So that's more usual."

The puzzle posed by Earl's combination of assertiveness and diffidence was becoming even more complex. Earl seemed to find it difficult to tell John that he did not usually read for pleasure. Furthermore, Earl started by declaring school fun, but he did not describe intellectual interests or personal projects. Earl talked easily and engagingly, yet the themes of his narrative were sometimes scattered: To go beyond a simple interview and keep his attention focused on schoolwork was quite a challenge.

During the following week, before school, Earl chose and flicked through one of the books on George Washington that Nancy had displayed. Earl was engrossed, looking at pictures, reading here and there, and passing quickly through the whole book: some involvement, but far from a thorough reading. Earl's behavior fit exactly into the impression that Nancy gave John when they first talked about the project. Earl could read well enough, but would read only when he had a buddy to read with him or Nancy to nudge him along. Otherwise he lost the context of the story, and could not savor the simple pleasure of reading a book.

Earl could sustain interest when a topic captured his imagination, but his dominant approach to schooling involved a struggle to monopolize everyone's attention. In this respect, he had a lot of difficulty behaving in the neighborly way that good citizenship calls for in a classroom.

That afternoon, for example, an assignment involved working in groups to fill a profile drawing of George Washington with things Washington could not have experienced. Earl worked with Ben and Tom. He dominated the activities almost totally, holding the paper himself and doing all the writing. Tom managed to get a word in and briefly wrestled the paper away, but Ben was completely closed out.

As was often the case, Earl's dominance did not produce major resentment. Nancy explained that when others objected and challenged Earl, he rarely flared up or bore a

Challenges and Controversies

- Is it possible for children to express too much self-determination?
- When children engage in social comparison to determine what is expected of them, can they learn incorrect ideas as easily as correct ideas?
- Given that most humans struggle with the needs to demonstrate superiority and avoid feelings of inferiority, how can caregivers determine if particular children need assistance managing their competence needs?
- Should caregivers intervene when children bully one another, even if the children themselves are not particularly distressed by such behavior?

grudge—his good nature made it difficult to sustain lingering resentment. Earl was amiable as he pushed his peers aside and his manner said, "nothing personal, just business." He was not particularly considerate of others, but there was little malice, and conflicts often dissipated.

At the end of this session, where groups were accumulating points for their ideas, Nancy said there was another way to get points—points in your mind for being a team player and for sharing ideas. John thought Earl had not heard this comment, yet he was often listening when he appeared not to be. Perhaps by encouraging Earl to collaborate with his peers, he would also learn a bit more about himself and be better able to coordinate his own needs.

Identifying Earl's Interests

Unlike the other boys in this project, Earl was easily attracted to a wide range of topics, but his interests were rather fleeting. Earl was so readily enticed into thinking about various people, places, and things that it was difficult to find themes in his choice of activities that conveyed identity-enhancing interests. Looking carefully, though, it eventually became possible to see that Earl's long-term interests pertained either to his emerging sense of self or to forms of aggression common in a stereotypical masculine world.

When studying about Martin Luther King, Jr., Earl found ideas that were pertinent to his emerging sense of self. He had an African American father and a Caucasian mother, and so was biracial. It was not surprising, therefore, to find Earl attracted to stories and activities focusing on interactions among people of different races. This interest was evident after a vigorous group discussion of freedom in preparation for the study of Martin Luther King, Jr. Nancy asked the class to write in their Learning Journals. Writing about what freedom meant to him, Earl wrote:

What does freadum mean to me.
to be free
Like Mati Luthr King

if it was not for him
Black PePl wold not
Be free or wold not be in the USA.
Black Pepl

He actively participated in class discussions about King and the era in which King's vision dominated the media. Earl was also obviously gripped by a video on King's life and sustained a commitment to learning as much as he could about this topic. This interest in racial themes surfaced whenever Nancy offered new ideas. Near the end of the year, for example, a day ended with a partially dramatized video of Abraham Lincoln's life. After obviously remaining engaged in the video, Earl asked, "Can we have another one?" as it ended.

"Journal your thoughts," was Nancy's answer, directed at the whole class. Earl worked quickly, writing, "*Abe free slaves and was presedent of the USA*." He wrote about facts and included no opinions or critiques of the film, but drew Lincoln on a horse. Identifying these interests was made somewhat more difficult by the fact that, unlike David, Earl did not find writing to be a powerful form of expression or an aid to reflection. Even on a topic of real interest, his peers wrote appreciably more and with greater complexity long after Earl stopped. Earl's behavior suggested a fascination with positive events in African American history, but offered no clues as to why these themes were important.

Earl was also interested in superheroes, confirming his preoccupation with demonstrating superiority over others. We can only speculate on the meaning that superheroes might have had for Earl, but theories of egotism can offer some clues. Research on children's willingness to engage in social comparison suggests that they engage in such comparisons, even at young ages. Some researchers presume that this ability to make comparisons implies that children and adults share the same understanding of the information gleaned in the process. Others have conducted a range of studies that suggest children do not have the same understanding of comparative information and of the educational events that adults take for granted.

A typical second grader, in the latter view, is likely to be unable to fully differentiate such concepts as luck, skill, current ability, long-term intelligence, and effort—key elements that are necessary for an adultlike interpretation of information about one's relative standing in a group. Although children may understand some aspects of each concept, they would probably confound issues in ways that adults would not. So, at second grade, Earl would naturally be inconsistent in his use of such key concepts. Whereas preschoolers who cannot fully differentiate luck and skill concepts are fascinated by luck-driven games, perhaps Earl's preoccupation with superheroes suggested that he was working on a richer differentiation between effort, current ability, and long-term intelligence. Earl talked incessantly about such competence and self-determination issues in the lives of superheroes. Normatively speaking, children his age are working to coordinate effort-related issues such as self-efficacy and autonomy with skill-related concepts such as ability and intelligence. And, because Earl expressed himself more powerfully through action than words, his struggles might have been more apparent than the struggles of his peers.

Helpful as these generalizations are for emphasizing children's limitations, Earl was no typical second grader. He could surprise everyone by demonstrating interests that were more unusual than those of his peers and found a variety of ways to alter classroom activities to sustain these interests. When the children were about to construct annotated albums on topics of their choice, for example, Nancy asked, "Has anyone come up with a topic for a photo album?"

At Earl's turn, he asked, "Can you do two topics?"

"What are they?"

"I want to do football, bugs, and Egyptian pyramids." These were not realistic options for a second grader to photograph, but Earl's choices were adventurous.

"What kind of bugs?" asked Nancy, choosing the most realistic of the options.

"All kinds." Earl was thinking big. Did he have a close-up camera? Or, was he planning to cut photographs from books and magazines?

"How are you going to get bugs at this time of the year?" asked Nancy.

"I do have a lot of bugs at my house." Earl continued by asserting that he would try the Field Museum if he could not find bugs at home.

Later, Nancy introduced a new topic of "Fish" and declared herself ignorant. She told the students that they would have to come up with ideas of what to study and how to study. Sticking with his interest in forms of aggression, Earl wanted to study "Sharks and pike. Fish that eat smaller fish."

This interest in fish continued until the second graders spent most of the day at the Shedd Aquarium, with its fabulous array of creatures. Earl often wanted to show his discoveries to Nancy and his classmates. Inventing his own language to describe his experience, he called one fish that was sucking on a rock a "kissing fish." Even in the fairly conventional, sit-down-and-listen lesson on fish, Earl was absorbed, leaning forward, intent on what was said.

Earl's attraction to aggression was generally not reinforced in class, yet he found ways to work the exploration of this topic into his schedule whenever possible. On the morning of February 8, for example, Earl tapped and twitched at his desk. He finished part of his initial assignment, and got out *Nintendo Secrets: The Power User's Guide,*[3] which he looked at until Nancy told him to put it away. The class was about to go over the work.

John stood behind Earl as he rushed to catch up on the assignment he should have been doing instead of reading *Nintendo*. Earl managed to finish the first of two blocks of problems, but had not finished a second task. Nancy reminded the class to put CT [corrected together] or DT [done together] on their papers before correcting them. CT was used for work the students had finished and DT was used for work corrected before someone was done. Earl put CT on both papers.

"Put a DT," said Nancy, passing by.

"I did that," he said, correctly pointing to the work he had done, but implying both papers.

"OK," said Nancy, now a couple of desks away.

Again, Earl marked both papers CT. He proceeded reasonably quickly and well, working to complete the problems he had not quite finished as they went along correcting them—everything at or just after the last minute. His behavior did not seem to be motivated by a sense of duty, obligation, or an intrinsic desire to master the material. Instead, his effort was directed only at getting done and achieving the public appearance of competence. Nancy's technique for helping slower learners keep up with their peers may have helped Earl avoid gaining knowledge by completing the assignment.

Challenges and Controversies

- Is it possible for children to have too many interests?
- Should children who are impulsive be encouraged to study one or two topics in depth?
- Should caregivers encourage interest in topics that support aggressive behavior?
- How can caregivers label identity-enhancing interests in children who seem to be interested in everything?

Nancy was aware of the ways in which students like Earl took shortcuts to create time for their own interests. "I've been thinking that a real draw to them is this computer, and I'm not giving them a chance. Why should Ted get to it because he's first done? That's wrong of me." Nancy's sensitivity to fairness was evident, taking the form that equal access to information is more important than equal attainment.

John continued her train of thought, "That's one of the inequalities that I think undermines their motivation. Because they take longer on the first thing, their life is less. . . ."

"Right!" Nancy coaxed. "School is just a series of unfinished things."

Fortunately, Earl showed little ambiguity about his interests and was not overwhelmed by the tedium of the tasks that Nancy assigned. His interest in aggressive pursuits was common enough among the boys in his class so that he found plenty of peers willing to collaborate in such inquiry. Finding ways to help Earl transform his fleeting approach to tasks into longer-term commitments remained a challenge.

Searching for the Limelight

It is unlikely that children as young as those in second grade differentiate such concepts as current ability, effort, long-term intelligence, and task difficulty well enough to hold an adultlike ego orientation. Nevertheless, Earl's search to be the center of attention was similar to behavior found among adults whose ego orientation dominates their approach to meeting competence needs. The way in which Earl actively sought to be the center of attention in his class, combined with a willingness to back off and admit that he didn't know an answer, made his behavior somewhat challenging. In the lesson on silly sentences, for example, when Nancy called, "OK. Silly sentence number 1. Who wants to read it?" Earl waved his hand. Nancy called on him, but he was not ready, and backed off.

Later, the children were doing arithmetic. Arleigh had put 95 + 95 = 190 on the board. Earl wanted to explain Arleigh's solution, but all he had was the desire to explain things and not the knowledge of how to do the problem. His explanation came out verbal fruit salad, and he faded into silence. Nancy coached Earl, asking him what 6 tens and 6 tens would equal and showed him blocks to make the problem concrete. Earl said, "60."

Earl muttered an explanation for this response, straining to be in the limelight rather than listening to Nancy's questions. He behaved like "children who are so impressed by themselves that they believe they know everything. In a tense situation, they feel they have to answer even when they have no idea about the question at hand."[4] Earl had the limelight, but cut himself off from the benefits of his teachers' and classmates' knowledge of mathematics.

The class moved on to math and spelling tests. Nancy handed out booklets the children had partially completed, and that she had graded. Earl picked up his test and drifted back to his seat, peering to see others' scores. "What did you get? Yeah!" He paid little attention to others' scores, reflecting a vague and egotistical, but reasonably amiable, self-assertion that suggested he was just checking his assumption that all was right with the world.

This possibility was challenged when, after lunch, Earl demonstrated a clear preoccupation with his standing in the intellectual distribution of his peers. While the class was on the rug waiting for Nancy, Earl waved his snowman collage around. "Mine's the best." He flapped around and talked noisily, then told his neighbor, "Yours is the baddest." Earl's need to demonstrate superiority was definitely apparent. This preoccupation with being superior over others was also apparent two days before when he was reading in the resource room. Earl noticed a marker with another student's name on it in his reader, "Someone's way behind!"

"We all go at our own pace here," said Alice. Knowing his own pace was not always enough for Earl.

Concern with rank in the hierarchy was also evident when Earl took the suggestions Nancy wrote in his journal as an assault rather than as alternative perspectives on his writing. Twice, John saw Earl's face sag as he read a perfectly constructive comment. Superheroes presumably do not need suggestions, and probably would not take them well.

Next was a spelling test. Earl had been wriggling off and on all afternoon, slipping his arms in and out of his striped, purple tee shirt. Now, he slipped his arms inside, covered his knees with the shirt, and pulled the neck above his head—a striped, animate circus tent, topped by a purple baseball hat.

With a handful of math papers still in her hand, Nancy bounced to the front. "I'm going to pull one out at random." She pulled a problem and called, "Earl!" Earl was then asked to choose someone to work the problem with him on the board.

"It's kind of hard," said Earl. Why should Earl find it hard to complete a problem that he had already been tested on? Perhaps, Earl's hesitation meant he wanted to avoid revealing incompetence. He certainly showed a tendency to see all positions one takes as an indication of competence rather than of values—defining life as a test rather than an opportunity to learn. In this instance, however, that possibility seemed far-fetched. Earl's response was similar in its ambivalence to the response he gave when John asked him about abolishing homework. Earl was uncommitted to a position on how to do these math problems and could not have relished the possibility that others would find fault with whatever stand he took as a starting point.

This hesitancy was more consistent with a private self-consciousness, or ability to be aware of the covert and hidden aspects of the self. Like others who exhibit this propensity, Earl censored himself before asserting an opinion. He may have become overly conscious of his own thoughts, feelings, attitudes, motives, and behavioral tendencies. Such self-consciousness would involve a much more calculated reaction than was suggested by Earl's know-it-all attitude, but may emerge once he attained the limelight he sought.

A third, simpler option also seems plausible. If Earl had thoughtlessly completed these problems, guided by Nancy's directions, perhaps he did not know where his answer came from. More interested in building a tent with his clothes, Earl could have been simply avoiding Nancy's request to reconstruct his previous thoughts.

After school the day before, Nancy—who had a recorder on her desk that she turned on at optimal moments—asked Earl, "How do you think the kids would like this if . . . maybe they could invent their own projects to do? What do you think?"

"It's hard because I can't judge," said Earl. "Some people would but I think . . ." and he mumbled something inconclusive. Given his status as the loudest person in class, and his wide range of interests, Earl's tone was unusually low. He seemed to need and appreciate the structured nature of the tasks Nancy assigned.

Saved by the bell, it was Earl's turn, along with half the class, to go to the learning center for the same Styrofoam cup construction task that Jack tried a week before and on which Bruce had tried to copy from his peers. As the task was being explained, Earl declared, "Me and Derek want to go out there." When no one answered, he repeated this command to himself, eager to start. Earl made an ingenious puppet using the upturned cup as a base to conceal the operator's hand. Sticking through a hole in the base was a plastic spoon. Stuck on the spoon was a dish-sponge head with string hair. Earl remained wholly absorbed, working longer than most, discussing the work amiably with Jill and occasionally with Derek. There was no need to structure this task for him. Furthermore, Earl's willingness to invent a task without paying attention to the instructions matched what Earl told John about how he learned. He learned by watching those around him while inventing his own sense of purpose.

In Catherine Jamison's lively discussion of ideas for increasing friendship and reducing conflict, Earl, once again, sought to be the center of attention. Nancy quietly mentioned to John that Earl looked around to see how votes on suggestions were going before adjusting his own position to emerge as the leader of popular movements. Earl made a coherent case for avoiding fights by talking about problems, and made other thoughtful comments. He offered contradictory suggestions, working to take over by talking about how to solve problems rather than by solving actual problems.

Nancy reminded the class of how people had said, "Ugh," when she assigned buddies.

"But," said Earl, "you can talk about why they say 'ugh,' and then you can get to be friends. At first you say 'ugh,' and after a while you get to be friends." This seemed like the comment of a flexible learner, yet Earl's actions were not consistent with such insight.

Shortly afterward, for example, when the class went to music, Earl cut in front of Ted to head the line as they approached the door to the music classroom. When challenged, Earl refused to budge. Words and deeds did not coincide: Talk of experience was disconnected from experience.

Back in class, the "silly sentences" procedure had evolved. "Who wants to be the teacher?" asked Nancy. After Beth took a turn, Nancy asked for someone who had not been the teacher to take a turn. She knew Earl had had a turn, but his hand was up and Nancy chose him anyway. There was an outcry from the class. "He had a turn!"

Amidst turmoil, Earl denied it, and would not retreat. Nancy muttered to John, "He is a politician," meaning this in the needs-to-be-the-center-of-attention sense. Noticing

Challenges and Controversies

- When students consistently demand time in the limelight, is it wise for teachers to help them become the center of attention?
- Could students' sense of self-efficacy be harmed if they are consistently rebuked for seeking attention?
- Is it possible that students' affiliation needs will remain unmet when they adopt an ego orientation toward competence?
- Politicians are successful when they can entice others into voting for them. Can students become so preoccupied with pleasing others that they lose their ability to sustain identity-enhancing interests?

Earl's need to achieve his goal of attaining the limelight, Nancy found a socially valued way of labeling the behavior. Nevertheless, Nancy's preoccupation with fairness meant that Earl's identity as a politician was not always allowed to dominate the flow of activities in this class. When asked to write in their journals about colonial times, for example, the students worked in pairs. The children reported their ideas to the class, and Earl wanted to repeat a George Washington story out of context. Ignoring him, Nancy brushed on in a manner that redirected Earl's attention.

Earl seemed aware that there are many socially valid reasons for seeking to be the center of attention, and Americans can be quite inconsistent in their attitudes about such behavior. We celebrate the skills of superstars and make icons out of unusual personalities. We also impose severe forms of exclusion and isolation on ordinary people who do not conform to particular group norms. Democracy works when a few people are willing to stand up to such inconsistent pressure, while the rest of us offer opinions about their suitability for particular jobs. It should not be surprising, therefore, to find families and schools that encourage children to practice attaining the limelight and asserting their uniqueness: Leadership skills need to be developed. Earl challenged these values when he became so preoccupied with attaining the platform that he avoided learning the skills necessary to do the job effectively and ignored identity-enhancing interests. He taught his caregivers to rethink the ways in which they encouraged his self-determination, but only after these more subtle behaviors escalated.

Discovering the Pain of Being Different

Watching Earl interact with his peers and listening to the consistent references to his political instincts raised the possibility that he might one day become a dynamic leader. While leadership may seem glamorous, it also requires a special set of skills and personal insight. Earl would have to become less impulsive when responding to others' needs and learn to respond constructively in the face of ridicule. He would also have to find ways to integrate his various motivational needs and respect his uniqueness. Future leaders need to find ways to coordinate their own motivational needs so as not to be overcome by the expectations of others. Sadly, such growth does not come without a degree of discomfort, and watching such discomfort can be challenging for thoughtful caregivers.

The tension that comes from watching one's children struggle was apparent when John met Mr. and Mrs. Norton in mid-February. Both parents had full-time occupations in order to provide the best possible opportunities for their children. "When my children came into this school," said Mrs. Norton, "they'd not had any preschool. I had the good fortune of having the same caregiver come to our home for six years. I thought this would be a good thing. When I brought the children into school, I was informed they lacked classroom skills. . . ."

John wondered if this was why Earl and his siblings participated in extracurricular activities before and after school. Like many of the children at Sprague, Earl attended a privately run, activity-based program called the 103 Club, held in the school gym and lunchroom. Mr. and Mrs. Norton clearly did not need the childcare services that the program offered for many families. But, extra involvement with peers may help Earl remember to be more considerate of others' needs and expectations.

"I [had] thought, do I hold them out a year?" Mrs. Norton continued. "My sister referred to it as red shirting. . . . From what I saw at home, the way they could pick things up, and were intuitive, I thought it would not be beneficial to hold them out. You know, they were eager. I didn't realize they were going to be going in with red shirts and in an aggressive [pressured] environment. . . ."

"I think Earl is . . . real selective about what he finds interesting, and that may indicate low emotional maturity. On the other hand, he's extremely mature in trying to understand how he fits into the world, and he's had to grapple with that."

Mrs. Norton was hinting at issues that Mr. Norton tried to make more explicit. He declared, "The idea of LD sort of throws me. I have a lot of problems with it. . . . The way I see it, Earl utilizes his brains well. Maybe not in the same way as others, but at least he's thinking."

"He's a very active person," John agreed.

"If he's feeling positive, he's doing things. That's why I have trouble with the LD label."

"First grade was very difficult for him," added Mrs. Norton.

"Partly because of the teacher," Mr. Norton explained, "[but] his grades were normal."

"Later [in first grade], the school said . . . we'd like him assessed. . . . This is the same teacher, when I said, ah. . . ."

"There was a racial problem there," Mr. Norton chipped in.

"People were calling him racial names and stuff," added Mrs. Norton.

"When we brought it to the attention of his teacher, she said, 'I don't want to deal with it because it's going to happen in the real world anyway. He's going to have to deal with it on his own in the real world.' But that's too much baggage for a young kid."

"We were taken aback," said Mrs. Norton.

John remembered that second grade had brought a couple of similar incidents. During an argument, Fred once called Earl "mud-face." Nancy dealt with this in group discussion, and several of the children found cogent ways to make Fred feel embarrassed. Nancy also used the study of Martin Luther King, Jr. to emphasize the evil of prejudice.

Likewise, Mr. Best, who made it clear to Earl that he wanted to know if this ever happened, and that he wanted none of it in Sprague School, dealt with another incident on the playground decisively.

Earl, because of his biracial status, faced difficulties that his peers did not. It would be problematic, however, to assume that biracial status was the sole cause of the difficulties Earl had relating to his peers. Normatively speaking, most people find *difference* to be fraught with anxiety and pain, irrespective of cultural background.[5] Yet, biracial children face the unusual difficulty of being different from many family members as well as from peers and other community members.[6] Learning to value racial difference in a culture that values conformity is a difficult task for many adults, and Earl was confronting this issue as a child.

Certainly some biracial children have found this uniqueness of their life struggle to be overpowering. Those children experience racial identity confusion, low self-esteem, ambivalence toward their families, rejection of their parents, and above average levels of aggression.[7] Nevertheless, when biracial children interact with accepting peers, extended family, and other community members, they can experience recognition, acceptance, and the same sense of belonging that facilitates a healthy self-acceptance of their biracial identities. Biracial children have the added benefits of learning to separate the evaluation of others from their own experience at relatively young ages. Like children in other studies, Earl seemed to be actively struggling to find a comfortable resolution to this type of identity conflict.

"Now, really," said Mr. Norton, changing the subject, "He's a dynamic kid. We think he's very intelligent."

"I'd agree," said John.

Mr. Norton backed up his position with examples. "In golf, in some cases he can analyze my swing. Now it takes an awful lot of intelligence to do that. When he tells me something I'm doing, he's actually right. . . . So when they said LD, I thought, maybe it's the way they are handling Earl and his behavior. I don't know. I still think he's a very bright kid—a lot of energy that needs to be channeled."

"I said to Nancy, right early [after hearing Earl in a discussion of Martin Luther King], 'Why is this kid in the LD category?' But there are also things that happen that really make learning difficult for him, too," noted John. John and Mr. Norton seemed to be captured by the lay stereotype of children with learning disabilities as somehow being less intelligent than their peers. They were not distinguishing the ability to process information from the ability to integrate and use information.

Rather than pursue this line of thought and the inevitable follow-up of who might be to blame for Earl's learning difficulties, John chose to focus on Earl's abilities. Adopting Mr. Norton's positive attitude, John described the range of academic projects he observed and Earl's involvement, wit, and focus when his imagination was captured. In turn, Mr. Norton described the knowledge and intelligence Earl displayed at a recent trip to a children's museum, at an opera, and with his collection of baseball and basketball cards. "He can talk about each NBA team, who the stars are. . . . He can tell you who is good and who is bad. He would not get ripped off. He knows the value of cards: He's got burned a couple of times. But, [his interest] says to me that there's a lot going on."

It is common enough to see knowledge of the status of players, and the value of cards as a sign of intelligence: This occurs when individuals focus on the crystallized forms of intelligence as an index of competence. For Earl, this interest in "winners" might have been an expression of his desire to dominate—a desire to learn merely to assert intellectual superiority that could ultimately serve to maintain Earl's learning difficulties. Finding ways to help Earl use his knowledge to solve problems and contribute to socially valued activities could help him move beyond the recitation of facts.

"I was wondering," asked John, "how he got to know so much [about dinosaurs]. Maybe some from TV?" John was thinking of what Bruce's parents had told him about the public television program on dinosaurs that had aired recently.

"No," said Mrs. Norton, "we got him a lot of dinosaur books."

"He can tell us the features, what they eat—things like that," said Mr. Norton.

"Well before he could read, he'd drag around my college anatomy book," said Mrs. Norton. "He was picking things up, or he'd ad lib it. 'This is the heart and this is where the blood vessels are.' The book is so worn the cover fell off." Earl seemed to have a solid, well-established interest in how the human body worked.

"I don't claim to have figured it out," John said, "but somehow written words haven't connected for him. The spoken word has. And I'm wondering if you have any ideas as to what might be done that would give the written word the power that the spoken word has—and his drawings."

Somewhat defensively, Mr. Norton said that Earl's reading had improved over the last three months. "It's very noticeable when we're in the car. Signposts. He will blurt it out. Some words, he begins to stumble. We say, sound it out. He really sounds it out. . . . And we are doing a lot of reading to him every night."

"We need to do that," added Mrs. Norton, "because that's the only way he can wind down. Since he was a baby. You know how you see a dog make a nest. He would do that. He could not get to sleep. He was very charged."

"Wired," said Mr. Norton. "But when I put all the pieces together—what he's doing with his mind—I have difficulty accepting that label. I refuse to believe that."

Mrs. Norton was also opposed to the LD label. "My compliance with—not my complacency with—but my compliance with the label was based on the idea that anything that gets my kid in a one-to-one situation with an instructor has got to be beneficial."

"With that logic we felt OK," Mr. Norton conceded.

". . . Now Earl was complaining. He'd say, 'This is baby stuff. I don't know why I'm seeing Miss Kay.' I say, 'Honey, you get past that stuff and she's going to give you more interesting things.' And I said to her, 'You know, maybe you want to give him more of a challenge.' He hasn't complained recently. . . ."

"If he thinks the task is stupid," said Mr. Norton, "He won't pursue it."

"And he's very stubborn," declared Mrs. Norton. "His baby-sitter, who raised him from three weeks old, doted on him, enormously. There was nothing this child could do wrong, and nothing this child ever got disciplined for. So . . . he has great difficulty coping with adults who don't just let him be."

"So," said John, "I'm wondering how much comes out of being picked on?"

"He was always assertive," said Mrs. Norton. "Three years old, he would go into a group of strangers and say, 'How are you?' when the other two were cowering. . . ."

Earl's parents did not accept psychoanalysts' propensity to see inadequate attachment and personality deficits as the cause of disruptive behavior. Nor, did they see the value of punishment or negative reinforcement contingencies advocated by many behaviorists. Instead, they saw the value of reinforcing positive behaviors and allowing Earl to experience, with careful monitoring, the natural consequences of his disruptive behavior. They were able to see patterns in Earl's aggression, step outside the situation enough to avoid punitive cycles of conflict, and still sanction Earl by teaching him the natural consequences of his actions.

"The day before, in the 103 Club," said Mrs. Norton, "they called me up. He went ballistic on them. . . . He told the 103 teacher, 'Fine, put me in the corner. I'll go kill myself.'"

"Yes. They [Mrs. Quimby and the other 103 Club directors] told me that too," said John.

"The kid is pushing for a reaction," said Mrs. Norton. "He has already announced that he is going to be an attorney, because he can argue so well."

Mrs. Norton described the struggle of trying to get Earl to find a lost shoe. "'Tonight you are going to find your other shoe.' [I got] twenty minutes of resistance. I kept my composure. I kept monotone. 'That's unfortunate. You have to find your shoes. . . .' Finally, there's the shoe. I said, 'Now Earl, tell me where you found the shoe.' He looks at me and sings, 'Somewhere over the rainbow. . . .'"

"That was impressive," said Mr. Norton of his wife's effort to be patient. "I've seen some calming down over the year."

John asked if Earl's parents thought Earl would fit in better if everyone encouraged him to engage in more helping behaviors. Mr. Norton said, "I think we could do a little more . . . getting Earl to be a little more helpful. He seems to enjoy that. He's not a vicious kid."

Earl's parents also seem to know that a natural next step in helping Earl was to alter his emotional attributions. The goal of this kind of intervention would be to help Earl feel the guilt that comes from analyzing his own behavior rather than the shame associated with being "found out" and punished. Helping Earl label aspects of his experience and find less aggressive ways of responding to his anger and frustration would assist him in developing a guilt-ridden rather than a shame-ridden approach to regulating his own behavior. Earl also had to know that he had every right to feel angry, hurt, and frustrated when he was the target of racial slurs.

"Let's be honest about it though," said Mrs. Norton. "There have been times when he has come home from a summer camp, extremely upset. Very volatile! He said, 'I want to, I really want to hit those people hard.'"

"Racial slurs," said Mr. Norton, defending Earl's right to be angry.

"A lot of racial slurs—real cruel treatment. He had an enormous amount of anger. . . ." Mrs. Norton elaborated.

"It's a multicultural society," said Mr. Norton, "and we want him to see that. One of the things our kids had a problem with, they had never heard these terms until they got into school. They said, 'I'm not black. You're not white. We're brown, we're tan.' And if you think about it, it makes a lot of sense. . . . They began to tell kids, 'No I'm brown.'"

"I don't know if you've seen Earl's older brother or sister," said Mrs. Norton. "They have my [fair] complexion. His brother insists [on the brown label]—last night he even said, 'I'm white!'"

"It's something the other kids don't have to deal with. Last night, at 103 Club, this kid said to his father, 'Is that a white person?' I yell out, 'Yeah, I'm white.' I thought it was important for my children to see me respond cheerfully, 'Yes, I'm white.' And that's what precipitated that conversation, 'cause it's not something we talk about until the kids bring home a problem."

John mentioned how interested Earl had been in Martin Luther King, and Mr. Norton said, "Well, [Earl] did say I'm so happy Martin Luther King lived, because if he did not live and do what he did, brown people would not have the freedom to do what they do today. And he said, you would have had to use the back doors . . . and he said, he did it for all people."

John and Earl's parents had talked for over 90 minutes. Mrs. Norton then asked John, "Did you have any questions?"

"Ah," mumbled John in surprise, "have there been any strains with homework or anything?"

"Not in second grade," said Mrs. Norton, cheerfully. "The family is all home by 6:30, and we've just got two hours left, and then it's getting ready for bed. So, during the week, the kids, they are on the job from 7:30 a.m. when they get here [to school], and [go] until 6:00, 6:15, or 6:30 p.m."

"They put in a full day. They really do," said Mr. Norton.

"And what about report cards?" asked John. "Have they been the focus of any concern?"

"Yes," said Mr. Norton. "He wasn't very pleased with the Ns [for not satisfactory]."

"What we do," said Mrs. Norton. "We say lets look at internal improvement. . . . Did you improve? They carry in some interesting baggage. 'I want to get As.' They must be hearing kids communicate those things."

"On the other hand—" Mr. Norton hinted at a small disagreement. "There is no excuse for the N you know. He can do better. He recognizes that." Mr. Norton accepted the authority of those in school who assessed Earl's performance.

"We try to praise the good things," Mrs. Norton qualified her encouraging stance.

"Yes, more positive than negative. In fact I said, 'Earl I don't want to see Ns in your next report card,'" confessed Mr. Norton.

"Here," Mrs. Norton interjected, "I would caution against that. . . . You strive harder, but at what a price? I didn't want to put [my harsh experience of school] on my kids."

In general, John and Earl's parents held similar views about Earl. They seemed to see the same boy. Mr. and Mrs. Norton were also pleased, and perhaps a little surprised, that John had seen so many strengths in Earl. "I'm of the long-term opinion that all things will sort out," said Mrs. Norton, optimistically. "I know basically where my children came from. And my gravest concern is that they don't lose that desire they have to learn and that excitement. That is the most critical step."

"I totally agree," said John who often defined the quality of one's intellectual life in terms of the ability to sustain interest in a topic.

As if to confirm the importance of this insight, Mr. Norton spoke of a brother, who "was going to be thrown out of school in third grade because he was so disruptive."

Mrs. Norton added, "They found he was at an eighth grade level. He was accelerated and entered college at 15. He [illegible] got a doctorate. But it was not a happy experience."

Challenges and Controversies

- How can caregivers help students who are obviously different from their peers find value in that difference?
- Focusing on leadership potential can help unusual students find a socially valued role. Can it also hinder children's growth by prematurely imposing adultlike responsibility on them?
- What can caregivers do to help children respond to racial slurs?
- How can caregivers validate legitimate anger without also encouraging aggressive behavior?
- What can caregivers do to help children distinguish the evaluation of others from their own experience?
- What strategies can caregivers use to help children who are assertive learn to respect the perspectives of others?

"It sure wasn't," agreed Mr. Norton. "He talks about it now. He is now retiring, and getting out of an emotional morass. There is a genetic basis for intelligent coping at some level, but my concern is that the children come to their talents in a healthy way and can enjoy them in a healthy way."

Within a week of this conversation, John combined drafts of his observations in school and a transcript of this interview. John sent his writing to Mr. and Mrs. Norton and called a week later to see if there were any queries, doubts, or suggestions.

"Beautiful," was Mrs. Norton's first comment. She then went on to worry about Earl's social standing and wondered aloud if they had an amiable psychopath on their hands. Mrs. Norton knew that she had overstated Earl's troubles, but she told John that she could not help but worry about him. She said that she had, some time ago, typed Earl as a senator—quite unlike her other children. "Interesting," John and Mrs. Norton reflected, "that Nancy described him as a politician." Mrs. Norton then added that she and her husband would continue to look for ways to encourage Earl's interest in the written word and in the value of helping and collaborating.

It is a long-standing observation by behavioral psychologists that troublesome children keep adults focused on their troublesome behavior, which helps maintain the troublesome behavior. Earl was very active in maintaining his way of life, and Mrs. Norton saw incidents at home that matched what Nancy had seen in school. In this respect, the amount of work it took to communicate about Earl's progress was less strenuous than was the case with Jack. Earl's behavior was every bit as troubling as Jack's, but for different reasons. Earl's impulsivity was coupled with a volatility that needed to be tempered before he was strong enough to hurt others with his anger.

Literacy among the "Bad Boys"

Progressive educators often argue that students benefit most when defining their own purposes for learning. Accepting that "ideas (which themselves are but parts of our experience) become true just in so far as they help us get into satisfactory relation with other parts of our experience,"[8] progressive educators can be overcome with romantic visions of perfectly task-involved students consistently adhering to the guidance of their teachers. As every teacher learns quickly enough, not all students who are exploring their experiences engage in appropriate activities. Nourishing students' interests often involves a process of association by which existing interests are paired with new or uninteresting constructs. Over time, if new and old ideas are consistently linked, the entire system of constructs can become connected and commitment to the system sustained. When students fracture their intellectual lives, they minimize the opportunity to associate new and old ideas by failing to coordinate their personal needs and/or considering others' expectations.

Earl and his friends reminded Nancy, John, and a host of educators of the need to monitor children's investigations. Their adventure began when Earl selected a book from the library on video games and superheroes, and walked back to class engrossed in the lives of superheroes. When he arrived, the children were asked to write about objects of personal meaning that they brought to school. This project was associated with author Laurie Lawlor's visit—the visit that helped inspire David's story of the "hewmen" boy who turned into a deer and back again. Earl and Derek created an entirely different world from the one David had constructed out of this assignment. They had books on warfare, weapons, and superheroes spread around them. Earl was busy drawing vigorous, heavily armed figures (see Figure 6.1). "Mrs. Brankis," he called, "I just drew this awesome weapon."

Those who study the way in which violent behavior is socialized would not be surprised to find that, after this literary adventure, Fred and Earl got into a fight at recess. Earl seemed to be learning how to bully others both from the direct experience of fighting and from the vicarious experience of following the lives of superheroes.

John recalled Earl's description of the joy of learning a game in gym. "One game . . . I really had no idea how to play it. But, you know, the kids were running and I had no idea what to do, so I just ran with them. Then, I never got tagged in the game." This seemed more and more like a description of Earl's typical mode of operation. Following the group worked poorly for workbooks and many class assignments that did not involve a public display of one's thought: Earl was quickly tagged out when he started running without looking at the instructions. But on more physical tasks, Earl became a creative apprentice trying to copy the best aspects of each master artist's work.

Superhero life involves avoiding the more communitarian aspects of social interaction in favor of a rugged individualism that is sustained by periodic social isolation. Earl's behavior conformed to this ideology, but it was difficult to discern the cause and effect of his aggression by simply observing him. Earl's macho and clumsy manner could have led to fights that he then justified by looking for parallels in the lives of superheroes. Or, Earl's favorite superheroes may have served as models, exemplifying an image he enjoyed. In a pattern of observational learning, Earl could have been vicariously conditioned to recast his desire to be liked by his peers into forms of dominance, and acted on this knowledge by fighting with his peers.

Those who have studied the concept of vicarious conditioning caution us to remember that "people are generally less affected emotionally by the adversities of strangers than by the suffering and joy of those close to them and on whom they depend."[9] Nevertheless, Earl seemed to resonate with the lives of superheroes in a way that made it difficult to

FIGURE 6.1 Earl's Superhero

presume that superheroes held stranger status in his world. So, although we could not discern a clear cause of Earl's aggression, we could conclude that he was busy identifying and regulating violent emotions more often than nurturing ones.

Dick Best [the principal] was called on to mediate the conflict between Earl and Fred, and both boys were grounded for several recesses. Back in the class, with Nancy's guidance, the boys had to talk toe to toe. Constructive suggestions were countered with assertions that the "enemy" could not be trusted and would just do bad things. Nancy asked the boys for suggestions about how to resolve this fight. Fred and Earl said they preferred to be put in separate rooms or to be separated in Nancy's classroom.

"Separate you two?" said Nancy. "You come together like magnets. You *like* to get together." Nancy's observations seemed right on target.

When a visitor interrupted to demand Nancy's attention, John told the boys that they seemed to be negotiating very well. "You are not fighting, and you are listening to each other pretty thoughtfully." Indeed, the boys were negotiating well in spite of their claims that trust was impossible. With a little time, they even calmed down enough to go back to work. It was amazing how one minute Earl could be so mean to his friends and the next everyone could be pals, yet Jack was consistently ignored by his peers or remained on the fringe of any activities.

Earl turned back to his superhero drawings. There were superhero comics all around him on the table. Wanting to call Earl's attention to the possibility of vicarious conditioning, John pointed out that boys read these and fight, while girls do not read them and do not fight as much. Earl abruptly said that he knew plenty of girls who fought. Recognizing the accuracy of Earl's challenge, John decided not to push this point, and Earl continued, relaxed in his drawing.

Still working on the task of writing about a personal object, Earl had written nothing. Yet, his drawings were lively. Earl was self-aware enough to explain to John, "I like drawing pictures." Earl had an extremely strong commitment to performing like superheroes and was committed to action rather than words. He could not find the aesthetic and reflective experience of writing to be as powerful a medium for self-expression as drawing weapons and imagining ways in which to use them.

John knew that it would be possible to channel the excessive activity levels and attraction to novel stimuli that he observed in Earl into more appropriate instrumental motor and attention responses. He hoped to facilitate this change in their attitude towards achievement by encouraging Nancy to let the children decide what materials to read and dramatize their experiences, "learn[ing] with their whole bodies instead of just their eyes."[10]

At the end of April, Nancy asked students to choose groups, based on interest, to prepare plays. Most boys wanted to invent plays based on comics and read comics to get ideas. Earl and those interested in superheroes sat around a low table discussing the "neat" qualities of different comic characters.

"I don't want anyone touching this comic except me," said Earl, signaling that ownership was an issue.

"You [should] share," said Ben.

"My mother won't let me," claimed super-Earl.

"Then you can't be part of this group."

"This is my oldest comic," said Earl, skimming through it, ignoring the rebuke. "D.C. It is my oldest one. It is very old."

The boys continued to talk about prices, ownership, and the relative powers of superheroes. No one seemed to be thinking about how to write an interesting play. In this respect, they did not deviate from the typical chatter of the more macho boys in the class. Earlier that week, for example, Earl challenged Shane: "No matter what, the Redskins are number one."

"They didn't win the Super Bowl." Shane was in Earl's face.

"They have never lost in the play-offs."

"Yes they did. They lost to San Francisco."

Shane and Earl went on in this vein for at least five minutes.

"[The University of] Alabama would kill the Dallas Cowboys," said Shane. Then, "Did you watch *Fried Green Tomatoes?*"[11]

"Yes," said Earl, who kept to the topic of dominance. "I liked the part where [a middle-aged woman rammed the car of two younger women, and] said, 'I'm older and I've got more insurance.'"

Allan, Earl's newest friend, ignored the debates about power and ownership, and read the available comics looking for ideas. In contrast, whether talking or silent, Earl flipped through comics, but never alighted for long on the printed word.

Nancy reminded the group that they agreed to read. "That's the only reason I agreed to let you have comics." Only Nancy's warning prompted everyone, including Earl, to begin reading.

Two days later, during snack time, Earl flicked through a large color catalogue of comics and related paraphernalia.

"What are comics for?" asked Fiona.

"For reading," said Earl.

"I get that part." Fiona was bemused, yet tolerant. "What do you read them *for?*"

Earl kept flipping pages, but Ben said, "There's excitement in them for boys."

John interjected, intensely "Why, Ben, is it for boys and not girls?"

"There's so much death and blood in them." The work of superheroes is apparently not women's work.

Later, when the group reading comic books formed, three third grade boys had been recruited to help. Earl delayed starting because he wanted to find a chair that was bigger than average, and to jostle for space "amongst the ordinary mortals" at the table.

Rhonda Newman, the assistant principal, was helping the group get organized. She efficiently arranged pairs of boys to read different comics.

Allan and Earl had *Spider-Man.*[12] Earl turned a page before Allan finished the last panel, and read, "Ha! The secret empire I presume. Hey! Cut me some slack. I ran into not one, but two super do-gooders. Spidey and that Darkhawk dweeb."

Earl mispronounced some words and missed others, but did not stall. In turn, the two boys read well enough. Soon, they began counting the members of the Wrecking Team described and illustrated in the comic book. Then, they tried to match the characters on the cover with those inside the book.

"Is he," Allan pointed, "just an ordinary human with a strong gun?" This occasioned a discussion of cyborgs, robots, and other comic book roles—certainly a form of intellectual work. John was looking for a germ of curriculum that would more thoroughly synthesize personal experience with popular, peer, and school culture. He searched for a way to make literacy personally meaningful for Earl. John was disheartened when, after Rhonda urged the group to finish reading and summarize, Allan and Earl simply flicked to the end.

"I gotta read this last page," said Earl. He then read the comprehension sheet Nancy had prepared, which asked, "What is the problem?"

"There is not a problem," Earl said. "They are just fighting." Then he read aloud, "What is the action?" Answering the question Earl said, "There is no action, it's a fight."

Sitting beside him, scribbling this down, John thought, "What you see is what you want." There certainly was fighting in the comic, but Earl recorded only that and not the rest of the story.

John was away the next day. When he returned, Nancy told him that the superheroes nearly destroyed one another. Apparently, when Nancy, Rhonda, or the third grade tutors made attempts to help the boys in the superhero group reflect on the intellectual features of acting out a story, they instigated only anger. The boys' anger escalated into progressively more intense forms of bickering that gradually became personal. Eventually, the boys were no longer pretending, and the violent world of Marvel Comics was becoming their world.

Because no one lives in isolation, children need to coordinate concepts of the self and concepts of group affiliation. When children perceive themselves as similar to others, they begin to formulate a social identity. As they develop stronger affiliations with a particular group, children begin to differentiate their group from other groups and create norms to sustain their group. The resulting sense of cohesion also affects children's relationships with other groups. If groups accept aggressive norms, they can sustain such norms for the life of the group. It is also common for in-group members to instigate conflict with out-group members. These possibilities were not lost on Nancy.

"Nothing has captured them like this stuff. But I don't think it is capturing their intellect. It has just captured their egos."

"All this big muscle stuff," agreed John.

"And there's not a girl in their group." Nancy laughed, but was still disturbed. "I can't take it. I've put a deadline of Friday. It's so awful. I liked it better [earlier in the year] when we were talking about fairness."

"I don't think it is good for Earl. I think the other things were so much better, like fairness, and looking out for each other. Since this comic book thing, he's deteriorated."

John and Nancy were trying to decide how Marvel Comic superheroes differed from the Greek gods, superheroes of another time, when Rhonda joined them. "If you are looking for a child-centered school, we . . . followed their lead. . . . They were where they needed to be. . . . They had fantasized all these times. I was destroying their fantasies. They were ready to kill me. I don't mind. I'm not afraid of anger."

"But Rhonda, what good is coming out of this?" asked Nancy.

Rhonda argued that the thwarted impulse to get what one wants is the beginning of social life, democracy, civilization, and laws.

"Superheroes don't make laws," said John.

"By the end of two weeks," Rhonda said, "they would have a democracy."

Challenges and Controversies

- If ideas should help children connect various parts of their experience, how can caregivers coach children into accepting constructive ideas?
- Should children be challenged when their ideas are socially inappropriate?
- How can educators limit behavior that goes awry without becoming overly controlling?
- How can educators encourage children who become preoccupied with power and self-determination needs to also consider their competence needs?
- Group dynamics can take on a life of their own. How can educators help students become aware of the ways in which they can undermine their personal identities in the service of accepting a group identity?

"You are going to have to get some girls in there, or it won't happen," said John.

"Yes, girls would help. . . . But, this is really what learning is."

"I'll never do Marvel Comics in my room again," said Nancy. Nancy, Rhonda, and John were serious but also breaking the tension with laughter. "Give me twenty sets of workbooks," called Nancy. They were discovering the frustrating effects of excessive classroom noise on the performance and activity levels of these boys.

Later in the day, when play preparation continued, Rhonda arrived in the doorway and called, "If I meet with the superheroes group, are they going to yell at me today?" She was serious, but relaxed.

"No," called the boys.

"We are not having a play," Rhonda proceeded. "You are [each] going to make a mask, but before you do. . . . Write down what you are going to say into the microphone. Remember, I don't know these superheroes. Are you good or bad? Who are your enemies? Why are bad guys afraid of you?" In such ways, Rhonda and Nancy tried fruitlessly to get motives and reasons added to the superheroes' muscles.

Earl wrote almost nothing. Nancy passed by to ask questions with the hope of provoking writing. Listening, Earl sat staring into space before slowly writing a few words. Earl was more productive when making his mask, although he did not color it.

Later, the superheroes wore their masks and delivered words to the class. But the hope of a vigorous conjunction of personal impulses with peer and popular culture in schoolwork remained unrealized. The boys adopted the stance that ordinary human or not, with or without a powerful gun, literacy, mutual respect, and collaboration were of no use to a superhero.

Tempering Aggression

If intrinsic interest in how people interact with one another must be tapped before literacy can play a central role in someone's life, educators need to be careful about how they manage children's aggressive behavior. Restricting children's opportunities to collaborate can limit their opportunities to learn communication skills, and text gains meaning only because it allows individuals to communicate with one another. When direct forms of communication are associated with textual forms of communication, children's moral as well as intellectual functioning can be enhanced. Active boys like Earl are unlikely to acquire an intrinsic understanding of the quieter pleasures of reading and writing until they see the value of communicating with others and learn to transfer those skills into their imagination. To make such associations, Earl would have to become less concerned with looking smart and beating the best player, and more concerned with considering others' needs and expectations. Only then is he likely to identify socially valued ends to pursue in school, and ultimately in life.

In John's first interview with Earl, he said of school, "They let you help littler children. . . . It's one of my favorite things to help kindergartners." John had edited this out of the manuscript because it seemed like a passing comment that was not supported in any way by Earl's behavior. Perhaps Earl's speech and action would become fully integrated and less aggressive if, like David, he constructed a world where helping and collaborating were more central.

When half the class was discussing fish around a table with Nancy, Earl dominated again. "Everyone is going to get a turn," said Nancy.

"Start with Ruth," said Earl, accepting the rebuke. Ruth happened to be beside Earl, and if she went first, he would go second. A bit of a stretch, this was an opportunity to attribute a concern for others to Earl and begin calling his attention to others' needs and expectations.

There was such consistency in Earl's aggressive behavior that positive labeling alone did not seem likely to help him become more thoughtful toward others. Earl's topic for discussion, for example, was predators—sharp-toothed superheroes of the deep (see Figure 6.2). Would Earl ever consider *Symbiosis Under the Sea?* Or, *Teamwork Among Fish?* His dominance theme was so consistent that the evolution of communitarian thoughts and actions seemed unlikely. To this extent, Earl's experience was fully connected, although he focused so much on self-determination and power needs that he closed off more emotional, aesthetic approaches to life.

At show and tell that same afternoon, Ben waited to show the class his gyroscope. "Just roll the stupid thing," demanded Earl.

"*You* are stupid," said Ben joking, but clearly defending himself. There was general laughter, and Earl appeared not to be put out. Yet, when the class went to the library, Earl acted out in a way that upset the librarian: He sprayed books around as if he was in a feeding frenzy for material on sharks.

Earl manipulated rules to achieve ends that were in his favor, regardless of whether they conformed to others' expectations. To be successful, he had to use skills he was still in the process of acquiring and imagine others' perspectives well enough to acquire their compliance with his agendas. To help Earl become aware of others' expectations, John began to look for opportunities to suggest prosocial behavior rather than correct Earl's somewhat insulting manner. He knew that these associations needed to be developed slowly and without the use of bullying tactics that might validate Earl's aggressive behavior. Speaking with Mrs. Quimby, who ran the 103 Club before and after school, John learned about her behavior modification program for encouraging Earl to become less

Shark'S Prey

When a Shak bites it's
prey the shark tilts its
Snot up out of the Way.
its jaws swing down and
forward So that the Shaks
mouth opens at the front
of it's body.

FIGURE 6.2 Earl's Approach to the Study of Fish

dominating. Mrs. Quimby agreed that, at the very least, the reinforcement might encourage Earl's mercenary tendencies and planned to label Earl's desire to help others, and consider their needs and expectations.

Progress was slow. After a small flu epidemic, for example, Nancy realized that everyone was back. "Stand up if you're one of the people who had the flu."

Earl, who was not sick, stood up. "I'm one of the people, but I didn't . . ." and he trailed off into silence. He seemed willing to do anything, even claiming sickness, to be in the limelight.

A week after Valentine's Day, Colleen gave out valentines that she had been too sick to hand out earlier. Earl came over to say, "Thank-you Colleen." John reinforced such polite behavior by telling Earl how thoughtful he had been, and that not many of his classmates were as nice. Unfortunately, Earl remained busy drawing and seemed not to hear John's compliment.

Later that day, Nancy began reading Alice Walker's book, *Finding the Green Stone.*[13] Set on an idyllic Caribbean island, the story was about how black children dealt with the themes of care and resentment: Perhaps such modeling would help Earl reflect on his priorities. "Which is Alice Walker?" asked Nancy, pointing to the photo of Walker and the white woman illustrator on the dust jacket. Grabbing the limelight, Earl came and pointed correctly—no simple grandstanding this time.

In Walker's story, Johnny and Katie had brightly glowing green stones that they loved, but Johnny soon lost his and coveted the sister's stone. When her brother made Katie angry, her stone lost brightness. When she decided that she loved her brother, and would help him find his stone, the glow returned to her stone.

When the siblings' mother appeared in the story with a very brightly shining stone, Nancy asked the class why this stone shined so brightly.

"Because she loves it," said Earl. Earl's attention was on the stone and not on the love between family members.

Earl's friend Ruth knew that the theme of this story was neither materialistic nor selfish: "She works with children. She's helping other people."

Recess arrived so Nancy suggested that, as the class left, the children ask themselves, "Why does Johnny have trouble finding his stone?"

During recess, Alice Kay, Catherine Jamison, and John discussed how to attribute prosocial motives to Earl and why these tendencies should be encouraged. Alice planned to ask Earl and Jack, right after recess, to compliment one another. Catherine also agreed to look for ways to encourage this change.

Alas, by the end of recess, this plan changed. The adults discovered that Earl had slugged someone—so much for his green stone. Catherine gently quizzed Earl in the hall about these events. Earl said he had swung around and accidentally clouted the boy. The story was fuzzy. John could not follow it. The discussion went for about five minutes and Catherine restrained herself from accusing Earl of deliberately hitting. Eventually, Catherine asked if John wanted to ask anything that might clarify events. John said, "It seems that Earl has been thoughtful of others already today. (Thank goodness for Colleen's valentine and his thanking her.) Probably, he wouldn't want to hurt someone, and he'd want to tell the person he didn't mean to hurt him."

Then, John asked if the boy who got hit was a good person. Earl said, "He's OK."

"Well maybe he'd be pleased," John suggested, "if you told him you were sorry and would like to be friends."

Catherine then took Earl to his regularly scheduled session with Alice, who found him calm. Alice elicited an exchange of compliments. Jack, who Alice said was afraid of Earl, complimented Earl first. Alice then asked Earl to do likewise. Earl simply said, "good." Alice prompted, saying, "We usually say the person's name when we compliment them."

"Jack," said Earl, without looking at him. Warming to the task, Earl finally said, "Jack, you are good."

Back in class, Nancy asked, "What questions were we asking before recess?" Then, "what will it take for Johnny to find his green stone?"

"Love, love," said Earl.

"Don't steal things," and similar suggestions of good conduct came out.

"What has he done that might help?"

"Said he's sorry."

"Why?"

"Maybe," said Earl. "He thinks if he bes nice, then the stone will light up."

"So you think he's being nice just to get the stone back?" asked Nancy.

"Yes," said Earl.

"Anyone else?" asked Nancy, but no one refuted Earl's interpretation. The class was locked into an instrumental preoccupation with doing good to get something in return. Moral action, in this view, satisfies one's own needs and occasionally the needs of others, but rules tend to be endorsed as a means to the end of serving one's self-interest. Earl remained engrossed in finding the green stone as Nancy read on.

After much searching, accompanied by everyone in the community, the characters came to rest under a big tree. "The tree's green stone was one of its millions of fat green leaves."

"That's his! [The tree's stone]" called Earl. Noticing the tree was the beginning of Johnny's change of heart and his discovery of his own stone—a discovery Earl could make only by having his own change of heart.

Nancy asked what the story showed.

Earl suggested, "love is better than. . . . Ah, hate can do something that is not good, and love is better than hate. If you love something and you're being mean, you could lose it." Earl's interpretation offered a mixture of materialism and altruism.

Nancy said, "Earl, since you spoke first, stand by me and we'll see if we can link our thoughts up." Nancy then held Earl's hand.

Next, Arleigh took a turn. "I think what Earl is saying is right. If you have something special, and you lose it, it's probably because you were bad. If you say sorry, you'll probably find it." Arleigh then held hands in the line with Earl.

Shane spoke about forgiveness. "Join the line," said Nancy.

In the line that formed as others had their say, Earl stopped listening and jostled for position. Lost in his own world, Earl did not seem to internalize any of the virtuous behaviors being discussed.

Earl surprised everyone the next day when, as soon as he arrived, he went to work on silly sentences before moving on to geography questions. This was unusual. Earl finished his work without prodding. Then, he moved on to spelling, and came over to work with Shane. Nancy called Earl to her and suggested that he help Jack as well. As the work session ended, Earl said proudly, "I helped them." Earl welcomed Nancy's attempt to help him become less domineering.

Later, the students went back to work on their fish projects. The day before, Earl and his group could not decide what to do and Nancy had told them to really take their time to decide. After a night's rest, they got together and immediately started writing. Earl produced some vigorous artwork and, for him, a fair quantity of writing.

Another group decided they wanted to work with clay. Earl stopped writing and blurted out, "I want the clay . . . we're doing clay now." Nancy handed him clay and he said, "I want the biggest." The writing was dropped and suddenly there was a wonderfully sculpted shark, with detailed gills, eyes, and teeth. Earl could be a loose cannon, but when there was no reading or writing involved, he was also competent, involved, and witty.

Perhaps it would be possible to channel Earl's appreciation for action into less violent activities. This seemed likely earlier in the day, when Dr. Kahne, the father of one of the students, came in with a cow's heart, kidney, and brains. Earl was to the fore, asking and answering questions in his most domineering style.

"Do you know what a kidney does?" asked Dr. Kahne.

"Pee pee," said Earl, with no trouble.

The children were issued surgical gloves. Earl held his hands up like a freshly scrubbed surgeon about to put on gloves.

"This is awesome," he said a little later, with half a brain on each hand. Then, "What's this?" he asked, poking at one of them.

"A blood vessel."

The organs were from cows. "What would be the worst thing about being a cow?" asked Dr. Kahne.

"They'd kill you," said Earl, lively and up with the play.

Near the end of day, after Earl and Fred had calmed down, the class went back to organ inspection. In the midst of this, Earl held his gloved hands up and called, "It's a success! The operation is a success."

Challenges and Controversies

- How can educators help children who prefer action more than words make constructive associations between the two modes of communication?
- Given that beneficence requires the ability to anticipate others' needs, what can educators do to help children associate beneficence and learning?
- Are there ways to help children understand the expectations of others without lecturing them?
- What models, other than superheroes, can be used to validate children's interest in action?
- For most second graders, working hard to learn takes on moral implications. Can teachers foster high levels of task-involvement by acknowledging children's commitment to fulfilling educational obligations?

"It is?" responded Nancy, looking at the mess and remembering Earl's fight with Fred.

With a flash, Earl startled and angered Nancy by putting his hand close to the scalpel as she cut open one of the arteries of the heart. The green stone seemed to produce a temporary change, but perhaps Earl's interest in physiology could be associated with the prosocial idea that doctors generally help people. Doctors would certainly offer models of action less violent than those of superheroes.

Impediments to Task Orientation

In an ideal world, students would find all of the activities in school to be as engaging as those that led Earl to declare his operation a success. In reality, one of the most controversial problems in the field of motivation involves the relationship between the nature of academic tasks and students' competence needs. Because task difficulty can be determined only by making comparisons, there are no absolute rulers for assessing whether students are engaged in appropriately challenging tasks. When students are task-oriented, they compare their current abilities with those required to master the task and feel competent when the two aspects of experience become aligned. When students are ego-oriented, they compare their current abilities with the abilities of others and feel competent when they can demonstrate superiority or avoid feeling inferior.

Earl was capable of adopting both task and ego orientations, but most often chose the latter. Classroom activities tend to pull for one orientation over another, but Earl did not always go along with such agendas. During the group's discussion of *Penny-Wise, Fun-Foolish,*[14] for example, Nancy asked the children to suggest possible interpretations of the title: "It doesn't have to be right. It's just a guess." Then, the students were told to read two pages and tell Nancy what the title meant.

Because students like Earl had a tendency to drift away from the printed word into their own thoughts of what the book should be about, Nancy's assignment provided them with structure they could or would not provide for themselves. By using questions to scaffold the process of thinking about a particular piece of text, children can organize their approach to reading, enhancing their understanding and ability to link a story to other aspects of their identity. When students are highly task-oriented, this approach works well. Students learn by associating old concepts with new ones, constructing new ideas in the process.

When students are ego-oriented, however, they look to others for validation of their ideas and can mistrust their own abilities. Going against the grain in his group, for example, Earl took the idea of guessing literally and suggested that a penny could be money. He stuck to this interpretation even though others, looking at pictures in the story, correctly argued that "Penny" was the name of a person. Preoccupied with out-performing his peers, Earl could have resisted others' interpretations because he thought his own ideas were superior. Or, wanting to avoid feeling inferior, Earl could have become preoccupied with defending his incorrect assumption rather than accepting the more correct interpretation of the word.

Ever resistant to teacher-structured tasks, John wondered if Nancy's use of group study questions pushed students like Earl into defining learning as a competition at the expense of promoting their independence. Perhaps, John thought, students would be better off with self-chosen tasks that were tailored more closely to their reading level. Of course, adjusting students' work could simply change the stigma of being labeled LD from a struggle to keep up to the shame of working on easier tasks.

A positive relationship between equal educational opportunity and motivation can occur because, when optimally motivated, individuals choose tasks that are moderately difficult rather than excessively easy or impossibly difficult to master. A well-run classroom offers students opportunities to choose their own learning activities, whenever it is practically possible to do so, because teachers gain insight into students' motivation. Worksheets and other adult-defined tasks establish guidelines for students that could undermine the intellectual struggle of determining what one is capable of mastering and the thrill of successful discovery. With worksheets, students are released from the burden of defining easy and hard tasks, assessing their own abilities in relation to a particular range of tasks, and linking their reactions to other parts of their experience. Nancy called John's attention to another shortcoming of adult- or textbook-structured tasks—the fact that social comparison is readily visible, making it impossible for students like Earl, who adopt an ego orientation, to ever feel comfortably competent.

Earl led John to question the preoccupation with relationships between task choice and motivation. As Earl finished, he told Nancy, "I know why the person who wrote it called him 'Ostrich.'" Earl did not have to give up his connection to money as a theme in the book. He had seen "rich" in "Ostrich" and recognized that there was a connection with this name and Ostrich's interest in money. Reinforcing this thoughtfulness, Nancy suggested that Earl write Ostrich on the chalkboard and underline "rich," so the others would realize this parallel. Earl seemed to be looking at the text metaphorically rather than passively decoding words to get to the end of the book.

This wisdom made John wonder why Earl had been classified as a student with learning disabilities. Earl seemed to understand much more about the text than John had given him credit for. And, he was willing to go beyond Nancy's request in a way that is often rare, even among graduate students. Of course, we could also wonder how often second graders read only parts of the words in a story and whether this was a habit that eventually needed to be challenged. But, Earl definitely had skills his peers did not.

"We are going to become critics," said Nancy after everyone finished. The students quickly divided themselves into a group with positive reviews and another with negative reviews.

Earl again demonstrated that he had been more skilled than a cipher. "It had a carnival and it talked about what you should and shouldn't do with money." None of the other students mentioned the moral of the story. Earl clearly came through this reading assignment able to keep up with his classmates. Like a literary critic, he was able to talk about interpretations that might help him construct his own identity.

These discussions were quite beneficial to Earl, who did not enjoy cut and dried worksheets—activities that Nancy called "crud." Earl was alert only when a public effect was about to be made. His preoccupation with facts rather than opinions made it difficult to know if he viewed school merely as a test that he had to dominate or as a series of public demonstrations of personal power. Earl's struggle to learn schoolwork certainly seemed subordinate to concerns about being in the limelight and living alongside superheroes: He tricked and manipulated his way along. More troubling, Earl seemed to trick himself, constructing false beliefs about what he knew and was learning.

Because Earl was grounded during lunch recess, John took the opportunity to talk with him about how he learned and his understanding of epistemology. John wanted Earl's views on the relative merits of memorizing facts versus developing personal positions on controversial matters. Several of us had been studying children's ability to distinguish these forms of knowledge. We found that students like Earl, who became preoccupied with memorizing factual information were likely to enjoy the work that Nancy called "crud" and that Earl sometimes cheated his way through. On the other hand, Earl's need for adventure seemed to lead him to prefer learning about topics that did not have a known answer.

Using dinosaur books and pictures, John presented the possibility of memorizing dinosaur names and sizes versus inquiring about the controversial matter of why they died out. To help Earl imagine the second alternative, John then showed Earl pictures illustrating different theories of extinction. Surprisingly, like adults who advocate "teacher-proof" curriculum, Earl said that learning names should be done before students explored controversial material. "What," John asked, "would happen if the boys and girls just did the remembering? Would it be good or bad if they stopped after that?"

"Be sort of not good because if somebody asked you a question you wouldn't know." Earl's purpose for knowing things was to be able to answer other people's questions. He did not raise the possibility of adventure, self-discovery, or the greater social utility that comes from exploring controversial topics. Earl's words fit with what John had just observed. Earl paid attention to schoolwork only when factual questions were to be discussed or scored. Accepting that some questions have no answers seemed to be outside his reach.

"What if it's a thing that not anyone knows, 'cause the scientists are really not sure. Like, it's such a long time ago it's hard to tell." John did not want to correct Earl's opinion by reasserting the controversial nature of the question, yet he sought greater insight into Earl's ability to accept the value of controversies.

"Well the scientists probably never thought of this, see. . . ." Earl faded into a long pause.

"Pretty hard to be sure?"

"There's a way of finding out." Earl kept talking—trying, but failing, to say how scientists might be certain about why the dinosaurs died out. Earl denied that the issue was fundamentally controversial and talked as if intellectual life was a test where the answers were known. Earl demonstrated a strong need for quick closure (urgency) and to maintain that closure for as long as possible (permanence) when thinking about academic tasks. These patterns were apparent only when knowledge to be learned was factual. Earl did not show such reactions to more active adventures such as fighting and dissecting animals.

Next, John wanted to see if Earl defined learning like the games in the gym, where Earl said he blundered to success. John reminded Earl that he once described his blundering and asked, "Do you think a lot of boys and girls learn that way, or do they learn different?"

"They learn all kinds of ways. . . ."

"Could you tell me more. Maybe you sometimes do things differently?"

"I do things all kinds of ways."

"OK. Could you tell me about those [ways], like [when you learn] school things."

"I look around and follow."

"You look at the other guys."

"Then I find out what it is, and then I try and go against the other person who is best at it, and see how I'm doing. If I can beat the one who is the best at it, I can find out that I'm getting to know the rules, like." On this score, there was no discontinuity in Earl's speech and action. Earl's words and deeds implied that his goal was to be number one, but this kind of ego orientation rarely allowed for reflection on the meaning of the printed word or the kind of self-discovery offered by higher levels of literacy.

"So, do you do schoolwork the same way sometimes?" asked John.

"Well in school, I come back from learning places [resource room] and I don't know what to do . . . then sometimes I look where the other kids are. Or, sometimes I read the instructions."

Unlike Bruce, Earl knew that instructions were important, and he did not think that pure blundering was the only way to learn. But, like Bruce, Earl's reasons for learning about dinosaurs were to prevent people from discovering that he did not know answers and for demonstrating that he could beat the best.

Ideally, science might teach tolerance and uncertainty, but not to Earl (or Bruce). Earl presumed that the answer to the riddle of the dinosaurs' demise must be known, and he bluffed about what he knew in a way that did not foster greater knowing. Earl also told us the only way that he knew when he knew something was when he was better than others. Unfortunately, it is possible to be better than others only when the world is a game where the endpoint is settled, the answers already exist, and the goal is to get them first.

Challenges and Controversies

- How can educators establish environments that encourage students to make growth-enhancing task choices?
- Are there tactful ways to help caregivers see that factual recall is only one form of knowledge valued in school?
- When students are ego-oriented, can caregivers persuade them to see the value of essential tasks? How?
- What should caregivers do when students consistently choose easy tasks? Impossible tasks?
- Can caregivers stimulate interest by helping children who resist teacher-designed tasks imagine relevant controversies?
- How can caregivers encourage children to distinguish factual and controversial knowledge while learning both types?
- Like Earl, most students learn "all kinds of ways." What can caregivers do to encourage various approaches to learning?

In thinking about the interview, John mused about his hopes for Earl. John knew that the desire to make sense, regardless of one's standing relative to others, is generally associated with the desire to collaborate in learning. Unfortunately, Earl's desire to be number one was in direct conflict with the skills necessary for effective collaboration, hampering his ability to learn the art of communication.

Writing to Communicate

Rather than trying to make Earl into a boy he was not, Nancy accepted his commitment to attaining the limelight and public displays. Using this information, she organized a series of conversations about fairness and the purpose of school activities that she hoped would help Earl and other classmates understand why so many people find value in writing. Students were encouraged to listen to one another as well as describe their reasons for writing. By working to communicate orally, and then using journals to reflect on that communication, Nancy hoped students would associate the two forms of communication. Earl was quick to speak up in class discussions, but slow to write. Perhaps his peers could teach him why writing was also worthwhile.

"Let me ask you this," encouraged Nancy. "Why do you think it's important for a kid to write?"

"I don't know," said Earl, seeing no reason.

"Why do I get you to write in your journals?"

Silence. Nancy called everyone's attention and put the question to the whole class.

"Because," said Erica, "when you look back at it, you'll remember what you did."

"OK. Can your brain remember enough things?"

"No," said many of the children in unison.

"So, writing works like an encyclopedia of the information you've encountered. What's another reason?"

Jack's hand was up, an encouraging sight. "If you get a ticket, you wouldn't know how to write."

"If you were a cop," said Earl.

"If you were a cop, you wouldn't know how to write," added Jack. The macho view of right and wrong continued to prevail.

"We don't just tell you things," said Ben. "We write to you."

"Communicate," said Jill.

Nancy probed a little more. "Why might thoughts on paper be valuable to other people?"

"They might get your idea."

"Communication," repeated Jill.

"Communication! Very good," said Nancy, hoping to encourage others to speak up as well. "What if you came to school and we had no writing? How much information could we have in our class? What do you think Earl?"

"If we had no books, there would be one good thing—no social studies." Earl was referring to an unhappy recent event with a substitute. He was not about to advocate writing as a means of passing information to one another.

"We couldn't communicate," repeated Jill. "Like if someone moved away, you wouldn't be able to write to them."

"We learn to read by writing," said Fiona.

"What if you know how to read perfectly? For you or me or John, why should we write?" In full scribble, John provided an excellent model for Nancy's point. Jill came over to watch, marveling at John's speed. While John tried to continue, Jill also counted the pages he had filled.

"If you read a book and you wrote about it, you wouldn't have to read it over again [if you wanted to remember]," said Fiona.

"How about our journals on plants [which the class had completed recently]?" Nancy asked. "Could you remember?" The lunch bell rang and, although Nancy released the class, about half the students lingered. "Earl, if you don't understand why you write, why do you draw?"

"It's a cool thing."

"Why is writing not cool and drawing is?"

"It is cool." Earl was adamant, but no more articulate.

"Writing is?" Nancy was a little surprised.

"It's pretty good," conceded Earl.

"Derek, why do you write stories?"

"I like writing my own stories," said Derek, tautologically.

"It's inventing. Writing is inventing," said Nancy.

"It helps your grades."

"What if there were no grades?" Nancy did not want children to see grades as the reason for writing.

"I'd keep writing," said Earl.

Jacob appeared at Nancy's elbow. "Look what you've written in your journal," marveled Nancy. Indeed, Jacob had been prolific. "We'll look at our journals after lunch," said Nancy, hinting that it was way past time to leave.

The session was intended to increase Earl's interest in writing. More than that, Nancy was trying to get Earl to see why others found writing "cool." And, Nancy was doing more than trying to give Earl sugar to help the medicine go down. These discussions encouraged Nancy's students to participate in the formation of the purposes governing their activities—to reflect on and reshape their reasons for action. In this respect, Nancy promoted the essence of intellectual freedom and perhaps the most important purpose of education.

After lunch, Nancy said, "Find your journals." Most of the children spontaneously began reading them. "The question is," said Nancy. "What are we doing with these?" The children seemed to ignore her and continued reading. "I want you to take the time to look back through to see what you've written."

"And drawn," said Earl.

"Who can find a treasure? You can be archaeologists. Earl, tell us something that is a treasure to you in your writing."

Earl made a couple of false starts, had trouble reading, and said, "Oh, never mind."

"I remember a piece of writing you did that I found so valuable. That list you made about what jazz was about."

Earl didn't take the hint, and Jack was drifting. Quietly and intently, almost all the girls and a collection of boys unearthed treasures from their journals. They ignored the way Nancy encouraged Earl.

"Jack, did you find a treasure?"

"At Christmas, I went to Derek's house."

"Let's think about Jack's entry. Is there anyone else who could write that?"

"No."

"That's what makes it special, 'cause Jack has his own story." Nancy was hoping that Jack would also sense the special qualities of his work.

"Jill, did you find a treasure?" encouraged Nancy. "Should only other authors give us input? Who is not an author in here?"

"Nobody."

"How do you become not an author?

"Don't write," said Earl.

"*You* should keep a journal," said Derek to Nancy, who then pulled out the journal she started earlier in the year.

"I wrote '*Perceptions of My Class,*'" Nancy read. "'*Active, noisy, indulged, spirited.*' You are a lot of action. '*Trouble listening.*' Look at yourselves. I wouldn't write that now!" Nancy then returned to the point of writing, "Earl? This started with you."

"I do like to write, and know how to communicate better, and learn more things, and keep old things." Earl gave reasons he did not have, or was unwilling to talk about, earlier in the day.

At the end of this discussion, everyone met on the rug to read Ron Bacon's large-type book, *Save Our Earth,* designed for groups.[15] "What if there were only pictures?" Nancy asked and read the words "protesting, pollution," and so on. "Can a superhero come and save the earth?"

"No."

"Who has to do it?"

"All of us."

"The author doesn't believe the superhero theory for saving the earth either," said Nancy after reading the blurb about the author.

As she read on, Earl drew a person sinking into a morass. A speech bubble said, "Help me." Earl's title said, "*Polishin [pollution] stinks.*" He was at least putting captions on his drawings.

Nancy drew attention to this. "You have a lot of stories you could write that are more exciting than those Choro Choro superheroes." The group laughed in a friendly fashion, and Earl was not put down. "I'm telling you!" added Nancy into the congenial hubbub.

Concluding, Nancy said, "What I hear coming out of this is all the stories you have to tell." The discussion turned to the autobiographies that the children were doing for homework. "Who," asked Nancy, "is better qualified than you to be authors about your own life?"

"No one."

"Your parents?"

"No."

"No one has seen our whole life," said Allan.

Over the next few weeks, the class continued to read and discuss the series about Richard Best and his trials in school. Sometimes Nancy read, but more often, pairs of students read and then wrote in their journals. "Take out your journals," said Nancy. "You will be sharing one book. Two chapters . . . Richard Best again. *Lazy Lions, Lucky Lambs*."[16]

Earl seemed to need more encouragement to write about his experience than most of the other students. Nancy caught Earl ripping out a page he started and interrupted him. "These are things we need to save. These are good things. See what else you can write about." Nancy prompted Earl to finish his sentence, and he worked with a flurry. "Boy are you writing away with ideas!" said Nancy. "What's making him learn more? Do you remember? Yes, he's learning to read, and who helped him?"

Soon, Nancy said, "Let's take two more minutes then we'll discuss."

"No," protested Earl. "I need more than two." The encouragement certainly worked.

"You need more? You sure have a lot there."

Earl's first words were large and wandered across the page. "*He made a frend. He went to the princiBl He may get pole [pulled or held] Back agian. He can not rite. But now Hes makeing a difers. Hes tincing [thinking] Befor he does it.*" Halfway down the page, Earl's script became smaller and tidier. "*Hes lirnig HOw to read. He Lerd How to spell word Becus His frend Matt taot him. He tried to lern the Bainer.*"

Earl protested, saying that he wanted to write about what might have happened at the party, a detail not found in the book. Nancy drew everyone's attention to the idea and agreed that it would be a good one. Earl continued writing, describing a fun party until Nancy asked, "Do we need more time?"

"Yeah," said Earl, barely lifting his head.

"If you think you are ready to share, go to the rug." called Nancy to the more restless students.

Earl continued with, "*[He] may not get pulld Back again Becus He may Have good grades*." When the bell signaled the end of the day, Earl kept writing. Nancy came back into the room and Earl said aloud to no one in particular, "I'm keeping writing." Finally Ben, determined to talk about Marvel Comics, distracted Earl. With the right encouragement, Earl could sustain high levels of task-involvement even though this was not his primary orientation toward schoolwork.

At the beginning of the year, on the school questionnaire, Earl's mother wrote, "Keep him busy with positive reinforcement, or he will turn into a stubborn mule." Not everyone can manage a stubborn mule, nor does "mule management" sum up the complexity of the many tricks Nancy tried to keep Earl committed to learning. Nancy was apparently successful, at least in the eyes of her student. In the last week, Nancy asked the class to write advice to next year's second graders, telling them what the class would be like. Earl wrote, "*You Have the niceit tecHer. She sings, she dansis She Reads. She Lets you liten to the Rado and shes the Best in the world.*"

Nancy the nice teacher also asked the children to draw and describe "a school of your dreams." Earl described his drawing to John. "It's the high-tech weapons school, and here is golf. The guards right here are Ninjas. I'm going to write about it afterwards."

As Nancy passed by she asked about a futuristic vehicle with a clearly warlike purpose, "Is that a tank?"

Challenges and Controversies

- What activities can educators use to help students identify constructive reasons for learning in school?
- How can educators sustain students' interest in hearing others' ideas?
- Can caregivers change students' competence orientations, encouraging a task orientation and eliminating ego- and work-avoidant orientations? Should they try?
- Why is it important to have reasons for learning?

"It's a time car," Earl lied. The boy-who-would-be-a-superhero knew what to say to please his teacher. He also showed no burning need for literacy in his imaginary school of high-tech weapons and broke a promise to John that he would write about the school as well as draw.

Lessons from Earl's Life

Earl taught us that some children simultaneously imitate others' expectations to gain the limelight and become overly preoccupied with self-determination. These contradictory values lead such children to fracture their experience in three ways. First, they become concerned with autonomy and self-efficacy to such an extent that they ignore their competence and affiliation needs. Second, because they will say or do whatever it takes to become the center of attention, they respond to others' expectations inconsistently. Third, because identity-enhancing interests are essential for self-determination and working to guess and imitate others' expectations undermines the ability to find such interests, these children will not be able to consolidate their needs and others' expectations. Adopting an ego orientation toward competence can help these children feel autonomous if they succeed in their quest for superiority. However, when they cannot perform well after attaining the limelight, such children fail to meet their needs and also incur the wrath of their would-be constituents. Faced with repeated disappointment, impersonal assertiveness can become anger-driven aggression unless someone intervenes to interrupt such a frustrating cycle.

Nancy and her colleagues taught us about six types of interventions that interrupt children's cycles of frustration. First, because children learn by associating action with ideas, they benefit from dramatizing various roles and events and then reflecting on their experience. Second, allowing attention-seekers time in the limelight, even when they are likely to fail, fosters an awareness of negative as well as positive consequences. Third, labeling negative as well as positive emotions validates legitimate sources of frustration and anger, helping children who may be acting out to define their experience. Fourth, inventing positive labels for children's character traits nurtures leadership potential, acknowledges identity-enhancing interests, and replaces negative stereotypes. Fifth, labeling the positive features of children's behavior reinforces associations between attention and effort, beneficence and learning, and behavior and emotions. Finally, asking groups of children to describe how and why they learn, label their emotions, and critique the social value of their group identities can help individuals imagine alternative approaches to consolidating their needs and others' expectations. When caregivers are careful to avoid responding to aggressive behavior in kind, they reduce the escalation of children's anger and frustration. Interventions that are used proactively can be paired with a positive attitude and calm demeanor to eliminate cycles of aggression, but only if children are encouraged to identify the sources of their experience and imagine alternative courses of action.

ENDNOTES

1. See Ladd & Profilet (1996).
2. See Adler (1930, p. 77).
3. See DeMaria (1990).
4. See Adler (1979, p. 77).
5. See Pinderhughes (1989).
6. See Miller & Miller (1990).
7. See Faulkner & Kich (1983), Gibbs (1989), and Ladner (1977) for examples of such research.
8. This is part of William James's definition of pragmatism (James, 1948, p.147).
9. See Bandura (1971, p. 14).
10. See Zentall (1980, p. 104).
11. This was a 1991 movie, directed by Jon Avnet, that made its way to television.
12. The children worked with books from a series (Michelinie, 1993a, 1993b, Michelinie & McFarlane, 1992).
13. See A. Walker (1991).
14. See Delton (1991).
15. See Bacon (1991).
16. See Giff (1985).

CHAPTER

7 Responding to Fractured Experience

Despite the holistic approach to learning advocated by the teachers, Laura B. Sprague School, located in an upper-middle-class suburb, conformed to the American preoccupation with defining success in terms of high scores on standardized tests. Average test scores placed Sprague above the 80th percentile of schools in the United States. Teachers kept their eye on children's daily progress, but administrators made sure that children were helped to attain test scores that would allow them an advantage when advancing to universities and occupations of prestige. Fractured experience could not be left to languish if administrators were to attain their goals.

Schools like Sprague attain such high marks on standardized tests, in part, because educators watch carefully for children who are having more difficulties than their peers and offer interventions to remedy those difficulties. At Sprague, high-stakes testing did not begin until third grade, but teachers of grades K through 2 were busy monitoring children's performance, looking for signs of trouble. When children were not progressing well, teachers made referrals to a Student Services Team. These "sending teachers" responded to a behavioral checklist (e.g., writes letters backwards, writes off the lines, does not listen to directions), offering clues about children's needs. They also described the interventions they had made to remedy poor performance. Attending a regularly scheduled weekly meeting of the Student Services Team, sending teachers might receive suggestions of new practices to try, parent volunteers could be assigned to work with the child, and/or children could be referred to specialists for a full case study.

Bruce, David, Jack, and Earl had all been referred for services in first grade, participated in a range of interventions in first and second grade, were involved in full case studies, and showed signs of marked difficulty on a battery of psychological tests.[1] These boys and others like them took an individualized IQ test (typically the WISC-R), and showed a gap of at least one standard deviation between their verbal and nonverbal performances. They took a test of processing ability (typically the Detroit Test of Learning Aptitude) and a nationally normed standardized achievement test (typically the Kaufman Test of Educational Achievement). The teachers' responses on the behavioral checklist offered clues as to which subtests were most important and whether additional testing should be conducted.

The most common difficulties involved auditory and visual discrimination and/or auditory or visual integration. Nevertheless, evaluation of speech and language production, physical and motor coordination, and social skills were also used when necessary. Specialists used these evaluations to clarify the accuracy of teachers' observations and explore the potential for overlooked disabilities. After testing was completed, the Student Services Team met with the sending teacher and relevant specialists (e.g., resource room coordinators, social workers, psychologists) to examine the evidence and make recommendations. At this meeting, educators discussed whether a child had learning disabilities or if more informal interventions and observations would be sufficient to meet the child's needs. The families were then invited to a Multiple Disciplinary Conference (MDC) that also included the sending teacher and any specialists that would be working with the child. Prior to that meeting, recommendations from the Student Services Team were incorporated into a formal Individualized Educational Plan (IEP) for the child. At the Multiple Disciplinary Conference, the families and educators discussed the formal test results and reviewed the criteria for special services eligibility. When eligibility criteria were met, the family and educators went through a list of relevant objectives and proposed services, editing the first draft of the IEP (a document that can range from 11 to 28 pages) until consensus was reached about each objective and intervention. Parents were then given as much time as they needed, either at the meeting or at home, to reevaluate the proposal and sign a consent form before services began.

Bruce, David, Jack, and Earl had all completed the identification process in the fall of second grade. During the year, Alice Kay took time each month to call the Johnsons, Richardsons, Davises, and Nortons, requesting information about any questions or concerns. In November's parent-teacher conference, the team of specialists servicing each student convened to discuss the student's progress. Parents were also free to request a conference whenever they saw a need. By the end of the year, a cohesive group of parents, classroom teachers, and specialists knew each boy's IEP as well as the details of his performance in class, on the teacher-designed second grade achievement tests, and on a second administration of the Kaufman Test of Educational Achievement.

In late spring, everyone involved with a particular student participated in an Annual Review to discuss the progress of each student receiving special services. For each student, Alice Kay consulted with the classroom teacher and all relevant Student Services Team members to form a viable third grade IEP. Caregivers from home and school designed plans for third grade, and imagined the child's needs in relation to larger institutional commitments. The boys' classroom teachers, various resource room teachers, and one or both parents typically attended the annual review.

Despite all this time and care, educators adopted a language of accountability in annual reviews that was transferred to education from business communities and treated absolute levels of achievement like tangible products. Others adopted a romantic language that focused so exclusively on descriptions of a child's experience that it was difficult to evaluate that experience. These were not languages that acknowledged the highly subjective nature of task difficulty and accomplishment, or the necessity of social comparison for determining competence. Sadly, preoccupation with a perfectly uniform product undermined the optimal levels of motivation and love for learning fostered by educators at Sprague. Preoccupation with literal descriptions of a child's work made it difficult to determine the degree of challenge and growth attained. Details of the year-end conferences revealed how talk focusing exclusively on accountability or storytelling causes misery for particular children and their families. The omnipotent director who sees the little sparrow fall—the one who is to be found in the details—was not in control of these conferences.

Challenges and Controversies

- What are the liabilities associated with treating achievement as a product that can be turned out in a perfect, uniform manner?
- In what ways can caregivers who enjoy children become overly romantic about their achievement, overlooking important developmental difficulties they may be facing?
- Are there procedures available to make the process of labeling children's difficulties less driven by absolute levels of achievement?

Bruce's Future

John missed the conference where Bruce's third grade year was discussed because he accepted an invitation to discuss future plans for research on child development. At the meeting, John and other researchers were asked to discuss directions for research on child mental health in schools and families. Arriving at this meeting with his head full of Bruce, David, Jack, and Earl, John found almost all the language to be harsh and alien. Television and radio news, along with many other public discussions of education, often rely on the kind of talk that made John so uncomfortable.

The system of thought that drives such language relies on a notion of truth as absolute and stable. Harmless in the armchair discussions of those working in think tanks, this vision of truth becomes dangerous when it spills over into how we characterize the teaching and parenting of children with learning disabilities. Consider the message to parents and teachers that emerge in the following: "Unreplicable research cannot be validated, and its results must be considered idiosyncratic because they cannot be generalized. . . . [We need to be] making our research in learning disabilities replicable and more respectable. We must have replicable research, because only replicable research can be validated, and only validated research can contribute to a usable and generalizable body of findings pertaining to learning disabilities. Creating this body of findings should be the mission of all researchers."[2]

To see this quest for certainty and, by implication, uniformity as something that should limit all research would be as unfortunate as Bruce's machismo. To seek universal knowledge on the understanding of human development is as fallible as any other form of human inquiry and can lead us to popularize false beliefs as easily as helpful ones. Generalizations are useful to those who seek uniform definitions of educational problems and uniform solutions to the problems so defined. They also drive the agendas of a type of administrator who makes it difficult for teachers to see particular children more clearly, and to work out, with those particular children and their classmates, exactly what to do. A simplified world of such generalizations does not offer a language about how specific purposes and practices can become the work of particular teachers, children, peer groups, and parents. John left his meeting frustrated by an overwhelming sense that he would be unable to stop a dangerous bandwagon that was headed in the wrong direction. The bandwagon of uniformity, John thought, moved away from helping schools learn to respect children's motivational needs and the challenge of coordinating personal needs and others' expectations.

Before going to the meeting of researchers, John had obtained permission from everyone attending Bruce's meeting to record those proceedings. The day after both meetings, when listening to the recording about Bruce, John felt the same sensation that emerged during his conversation with the researchers. The directors of both meetings were detached, far above the children, looking for algorithms to apply to Bruce's case.

Bruce's mother met with Alice Kay and Thyra DeBolt. Comparing Bruce's performance with those of his peers, Alice began, "He is gaining confidence in his own ability. Math is an area of strength. . . . His total math composite puts him just about in the middle of second grade. Although he's made progress, he is still a little bit behind.

"In reading, Bruce has made progress in his sight word vocabulary and various decoding strategies. However, I . . . feel there is very little carry over into the assignments or reading that he does with Thyra. . . . We are talking, reading at the beginning of second grade. Spelling and written expression are Bruce's weakest. . . .

". . . Next year, Bruce will continue to need intensive remedial help in language arts. I feel that he really needs a structured, supportive environment for next year. . . .

"Thyra, do you have anything to add?"

"Well, I agreed with that. I think in the classroom, in math computation, he performs higher than he did on the test. . . . He seems to remember most of the things we have learned this year. I think he feels very good about himself in math, and if we are having class discussion and it involves math and science, he is right up there with all the kids. But when it comes to spelling and writing, he has problems. But . . . he is not afraid to put things down on paper. . . ."

"I think," said Alice, "his writing was difficult to read because he wasn't doing any phonics. Now he is. . . .

"But . . . the whole battery came out at the beginning of the second grade. And I think we have to consider, very, very seriously what type of placement for next year. He is going to go on to third grade. There is no question of that."

"I'd been wondering," said Mrs. Johnson, "if it might not be better to keep him in second?"

Everyone talked at once, making the recording of individual voices a blur. Then:

"I don't think," said Alice, "in Bruce's case. . . ."

"I think," interrupted Thyra, "that would hurt his macho image of himself."

"Well, yes," said Mrs. Johnson, "but might it fit academically?"

"OK," said Alice, "what we are going to propose is to hire another LD teacher. I have a group of four boys that are in the same position as Bruce. . . . The teacher would be here in the morning, and she would be . . . responsible for their academic subjects. And she is trained, as I am, in learning disabilities. So rather than get me three days a week for 30 minutes, they would be with her most of the morning, five days a week. . . ."

This proposal had already been briefly presented to Bruce's father over the phone. Mr. Johnson had told John that he felt the family was being punished. John was not the least bit surprised by Mr. Johnson's feeling. Although John saw no evidence whatsoever that anyone intended to punish Bruce and his family, to feel punished because one is different from others is an everyday law of this contemporary jungle.

Nothing in the conversation could counter the flavor of a rather sweeping judgment: If you can't provide the books and activities most affluent families in the area can, then your child will be cut off from the world of the worthy. Bruce's classmates were complicit in the gestures that cut him off from a comfortable life in the community. Similarly, Bruce himself helped to invite it. He, in turn, cut off geeks and offered no succor to the weak. The sense of feeling punished did not originate in one place or with one person. It was not as if someone had been unreasonable or adopted a behavior that could easily be changed. The cycle of miscommunication perpetuated itself.

After the decision to offer him more intensive services the following year, Bruce seemed more tense, or intense, than usual. When John watched Thyra, Dick Best, and another teacher enrolling him (and another student), as gently as possible, in summer school, Bruce behaved like a wild man. His typically well-groomed hair looked like that of a punk rocker and his expression matched it. Surrounded by adults, Bruce glanced about furtively as if to escape. Summer school was hardly welcomed in his agenda.

The school picnic for the second grade came a week after the conference. It was held in a park with grass, lakes, and trees. Bruce played with friends, but twice John noticed him stalking alone, muttering intensely, with his hands out wide, palms up, in his most exasperated, "give me a break you spastic geek" manner.

The next day, John mentioned Bruce's behavior change to another teacher. The teacher elaborated, saying that at the picnic Bruce was caught waving a big stick through a group of parents in pursuit of two smaller boys. "One little kid got away from him, and then he ran and threw this club—he just hauled off and threw it as hard as he could, and it happened to land where there was nobody. A mother said, . . . 'I'm glad we don't have to put up with that [in our class].' The parent's reaction was—this boy doesn't belong."

This teacher also recognized Bruce's role in maintaining his marginal place: "I got Bruce and said, 'We can't throw the sticks or anything in this crowded place.' But he didn't even register. Then I realized I hadn't said his name right. So I said, 'You're Bruce, aren't you?' I wasn't harsh with him, but I saw how difficult it is to penetrate somebody like that as far as school is concerned. He was very, very tough."

As others observed, an important function of special education is to legitimize regular education by affirming that the problem is with the children diagnosed as having disabilities, not with the practices of regular education.[3] There need be no formal punishment for this function to be fulfilled or for punishment to be felt. Such pain could be prevented only in a school and classroom that gave Bruce no reason for his macho, defensive motives; actively provoked him to abandon them; and actively embraced him in a fashion that seemed fair to him and everyone else. The meeting about Bruce's progress proceeded without critical analysis of Bruce's ethical choices, or of the context within which he made those difficult choices.

Back in the meeting, Alice continued, "After lunch, they will have 50 minutes with their peers in the [regular] classroom. Then they go to gym for a half-hour, whatever. Then they come back and they have another 50 minutes with their peers. So this teacher would be doing science, social studies, or maybe math, in the afternoon. The LD teacher, in the morning, would preview the lesson so they are one up on everyone. So the next day they can review it. So I see this as a real viable package."

"I like that part of it," said Mrs. Johnson. "I'm just concerned about the kids. I mean, how do you think the other kids are going to react? Are they going to be singled out as four dumb kids?"

Thyra said, "The kids don't really notice."

"They don't notice," said Alice. "They don't really care. They don't know, you know."

"That would be great. That's what I'm looking for, that they don't know."

Many children at the school do not see going to the resource room as a stigma.[4] Bruce, however, was preoccupied with status, and occasionally resisted going to the resource room. He had also been taunted as slow, and it stung him. The hope that others would not know that Bruce was having trouble with schoolwork is a hope that the problem might be solved without creating classroom communities wherein each student's particularities are known, respected, and worked with by everyone. On this point, Mrs. Johnson and Bruce's teachers seemed, for the moment, agreed.

Listening to the tape, John did not agree with them. John saw a contradiction in the caregivers' hope that things can be made to "work" if educators remove from regular education classrooms the problems associated with respecting individual differences—real communities in classrooms cannot be created if some children have secret lives. Like John, many researchers also hoped to deal with the consequences of differential levels of ability by obscuring them from children. Yet, the desire to obscure differences in competence is not the same as respecting people regardless of their competence. On the contrary, obscuring differences seems to deny respect by denying the identities that make individual children interesting to know.

"Even if they know," Alice continued, "they say, 'I am going to a special teacher.'. . . We have to go to the speech teacher. Or music."

"Violin lessons," added Thyra.

Alice noted that some new action was needed because, "The demands of the third grade are so much greater."

"Oh," said Mrs. Johnson. "It has my consent. If I wasn't a working mother, I would consider taking him out for a year and home schooling him; just to give him time to mature, and keep his self-esteem as high as I can. I don't expect all of my kids to be A students, but they are great kids, and I want them to survive."

Bruce's "regular education" teacher for next year was introduced. Mrs. Johnson agreed with her, that positive feedback from the teacher was important, but added, "They also need positive feedback from their peers." John was comforted by this more honest acknowledgment about what peers would know.

Mrs. Johnson continued, "Bruce came home a few weeks ago and he was really upset, because some girl made fun of him, and said he couldn't read. . . . He could have a bunch of kids make fun of him."

"At the beginning of the year," said Bruce's future teacher, "we have a talk about differences and that people are different, and if I catch people doing things [like that] we sit down and have a talk about it as a class. This is not how we treat other people. . . . I'm letting them know that everyone is human, and people have different strengths and weaknesses."

The established practices of special education, the language we use for talking about children like Bruce, and the cultures of our schools do not support the vision this teacher began to articulate. It became hard, in this language, to confront Bruce with his moral choice to stand up for himself in an assertive, macho way. The language of assimilation

Challenges and Controversies

- In what ways do educators imitate the language of researchers who are interested in discovering general laws of child development?
- How can caregivers find a language for communicating what they know about particular children that does not overemphasize absolute levels of achievement?
- How can caregivers help children who recognize implicit assertions about their relative incompetence sustain self-respect and manage their anger?
- How can caregivers help children who receive special services understand the wisdom of these decisions?
- Is it always beneficial to offer children with learning disabilities extra schooling?

did not capture the limits of the narrow, right-wrong world Bruce constructed for himself and that constrained him. Nor did it capture the ways the classroom ethos maintained his identity and curriculum.

The adults in the picture were anxious about Bruce's plight, and went extra miles for him. During class time, Thyra, worried, but both encouraged and helped Bruce more than most of her children. She even fed him snacks more often than the others, and helped him after school. But, individual action was constrained by the language of professional specialization. The language used to characterize Bruce was the technical language of nomothetic psychology and its dialects in special education: the dialects of achievement levels and deficiencies in cognitive processes. In such a world, the student's unique experience of school has little place in the decisions about how to help him or her come to respect personal needs and consolidate those needs with others' expectations.

David's Future

The language of absolute levels of achievement also dominated David's annual review, in which Mrs. Richardson joined Alice, Catherine Jamison [the social worker], Ann Bates, and John. Ann also introduced a romantic language when describing David's classroom performance. Alice began, "David has had a very productive and successful year in second grade. He is becoming a more fluent reader, and his sight vocabulary has improved. He still benefits from rereading familiar material. He made about a year's gain in everything, although his reading is still below grade level—about the middle of second grade. Yet, he did make a year's progress.

"David is proud of his personal writing, and his cursive writing is improving. David finds it difficult to retain previously learned math materials. The test I gave him showed very minimal progress in math. . . . Maybe this is an underestimation of his ability. . . .

"His spelling is at the beginning of second grade.

"His reading and math skills are still well below grade level expectations. He needs continued guidance and support in these areas. . . .

"So, for next year, I said he needed a structured, supportive, and nurturing classroom with a project-orientated teacher willing to include activities addressing science, art, and nature."

Catherine Jamison summarized a parallel position, and then Alice asked, "Ann, anything to add?"

"I feel that David has had a very good year," said Ann. "Particularly now, we are seeing him feel so much a part of the class. And he has developed, just in the last week or so, some interesting new friendships." Ann worked hard to introduce the language of details into the conversation about absolute levels of achievement.

"He and a group of boys put together a very spontaneous play about endangered animals, where they used the stuffed animals. . . . They worked on it yesterday, and did it this morning. While they were doing it, they were behind a bookshelf. David was working the leopard. Suddenly, one of the kids said, 'Who is doing the leopard? He is really good.' Someone said, 'I think it is David.' And when it was over, they all went up to him and said, 'You were good.' He was really pleased. This is happening more and more.

"In that play, he really stayed on the subject. He . . . made the animal say, 'My parents have been killed, and I am the only one left.' He was trying to get the idea of being endangered. The others were not staying on it.

"And his writing has emerged. . . . Listening and speaking are other strands of language arts he's made a lot of progress in, too. He contributes now, every morning. He really didn't do that at the beginning. And he listens to other people, and he'll respond to what they say, or come to me later if he thinks there is some inconsistency. . . .

"This piece that he wrote about *Puss in Boots,* I think, shows how far his writing has really come. He had some nice complex sentences. . . . His writing is something he can be proud of. There's a lot of personal voice to it. He sees writing as a way to express himself. His progress in that has been, I would say, right up there with most of the children's progress, if not better. . . . For David, it's more than just a skill area.

"And his reading is coming along very, very well. . . . He has such an appreciation for good literature. I see him so engaged when I read to the children—completely engaged, waiting for the page to turn."

"He's like that at home too," Mrs. Richardson chuckled, clearly recognizing the son she saw at home.

Ann's detailed and personal picture of David fit with what is expected of teachers who adopt a whole language approach to literacy. Each student's idiosyncratic experience—interests and forms of expression—becomes central to assessing his or her progress. Ann provided a detailed and caring portrait of David: Reading levels and test scores did not define this student.

"Well," said Mrs. Richardson, matching Ann's warm spirit, "I've seen a lot of improvement, too . . . socially he's doing much better." She described new friendships.

"And on the math, we have not done very much. We were concentrating on reading and spelling." Mrs. Richardson was upset about the math progress, and hoped that David's grandfather would be able to help him catch up over the summer.

"Between that, and the deer, and the wild things, and everything that's out there . . . it's very educational, and he does enjoy it. My Dad's very much into nature."

Alice asked Catherine what she proposed as David's itinerary for the following year.

"I'd like to check in with his teacher and see what appears. Then, if he needs to be seen, I'd be happy to see him. But if he has no need, then I won't pester him."

"'Cause he really likes to be in [regular] class," Mrs. Richardson explained, indirectly stating a strong hope. "Toward the end, he kind of didn't want to go [to the resource room]. He was, like, very interested in staying in the classroom."

"Yeah," agreed Catherine.

"For me too. He, he," Alice chuckled.

"I gave him the choice recently," said Catherine, "and, about half the time, he wanted to stay in the class."

"Well," said Alice, "I think that, for LD services, I would really like to continue to see him—to work on the math skills, perhaps. I would really like to start out seeing him three times a week again. I would rather start off big, then go back. . . . For the math especially."

"That will continue in the summer months," said Mrs. Richardson. "And we can get third grade math materials."

Based on Mrs. Richardson's manner and from what she told him earlier, John believed that Mrs. Richardson was asserting her fond hope that David would be judged to need no special services. Yet, she did not say this directly and nothing came of it. It sure seems hard for a parent, trying to assimilate all that comes across the table in these brief meetings, to make his or her own hopes seem reasonable. Mrs. Richardson implicitly accepted that the test scores should be the basis for decisions about where to place David. She was less inclined than Ann to disaffection with these measures.

"So," said Alice, "what I've written here is, Catherine's going to monitor, and I'm going to see him."

"OK," said Mrs. Richardson. "And John, how do you think he's done?"

"Well, I think Ann really summed up how he'd really come together, and I hope that continues." John was annoyed with how ineffectual he was, but he could not analyze his reaction clearly enough to speak without speaking falsely. John did not really support Mrs. Richardson. He believed that everything David needed from school should be—and could be—provided in a classroom, like Ann's, where children support one another. The situation was not constituted so as to make it easy to say that without undermining the other well-meaning professionals who were teaching John about the tension educators face while trying to find a language of synthesis to describe their efforts. Alice was not responsible for the organization of regular classrooms. Nor was it Ann's business to decide how the third grade classes should run. Similarly, John questioned his right to say what he thought and was puzzled about who in this group should even hear his views.

"I think he's going to have a really good year next year," Mrs. Richardson continued. Like her son, she was hopeful and tough, but a touch sad.

"I think the way Ann's caught his imagination is important," John finally said, trying to make his most general point.

"He certainly has one," agreed Mrs. Richardson.

"He has a lot to contribute," said Ann. "I think he feels that, and it's our task to be sure in school that those things are valued and are a major part of the curriculum."

"Hmmm," Mrs. Richardson mused.

"Because what he has to contribute is important for all children. I truly believe that. I think he has some things that we need to foster in other children."

"That don't show up on scores," John added, emphatically.

"It's not," said Ann, "a measurement kind of thing. . . . We have to work on changing schools more than changing kids. And I think that he kind of demonstrates that a lot, because he has things that should be a major part of the curriculum." As Singing Bird hoped, Quiet Bird had something to contribute. David had sensitivity, integrity, aesthetic values, and an ethical sense. David's strengths were announced and the system, at last, was critiqued. And, even though they did not always use a language of synthesis, David's teachers were well aware of the contradictory goals they faced in these annual reviews.

"But," said Mrs. Richardson, accepting the way things appeared to be, "We can't go putting a sandbox in the room."

"What will happen," said Alice, "is we have an IEP [Individual Educational Plan] we signed when he entered the program. That was in November. I looked it over, and I still can work on those goals; you know, the math and reading and things." Respecting David's interests did not mean ignoring his educational difficulties.

"Could he improve a lot over the summer," asked David's mother, "especially on the reading?" Then she whispered, "I hope he does." And louder, "Um, then you'll just go into the math, or you'll stay with both?"

"Normally, I work on both areas," said Alice. "I kind of try and work with the classroom teacher."

"OK. I mean, they [David and his Grandpa] will be reviewing and all that. My dad is really good with that. He does a lot more with him than he did with me. He, he." Mrs. Richardson chuckled, but her hope and disappointment were real.

David put his personal, social, and academic life together in an admirable fashion. Most of the time, he was wholeheartedly engaged in school learning. Sadly, David's integrity, determination, and attempts to put the different aspects of his experience into satisfactory relation to one another was of little consequence in the world of absolute levels of achievement.

Challenges and Controversies

- In what ways can educators rely too much on parables or examples to convey what they know about children's needs and accomplishments?
- Is it possible to combine stories about a particular child with more general conclusions when representing their accomplishments?
- How can schools offer parents hopeful information about their child's need for special services?
- To what extent should educators help parents see the future value of a child's current abilities in meetings designed to plan a future course of action?
- How common is it for educators to reify grade level by assuming that grade level represents a set of specific skills rather than a statistical mean?

Children might benefit if teachers' ability to help their students remain wholeheartedly engaged, offering access to the information necessary for sustaining that engagement, were celebrated more often in schools. Critics of schools benefit from reminders that grade level is nothing more than a statistical mean number of correct answers attained by children in each grade. Half the population will be declared inevitable failures when we reify grade level and use it to identify particular forms of knowledge to be acquired by everyone. The social difficulties that standardized IQ tests were intended to help solve can, in this way, be seen to maintain a new social difficulty of allowing room for children to integrate aspects of their experience.

Jack's Future

Bob and Cara Davis both came to meet with Alice, Catherine, Marty Kremer [the speech teacher], Nancy Brankis, and John. Jack's conference involved a more integrated language than was evident for Bruce or David. The nature of Jack's difficulties meant that caregivers had to meet more often to construct a collective image of the same boy. Perhaps their familiarity with one another made it easier to imagine a more cohesive language.

Alice began, "Let me just review the little report I'm going to be giving you. . . . Jack has had a difficult year. Any interest has been minimal. He lacks voice, self-esteem, and confidence; and we are not sure why. Movement in and out of the classroom has been difficult for him. However, there has been an improvement of late, since all but social services have ceased. His parents are connecting him with friends, and the classroom teacher is forcing accountability. As well, the social work has benefited Jack.

"Jack has good oral reading skills, and comprehension skills improved with guided intervention."

"Now, we went over some of the scores last time we met. . . . In reading, we saw a growth of just about a year—a year and two months. . . ."

"Writing skills are his weakest area, with spelling skills at the beginning of second grade at the best. . . ."

"Although math skills are progressing, they are far below grade level . . . and weaker than reading."

Marty was next. "Speech and language skills were temporarily suspended after the parents made this decision. Thus, it is difficult to ascertain Jack's speech and language skills at this point. This report is based on the observations noted when Jack was still receiving speech and language services. . . . He was still not articulating the emphasis correctly. Jack's understanding of vocabulary was also weak. It was also difficult for Jack to explain his ideas. Jack's written expression was often very brief and contained many grammatical errors. When I tested him, his expressive and receptive language skills were below one standard deviation of the mean, so they were weak. And, I also gave him [a test that] emphasizes retrieval, and he fell within the third stanine, and the average range is the fifth stanine. So he still has needs in those areas. Thus, continued services for speech and language are recommended for the fall."

Catherine was next. "Jack . . . has continued to do well in social work, but is not transferring it much to the classroom. For next year I'm recommending seeing him more in the classroom."

"Nancy," said Alice, "do you have anything to add?"

"Yeah. I think that we have heard a lot of negatives here, but I think there are some positives. I don't think that we can expect overnight change. We realize that he needs voice, that he needs interests, that he needs friendships. I think voice is vital, but in his mind, I think friendships are [vital]. And he has become more connected with kids. . . . He puts himself into the thick of things. Before, he would not have even taken the risk."

"Right," said Mr. Davis.

"He is much more willing to work with me. . . . Recently he's had some nice writing. It's too bad we are at the end of the year and it's not Christmas."

"But there is progress," said Mrs. Davis.

"There is progress," Nancy agreed. "Are you finding any difference on medication? He says, 'I take a different medication because it helps me sleep.'

"That's 'cause he takes it at night," said Mr. Davis.

"So are you finding his sleep patterns are better?"

"Yes."

"Because," said Nancy, "this is evidently how he is visualizing it. 'I take it because it helps me sleep.'"

"Interesting," said Mr. Davis. "Probably, he heard us talking about the possible side effects. On the first night, he said, 'I'm tired dad.' It can make him sleepy."

"But we upped his dosage a little bit, 'cause we were having great big, noncompliance. I mean, he had a voice all right. He was telling us just about everything he wanted to tell us."

"And then some," said Mrs. Davis.

"'This is my room, and I do what I want to do.'"

"Yes," Mrs. Davis agreed.

"I said, 'I own the house so. . . .'"

Mrs. Davis added, "[He said,] 'it's a free country, and I do what I want to do.'"

"It's that lesson [on rights] back there in November," said Nancy. "Good for him!"

"'I have rights,' he said," said Mr. Davis, smiling.

"Yes he does," chuckled Nancy. "Good for him!"

There was plenty of good-natured chuckling during this, but Nancy's difference of opinion with the Davises was real. Jack's parents sought compliance whereas Nancy sought open expression of ideas.

"He'd better play in his room," said Mrs. Davis.

"Make his bed. He, he," Mr. Davis chuckled.

Alice outlined the arrangement planned for Jack. He would receive the same plan that was outlined for Bruce, becoming one of the children in the intensive services group.

"It's not pulling out and pulling in," said Alice. "Which we thought was not doing a service to Jack."

"I think," said Nancy, "this could be a good—not solution, but opportunity for Jack—because of the cohesiveness. I'm looking for cohesiveness in this group. If he can work well in the small social work group, can he take that into the academic arena, with these boys?"

"How are you handling the academics?" asked Mr. Davis.

"They will all have individualized programs," said Alice. "I hate to use the word 'self-contained,' but it's that kind of work. . . . Everything is individualized. . . ." The boys would spend every morning with a single special education teacher rather than receive services three days a week for 90 minutes.

Nancy held a different impression. "I'm hoping that this teacher uses him to help the other children to decode and use the skills that he has and bring some leadership. . . . Because that's when you get voice, when you get confidence. And, I'm hoping they don't go in six directions."

Mr. Davis asked, "When they go into fourth grade, will they . . . be as prepared as the other third graders?" Clearly he expressed the hope of many parents of children receiving special services, but the question produced a silence. Knowing that, if the tests are done right, half the nation will always be below grade level meant that many families are doomed to disappointment when they see special education as facilitating an opportunity for children to "catch up" with their peers.

"Well," started Alice, "what do you mean, subject matter wise, or academic wise? There's a difference."

"What they need to be ready for fourth grade. . . ."

Nancy explained, "He has been exposed to the same thing as all my second graders. Is he at the same level? No he is not, and you'll be looking at the same situation [in third grade]. . . ." Sprague was unusual in that the teachers established a second grade curriculum that all children were exposed to, no matter who taught them. Nancy did her best to communicate this to Jack's naturally anxious parents, but may have taken that information so for granted that she did not realize the source of their confusion.

Nancy was imagining Jack's character and not classroom activities or test scores. "You can look at Jack and say, he's at this level or that level. I look at Jack and I say, 'let's look at this whole kid and what he needs as a child.' And I am going to be jumping for joy if he is part of the group. And to hell with the academics right now, because that's going to come."

Challenges and Controversies

- What kinds of relationship-building activities are necessary for helping a diverse team of experts communicate with one another?
- When parents and educators disagree about how much information to share with children, how likely is it that they will be able to share a comfortable conversation about such differences?
- Is it wise for educators to assign children who are as different as Jack and Bruce to the same special education program? What are the likely benefits? Liabilities?
- How often do schools establish a standard curriculum for each grade level, but offer different methods of addressing that curriculum?
- How does such a standard curriculum facilitate equal educational opportunity among children with diverse needs and abilities?

"You sound like me in the last meeting," said Mr. Davis.

"Well you convinced us," said Nancy. Jack's progress was also convincing.

Earl's Future

More positive than any of the others, the meeting on Earl involved Alice, Catherine, Mr. Norton, Nancy, and John. Alice began, "Earl has had a very good year, he has been motivated and learning in project-orientated, artistic, or group work. Earl's reading ability in both decoding and comprehension has greatly improved. . . . When I tested him in February, he was reading about middle first grade. And, when I tested him now, he tested out almost fourth grade. His comprehension skills are stronger than his skill in decoding. . . . His attention span is poor, and conceptualizing ideas and placing ideas within a stated framework remain problematic. . . ."

"His math skills are not as strong as his reading skills, but at least he is on grade level. I was reading the problems. . . . If he had to read the problems to himself and do the problems independently, maybe the score wouldn't have been so high. But we certainly have seen growth.

"Spelling is his weakest academic area although he showed just over a year's growth. Earl needs, for next year, a less structured environment, a classroom stressing group work, a project-orientated environment, and a teacher who is flexible to Earl's learning style. I think he's had a good year."

"Agreed," said Mr. Norton.

"I have a shorter summary," said Catherine, Earl's social worker. Catherine felt Earl had made significant gains in her sessions. Also, "Earl bloomed in his classroom. He . . . became a strong positive force. I am not thinking that I necessarily need to continue."

"Nancy," said Alice, "did you have anything to say?"

"Lots of things. He, he. Well! Earl! First of all, I actually adore him. We've had a great year together. He's a wonderful kid. He has a power about him. . . . One of my goals, not just academically, but on the social front was to take that power and put it in a more positive way. . . . He does emerge as a leader often, but now he is also able to mesh with the group and integrate well. . . .

"I've seen instead of getting in tangles and fights, he will cry. . . . Instead of trying to overpower the situation, he's sensitive to it now. Certainly we don't want to keep crying in school, but it shows a sensitivity that I think is real growth. . . ."

"Friendships. He's really come a long way. . . . He has really developed his own interests. He is really artistic, and has just started to have a writing connection. . . ."

"I find that, in some ways, he's so mature. He's so worldly. Then, in other ways, he is very much a little boy. Some of his comments are just. . . ."

"Astounding," said Mr. Norton. "I know."

"Yes. He is quite bright."

"He is quite bright," said Alice, "but he has some needs."

"What I have found, in reading, if he reads with someone—has that social support—his reading is absolutely fine. . . . He has to become more independent. So, as much as you can, encourage that this summer. . . ."

"Any questions you have for us?" asked Nancy.

"My comments," said Mr. Norton, "go along the line of [Nancy's]. We've seen so much growth and development. But what I really want to say is, hats off to you [Nancy]."

"Well thanks."

"You know, you are his idol. You are on that pedestal with mom."

"Oh my!" Nancy laughed.

"Seriously! Ah."

"It's a big place to be," said Nancy. (A place, we learned a year or so later, that Nancy fell from with the usual Freudian crash that follows from a strong transference experience.)

"You have certainly made a difference," continued Mr. Norton. "We are very proud of him. We've always felt that Earl was a very intelligent kid. But we think those first four or five years in his life weren't the most solid. We think he is coming into his own. We think he is going to excel as time goes on." Mr. Norton went on to describe more of Earl's achievements.

"But within the school," said Nancy, "there are skills he misses from not having that focusing ability. . . . I think sometimes he buys a little too heavily into competition, for my comfort. . . ."

"I don't think it's quite as much as it was,"

"Not as much, but it's still there."

Catherine added, "I've seen him encouraging the other boys to become more competitive, to be like him."

"There is," said Nancy, "a difference between competition and striving to be your best. . . . 'I have to be a winner, winner, winner.' That's different than, 'I'm really trying to achieve a goal.'" Intuitively, Nancy seemed to know the distinction researchers make between ego-involving, competence motives and exchange-promoting, affiliation motives. Earl still needed more work on the latter, and to become more aware of the extent to which his sense of competence hinges on approval from others.

"Do you really think he is egotistical?"

"Yes. What do you think John?"

"I think that's part of the reason he finds it hard to get absorbed in a book, and to sit and write. Because he hasn't seen those things as social communication, or he only partly sees them as communication. . . . I think the egotistical thing doesn't carry him through solitary reading and writing. Nancy has got the writing to come along, as he has a sense that he is communicating with her." John was committed to understanding the nature of Earl's ego orientation rather than ridiculing this approach to competence.

"What I put down for next year," said Alice, "is that he's going to be in a regular classroom, with a continuation of LD services. I would like to see him twice a week next year. And we will monitor with the social work services." Alice was aware that there were still inconsistencies in the data that Nancy, John, and the Nortons seemed to be overlooking.

"OK."

Nancy noted Earl's friendship with Allan.

"I don't know how that happened," said Mr. Norton, "but boy it has certainly done wonders for him. . . . Allan's mother, she called and said, 'I can't believe the bonding

Challenges and Controversies

- When a child makes as much growth in absolute levels of achievement as Earl did in one year, is it wise to still think of him or her as having learning disabilities?
- Can caregivers become so excited about signs of growth that they forget about the limitations of available test information?
- Is it possible that strong gains in one area can create a general halo effect on everyone's assessment of a child's growth?
- How common is it for children to "outgrow" their disabilities?
- When children's achievement is highly dependent on their relationships with their teachers, is it possible to see gains disappear when those relationships change?
- Is a conservative approach to withdrawing services generally a wise approach?

between these kids.' And it snuck up on us. . . . He has several friends now, whereas nine months ago he didn't."

"I know," said Nancy.

"He is beginning to learn the art of compromising," said Mr. Norton. "Now he says, 'If you want to have a friend, you have to be a friend.' Three months ago, it would be confrontation time. Now it's, 'Let me think about that.'"

"We think the system here, it's really doing a job. . . . We know this could have been a disaster. We now feel that, yes. Earl is going to make it and do real well. . . ."

"Before," said Nancy, "if there was any confrontation, his eyes would glaze . . . I didn't even know if he could hear me. It was worrisome. . . . Now he will have some tears; a little boy who has some feelings and some hurts, and wants to work through situations. That's so different!"

"Well," said Nancy as the session ended, "thanks for sending me that nice boy."

"Thanks for the relationship with Allan. That's wonderful."

"Yeah! That's been one of my accomplishments this year. You look for those."

The Conference We Need

In an autobiography written near the end of the year, Earl recounted car rides into Chicago with his father. "Sometimes," he wrote, "I was kind of scared, because there were gang signs on the walls." Earl lived far from walls with gang signs—partly to avoid the poverty, the unpredictable life, and the "poor" schools.

The divisions between the lives of different parts of our society parallel the fractures in the experiences of Earl and the other children included in this project. Some of the parents at Sprague consciously chose the school district because it was a "good" one—with high test scores. But the boys with learning disabilities didn't match up. In a variety of ways, they were victims of the very impulse to be superior over others that created the gap between "good" schools and "poor" schools. This impulse symbolically and physically separated the boys from their peers, parallel to the ways in which the different aspects of the boys' own experiences were separated from one another.

Most effective practices for fostering a sustained commitment to learning allow individuals to integrate their personal and academic lives, and join a community of others who support such intellectual quests. Nevertheless, when there is a mismatch between the edicts of educational authorities and children's personal preferences and values, it is rational for them to begin fracturing their experience, and seek happiness outside of school. Likewise, when the behavior of a community member is overly disruptive, it is rational to want to remove that individual from the community and work to change disruptive behaviors. Mediating such tensions between personal and collective goals in a classroom can be difficult, but can offer rewards that are well worth the energy.

Bruce, David, Jack, and Earl teach us that schools are faced with a no-win situation when they label children and offer them extra help. On the one hand, these boys could not have mastered the second grade curriculum without the extra help. On the other hand, such help sometimes undermined the very will that drove their achievement motivation: Extra help taught the boys to ignore their personal interests and define school as a test or a contest in which others determined what was worthwhile to know and experience.

Given these tensions, how can attempts to humanize schools be legitimized so that all participants feel free to integrate their needs and the various aspects of their school and personal lives? How can individuals at extreme ends of the achievement distribution be welcomed in their respective classroom communities rather than ridiculed for their uniqueness?

We began by looking for better ways to help children feel pleasure from exploring new ideas and establishing comfortable relationships with others. Looking for patterns in the connected experiences of Bruce, David, Jack, and Earl, we learned that their most treasured interests emerged in life at home. Furthermore, the events that precipitated egotistical behavior in Bruce and Earl and egocentric behavior in David and Jack most often occurred in communal settings wherein the boys felt a sense of ridicule and/or disconnectedness from the dominant agendas. That disconnectedness naturally led them to fracture their intellectual lives, and ultimately undermine their academic growth.

To identify fractured experience, we explored children's sense of their identities. Yet, we could not help these boys improve the overall quality of their academic life by simply encouraging them and their families to turn inward and explore personal interests and values. The boys and their adult guardians also had to step outside their own respective worldviews to consider the perspectives and needs of other community members. In other words, they needed to coordinate the dual philosophies of individualism and communitarianism in their educational lives.

Balancing personal and communal needs was made especially difficult when school was defined as a test or a contest. Psychologically speaking, when life became a test or a contest, the children were confronted with a hierarchical world wherein the values of authorities were deemed more important than their intuitions and thoughts. Children moved away from the position of "loser" in the competition to pass tests when, in lieu of becoming fixated on their own and others' academic competence, they learned to value thinking while discussing ideas. Yet, in accepting such a value change, children could not passively receive or accept whatever lessons teachers chose to deliver: Authoritarian approaches to teaching undermined children's initiative and implicitly offered subtle forms of disrespect rather than encouragement.

Alternatively, it was easier for children to remain committed to the learning enterprise when they were treated like active moral agents, capable of setting goals and theorizing about their educational experiences. Persistence in the learning enterprise occurred when children felt a sense of freedom and recognized that "every 'I-will' arises out of a notion of freedom" and "the natural revulsion of humans towards doing someone else's bidding."[5] They complied with caregivers' attempts to "let [the child] always think he is master while you are really master. There is no subjection so complete as that which preserves the forms of freedom; it is thus that the will itself is taken captive. . . . No doubt he ought only to do what he wants, but he ought to want to do nothing but what you want him to."[6]

Sociologically speaking, classroom situations were often ambiguous and teachers rarely had time to fully consider individual differences in what children wanted to do. Instead, the children were expected to step outside their own worldview, follow teacher-established rules, and consider the perspectives and needs of other community members. Each classroom contained a unique combination of relatively common rituals, and conflict occurred from misunderstandings about the nature of those rules. The misunderstandings of Bruce, David, Jack, and Earl, who regularly missed details about others' expectations, exacerbated normal levels of confusion about the nature of the curriculum and the purposes of particular tasks.

Our Future

For many parents and teachers who work with confused children, traditional psychological and sociological conclusions may seem obvious. Of course children's experiences are fractured: Caregivers live with daily reminders of the ways in which their children make embarrassing or frustrating mistakes and struggle painfully to rectify those mistakes. It is also obvious that such children find it difficult to fit into their classroom communities—why else would they be labeled *students with learning disabilities?* To move beyond labels and make progress in the struggle to assist children who fracture their experience, it seems more useful to invent a language that synthesizes generalizations and details of particular lives that can reveal some of the concrete ways in which caregivers have assisted struggling children. At this point, our new language involves a commitment to several ideas:

Revise Definitions of Equal Educational Opportunity

First, we would like to see a revised definition of equal educational opportunity, focusing on the search for a level motivational playing field rather than equality in test scores. If lives in school are about sustaining motivation to learn rather than gaining high test scores or special prizes, everyone, even the most confused or alienated members of the community, can engage in meaningful work that is valued by others. (For some children, of course, performing well on tests will naturally follow from such commitments.) We will know that we are successful in promoting equal educational opportunity when all children—even those like Bruce, David, Jack, and Earl—are free to reveal their vulnerabilities without being ridiculed and to negotiate effective ways of developing their talents. This will be fair because most of the skills for living healthy lives, raising families, and contributing to the larger social good involve subtle forms of give and take rather than simplistic values associated with winning and losing.

Strengthen Attempts to Consolidate Experience

We would like to see children and their caregivers find ways to integrate aspects of their experience so that ideas generated from one aspect of experience offer direction and meaning to other aspects of experience. To succeed, individuals will have to respond fully to their self-determination, competence, and affiliation needs. Although individuals share the same needs, differences in their orientations to the world affect their ability to meet such needs and their approaches to doing so. Commitment to interests that enhance self-awareness helps individuals respect their need for autonomy and self-efficacy. Willfully attending to the specific demands of meaningful tasks rather than remaining overly preoccupied with demonstrating superiority and avoiding inferiority can facilitate respect for competence needs. And, recognizing that every identity-enhancing exchange with another person affects future intimacy can nurture affiliation needs. Individuals who recognize the interdependency of these agendas are less likely to become cut off from growth-enhancing experience.

Ideally, individuals should be able to find identity-enhancing ways of integrating aspects of their experience across the different spheres of their lives. Expectations for children differ in school, at home, and in peer groups, but children may consolidate information from these various sources when constructing a comfortable sense of who they are and who they would like to become. Taking responsibility for responding to the expectations of others while revealing vulnerabilities and commitments is a complex enterprise that many adults find challenging. Children need guidance with labeling essential needs and expectations in their lives well enough to imagine coordinating them.

Label Educational Experience

We would also like to see greater respect for the challenge of labeling educational experience. Educators quickly learn that when fully gripped by an intellectual task, all children can sustain attention and commitment to that task until it is complete. When engaged, children can defy all statistical description of what might be "developmentally appropriate." Teachers can also discover a myriad of surprises when they spend their diagnostic energies helping children construct intellectual interests and critiques of the learning process.

Children react to implicit messages evident in their experience. Bruce, David, Jack, and Earl showed us how children who fail to understand the necessity of particular curricula and educational practices can react with levels of alienation that undermine any chance they have for solid intellectual growth. Aggressive and avoidant behavior becomes prevalent, even among children who are well cared for, if they fail to understand the purposes of particular activities. When caregivers offer positive, detailed descriptions of particular acts of learning, they offer an alternative interpretation of learning. In time children tend to look for similar ways to diminish misunderstandings.

Encourage Children to Become Educational Theorists

We would like to see children persuaded to think like educational theorists. If children look for ways in which school knowledge can be made responsive to personal knowledge, their overall growth can remain lively and continuously constructive, even when they are learning the routine skills that others take for granted. Children can keep the academic diet of easily testable, discrete "facts" and "truths," of the type typically found on achievement tests, in its proper perspective. As theorists, children can learn that to converse with others requires knowledge about our shared culture. Recognizing that personal needs and expectations are unique, children can learn how to reject educational environments wherein:

> The mere absorbing of facts and truths is so exclusively individual an affair that it tends very naturally to pass in to selfishness. . . . Indeed, almost the only measure for success is a competitive one, in the bad sense of that term—a comparison of results in the recitation or in the examination to see which child has succeeded in getting ahead of others in storing up, in accumulating, the maximum of information.[7]

Like Helen Cordero, the woman who invented a new form of Pueblo art, children who behave like educational theorists offer creative metaphors for experience that combine personal interests and cultural norms. Helen did not simply try harder or more ingeniously to perform a task that was clearly set before her. She had to create a task that simultaneously had personal relevance and appeared meaningful or legitimate to other individuals within her culture. Likewise, children, even those with learning disabilities, can learn to create meaningful intellectual lives for themselves.

Call Attention to Moral Agency

We would also like to see attention called to the importance of moral agency whenever it is practical to do so. Classroom conversations should involve particularistic concerns with social justice and personal responsibility in which children and teachers consciously examine the moral implications of their words and deeds. When teachers establish environments in which their corrections feel like love rather than ridicule, children can be expected to take responsibility for their actions. When children see themselves as active moral agents who are responsible for their own growth as well as the growth of others in the community, they can work to build comfortable communities while meeting their affiliation needs. Caregivers can facilitate conversations about how personal and communal interests converge, exploring fair ways to organize a classroom, good and bad conduct, and multiple forms of meaning making. Examining lives in progress, with all their triumphs and failures, can teach individuals that thoughtful social interactions also foster intellectual growth, validating personal interpretations of the world while sustaining fair and compassionate relationships.

Teachers who are willing to help their children examine and deal with negative as well as positive emotions facilitate a process of action and reflection that enhances moral functioning. With guidance, children can imagine a comfortable world wherein it is safe to make mistakes and fun to work on difficult tasks. However, children cannot be successful in this endeavor if they are unwilling to accept new ideas or reciprocate with respect for the talents of their teachers and classmates. Negotiating which activities are educative and which are not can be effective only if children and their caregivers establish meaningful ground rules.

Negotiating ground rules is not always as easy as it might sound. On a systemic level, it is problematic to assume that everyone understands the definitions of the situations they face in identical ways. At the most basic level, after determining that it is important to come to school, children and their caregivers probably need to discuss whether a particular task should be construed as an opportunity to learn, show what you know, or outperform others. Yet, even when it is agreed that a situation involves learning, some children will assume that tasks require peer collaboration whereas others will assume they require solitary work. These discrepancies in understanding the definition of the situation can, at the very least, lead to embarrassment or, more seriously, to conflicts that undermine children's ability to attend to the task at hand.

Establish an Engaging Learning Environment

We would like to see caregivers and students alike participating in educational environments that are exciting and comfortable. No matter how self-aware learners can become, they will inevitably fracture their experience if they work in settings that are disrespectful of their emerging identities. Robert White's longitudinal studies of adult lives in progress exemplify the view that an internal sense of competence and understanding of institutional practices will not always lead to comfortable levels of productivity. Bruce, David, Jack, and Earl offer parallel examples of young lives in progress with similar highs and lows. Knowing about these lives can teach us the importance of helping children and teachers strike a balance between public, communal needs and private, individual concerns.

In schools, because no one is free to avoid communal life, everyone's quality of life might be improved if they explicitly negotiate the practices that are used to facilitate various learning, testing, and contest agendas, seeking ways to create balance among these types of situations. In looking at the daily struggles of Bruce, David, Jack, and Earl, we see educators and family members stepping outside of their own perspectives to consider the views of others who sought to help the boys learn. There are, however, traditional roles for parents, children, and teachers that need to be considered when establishing a comfortable community. Ultimately, like the Johnsons, Richardsons, Davises, and Nortons, most parents comply with the edicts of the educational professionals who make decisions about how their children should be educated. Like Bruce, David, Jack, and Earl, children find comfortable ways of living within the communities to which they are assigned or face unpleasant consequences of ridicule and punishment. Furthermore, educators like Thyra, Ann, Nancy, and their colleagues usually respond to the edicts of those who establish social and intellectual policies for their school and district.

A productive learning environment can be constructed by acknowledging these different perspectives on education and limits on personal freedom. To facilitate moral and intellectual growth as well as healthy learning environments, it might be helpful to include all of these individuals in conversations about how schools ought to be organized. Ideas that seem exciting and important to adults may not be so interesting to children. Experience can be consolidated when positive associations are made between student-selected and teacher-selected material, and new ideas emerge from such associations.

Invent Constructive Responses to Resistance

We would like to see everyone be more tolerant of students' mistakes while learning to coordinate their needs. A language of synthesis will be valuable only if those using it find ways to understand one another and the anxiety provoked by growth-enhancing activities. Facilitating children's ability to formulate constructive critiques of their educational experiences will require sensitivity to their incomplete knowledge of how schools function.

David's emerging poetry teaches us that children with problems adjusting to school could easily have confused interpretations of the task before them—failing to define the school curriculum in ways that allow one experience to give direction and meaning to another. David and Jack imposed a testing framework on learning and could not experience the freedom of inquiry necessary to fully integrate new and old knowledge. Likewise, when Bruce and Earl defined learning situations as contests, they could not put the various parts of the intellectual task at hand into satisfactory relation with one another or with other aspects of their lives. All four boys, in other words, wounded themselves by creating internal barriers and conflicts that resisted meaningful resolution until they were encouraged to reflect on the nature of their experiences.

To remain tolerant of one another, children will need structured introductions to educational dilemmas and permission to speak their minds. Classrooms are generally noisy, crowded places in which it is difficult to organize activities so that everyone's perspective can be heard. Without encouragement from caregivers, children have difficulty polishing their thoughts in ways that promote constructive reflection. Children learn as part of a collective group of learners and some are more easily distracted from the topic at hand than others.

Facilitating parents' participation in such adventures will also require careful attempts to consider their views. The unusual problems faced by the parents of Bruce, David, Jack, and Earl accentuated the typical sources of frustration among parents trying to coordinate family and work demands. Mr. and Mrs. Johnson were confronted with the added challenge of an overly defensive child who was continually fighting for adult attention both at home and at school. Mr. and Mrs. Richardson learned about a boy who behaved at home in ways that were entirely different from the ways in which he behaved at school. The Davises were overwhelmed with the task of coordinating the multiple languages of various experts who rarely considered the "whole boy" when addressing the particular behavioral symptoms they were charged to treat. Finally, the Nortons faced the added burden of raising a family with a dual-ethnic identity. The children needed direct conversations about the value of celebrating difference so they would not succumb to the messages implicit in the kinds of teasing they faced. Like these parents, those who alter their home lives to encourage connections with school's agendas enhance children's ability to come to school ready to participate in exciting adventures.

Educators also need to strike a balance between their own resistance to a language of synthesis and their awareness of students' resistance. Bruce's dependence on Thyra's help offers the most compelling example of how teachers struggle to set priorities for themselves and their students. Some children actively avoid taking charge of their own learning, and it would seem cruel and unusual punishment to avoid helping them. Yet when such students find themselves "stuck" or unwilling to do the intellectual work necessary to successfully label their own educative experiences, teachers should confront them with the fact that their behavior is sometimes irresponsible. Such confrontations may involve parents, administrators and other teachers as well as students in ways that inevitably became public and affect the classroom ethos. Confrontations are unpleasant, but potentially rewarding. Children like Bruce can enhance their own growth if they accept their membership in the discourse community of their respective classrooms and collaborate with others to establish fair and effective practices, but they will need gentle coaching in how to do so in a language they can understand.

Despite educators' commitment to nurturing children's growth, most find themselves shifting back and forth between the languages understood by parents and children and the varied languages of educational researchers and policy makers. Such coordination is difficult and it is easier to choose one audience over another. Although, for this project, we carefully selected teachers who respectfully listened to the concerns of children, many teachers choose an adult audience and are not so willing to respectfully listening to children's needs and critiques. In such classrooms it becomes difficult to thoughtfully negotiate practices that enhance everyone's ability to integrate aspects of their experience.

Fortunately, the collection of educators and parents involved in this project knew that they would benefit from discovering the richness of one another's lives, both in and out of school. When families were invited to participate in conversations about how best to educate their children, opportunities for miscommunication were thwarted. When students were free to act and describe the nature of their experiences, repeating this action-reflection process until everyone felt confident, their caregivers learned about themselves and about the world outside of their classroom. Everyone learned that children's critiques of their educational experiences, like those evident in the poems and journal entries of David, Jack, and Earl, bear tasty intellectual fruit when nurtured in an environment that is designed to promote education as an adventure.

Ultimately, the conversations represented in this book reflect a shared vision for what is important to do and know in second grade as well as a sense of what has been done and known. When individuals learn about the limitations of their own perspectives, groups learn about the needs of particular members. When the fit between educational practices and individual needs and interests is comfortable, the facts of life in school can be greeted with the feelings of warmth and safety that come from knowing that one is loved and respected. When the fit is uncomfortable, community members who define themselves as responsible moral agents will struggle (sometimes unsuccessfully) to resist mocking those individuals who challenge their comfort. Finding ways to consolidate issues of motivation, fairness, and the struggle to learn can help individuals continue to associate old and new ideas, inventing new knowledge in the process.

ENDNOTES

1. Details of these tests are obfuscated to preserve confidentiality.

2. See Hammill (1993, pp. 305–306). Moats & Lyon (1993) offer a similar approach to helping children with learning disabilities find meaning in school.

3. See Skrtic (1991).

4. See Nicholls, McKenzie, & Shufro (1994). Padeliadu and Zigmond (1996) also noticed that elementary children move in and out of class for many reasons and appreciate the extra attention they receive from adults.

5. See Arendt (1978, p. 69).

6. See Rousseau (1762/1911, p. 84).

7. See Dewey (1943, pp. 15–16).

REFERENCES

Ackerman, D., & Howes, C. (1986). Sociometric status and after-school social activity of children with learning disabilities. *Journal of Learning Disabilities, 19*, 416–419.

Adalbjarnardottir, S., & Selman, R. L. (1989). How children propose to deal with the criticism of their teachers and classmates: Developmental and stylistic variations. *Child Development, 60*, 539–550.

Adelman, H. S. (1978). The concept of intrinsic motivation: Implications for practice and research with the learning disabled. *Learning Disability Quarterly, 1*, 43–54.

Adelman, H. S., & Chaney, L. A. (1982). Impact of motivation on task performance of children with and without psychoeducational problems. *Journal of Learning Disabilities, 15*, 242–244.

Adelman, H. S., & Taylor, L. (1983). Classifying students by inferred motivation to learn. *Learning Disability Quarterly, 6*, 201–206.

Adler, A. (1930). *The education of children*. Chicago: George Allen and Unwin.

Adler, A. (1979). *Superiority and social interest*. New York: W. W. Norton & Company. [Essays translated with comments by H. L. Ansbacher and R. R. Ansbacher.]

Ainsworth, M. D. (1985). Patterns of attachment. *Clinical Psychologist, 38*, 27–29.

Ainsworth, M. D. S., & Marvin, R. S. (1995). On the shaping of attachment theory and research: An interview with Mary D. S. Ainsworth. *Monograph of the Society for Research in Child Development, 60* (2–3, Serial No. 244, pp. 3–21).

Ainsworth, M. S. (1979). Infant-mother attachment. *American Psychologist, 34*, 932–937.

Allport, G. W. (1961). *Pattern and growth in personality*. New York: Holt, Rinehart, & Winston.

Anno, M. (1992). *Anno's USA*. New York: Putnam Press.

Arendt, H. (1978). *The life of the mind: Thinking and willing*. New York: Harcourt Brace Jovanovich. (Originally published in 1971.)

Arsenio, W., & Cooperman, S. (1996). Children's conflict-related emotions: Implications for morality and autonomy. In M. Killen (Ed.), Children's autonomy, social competence, and interactions with adults and other children: Exploring connections and consequences (pp. 25–39). *New Directions for Child Development, 73*.

Arsenio, W. F., & Fleiss, K. (1996). Typical and behaviourally disruptive children's understanding of the emotional consequences of socio-moral events. *British Journal of Developmental Psychology, 14*, 173–186.

Asher, S. R., & Coie, J. D. (1990). *Peer rejection in childhood*. New York: Cambridge University Press.

Asher, S. R., & Rose, A. J. (1997). Promoting children's social-emotional adjustment with peers. In P. Salovey & D. J. Sluyter (Eds.), *Emotional development and emotional intelligence. Educational implications* (pp. 196–230). New York: BasicBooks, Inc.

Astor, R. A. (1994). Children's moral reasoning about family and peer violence: The role of provocation and retribution. *Child Development, 65*, 1054–1067.

Atkinson, J. W., Heyns, R. W., & Veroff, J. (1954). The effect of experimental arousal of the affiliation motive on thematic apperception. *Journal of Abnormal and Social Psychology, 49*, 405–410.

Babcock, B. A. (1986). Modeled selves: Helen Cordero's "Little People." In V. W. Turner & E. M. Bruner (Eds.), *The anthropology of experience* (pp. 316–343). Chicago: University of Illinois Press.

Bacon, R. (1991). *Save our earth*. Crystal Lake, IL: Rigby.

Baker, L., Scher, D., & Mackler, K. (1997). Home and family influences on motivations for reading. *Educational Psychologist, 32*, 69–82.

Bandura, A. (1971). *Social learning theory*. Morristown, NJ: General Learning Press.

Bandura, A. (1997). *Self-efficacy: The exercise of control*. New York: W. H. Freeman & Co.

Bandura, A., Barbaranelli, C., Caprara, G. V., & Pastorelli, C. (1996). Multifaceted impact of self-efficacy beliefs on academic functioning. *Child Development, 67*, 1206–1222.

Banerji, M., & Dailey, R. A. (1995). A study of the effects of an inclusion model on students with specific learning disabilities. *Journal of Learning Disabilities, 28*, 511–522.

Barkley, R. A. (1997a). Behavioral inhibition, sustained attention, and executive functions: Constructing a unifying theory of ADHD. *Psychological Bulletin, 121*, 65–94.

Barkley, R. A. (1997b). *ADHD and the nature of self-control*. New York: The Guilford Press.

Baumrind, D. (1966). Effects of authoritative control on child behavior. *Child Development, 37*, 887–907.

Baumrind, D. (1971). Current patterns of parental authority. *Developmental Psychology, 4*, 1–103.

Baumrind, D. (1989). Rearing competent children. In W. Damon (Ed.), *Child development today and tomorrow* (pp. 349–378). San Francisco: Jossey-Bass.

Berndt, T. J., & Ladd, G. W. (1989). *Peer relationships in child development*. New York: John Wiley & Sons.

Berndt, T. J., & Perry, T. B. (1986). Children's perceptions of friendships as supportive relationships. *Developmental Psychology, 22*, 640–648.

Berndt, T. J., Perry, T. B., & Miller, K. E. (1988). Friends' and classmates' interactions on academic tasks. *Journal of Educational Psychology, 80*, 506–513.

Beyer, S. (1995). Maternal employment and children's academic achievement: Parenting styles as mediating variable. *Developmental Review, 15*, 212–253.

Bierman, K. L., & Welsh, J. A. (1997). Social relationship deficits. In E. J. Mash & L. G. Terdal (Eds.), *Assessment of childhood disorders* (3rd ed., pp. 328–365). New York: The Guilford Press.

Bigelow B. J., & LaGaipa, J. J. (1995). The development of friendship values and choice. In H. C. Foot, A. J. Chapman, & J. R. Smith (Eds.), *Friendship and social relations in children* (pp. 15–44). New Brunswick, NJ: Transaction Publishers.

Boivin, M., & Hymel, S. (1997). Peer experiences and social self-perceptions: A sequential model. *Developmental Psychology, 33*, 135–145.

Bowes, J. M., & Goodnow, J. J. (1996). Work for home, school, or labor force: The nature and sources of changes in understanding. *Psychological Bulletin, 119*, 300–321.

Bradley, R. H., Caldwell, B. M., & Rock, S. L. (1988). Home environment and school performance: A ten-year follow-up and examination of three models of environmental action. *Child Development, 59*, 852–867.

Bretherton, I., Golby, B., & Cho, E. (1997). Attachment and the transmission of values. In J. E. Grusec & L. Kuczynski (Eds.), *Parenting and children's internalization of values: A handbook of contemporary theory* (pp. 103–134). New York: John Wiley & Sons.

Bringuier, J-C. (1980). *Conversations with Jean Piaget*. Chicago: University of Chicago Press.

Brown, J. R., Donelan-McCall, N., & Dunn, J. (1996). Why talk about mental states? The significance of children's conversations with friends, siblings, and mothers. *Child Development, 67*, 836–849.

Buhrmester, D., & Furman, W. (1987). The development of companionship and intimacy. *Child Development, 58*, 1101–1113.

Bukowski, W. M., & Sippola, L. K. (1996). Friendship and morality: (How) are they related? In W. M. Bukowski, A. F. Newcomb, & W. W. Hartup (Eds.), *The company they keep: Friendship in childhood and adolescence* (pp. 238–261). New York: Cambridge University Press.

Burhans, K. K., & Dweck, C. S. (1995). Helplessness in early childhood: The role of contingent worth. *Child Development, 66*, 1719–1738.

Burnett, P. C., & Demnar, W. J. (1996). The relationship between closeness to significant others and self-esteem. *Journal of Family Studies, 2*, 121–129.

Bursuck, W. D., & Asher, S. R. (1986). The relationship between social competence and achievement in elementary school children. *Journal of Clinical Child Psychology, 15*, 41–49.

Bus, A. G., Belsky, J., van IJzendoorn, M. H., & Crnic, K. (1997). Attachment and book reading patterns: A study of mothers, fathers, and their toddlers. *Early Childhood Research Quarterly, 12*, 81–98.

Butler, R. (1987). Task-involving and ego-involving properties of evaluation: The effects of different feedback conditions on motivational perceptions, interest, and performance. *Journal of Educational Psychology, 79*, 474–482.

Butler, R. (1989). Mastery versus ability appraisal: A developmental study of children's observations of peer's work. *Child Development, 60*, 1350–1361.

Butler, R., & Neuman, O. (1995). Effects of task and ego achievement goals on help-seeking behaviors and attitudes. *Journal of Educational Psychology, 87*, 261–271.

Cashmore, J. A., & Goodnow, J. J. (1985). Agreement between generations: A two-process approach. *Child Development, 56*, 493–501.

Chapman, J. W. (1988). Cognitive-motivational characteristics and academic achievement of learning disabled children: A longitudinal study. *Journal of Educational Psychology, 80*, 357–365.

Chen, L. (1990). The effects of attributional feedback and strategy training on achievement behaviors with mathematical learning disabled students. *Bulletin of Educational Psychology, 23*, 143–158.

Chiu, C., Hong, Y., & Dweck, C. S. (1997). Lay dispositionism and implicit theories of personality. *Journal of Personality and Social Psychology, 73*, 19–30.

Clark, M. S., & Mills, J. (1993). The differences between

communal and exchange relationships: What is and is not. *Personality and Social Psychology Bulletin, 19*, 684–691.

Cobb, P., Wood, T., Yackel, E., Nicholls, J., Wheatley, G., Trigatti, B., & Perlwitz, M. (1991). Assessment of a problem-centered second-grade mathematics project. *Journal for Research in Mathematics Education, 22*, 3–29.

Coie, J. D., & Dodge, K. A. (1983). Continuities and changes in children's social status: A five-year longitudinal study. *Merrill-Palmer Quarterly, 29*, 261–282.

Coie, J. D., & Krehbiel, G. (1984). Effects of academic tutoring on the social status of low-achieving, socially rejected children. *Child Development, 55*, 1465–1478.

Coie, J. D., & Kupersmidt, J. B. (1983). A behavioral analysis of emerging social status in boys' groups. *Child Development, 54*, 1400–1416.

Colby, A., Kohlberg, L., Gibbs, J., & Lieberman, M. (1983). A longitudinal study of moral development. *Monographs for the Society for Research in Child Development, 48*, 1–96.

Coles, G. (1987). *The learning mystique: A critical look at "learning disabilities."* New York: Fawcett Columbine.

Collins, R. L. (1996). For better or worse: The impact of upward social comparison on self-evaluations. *Psychological Bulletin, 119*, 51–69.

Collins, R. L., & DiPaula, A. (1997). Personality and the provision of support: Emotions felt and signaled. In G. R. Pierce, B. Lakey, I. G. Sarason, & B. R. Sarason (Eds.), *Sourcebook of social support and personality* (pp. 429–443). New York: Plenum Press.

Cordova, D. I., & Lepper, M. (1996). Intrinsic motivation and the process of learning: Beneficial effects of contextualization, personalization, and choice. *Journal of Educational Psychology, 88*, 715–730.

Cowan, P. A. (1997). Beyond meta-analysis: A plea for a family systems view of attachment. *Child Development, 68*, 601–603.

Crick, N. R., & Dodge, K. A. (1994). A review and reformulation of social information-processing mechanisms in children's social adjustment. *Psychological Bulletin, 115*, 74–101.

Csikszentmihalyi, M. (1990). *Flow: The psychology of optimal experience*. New York: Harper & Row.

Damon, W. (1977). *The social world of the child.* San Francisco: Jossey-Bass, Inc.

Damon, W. (1984). Peer education: The untapped potential. *Journal of Applied Developmental Psychology, 5*, 331–343.

Damon, W., & Killen, M. (1982). Peer interaction and the process of change in children's moral reasoning. *Merrill-Palmer Quarterly, 28*, 347–367.

Damon, W., & Phelps, E. (1989). Strategic use of peer learning in children's education. In T. J. Berndt & G. W. Ladd (Eds.), *Peer relationships in child development* (pp. 135–157). New York: John Wiley & Sons.

deCharms, R. (1984). Motivation enhancement in educational settings. In R. Ames & C. Ames (Eds.), *Research on motivation in education, Vol. 1, Student motivation* (pp. 255–310). New York: Academic Press.

Deci, E. L., & Chandler, C. L. (1986). The importance of motivation for the future of the LD field. *Journal of Learning Disabilities, 19*, 587–594.

Deci, E. L., Hodges, R., Pierson, L., & Tomassone, J. (1992). Autonomy and competence as motivational factors in students with learning disabilities and emotional handicaps. *Journal of Learning Disabilities, 25*, 457–471.

Deci, E. L., & Ryan, R. M. (1985). *Intrinsic motivation and self-determination in human behavior.* New York: Plenum.

Delton, J. (1991). Penny-wise, fun-foolish. In V. A. Arnold, C. B. Smith, J. Flood, & D. Loop (Eds.), *Bit by Bit* (pp. 238–248). New York: Macmillan Publishing Co.

DeMaria, R. (1990). *Nintendo secrets: The power user's guide*. New York: Prima Publishers.

DeVries, R. (1970). The development of role-taking as reflected by behavior of bright, average, and retarded children in a social guessing game. *Child Development, 41*, 759–770.

Dewey, J. (1943). *The child and curriculum.* Chicago: University of Chicago Press. (Originally published in 1902.)

DeWolff, M., & van IJzendoorn, M. H. (1997). Sensitivity and attachment: A meta-analysis on parental antecedents of infant attachment. *Child Development, 68*, 571–591.

Dodge, K. A., Coie, J. D., Pettit, G. S., & Price, J. M. (1990). Peer status and aggression in boys' groups: Developmental and contextual analyses. *Child Development, 61*, 1289–1309.

Dodge, K. A., Price, J. M., Coie, J. D., & Christopoulos, C. (1990). On the development of aggressive dyadic relationships in boys' peer groups. *Human Development, 33*, 260–270.

Dunn, J., & Brown, J. (1994). Affect expression in the family, children's understanding of emotions, and their interactions with others. *Merrill-Palmer Quarterly, 40*, 120–137.

Dunn, J., Brown, J. R., & Maguire, M. (1995). The development of children's moral sensibility:

Individual differences and emotion understanding. *Developmental Psychology, 31*, 649–659.

Dunn, J., Creps, C., & Brown, J. (1996). Children's family relationships between two and five: Developmental changes and individual differences. *Social Development, 5*, 230–250.

Dunn, J., & Herrera, C. (1997). Conflict resolution with friends, siblings, and mothers: A developmental perspective. *Aggressive Behavior, 23*, 343–357.

Eisenberg, N. (1992). *The caring child*. Cambridge, MA: Harvard University Press.

Eisenberg, N., Fabes, R. A., & Murphy, B. C. (1996). Parents' reactions to children's negative emotions: Relations to children's social competence and comforting behavior. *Child Development, 67*, 2227–2247.

Eisenberg, N., Guthrie, I. K., Fabes, R. A., Reiser, M., Murphy, B. C., Holgren, R., Maszk, P., & Losoya, S. (1997). The relation of regulation and emotionality to resiliency and competent social functioning in elementary school children. *Child Development, 68*, 295–311.

Eisenberg, N., & Miller, P. (1987). The relation of empathy to prosocial and related behaviors. *Psychological Bulletin, 101*, 91–119.

Eisenberg, N., & Mussen, P. H. (1989). *The roots of prosocial behavior in children*. New York: Cambridge University Press.

Ellsworth, M. E. (1997). *Gertrude Chandler Warner and 'The Boxcar Children.'* Morton Grove, IL: Albert Whitman & Company.

Emmons, R. A. (1997). Motives and life goals. In R. Hogan, J. Johnson, & S. Briggs (Eds.), *Handbook of personality psychology* (pp. 485–512). New York: Academic Press.

Epstein, J. L. (1989). The selection of friends: Changes across the grades and in different school environments. In T. J. Berndt & G. W. Ladd (Eds.), *Peer relationships in child development* (pp. 158–187). New York: John Wiley & Sons.

Erdley, C. A. (1996). Motivational approaches to aggression within the context of peer relationships. In J. Juvonen & K. R. Wentzel (Eds.), *Social motivation: Understanding children's social adjustment* (pp. 98–125). New York: Cambridge University Press.

Erdley, C. A., & Asher, S. R. (1996). Children's social goals and self-efficacy perceptions as influences on their responses to ambiguous provocation. *Child Development, 67*, 1329–1344.

Erikson E. H. (1963). *Childhood and society*. New York: W. W. Norton & Co. (Originally published in 1950.)

Evans, I. M., Salisbury, C., Palombaro, M., & Goldberg, J. S. (1994). Children's perceptions of fairness in classroom and interpersonal situations involving peers with learning disabilities. *Journal of the Association for Persons with Severe Handicaps, 19*, 326–332.

Farmer, T. W., Pearl, R., & VanAcker, R. M. (1996). Expanding the social skills deficit framework: A developmental synthesis perspective, classroom social networks, and implications for the social growth of students with disabilities. *Journal of Special Education, 30*, 232–256.

Farnham-Diggory, S. (1992). *The learning-disabled child*. Cambridge, MA: Harvard University Press.

Faulkner, J., & Kich, F. (1983). Assessment and engagement stages in therapy with the interracial family. *Family Therapy Collections, 6*, 78–90.

Fontaine, A. M. (1994). Achievement motivation and child rearing in different social contexts. *European Journal of Psychology of Education, 9*, 225–240.

Fox, N. A., Kimmerly, N. L., & Schafer, W. D. (1991). Attachment to mother/attachment to father: A meta-analysis. *Child Development, 62*, 210–225.

Freeman, B. (1994). Power motivation and youth: An analysis of troubled students and student leaders. *Journal of Counseling and Development, 72*, 661–671.

Freeman, J. (1993). Parents and families in nurturing giftedness and talent. In K. A. Heller, F. J. Monks, & A. H. Passow (Eds.), *International handbook of research and development of giftedness and talent* (pp. 669–683). Oxford, England: Pergamon Press.

Freitag, M. K., Belsky, J., Grossmann, K., Grossmann, K. E., & Scheuerer-Englisch, H. (1996). Continuity in parent-child relationships from infancy to middle childhood and relations with friendship competence. *Child Development, 67*, 1437–1454.

Friedman, D. E., & Medway, F. J. (1987). Effects of varying performance sets and outcome on the expectations, attributions, and persistence of boys with learning disabilities. *Journal of Learning Disabilities, 20*, 312–316.

Fromm, E. (1942). *Fear of freedom*. London: Routledge.

Fuchs, L. S., Fuchs, D., Karns, K., Hamlett, C. L., Katzaroff, M., & Dutka, S. (1997). Effects of task-focused goals on low-achieving students with and without learning disabilities. *American Educational Research Journal, 34*, 513–543.

Furman, W., & Buhrmester, D. (1992). Age and sex differences in perceptions of networks of personal relationships. *Child Development, 63*, 103–115.

Gagne, E. E. (1975). Motivating the disabled learner. *Academic Therapy, 10*, 361–362.

Gambetta, D. (Ed.). (1988). *Trust: Making and breaking cooperative relations*. Cambridge, MA: Basil Blackwell.

Garner, P. W. (1996). The relations of emotional role taking, affective/moral attributions, and emotional display rule knowledge to low-income school-age children's social competence. *Journal of Applied Developmental Psychology, 17*, 19–36.

George, T. P., & Hartmann, D. P. (1996). Friendship networks of unpopular, average, and popular children *Child Development, 67*, 2301–2316.

Gibbs, J. T. (1989). Biracial adolescents. In J. T. Gibbs & L. N. Huang (Eds.), *Children of color: Psychological interventions with minority youth* (pp. 322–350). San Francisco: Jossey-Bass Publishers.

Giff, P. R. (1984). *The beast in Ms. Rooney's room.* New York: Bantam Doubleday Dell Publishing.

Giff, P. R. (1985). *Lazy lions, lucky lambs.* New York: Bantam Doubleday Dell Publishing.

Glassco, J. A., Milgram, N. A., & Youniss, J. (1970). Stability of training effects on intentionality in moral judgment in children. *Journal of Personality and Social Psychology, 14*, 360–365.

Goldberg, W. A., Greenberger, E., & Nagel, S. K. (1996). Employment and achievement: Mothers' work involvement in relation to children's achievement behaviors and mothers' parenting behaviors. *Child Development, 67*, 1512–1527.

Goodnow, J. J. (1995). Parents' knowledge and expectations. In M. Bornstein (Ed.), *Handbook of parenting, Vol. 3: Status and social conditions of parenting* (pp. 305–332). Mahwah, NJ: Lawrence Erlbaum.

Goodnow, J. J. (1997). Parenting and the transmission and internalization of values: From social-cultural perspectives to within-family analyses. In J. E. Grusec & L. Kuczynski (Eds.), *Parenting and children's internalization of values: A handbook of contemporary theory* (pp. 333–361). New York: John Wiley & Sons.

Gottman, J. M. (1983). How children become friends. *Monographs of the Society for Research in Child Development, 48* (3, Serial No. 201).

Gottman, J. M., Guralnick, M. J., Wilson, B., Swanson, C. C., & Murray, J. D. (1997). What should be the focus of emotion regulation in children? A nonlinear dynamic mathematical model of children's peer interaction in groups. *Development and Psychopathology, 9*, 421–452.

Graham, S., & Hoehn, S. (1995). Children's understanding of aggression and withdrawal as social stigmas: An attributional analysis. *Child Development, 66*, 1143–1161.

Graziano, W. G. (1978). Standards of fair play in same-age and mixed-age groups of children. *Developmental Psychology, 14*, 524–530.

Graziano, W. G. (1994). The development of agreeableness as a dimension of personality. In C. F. Halverson Jr., G. A. Kohnstamm, & R. P. Martin (Eds.), *The developing structure of temperament and personality from infancy to adulthood* (pp. 339–354). Hillsdale, NJ: Lawrence Erlbaum.

Graziano, W. G., Brody, G. H., & Bernstein, S. (1980). Effects of information about future interaction and peer's motivation on peer reward allocations. *Developmental Psychology, 16*, 475–482.

Graziano, W. G., & Eisenberg, N. (1997). Agreeableness: A dimension of personality. In R. Hogan, J. A. Johnson, & S. R. Briggs (Eds.), *Handbook of personality psychology* (pp. 795–824). San Diego, CA: Academic Press.

Graziano, W. G., Leone, C., Musser, L. M., & Lautenschlager, G. J. (1987). Self-monitoring in children: A differential approach to social development. *Developmental Psychology, 23*, 571–576.

Graziano, W. G., Musser, L. M., Rosen, S., & Shaffer, D. R. (1982). The development of fair-play standards in same-race and mixed-race situations. *Child Development, 53*, 938–947.

Greenberger, E., & Goldberg, W. A. (1989). Work, parenting, and the socialization of children. *Developmental Psychology, 25*, 22–35.

Gresham, F. M., & MacMillan, D. L. (1997). Social competence and affective characteristics of students with mild disabilities. *Review of Educational Research, 67*, 377–415.

Griffith, J. W., & Frey, C. H. (Eds.). (1981). *Classics of children's literature.* New York: Macmillan Publishing Company.

Grolnick, W. S., Deci, E. L., & Ryan, R. M. (1997). Internalization within the family: The self-determination theory perspective. In J. E. Grusec & L. Kuczynski (Eds.), *Parenting and children's internalization of values: A handbook of contemporary theory* (pp. 135–161). New York: John Wiley & Sons.

Grolnick, W. S., & Ryan, R. M. (1990). Self-perceptions, motivation, and adjustment in children with learning disabilities: A multiple group comparison study. *Journal of Learning Disabilities, 23*, 177–184.

Grotpeter, J. K., & Crick, N. R. (1996). Relational aggression, overt aggression, and friendship. *Child Development, 67*, 2328–2338.

Grusec, J. E., & Goodnow, J. J. (1994). Impact of parental discipline methods on the child's internalization of values: A reconceptualization of current points of view. *Developmental Psychology, 30*, 4–19.

Grusec, J. E., Goodnow, J. J., & Cohen, L. (1996). Household work and the development of concern for others. *Developmental Psychology, 32*, 999–1007

Grusec, J. E., & Kuczynski, L. (Eds.). (1997). *Parenting and children's internalization of values: A handbook of contemporary theory*. New York: John Wiley & Sons.

Guralnick, M. J., Gottman, J. M., & Hammond, M. A. (1996). Effects of social setting on the friendship formation of young children differing in developmental status. *Journal of Applied Developmental Psychology, 17*, 625–651.

Hagen, J. W., Barclay, C. R., & Newman, R. S. (1982). Metacognition, self-knowledge, and learning disabilities: Some thoughts on knowing and doing. *Topics in Learning and Learning Disabilities, 2*, 19–26.

Hammill, D. D. (1993). A brief look at the learning disabilities movement in the United States. *Journal of Learning Disabilities, 26*, 295–310.

Harrell, L. G., Doelling, J. E., & Sasso, G. M. (1997). Recent developments in social interaction interventions to enhance inclusion. In P. Zionts (Ed.), *Inclusion strategies for students with learning behavior problems: Perspectives, experiences, and best practices* (pp. 273–295). Austin, TX: PRO-ED.

Harrist, A. W., Zaia, A. F., Bates, J. E., Dodge, K. A., & Pettit, G. S. (1997). Subtypes of social withdrawal in early childhood: Sociometric status and social-cognitive differences across four years. *Child Development, 68*, 278–294.

Heavey, C. L., Adelman, H. S., Nelson, P., & Smith, D. C. (1989). Learning problems, anger, perceived control, and misbehavior. *Journal of Learning Disabilities, 22*, 46–50.

Henker, B., & Whalen, C. K. (1989). Hyperactivity and attention deficits. *American Psychologist, 44*, 216–223.

Hetherington, E. M., & Martin, B. (1986). Family factors and psychopathology in children. In H. C. Quay & J. S. Werry (Eds.), *Psychopathological disorders of childhood* (3rd ed., pp. 332–390). New York: John Wiley & Sons.

Hidi, S., & Harackiewicz, J. M. (2000). Motivating the academically unmotivated: A critical issue for the 21st century. *Review of Educational Research, 70*, 151–179.

Hill, C. A. (1987). Affiliation motivation: People who need people . . . but in different ways. *Journal of Personality and Social Psychology, 52*, 1008–1018.

Hinde, R. A., & Groebel, J. (Eds.). (1991). *Cooperation and prosocial behavior*. New York: Cambridge University Press.

Hinshaw, S. P., Zupan, B. A., Simmel, C., Nigg, J. T., & Melnick, S. (1997). Peer status in boys with and without attention-deficit hyperactivity disorder: Predictions from overt and covert antisocial behavior, social isolation, and authoritative parenting beliefs. *Child Development, 68*, 880–896.

Holmes, J. (1997). Attachment, autonomy, intimacy: Some clinical implications of attachment theory. *British Journal of Medical Psychology, 70*, 231–248.

Hopmeyer, A., & Asher, S. R. (1997). Children's responses to peer conflicts involving a rights infraction. *Merrill-Palmer Quarterly, 43*, 235–254.

Howes, C. (1983). Patterns of friendship. *Child Development, 54*, 1041–1053.

Howes, C. (1987). Social competence with peers in young children: Developmental sequences. *Developmental Review, 7*, 252–272.

Howes, C. (1988). Peer interaction in young children. *Monographs for the Society for Research in Child Development, 53* (1, Serial No. 217).

Howes, C. (1990). Social status and friendship from kindergarten to third grade. *Journal of Applied Developmental Psychology, 11*, 321–330.

Howes, C. (1997). Teacher-sensitivity, children's attachment and play with peers. *Early Education and Development, 8*, 41–49.

Howes, C., Hamilton, C. E., & Matheson, C. C. (1994). Children's relationships with peers: Differential associations with aspects of the teacher-child relationship. *Child Development, 65*, 253–263.

Howes, C., Matheson, C. C., & Hamilton, C. E. (1994). Maternal, teacher, and child care history correlates of children's relationships with peers. *Child Development, 65*, 264–273.

Howes, C., Sakai, L. M., Shinn, M., Phillips, D., Galinsky, E., & Whitebook, M. (1995). Race, social class, and maternal working conditions as influences on children's development. *Journal of Applied Developmental Psychology, 16*, 107–124.

Hubbard, J. A., & Coie, J. D. (1994). Emotional correlates of social competence in children's peer relationships. *Merrill-Palmer Quarterly, 40*, 1–20.

Imber, S. (1973). Relationship of trust to academic performance. *Journal of Personality and Social Psychology, 28*, 145–150.

Jacobsen, T., & Hofmann, V. (1997). Children's attachment representations: Longitudinal relations to school behavior and academic competency in middle childhood and adolescence. *Developmental Psychology, 33*, 703–710.

James, W. (1948). *Essays in pragmatism*. New York: Hafner Publishing Company.

Jones, E. F., & Nelson-LeGall, S. (1995). The influence of personal effort cues on children's judgments of morality and disposition. *Merrill-Palmer Quarterly, 41*, 53–69.

Juvonen, J., & Wentzel, K. R. (1996). *Social motivation:*

Understanding children's school adjustment. New York: Cambridge University Press.

Kavale, K. A., & Reese, J. H. (1992). The character of learning disabilities: An Iowa profile. *Learning Disabilities Quarterly, 15*, 74–94.

Kelly, G. (1985). Motivation in learning disabled children. *British Journal of Occupational Therapy, 48*, 340–342.

Kindermann, T. A. (1996). Strategies for the study of individual development within naturally existing peer groups. *Social Development, 5*, 158–173.

Kistner, J. A., & Törgesen, J. K. (1987). Motivational and cognitive aspects of learning disabilities. In B. B. Lahey & A. E. Kazdin (Eds.), *Advances in clinical child psychology* (Vol. 10, pp. 289–333). New York: Plenum Press.

Klann-Delius, G., & Hofmeister, C. (1997). The development of communicative competence of securely and insecurely attached children in interactions with their mothers. *Journal of Psycholinguistic Research, 26*, 69–88.

Kochenderfer, B. J., & Ladd, G. W. (1996). Peer victimization: Cause or consequence of school maladjustment? *Child Development, 67*, 1305–1317.

Kochenderfer, B. J., & Ladd, G. W. (1997). Victimized children's responses to peers' aggression: Behaviors associated with reduced versus continued victimization. *Development and Psychopathology, 9*, 59–73.

Koestner, R., & McClelland, D. C. (1992). The affiliation motive. In C. P. Smith, J. W. Atkinson, D. C. McClelland, & J. Veroff (Eds.), *Motivation and personality: Handbook of thematic content analysis* (pp. 205–210). New York: Cambridge University Press.

Kontos, S., Howes, C., Shinn, M., & Galinsky, E. (1997). Children's experiences in family child care and relative care as a function of family income and ethnicity. *Merrill-Palmer Quarterly, 43*, 386–403.

Koski, L. R., & Shaver, P. R. (1997). Attachment and relationship satisfaction across the lifespan. In R. J. Sternberg & M. Hojjat (Eds.), *Satisfaction in close relationships* (pp 26 55). New York: The Guilford Press.

Kruger, A. C. (1992). The effect of peer and adult-child transductive discussions on moral reasoning. *Merrill-Palmer Quarterly, 38*, 191–211.

Ladd, G. W. (1981). Effectiveness of a social learning method for enhancing children's social interaction and peer acceptance. *Child Development, 52*, 171–178.

Ladd, G. W. (1983). Social networks of popular, average, and rejected children in school settings. *Merrill-Palmer Quarterly, 29*, 283–307.

Ladd, G. W. (1988). Friendship patterns and peer status during early and middle childhood. *Journal of Developmental and Behavioral Pediatrics, 9*, 229–238.

Ladd, G. W. (1990). Having friends, keeping friends, making friends, and being liked by peers in the classroom: Predictors of children's early school adjustment. *Child Development, 61*, 1081–1100.

Ladd, G. W., & Coleman, C. C. (1997). Children's classroom peer relationships and early school attitudes: Concurrent and longitudinal associations. *Early Education and Development, 8*, 51–66.

Ladd, G. W., & Emerson, E. S. (1984). Shared knowledge in children's friendships. *Developmental Psychology, 20*, 932–940.

Ladd, G. W., & Golter, B. S. (1988). Parents' initiation and monitoring of children's peer contacts: Predictive of children's peer relations in nonschool and school settings? *Developmental Psychology, 24*, 109–117.

Ladd, G. W., & Mize, J. (1983). A cognitive-social learning model of social-skill training. *Psychological Review, 90*, 127–157.

Ladd, G. W., & Price, J. M. (1986). Promoting children's cognitive and social competence: The relation between parents' perceptions of task difficulty and children's perceived and actual competence. *Child Development, 57*, 446–460.

Ladd, G. W., & Profilet, S. M. (1996). The Child Behavior Scale: A teacher-report measure of young children's aggressive, withdrawn, and prosocial behaviors. *Developmental Psychology, 32*, 1008–1024.

Ladd, G. W., Profilet, S. M., & Hart, C. H. (1992). Parents' management of children's peer relations: Facilitating and supervising children's activities in the peer culture. In R. D. Parke & G. W. Ladd (Eds.), *Family-peer relationships: Modes of linkage* (pp. 215–254). Hillsdale, NJ: Lawrence Erlbaum.

Ladner, J. (1977). *Mixed families*. Garden City, NY: Anchor/Doubleday.

Laupa, M. (1995). Children's reasoning about authority in home and school contexts. *Social Development, 4*, 1–16.

Laursen B., Hartup, W. W., & Koplas, A. L. (1996). Towards understanding peer conflict. *Merrill-Palmer Quarterly, 42*, 76–102.

Lawlor, L. (1988). *How to survive the third grade*. New York: Pocket Books.

Lawlor, L. (1994). *The worm club*. New York: Pocket Books.

Leahy, R. L., & Hunt, T. M. (1983). A cognitive-developmental approach to the development of conceptions of intelligence. In. R. L. Leahy (Ed.), *The child's construction of social inequality* (pp. 135–160). New York: Academic Press.

Leve, L. D., & Fagot, B. I. (1997). Prediction of positive peer relations from observed parent-child interactions. *Social Development, 6*, 254–269.

Licht, B. G. (1983). Cognitive-motivational factors that contribute to achievement of learning disabled children. *Journal of Learning Disabilities, 16*, 483–490.

Licht, B. G. (1993). Achievement-related beliefs in children with learning disabilities: Impact on motivation and strategic learning. In L. J. Meltzer (Ed.), *Strategy assessment and instruction for students with learning disabilities: From theory to practice* (pp. 195–220). Austin, TX: PRO-ED, Inc.

Lincoln, A., & Chazan S. (1979). Perceived competence and intrinsic motivation in learning disability children. *Journal of Clinical Child Psychology, 8*, 213–216.

Lobel, A. (1970). The letter. In A. Lobel's *Frog and toad are friends*. New York: HarperTrophy.

Loehlin, J. C. (1997). A test of J. R. Harris's theory of peer influences on personality. *Journal of Personality and Social Psychology, 72*, 1197–1201.

Lollis, S. P., Ross, H. S., & Tate, E. (1992). Parents' regulation of children's peer interactions: Direct influences. In R. D. Parke & G. W. Ladd (Eds.), *Family-peer relationships: Modes of linkage* (pp. 255–281). Hillsdale, NJ: Lawrence Erlbaum.

Maccoby, E. E. (1984). Socialization and developmental change. *Child Development, 55*, 317–328.

Maccoby, E. E. (1992). The role of parents in the socialization of children: An historical overview. *Developmental Psychology, 28*, 1006–1017.

Maccoby, E. E., & Martin, J. A. (1983). Socialization in the context of the family: Parent-child interaction. In P. H. Mussen (Series Ed.) & E. M. Hetherington (Vol. Ed.), *Handbook of child psychology: Vol. 4. Socialization, personality, and social development* (4th ed., pp. 1–101). New York: John Wiley & Sons.

MacDonald, K. (1997). The coherence of individual development: An evolutionary perspective on children's internalization of parental values. In J. E. Grusec & L. Kuczynski (Eds.), *Parenting and children's internalization of values: A handbook of contemporary theory* (pp. 362–397). New York: John Wiley & Sons.

MacKinnon-Lewis, C., Starnes, R., Volling, B., & Johnson, S. (1997). Perceptions of parenting as predictors of boys' sibling and peer relations. *Developmental Psychology, 33*, 1024–1031.

Malik, N. M., & Furman, W. (1993). Problems in children's peer relations: What can the clinician do? *Journal of Child Psychology and Psychiatry and Allied Disciplines, 34*, 1303–1326.

Manion, V., & Alexander, J. M. (1997). The benefits of peer collaboration on strategy use, metacognitive causal attribution, and recall. *Journal of Experimental Child Psychology, 67*, 268–289.

Markman, E. M. (1979). Realizing that you don't understand: Elementary school children's awareness of inconsistencies. *Child Development, 50*, 643–655.

McAdams, D. P. (1980). A thematic coding system for the intimacy motive. *Journal of Research in Personality, 14*, 413–432.

McAdams, D. P., & Constantian, C. A. (1983). Intimacy and affiliation motive in daily living. An experience-sampling analysis. *Journal of Personality and Social Psychology, 45*, 851–861.

McClelland, D. C. (1985). *Human motivation*. Glenview, IL: Scott, Foresman.

McGillicuddy-DeLisi, A. V., Watkins, C., & Vinchur, A. J. (1994). The effect of relationship on children's distributive justice reasoning. *Child Development, 65*, 1694–1700.

McLeskey, J. (1992). Students with learning disabilities at primary, intermediate, and secondary grade levels: Identification and characteristics. *Learning Disabilities Quarterly, 15*, 13–19.

Meins, E. (1997). *Security of attachment and the social development of cognition*. Hove, England: Taylor & Francis.

Melton, G. B. (Ed.). (1995). The individual, the family, and social good: Personal fulfillment in times of change. *Nebraska Symposium on Motivation, 42*.

Michelinie, D. (1993a). *Spider-man: Carnage*. Marvel Entertainment.

Michelinie, D. (1993b). *Spider-man: The return of venom*. Marvel Entertainment.

Michelinie, D., & McFarlane, T. (1992). *Spider-man versus venom*. Marvel Entertainment.

Miller, A. T. (1985). A developmental study of the cognitive basis of performance impairment after failure. *Journal of Personality and Social Psychology, 49*, 529–538.

Miller, A. T., & Hom, H. L. (1990). Influence of extrinsic and ego incentive value on persistence after failure and continuing motivation. *Journal of Educational Psychology, 82*, 539–545.

Miller, P. A., Eisenberg, N., Fabes, R. A., & Shell, R. (1996). Relations of moral reasoning and vicarious emotion to young children's prosocial behavior toward peers and adults. *Developmental Psychology, 32*, 210–219.

Miller, R. L., Brickman, P., & Bolen, D. (1975). Attribution versus persuasion as a means for modifying behavior. *Journal of Personality and Social Psychology, 31*, 430–441.

Miller, R. L., & Miller, B. (1990). Mothering the biracial child: Bridging the gaps between African-American and White parenting styles. *Women & Therapy, 10*, 169–179.

Mink, I. T., & Nihira, K. (1986). Family life-styles and child behaviors: A study of direct effects. *Developmental Psychology, 22*, 610–616.

Moats, L. C., & Lyon, G. R. (1993). Learning disabilities in the United States: Advocacy, science, and the future of the field. *Journal of Learning Disabilities, 26*, 282–294.

Morrow, L. M., & Young, J. (1997). A family literacy program connecting school and home: Effects on attitude, motivation, and literacy achievement. *Journal of Educational Psychology, 89*, 736–742.

Musser, L. M., Graziano, W. G., & Moore, J. S. (1987). Developmental and contextual influences on the processing of information about peers. *Journal of Psychology, 121*, 387–400.

Nadler, A. (1997). Personality and help seeking: Autonomous versus dependent seeking of help. In G. R. Pierce, B. Lakey, I. G. Sarason, & B. R. Sarason (Eds.), *Sourcebook of social support and personality* (pp. 379–407). New York: Plenum Press.

Neckerman, H. J. (1996). The stability of social groups in childhood and adolescence: The role of the classroom social environment. *Social Development, 5*, 131–145.

Nelson-LeGall, S., & Glor-Scheib, S. (1986). Academic help-seeking and peer relations in school. *Contemporary Educational Psychology, 11*, 187–193.

Newcomb, A. F., Bukowski, W. M., & Pattee, L. (1993). Children's peer relations: A meta-analytic review of popular, rejected, neglected, controversial, and average sociometric status. *Psychological Bulletin, 113*, 99–128.

Newman, R. S. (1990). Children's help-seeking in the classroom: The role of motivational factors and attitudes. *Journal of Educational Psychology, 82*, 71–80.

Newman, R. S., & Goldin, L. (1990). Children's reluctance to seek help with schoolwork. *Journal of Educational Psychology, 82*, 92–100.

Newman, R. S., & Hagen, J. W. (1981). Memory strategies in children with learning disabilities. *Journal of Applied Developmental Psychology, 1*, 297–312.

Newman, R. S., & Wick, P. L. (1987). Effect of age, skill, and performance feedback on children's judgments of confidence. *Journal of Educational Psychology, 79*, 115–119.

Nicholls, J. G. (1960). The south-east buttress of green. *The New Zealand Alpine Journal, 47*, 292–293.

Nicholls, J. G. (1962). And the weather stayed fine. *The New Zealand Alpine Journal, 49*, 78–82.

Nicholls, J. G. (1984). Achievement motivation: Conceptions of ability, subjective experience, task choice, and performance. *Psychological Review, 91*, 328–346.

Nicholls, J. G. (1989). *The competitive ethos and democratic education*. Cambridge, MA: Harvard University Press.

Nicholls, J. G., Cobb, P., Wood, T., Yackel, E., & Patashnick, M. (1990). Assessing students' theories about success in mathematics: Individual and class differences. *Journal for Research in Mathematics Education, 21*, 109–122.

Nicholls, J. G., & Hazzard, S. P. (1993). *Education as adventure: Lessons from the second grade*. New York: Teachers College Press.

Nicholls, J. G., McKenzie, M., & Shufro, J. (1994). Schoolwork, homework, life's work: The experience of students with and without learning disabilities. *Journal of Learning Disabilities, 27*, 562–569.

Nicholls, J. G., & Nelson, J. R. (1992). Students' conceptions of controversial knowledge. *Journal of Educational Psychology, 84*, 224–230.

Nicholls, J. G., Nelson, J. R., & Gleaves, K. (1995). Learning "facts" versus learning that most questions have many answers: Student evaluations of contrasting curricula. *Journal Educational Psychology, 87*, 253–260.

Nicholls, J. G., & Thorkildsen, T. A. (1988). Children's distinctions among matters of intellectual convention, logic, fact, and personal preferences. *Child Development, 59*, 939–949.

Nicholls, J. G., & Thorkildsen, T. A. (1989). Intellectual conventions versus matters of substance: Elementary school students as curriculum theorists. *American Educational Research Journal, 26*, 533–544.

Nicholls, J. G., & Thorkildsen, T. A., with Bates, A. (1997). Experience through the eyes of Quiet Bird: Reconnecting personal life and school life. In A. Pollard, D. Thiessen, & A. Filer (Eds.), *Children and their curriculum: The perspectives of primary and elementary school children* (pp. 122–140). London: The Falmer Press.

Noddings, N. (1996). On community. *Educational Theory, 46*, 245–267.

Olszewski, P., Kulieke, M. J., & Buescher, T. (1987). The influence of the family environment on the development of talent: A literature review. *Journal for the Education of the Gifted, 11*, 6–28.

O'Neil, R., Welsh, M., Parke, R. D., Wang, S., & Strand, C. (1997). A longitudinal assessment of the academic correlates of early peer acceptance and rejection. *Journal of Clinical Child Psychology, 26*, 290–303.

Opie, I., & Opie, P. (1974). *The classic fairy tales*. New York: Oxford University Press.

Padeliadu, S., & Zigmond, N. (1996). Perspectives of students with learning disabilities about special education placement. *Learning Disabilities Research & Practice, 11*, 15–23.

Parker, J. G., & Asher, S. R. (1993). Friendship and friendship quality in middle childhood: Links with peer group acceptance and feelings of loneliness and social dissatisfaction. *Developmental Psychology, 29*, 611–621.

Parker, J. G., & Seal, J. (1996). Forming, losing, renewing, and replacing friendships: Applying temporal parameters to the assessment of children's friendship experiences. *Child Development, 67*, 2248–2268.

Patterson, G. R. (1980). Mothers: The unacknowledged victims. *Monographs of the Society for Research in Child Development, 45* (5, Serial No. 186).

Pearl, R. (1992). Psychosocial characteristics of learning disabled students. In N. N. Singh & I. L. Beale (Eds.), *Learning disabilities: Nature, theory, and treatment* (pp. 96–125). New York: Springer-Verlag.

Pearl, R., & Bay, M. (1999). Psychosocial correlates of learning disabilities. In V. L. Schwean & D. H. Saklofske (Eds.), *Handbook of psychosocial characteristics of exceptional children* (pp. 443–470). New York: Kluwer Academic/Plenum Publishers.

Pearl, R., & Bryan, T. (1992). Students' expectations about peer pressure to engage in misconduct. *Journal of Learning Disabilities, 25*, 582–585, 597.

Pearl, R., & Cosden, M. (1982). Sizing up a situation: Learning disabled children's understanding of social interactions. *Learning Disability Quarterly, 3*, 3–9.

Phelps, E., & Damon, W. (1991). Peer collaboration as a context for cognitive growth. In L. T. Landsmann (Ed.), *Culture, schooling, and psychological development: Human development* (Vol. 4, pp.171–184). Norwood, NJ: Ablex Publishing.

Piaget, J. (1965). *The moral judgment of the child*. New York: Free Press. (Original work published in 1932.)

Pinderhughes, E. (1989). *Understanding race, ethnicity, and power*. New York: The Free Press.

Pintrich, P. R., Anderman, E. M., & Klobucar, C. (1994). Intraindividual differences in motivation and cognition in students with and without learning disabilities. *Journal of Learning Disabilities, 27*, 360–370.

Plume, I. (1980). *The Bremen-town musicians*. New York: Doubleday & Company.

Plummer, D. L., & Graziano, W. G. (1987). Impact of grade retention on the social development of elementary school children. *Developmental Psychology, 23*, 267–275.

Poresky, R. H., & Whitsitt, T. M. (1985). Young girls' intelligence and motivation: Links with maternal employment and education but not systems theory. *Journal of Psychology, 119*, 475–480.

Power, F. C., Higgins, A., & Kohlberg, L. (1989). *Lawrence Kohlberg's approach to moral education*. New York: Columbia University Press.

Putnam, J., Markovchick, K., Johnson, D. W., & Johnson, R. T. (1996). Cooperative learning and peer acceptance of students with learning disabilities. *Journal of Social Psychology, 136*, 741–752.

Ray, G. E., Cohen, R., Secrist, M. E., & Duncan, M. K. (1997). Relating aggressive and victimization behaviors to children's sociometric status and friendships. *Journal of Social and Personal Relationships, 14*, 95–108.

Richards, H. C., Bear, G. G., Stewart, A. L., & Norman, A. D. (1992). Moral reasoning and classroom conduct: Evidence of a curvilinear relationship. *Merrill-Palmer Quarterly, 38*, 176–190.

Robinson, J. L., Zahn-Waxler, C., & Emde, R. N. (1994). Patterns of development in early empathic behavior: Environmental and child constitutional influences. *Social Development, 3*, 125–145.

Rosen, L. A., Furman, W., & Hartup, W. W. (1988). Positive, negative, and neutral peer interactions as indicators of children's social competency: The issue of concurrent validity. *Journal of Genetic Psychology, 149*, 441–446.

Rosier, K. B., & Corsaro, W. A. (1993). Competent parents, complex lives: Managing parenthood in poverty. *Journal of Contemporary Ethnography, 22*, 171–204.

Rotenberg, K. J. (1984). Sex differences in children's trust in peers. *Sex Roles, 11*, 953–957.

Rotenberg, K. J. (1995). The socialization of trust: Parents' and children's interpersonal trust. *International Journal of Behavioral Development, 18*, 713–726.

Rotenberg, K. J., & Morgan, C. J. (1995). Development of a scale to measure individual differences in children's trust-value basis of friendship. *Journal of Genetic Psychology, 156*, 489–502.

Rotenberg, K. J., & Pilipenko, T. A. (1983–84). Mutuality, temporal consistency, and helpfulness in children's trust in peers. *Social Cognition, 2*, 235–255.

Rousseau, J-J. (1911). *Emile, or education*. (B. Foxley, Trans.). London: J. M. Dent. (Original work published in 1762.)

Ryan, R. M., & Connell, J. P. (1989). Perceived locus of

causality and internalization: Examining reasons for acting in two domains. *Journal of Personality and Social Psychology, 57*, 749–761.

Ryan, R. M., & Deci, E. L. (2000). Intrinsic and extrinsic motivations: Classic definitions and new directions. *Contemporary Educational Psychology, 25*, 54–67.

Sabatino, D. A. (1982). Research on achievement motivation with learning disabled populations. *Advances in Learning & Behavioral Disabilities, 1*, 75–116.

Sale, R. (1978). *Fairy tales and after: From Snow White to E. B. White*. Cambridge, MA: Harvard University Press.

Saunders, B., & Chambers, S. M. (1996). A review of the literature on attention-deficit hyperactivity disorder children: Peer interactions and collaborative learning. *Psychology in the Schools, 33*, 333–340.

Scheinfeld, D. R. (1983). Family relationships and school achievement among boys of lower-income urban Black families. *American Journal of Orthopsychiatry, 53*, 127–143.

Schunk, D. H. (1982). Effects of effort attributional feedback on children's perceived self-efficacy and achievement. *Journal of Educational Psychology, 74*, 548–556.

Schunk, D. H. (1984). Sequential attributional feedback and children's achievement behaviors. *Journal of Educational Psychology, 76*, 1159–1169.

Schunk, D. H. (1985). Participation in goal setting: Effects on self-efficacy and skills of learning-disabled children. *Journal of Special Education, 19*, 307–317.

Schunk, D. H. (1989a). Self-efficacy and achievement behaviors. *Educational Psychology Review, 1*, 173–208.

Schunk, D. H. (1989b). Self-efficacy and cognitive achievement: Implications for students with learning problems. *Journal of Learning Disabilities, 22*, 14–22.

Schunk, D. H. (1995). Self-efficacy and education and instruction. In J. E. Maddux (Ed.), *Self-efficacy, adaptation, and adjustment: Theory, research, and application* (pp. 281–303). New York: Plenum Press.

Schunk, D. H. (1996). Goal and self-evaluative influences during children's cognitive skill learning. *American Educational Research Journal, 33*, 359–382.

Schunk, D. H., & Cox, P. D. (1986). Strategy training and attributional feedback with learning disabled students. *Journal of Educational Psychology, 78*, 201–209.

Schunk, D. H., & Rice, J. M. (1993). Strategy fading and progress feedback: Effects on self-efficacy and comprehension among students receiving remedial reading services. *Journal of Special Education, 27*, 257–276.

Schunk, D. H., & Swartz, C. W. (1993). Goals and progress feedback: Effects on self-efficacy and writing achievement. *Contemporary Educational Psychology, 18*, 337–354.

Schunk, D. H., & Zimmerman, B. J. (1996). Modeling and self-efficacy influences on children's development of self-regulation. In J. Juvonen & K. R. Wentzel (Eds.), *Social motivation: Understanding children's school adjustment* (pp. 154–180). New York: Cambridge University Press.

Schwartz, D., Dodge, K. A., & Coie, J. D. (1993). The emergence of chronic peer victimization in boys' play groups. *Child Development, 64*, 1755–1772.

Schwartz, D., Dodge, K. A., Pettit, G. S., & Bates, J. E. (1997). The early socialization of aggressive victims of bullying. *Child Development, 68*, 665–675.

Selman, R. L. (1980). *The growth of interpersonal understanding: Developmental and clinical analyses*. New York: Academic Press.

Selman, R. L. (1981). The development of interpersonal competence: The role of understanding in conduct. *Developmental Review, 1*, 401–422.

Selman, R. L. (1989). Fostering intimacy and autonomy. In W. Damon (Ed.), *Child development today and tomorrow* (pp. 409–435). San Francisco: Jossey-Bass Publishers.

Selman, R. L., & Demorest, A. P. (1984). Observing troubled children's interpersonal negotiation strategies: Implications of and for a developmental model. *Child Development, 55*, 288–304.

Selman, R. L., & Lieberman, M. (1975). Moral education in the primary grades: An evaluation of a developmental curriculum. *Journal of Educational Psychology, 67*, 712–716.

Selman, R. L., Schorin, M. Z., Stone, C. R., & Phelps, E. (1983). A naturalistic study of children's social understanding. *Developmental Psychology, 19*, 82–102.

Selman, R. L., & Schultz, L. H. (1989). Children's strategies for interpersonal negotiation with peers: An interpretive/empirical approach to the study of social development. In T. J. Berndt & G. W. Ladd (Eds.), *Peer relationships in child development* (pp. 371–406). New York: John Wiley & Sons.

Sharmat, M. W. (1972). *Nate the great*. New York: Bantam Doubleday Dell Publishing.

Short, E. J. (1992). Cognitive, meta-cognitive, motivational, and affective differences among normally achieving, learning-disabled, and developmentally handicapped students: How much do they affect school achievement? *Journal of Clinical Child Psychology, 21*, 229–239.

Sigelman, C. K., & Waitzman, K. A. (1991). The development of distributive justice orientations: Contextual influences on children's resource allocations. *Child Development, 62*, 1367–1378.

Siperstein, G. N., Leffert, J. S., & Wenz-Gross, M. (1997). The quality of friendships between children with and without learning problems. *American Journal of Mental Retardation, 102*, 111–125.

Skaalvik, S. (1993). Ego-involvement and self-protection among slow learners: Four case studies. *Scandinavian Journal of Educational Research, 37*, 305–315.

Skrtic, T. M. (1991). *Behind special education: A critical analysis of professional culture and school organization*. Denver, CO: Love Publishing.

Sletta, O., Valas, H., Skaalvik, E., & Sobstad, F. (1996). Peer relations, loneliness, and self-perceptions in school-aged children. *British Journal of Educational Psychology, 66*, 431–445.

Smetana, J. (1994). Parenting styles and beliefs about parental authority. In J. Smetana (Ed.), Beliefs about parenting: Origins and developmental implications (pp. 21–36). *New Directions for Child Development, 66*.

Smith, P. K., & Boulton, M. (1990). Rough-and-tumble play, aggression, and dominance: Perception and behaviour in children's encounters. *Human Development, 33*, 271–282.

Steig, W. (1969). *Sylvester and the magic pebble*. New York: Simon & Schuster.

Steig, W. (1976). *The amazing bone*. New York: Farrar, Straus, & Giroux.

Steig, W. (1982). *Dr. DeSoto*. New York: Farrar, Straus, & Giroux.

Sternberg, R. J., & Kolligian, J., Jr. (1990). *Competence considered*. New Haven, CT: Yale University Press.

Sternlieb, J. L., & Youniss, J. (1975). Moral judgments one year after intentional or consequence modeling. *Journal of Personality and Social Psychology, 31*, 895–897.

Stevenson, H. W., & Newman, R. S. (1986). Long-term prediction of achievement and attitudes in mathematics and reading. *Child Development, 57*, 646–659.

Stipek, D. J. (1997). Success in school—for a head start in life. In S. S. Luthar, J. A. Burack, D. Cicchetti, & J. R. Weisz (Eds.), *Developmental psychopathology: Perspectives on adjustment, risk, and disorder* (pp. 75–92). New York: Cambridge University Press.

Stipek, D. J., & MacIver, D. (1989). Developmental change in children's assessment of intellectual competence. *Child Development, 60*, 521–538.

Stremmel, A. J., & Ladd, G. W. (1985). Children's selective use of peer informants: Criteria for making information-seeking decisions. *Journal of Genetic Psychology, 146*, 541–550.

Swanson, J. M., Cantwell, D., Lerner, M., McBurnett, K., & Hanna, G. (1991). Effects of stimulant medication on learning in children with ADHD. *Journal of Learning Disabilities, 24*, 219–227.

Tassi, F., & Schneider, B. H. (1997). Task-oriented versus other-referenced competition: Differential implications for children's peer relations. *Journal of Applied Social Psychology, 27*, 1557–1580.

Thorkildsen, T. A. (1989a). Justice in the classroom: The student's view. *Child Development, 60*, 323–334.

Thorkildsen, T. A. (1989b). Pluralism in children's reasoning about social justice. *Child Development, 60*, 965–972.

Thorkildsen, T. A. (1991). Defining social goods and distributing them fairly: The development of conceptions of fair testing practices. *Child Development, 62*, 852–862.

Thorkildsen, T. A. (1994). Toward a fair community of scholars: Moral education as the negotiation of classroom practices. *Journal of Moral Education, 23*, 371–385.

Thorkildsen, T. A. (2000). The way tests teach: Children's theories of how much testing is fair in school. In M. Leicester, C. Modgil, & S. Modgil (Eds.), *Education, culture, and values, Vol. III: Classroom issues: practice, pedagogy, and curriculum* (pp. 61–79). London: Falmer Press.

Thorkildsen, T. A., & Jordan, C. (1995). Is there a right way to collaborate? When the experts speak can the customers be right? In J. G. Nicholls & T. A. Thorkildsen (Eds.), *Reasons for learning: Expanding the conversation on student-teacher collaboration* (pp. 137–161). New York: Teachers College Press.

Thorkildsen, T. A., & Nicholls, J. G. (1991). Students' critiques as motivation. *Educational Psychologist, 26*, 347–368.

Thorkildsen, T. A., Nolen, S. B., & Fournier, J. (1994). What is fair? Children's critiques of practices that influence motivation. *Journal of Educational Psychology, 86*, 475–486.

Törgesen, J. K., (1982). The study of short-term memory in learning disabled children: Goals, methods, and conclusions. *Advances in Learning and Behavioral Disabilities, 1*, 117–149.

Turiel, E. (1983). *The development of social knowledge: Morality and convention*. New York: Cambridge University Press.

Underwood, M. K., Coie, J. D., & Herbsman, C. R. (1992). Display rules for anger and aggression in school-age children. *Child Development, 63*, 366–380.

Van Lange, P. A. M., DeBruin, E. M. N., Otten, W., & Joireman, J. A. (1997). Development of prosocial, individualistic, and competitive orientations: Theory and preliminary evidence. *Journal of Personality and Social Psychology, 73*, 733–746.

Vaughn, S., Elbaum, B. E., & Schumm, J. S. (1996). The effects of inclusion on the social functioning of students with learning disabilities. *Journal of Learning Disabilities, 29*, 598–608.

Volling, B. L., Youngblade, L. M., & Belsky, J. (1997). Young children's social relationships with siblings and friends. *American Journal of Orthopsychiatry, 67*, 102–111.

Von Leyden, W. (1985). *Aristotle on equality and justice: His political argument*. New York: St. Martin's Press.

von Salisch, M. (1996). Relationships between children: Symmetry and asymmetry among peers, friends, and siblings. In A. E. Auhagen & M. von Salisch (Eds.), *The diversity of human relationships* (pp. 59–77). New York: Cambridge University Press.

Walker, A. (1991). *Finding the green stone*. New York: Harcourt Brace Jovanovich.

Walker, L. J. (1991). Verbal interactions within the family context. *Canadian Journal of Behavioral Science, 23*, 441–454.

Walker, L. J., & Hennig, K. H. (1997). Parent/child relationships in single-parent families. *Canadian Journal of Behavioral Science, 29*, 63–75.

Walker, L. J., & Taylor, J. H. (1991). Family interactions and the development of moral reasoning. *Child Development, 62*, 264–283.

Warner, G. C. (1992). *The boxcar children*. New York: Buccaneer Books. (Originally published in 1942.)

Warton, P. M., & Goodnow, J. J. (1991). The nature of responsibility: Children's understanding of "your job." *Child Development, 62*, 156–165.

Weiner, B. (1992). *Human motivation: Metaphors, theories, and research*. Newbury Park, CA: Sage Publications.

Weiner, B. (1994). Ability versus effort revisited: The moral determinants of achievement evaluation and achievement as a moral system. *Educational Psychologist, 29*, 163–172.

Weiner, B. (1996). Searching for order in social motivation. *Psychological Inquiry, 7*, 199–216.

Weisner, T. S., & Garnier, H. (1992). Nonconventional family life-styles and school achievement: A 12-year longitudinal study. *American Educational Research Journal, 29*, 605–632.

Wentzel, K. R. (1998). Social relationships and motivation in middle school: The role of parents, teachers, and peers. *Journal of Educational Psychology, 90*, 202–209.

Wentzel, K. R., & Asher, S. R. (1995). The academic lives of neglected, rejected, popular, and controversial children. *Child Development, 66*, 754–763.

White, R. W. (1959). Motivation reconsidered: The concept of competence. *Psychological Review, 66*, 297–333.

White, R. W. (1975). *Lives in progress* (3rd ed.). New York: Holt, Rinehart, and Winston. (Originally published in 1952.)

Wiebe, D. J., & Smith, T. W. (1997). Personality and health: Progress and problems in psychosomatics. In R. Hogan, J. Johnson, & S. Briggs (Eds.), *Handbook of personality psychology* (pp. 891–918). New York: Academic Press.

Wigfield, A., & Guthrie, J. T. (1997). Relations of children's motivation for reading to the amount and breadth of their reading. *Journal of Educational Psychology, 89*, 420–432.

Wiggins, J. S. (1991). Agency and communion as conceptual coordinates for the understanding and measurement of interpersonal behavior. In D. Cicchetti & W. Grove (Eds.), *Thinking critically in psychology: Essays in honor of Paul E. Meehl* (pp. 89–113). New York: Cambridge University Press.

Wilson, D. R., & David, W. J. (1994). Academic intrinsic motivation and attitudes toward school and learning disabled students. *Learning Disabilities Research & Practice, 9*, 148–156.

Winter, D. G. (1996). *Personality: Analysis and interpretation of lives*. New York: McGraw Hill.

Winter, D. G., & Stewart, A. J. (1978). The power motive. In H. London & J. E. Exner, Jr. (Eds.), *Dimensions of personality* (pp. 391–448). New York: John Wiley & Sons.

Wood, A. (1987). *The heckedy peg*. New York: Harcourt, Brace, & Company.

Yeates, K. O., & Selman, R. L. (1989). Social competence in the schools: Toward an integrative developmental model for intervention. *Developmental Review, 9*, 64–100.

Young, M. C. (1994). (Ed.). *The Guinness book of records*. New York: Bantam Books/Doubleday-Dell Publishing.

Youniss, J. (1980). *Parents and peers in social development: A Sullivan-Piaget perspective*. Chicago: University of Chicago Press.

Youniss, J. (1994). Children's friendship and peer culture: Implications for theories of networks and support. In F. Nestmann & K. Hurrelmann (Eds.), *Social networks and social support in childhood and adolescence. Prevention and intervention in childhood and adolescence* (Vol. 16, pp. 75–88). Berlin, Germany: Walter de Gruyter.

Zakriski, A. L., & Coie, J. D. (1996). A comparison of aggressive-rejected and nonaggressive-rejected children's interpretations of self-directed and other-directed rejection. *Child Development, 67*, 1048–1070.

Zakriski, A., Jacobs, M., & Coie, J. (1997). Coping with childhood peer rejection. In S. A. Wolchik & I. N. Sandler (Eds.), *Handbook of children's coping: Linking theory and intervention issues in clinical child psychology* (pp. 423–451). New York: Plenum Press.

Zarbatany, L., & Pepper, S. (1996). The role of the group in peer group entry. *Social Development, 5*, 251–260.

Zarbatany, L., Van Brunschot, M., Meadows, K., & Pepper, S. (1996). Effects of friendship and gender on peer group entry. *Child Development, 67*, 2287–2300.

Zentall, S. S. (1980). Behavioral comparisons of hyperactive and normally active children in natural settings. *Journal of Abnormal Child Psychology, 8*, 93–109.

GLOSSARY

ability The mental power or capacity to do something. When used as an attribution, ability generally refers to a cleverness, talent, or mental power.

academic alienation An orientation toward academic work that promotes avoidance.

academic competence Skill or talent for performing academic tasks.

academic disengagement Active avoidance of academic activities.

academic engagement Active participation in academic activities.

active-isolated behavior A type of withdrawal in which individuals work toward achieving solitude.

affective processes Mental and neural desires, feelings, or emotions believed to be a part of someone's intrapersonal experience.

affiliation orientations The means by which individuals seek to meet their needs for approval and intimacy.

aggression A hostile or potentially destructive form of reasoning or behavior usually initiated without provocation. In families, aggression involves actions that are punitive, hostile, or abusive. Among peers, aggression involves attacking others without provocation.

agreeableness A personality characteristic that involves complying with the expectations of others.

amotivation The absence of goals and energy that might be directed toward action, emotion, or reasoning.

anxious/ambivalent attachments Intermittent attention exhibited by children in response to overcontrolling or overstimulating behavior.

anxious/avoidant attachments Avoidance by children and their caregivers of direct response to one another.

asymmetrical relationships A hierarchical structure in which one individual is placed in a role that is superior to another.

attachment Emotional bonds that individuals form with their caregivers early in life.

attachment theory A description of how children's needs are created and met through bonds with significant caregivers.

attention A mental focus that occupies a person's consciousness. Attention is often equated with working memory as individuals notice the details of external stimuli.

attributions Characteristics ascribed to an effect to explain the cause of that effect.

attribution theory The study of how people use causal or commonsense explanations to explain human behavior.

autonomy A freedom of the will to govern the self. Among adults, this term is used to reflect freedom to act independently as well as freedom from oppression. Among children, autonomy often involves a willingness to select and maintain identity-enhancing interests that reflect a commitment to particular ideas and values.

average social status The position in a social group characterized by being moderately well-liked by the others in that group.

behavioral observations A systematic process by which individuals notice and record the actions of others.

behaviorism A set of psychological theories of how individuals' behavior evolves and is modified over a lifetime.

behavior modification An intervention used to alter the habitual behavior of particular people. It is often used with children to reduce aggression and/or self-destructive behavior and with groups to alter the climate of that group.

care A process by which individuals offer serious attention, interest, caution, and worry. When directed toward children, this often involves protection and attempts to provide for their needs.

casual friendships Relationships between two people that reflect occasional or temporary contact and moderate to low levels of intimacy.

cheating Gaining an unfair advantage either by breaking rules or deceiving others in order to appear more competent and/or superior to others.

close friendships Relationships between two people

that reflect regular contact and moderate to high levels of intimacy.

coaching The act of tutoring or giving advice to assist another person in improving his or her performance.

cognitive processes Mental and neural forms of reasoning or thinking believed to be a part of someone's intrapersonal experience.

cognitive strategies The mental mechanisms that individuals use to acquire, retrieve, and/or organize information.

communal goals Goals based on the assumption that anyone belonging to a group is entitled to a share of most of the resources of that group and that everyone's needs should be met.

companionship A relationship in which two people associate with one another in good fellowship.

competence A collection of adequate qualifications or capabilities.

competence orientations The means by which individuals seek to meet their need to demonstrate adequate qualifications or capabilities.

competitive orientation An individual's tendency to strive toward winning or demonstrating superiority over others.

conative processes Mental and neural readiness for action believed to be a part of someone's intrapersonal experience. Conative processes are now commonly referred to as volition.

conduct problems A set of difficulties that arise from the aversive qualities of a person's behavior.

conscience An inner moral sense as to individuals' relative goodness that affects their behavior.

controllability The degree of volitional influence that can be exerted over a cause.

controlling behavior Behavior that undermines the effect of volition on a cause.

controversial knowledge Information that is likely to be the subject of prolonged argument or dispute.

controversial social status The position in a social group characterized by being actively disliked as well as actively liked by other members of the group.

crystallized intelligence The collection and organization of information that is definite, most commonly in verbal form. This form of intelligence is heavily influenced by education and socialization processes.

direct instruction A structured teaching method in which tasks are broken into subskills, and sequential instruction is used to assist children in acquiring a standard set of academic skills.

effort The exertion of physical or mental power. When used as an attribution effort is generally defined as a vigorous or determined attempt to meet a goal.

effort-focused feedback Information on the correspondence between desired and actual effort and how that effort affected the results of an activity.

ego control The process by which an individual is aware of his or her coping and defense mechanisms and is able to use that knowledge to alter behavior.

ego-focused feedback Information on the correspondence between the self and desired performance on a task. (e.g., You need to work harder.) This has also been referred to as praise and usually involves global attributions.

ego involvement A motivational state in which individuals cope and/or defend themselves from the demands of a task by seeking to demonstrate superiority over others and/or avoid appearing inferior.

ego orientation A habitual tendency to cope and/or defend oneself by striving to demonstrate superiority over others or to avoid appearing inferior. Task mastery generates feelings of success only if one's performance is better than the performance of others.

egotism An approach to life in which self-enhancement and superiority over others is more important than any other values.

emotional attributions Emotional characteristics (e.g., guilt, shame) ascribed to an effect to explain the cause of that effect.

emotional support Assistance with labeling someone's reactions to personally significant events.

emotions Reactions to personally significant events that involve physiological, behavioral, and cognitive valence, usually associated with subjective feelings of pleasure or displeasure.

empathy Feeling vicarious emotional responses consistent with the emotions or situation of another (e.g., sadness, fear, loathing).

encouragement A type of feedback in which something positive about an individual's performance is noted and paired with a suggestion for improvement (e.g., you found many good ideas, now try to put them in a logical order).

engagement The process of being occupied or busy.

equilibrium A state in which individuals attain physical, mental, and emotional balance.

exchange orientation Seeking relationship by giving one thing and receiving another, often as equals.

expectations Demand characteristics in particular

contexts that offer structure to the needs that individuals come to value.

expressiveness A personality characteristic used to represent individuals' willingness to share their emotional states with others through gesture and words.

external influences Sources outside a person that affect his or her behavior.

external locus of control The belief that events or outcomes result from forces outside of one's own thoughts and actions.

extrinsic goals Objects of a person's ambition or effort that originate from expectations outside the person.

extrinsic rewards A tangible form of return or recompense originating outside a person and used to acknowledge service or merit (e.g., prizes, food).

failure attributions Characteristics ascribed to a failure experience to explain the cause of that failure.

family stability The degree to which the composition of a family remains fixed and the household norms remain predictable.

feedback Information on the correspondence between desired and actual attainment.

flow A state in which individuals find an experience so enjoyable that nothing else seems to matter.

fluid intelligence The collection and organization of information that is novel, most commonly involving abstract, nonverbal reasoning, and problem solving. This type of intelligence is not influenced by education or socialization processes.

fractured experience The inability to coordinate personal needs and others' expectations, often by ignoring particular needs/expectations or responding simultaneously to contradictory needs/expectations.

friendship Maintaining a relationship in which both parties enjoy mutual affection and regard.

friendship quality The characteristics of mutual affection that facilitate particular levels of intimacy.

goals The aim of a person's ambition and effort. Goals are usually more narrowly defined than orientations and involve a tangible destination or objective.

group affiliation The process by which an individual maintains a commitment to a group and/or groups maintain commitments to one another.

group dynamics The physical and moral forces that drive behavior between individuals and groups.

group membership The degree to which an individual is perceived to be a member of a group.

guilt A person's mental obsession with the idea of having engaged in a specific blameworthy action.

habits An automatic reaction to a particular set of circumstances.

happiness A feeling of internal harmony, pleasure, or contentment.

heteronomous morality An orientation that involves obedience for its own sake and a search for evidence that rules have been enforced.

hyperactive-distractible behavior Unusually high levels of activity that involve restlessness, fidgeting, impulsivity, and inattention to the tasks at hand.

imitation The process by which individuals mimic, copy, and/or repeat the speech and actions of another.

identity The socially defined condition and characteristics that comprise an individual's personality.

identity-enhancing choices Choices that allow one part of someone's experience to give direction and meaning to other parts of his or her experience.

identity-enhancing interests Exciting curiosity or holding attention to subjects that permit all parts of one's experience to give direction and meaning to one another.

individualistic orientation Being preoccupied with autonomy for it's own sake when organizing social information.

inferiority complex An abnormal sentiment of inadequacy that magnifies obstacles and undermines courage while nurturing a commitment to easy compensation or specious satisfactions.

in-group members A term used to distinguish members of a high-status, target group from members of other groups.

instruction A process of teaching or instructing another.

instrumental morality Preoccupation with doing good to get something in return.

instrumental motor response Behavior that involves using parts of the body as a tool to produce a particular outcome (e.g., using the hand to hold a pencil).

integrated experience A style of life in which all parts of an individual's experience give direction and meaning to one another. This usually involves the ability to respond to personal needs, distinguish personal concerns from the concerns of others, and coordinate others' hopes and expectations with personal needs.

interests Subjects or actions that hold one's curiosity and/or attention.

internal locus of control The belief that events or outcomes result from one's own thoughts and actions.

interpersonal competition An event or contest in which people strive for superiority or supremacy over one another. This term is distinguished from competition between groups, such as different species.

interpersonal exchange The reciprocal process between two persons of giving one thing and receiving another.

interpersonal experiences Forms of communication that occur between persons.

intimacy A state of being closely acquainted with private and/or personal thoughts of another. In friendship, this closeness should be reciprocated.

intrapersonal experiences Mental and neural states that occur within a person.

isolation The process of being cut off from other members of a social network.

leadership opportunity Situations in which an individual has a chance to be followed by others.

learned helplessness A belief that future events will be completely uncontrollable, derived from experiences where volitional influence had no influence over a cause. This state of mind can be sustained when individuals attribute their successes to external, unstable, specific events (e.g., an easy task) and their failures to internal, stable, and global traits (e.g., low ability).

learning The process of acquiring knowledge.

learning disabilities A wide range of difficulties that some individuals experience when they process and interpret information necessary for learning to occur. Common definitions generally involve psychological processes, the use and understanding of language and other symbols, and neurological components that cannot be linked to other handicaps.

learning-focused goals Aims addressing the process of acquiring knowledge used to direct a person's ambition and effort.

locus of causality The location of that which produces an effect in relation to a person. An internal locus of causality addresses factors inside a person whereas an external locus of causality addresses factors outside a person.

loneliness A state of feeling discomfort because one is without friends or companionship.

luck An attribution to chance as the source of good or bad fortune.

meta-cognitive strategies Approaches to labeling, reflecting on, and deliberately selecting particular mental mechanisms to acquire, retrieve, and/or organize information.

modeling A process of observational learning by which individuals imitate others. This type of learning may be conscious or unconscious.

moral agency An active attempt to respond to ethical issues associated with doing good and right.

moral reasoning The intellectual faculty used to draw conclusions about issues of ethics, justice, and care.

moral values A set of principles or standards that govern one's judgments of what is important in life.

motivation Internal factors or circumstances that induce a person to think and/or act in a certain way.

mutual friendship Pairs of individuals who both choose one another as friends.

need for achievement A force that organizes individuals' quest for demonstrating competence. Currently referred to as a need for competence.

need for affiliation A force that organizes individuals' quest for close ties with others. In children, this force organizes their willingness to seek help or comfort from others. It is sometimes referred to as a need for relatedness.

need for competence A force that organizes individuals' quest for achievement and expertise. Historically, it has been referred to as a need for achievement.

need for power A force that organizes individuals' quest for prestige, agency, and independence. In children, this need is restricted by the continuing growth of their cognitive capacities.

need for relatedness A force that organizes individuals' quest for interactions with others. This is sometimes referred to as a need for affiliation.

need for self-determination A force that organizes individuals' quest for power, autonomy, and self-efficacy. In adults, this is one aspect of their need for power.

needs Internal forces that organize how individuals perceive, define, and respond to their experience.

negative reinforcement Rewarding someone by taking away something aversive (e.g., eliminating tedious lectures).

neglected social status The position in a social group characterized by having no nominations as being liked or disliked by members of the group.

novel stimuli A previously unknown thing that stirs activity or energy.

observational learning The process of acquiring new knowledge by watching others.

optimal experience A state where individuals are in control of their actions and feelings, believing they are masters of their own fate. Such a state generally requires a commitment to seeking happiness for its own sake.

optimal motivation A state in which personal needs and others' expectations are coordinated. Such a state generally leads individuals to choose moderately difficult tasks and persist in completing such tasks.

orientations Styles for locating oneself in an environment with reference to time, place, and/or people. Orientations are often represented as general attitudes or forms of adjustment in relationship to particular circumstances.

outcomes-based education A structured teaching method in which behavioral objectives are defined and sequential instruction is used to assist children in acquiring a standard set of academic skills. This is a current term used for direct instruction.

out-group members A term used to distinguish members of a low status group from members of an in-group.

parenting styles A characterization of the systematic ways in which caregivers interact with target children.

parsimony The goal of introducing no more causes or forces than necessary to account for all the available facts or evidence.

passive-anxious behavior A form of withdrawal in which individuals take no action to initiate contact with others and remain concerned about imminent danger.

peer collaboration A process in which individuals of the same age work jointly toward a common goal.

peer relations A field of inquiry in which researchers explore how individuals of the same age interact with one another to establish and maintain exchange relationships.

perceived competence The extent to which an individual would define himself or herself as being adequately qualified or capable.

performance-focused goals Aims addressing the outcomes or skills acquired from the learning process.

popular social status The position in a social group characterized by being actively liked by other members of the group.

positive reinforcement Rewarding people by giving them something they covet (e.g., privileges, attention, tangible objects).

positive stimulation Pleasing thoughts or events that arouse, excite, and animate a person's attention.

praise A type of feedback where information on the correspondence between the self and desired performance on a task is noted (e.g., You have high ability). This has also been referred to as ego-focused feedback and usually involves global attributions.

private self-consciousness Excessive awareness of one's inner thoughts, emotions, and needs.

prosocial behavior Interpersonal actions that are evaluated favorably with reference to cultural or social standards (e.g., helping, sharing, comforting).

prosocial reasoning The intellectual faculty used to draw conclusions about positive social interactions.

protective factors Elements in someone's personality and/or environment that shield him or her from harm.

public self-consciousness Excessive awareness of one's appearance to external observers.

punishment Inducing a penalty or form of suffering for an offense. This can occur either by depriving others of something they value or by enforcing a harmful sanction.

reciprocity Give and take between persons in a relationship.

rejected social status The position in a social group characterized by being actively disliked by other members of the group.

relatedness The establishment of close ties between two people.

relational aggression Hostile or potentially destructive reasoning or behavior involving how one person maintains connection with another.

reward contingencies A plan for acknowledging service or merit that considers future uncertain occurrences.

rewards A form of return or recompense used to acknowledge service or merit.

Ritalin A drug that is used to help individuals regulate their attention.

sad-depressed behavior A type of withdrawal wherein individuals are extremely dispirited or overcome with feelings of hopelessness and inadequacy.

scaffolded-instruction A teaching technique in which educators conduct a task analysis, breaking tasks into subskills, and then teaching those subskills in a sequential manner.

secure attachments Children behave like effective agents when interacting with their world. They are able to engage in healthy forms of protest, and differentiate their own needs from those of others.

self-awareness Individuals' awareness of their own inner states and how they appear to others.

self-concept Individuals' sense of how they compare to others.

self-determination orientations The means by which individuals seek to meet their needs for power and independence.

self-efficacy Individuals' sense that they will succeed when devoting energy toward fulfilling a goal.

self-esteem The degree to which individuals like themselves.

self-regulated behavior The ability to control how one approaches and avoids particular tasks.

self-regulated learning The ability to make and act on responsible choices when working to discover something new.

shame A person's mental obsession with the inadequacy of the self that promotes a desire to hide from interpersonal situations.

skill An attribution used to reflect individuals' practiced ability, expertise, and/or dexterity in an action.

social acceptance The degree to which someone is liked or disliked by peers.

social comparison The process of finding similarities and differences with other people and the effects of those results on cognition, behavior, and emotion. Such comparisons are used to obtain correct or accurate assessments of abilities and opinions. Social comparisons are also used to maintain and enhance self-evaluations and/or for the relational purpose of connecting with others.

social competence The degree of skill an individual has for establishing and maintaining relationships with others.

social development The process of acquiring appropriate abilities for interacting with others measured over time.

social identity An individual's self-definition in relation to the properties of an in-group that is both prescriptive and evaluative.

socialization theory A description of how children's needs are created and met through a meticulous process of mutual reinforcement among family members.

social learning theory A collection of explanatory mechanisms for how social influences alter human thought, affect, and action. Reciprocal interactions among environmental factors, cognition, behavior, and biology produce such changes. Recently renamed *social cognitive theory.*

social norms Accepted ways of thinking, feeling, and acting, preferred because it is believed to be correct, just, and/or appropriate.

social preference The degree to which children like or dislike other children, usually measured using sociometric procedures.

social self-perceptions The degree to which individuals come to know their internal reactions to social situations. Individuals can come to this awareness by introspection—a process of turning thoughts inward, tuning out external stimuli—or by inferring them from observations of their own behavior.

social skills A set of learned behaviors that are coordinated to produce mutual relationships between people.

social spheres Naturally occurring categories used to organize norms and expectations when producing mutual relationships between people (e.g., family, school, church, peer groups). These categories sometimes hold overlapping expectations, but also have norms that differ from other categories.

social status The degree to which children are liked or disliked by members of a group.

social transgression A violation of norms used to produce mutual relationships between people.

sociometric measures A process of nominating individuals as liked and disliked for the purpose of determining their social status.

stability The temporal nature of a cause varying from fixed or not easily adjusted to variable or highly fickle.

subjective experience A means of interpreting events that proceeds from personal idiosyncrasy, emerging from an individual's distorted or partial consciousness.

success attributions Characteristics ascribed to a success experience to explain the cause of that success.

symmetrical relationships A structure of reciprocity that places individuals in equal roles.

sympathy Vicarious emotional reactions that are based on an appreciation for, but not an in-kind response to, another's emotional state or condition (e.g., sorrow, compassion, concern for another).

task choice The process of selecting an appropriate activity. Monitoring individuals' task choice in relation to task difficulty is used to gain insight into their motivational states. When individuals select tasks that are excessively easy or impossibly difficult, they reveal motivational difficulties. When they select tasks that are moderately difficult, optimal motivation is likely to occur.

task difficulty The degree to which an activity needs much skill and/or effort. When considered in relation to task choice, it is possible to infer an individual's motivational states.

task engagement The process of being occupied, busy, or involved in completing a task.

task-focused feedback Information on the correspondence between desired and actual attainment in acquiring comprehensive knowledge and/or skill about a particular piece of work (e.g., You read the whole book, now tell me about your favorite part).

task involvement A motivational state in which individuals find tasks meaningful in their own right and task mastery generates feelings of success and pleasure.

task orientation A disposition to find tasks meaningful in their own right and to feel successful by mastering tasks that enhance personal interests and knowledge. Historically, this has been referred to as approach motivation.

task mastery Comprehensive knowledge and/or skill concerning a particular piece of work.

teacher-proof curriculum A movement to standardize the curriculum by making the teachers' role redundant, emerging from the belief that teachers cannot sufficiently establish appropriate reinforcement schedules.

trust The sense that a person is reliable, honest, and/or committed enough to fulfill commitments and responsibilities. As a subjective state, trust is represented as a readiness or predisposition to evaluate others as reliable and honest. It is also seen as a set of behaviors that conveys confident expectations regarding the benevolence of others' intentions.

unilateral friendships Pairs of individuals in which one person sees a friendship and the other does not.

unsociable behavior A type of withdrawal wherein individuals do not respond to others so as to develop mutual understanding.

values The relative utility, worth, desirability, or importance of ideas.

vicarious conditioning The process by which individuals learn from scheduled reinforcement associated with modeling.

vicarious learning The process of acquiring new knowledge by observing the experiences of others.

victimization The process of singling out someone for punishment, unfair treatment, or as a target for inflicting harm.

volition The exercise of the will toward action.

withdrawn behavior Actions that involve retiring from, avoiding, or remaining mentally detached from others.

work avoidance A motivational state in which individuals seek to minimize effort and/or engage in easy tasks. Historically, this has also been referred to as avoidance motivation.

INDEX